P9-CBE-314

Midsummer Moon

Midsummer Moon

KAREN LYNN

DOUBLEDAY & COMPANY, INC.

GARDEN CITY, NEW YORK

All of the characters in this book
are fictitious, and any resemblance
to actual persons, living or dead,
is purely coincidental.

Library of Congress Cataloging in Publication Data
Lynn, Karen.
Midsummer moon.
I. Title.
PS3562.Y4447M5   1985   813'.54
ISBN 0-385-19861-2

Library of Congress Catalog Card Number 85-4421
Copyright © 1985 by Karen Maxfield & Lynn Taylor
All Rights Reserved
Printed in the United States of America

First Edition

Midsummer Moon

CHAPTER 1

It was typical Wellington weather. The heavy rain, creating a river of mud, and an eerie grey light heralded the commencement of the imminent battle. It always stormed before his battles and the troops knew to a man that they would be engaged before the day was over. The day was the eighteenth of June, 1815, and the place was Waterloo, a small town in France near the Flemish border.

Captain Jeremy Ainsworth, known outside military circles as Lord Marsden, led his company toward the Hougoumont farmhouse, where the 1st Guard Brigade together with the 3rd Guards and the 2nd Battalion Coldstream Guards was ordered to hold the orchard. Captain McDonnell was already there defending the château.

Ainsworth's aristocratic features were grim as he and his company galloped toward the spot Wellington had decided was critical. The long, patricianly thin face was marred with tension lines and deep-set brown eyes that narrowed while he scanned the horizon. The tall, lithe figure swayed easily in the saddle and, seeing nothing suspicious, let his mind drift back to the previous evening and his fellow officers' toasts and scrawled dispositions of property. The men all realized that they'd be lucky to see the next sunset.

His conscience smote him as he remembered he'd failed to fill his father's wish for him to marry and beget an heir. If he fell he was the last of his line. Everything would go to his cousin Jessamy—if Jessamy survived—but if they both died—Well, he wouldn't think about that. At the first opportunity, he'd remedy the situation. He'd marry the first presentable lady that came along. That was a silent promise to his father.

As the first cannon explosion was heard, the captain's thoughts were recalled to the battle at hand. Piercing brown eyes surveyed the scene about him. With a determined thrust of his chin, he hailed his men to ready themselves. He waited in anticipation of the battle to come, a surge of blood beginning to pump harshly through his system.

Larla Somerset, her pale gold curls damp and curling riotously about her oval face, calmly walked through the entrance to the Hôtel de Bien Ville in Brussels in search of her maid. She presented quite a contrast to the present occupants and camp followers wandering about the noted hostelry.

Larla's boat cloak had kept her reasonably dry but her hat was soaked. She brushed the wildly curling tendrils away from her ivory cheeks and slowly perused the room. The generous curve of her smile hinted at a warm, loving nature. Startling blue eyes held a quick intelligence that swiftly summed up any situation at hand.

Anyone watching was stirred to stare at the lovely damsel seemingly alone, undaunted and commanding in her posture. Her chin was tilted up defiantly and her eyes sparkled their intensity.

"Innkeeper!" called Larla imperiously. The man appeared almost magically. "Has my maid bespoken a room for Lord Somerset's granddaughter?"

"Non, mam'selle, she has not yet arrived."

"Do you have a room for Lord Somerset's granddaughter?" In situations such as this, appearing without one's maid, one had to command respect. Larla, being quite tall, looked down her aristocratic nose at the little man.

"Oui, mam'selle," he replied, managing a momentary curve in his otherwise grim countenance. He showed the way to the stairs, carrying her bag, making no comment.

Jenny Bailey, who usually followed closely in Larla's wake,

could always be counted upon to set the most officious of innkeepers in his place. The tall burly woman served more as a buffer against some of the harder aspects of following the army than lady's maid, but couldn't be faulted on her devotion to her mistress.

Larla didn't worry herself over Jenny's absence. That woman could take care of herself.

After unpacking, Larla could hear the rumbling sounds of wagons bearing the first loads of wounded from Waterloo. Rushing to the window, she scanned the horizon. There in the distance were assorted wagons lumbering along toward the town.

Larla didn't hesitate for a moment. She tore the comforter from her bed and pulled the top sheet loose. Opening her saddle bags, she found her scissors and cut and tore the sheet into strips. Stuffing the makeshift bandages under her cloak, she headed for the door despite the innkeeper's voice urging her to stay inside.

As Larla reached the street, other women were already opening their doors and ushering men inside, but the train of men was endless and there would be more soldiers than accomodations. Those who could walked, others were helped, while most had to be carried.

The sounds of moaning, wheels bumping, harnesses straining, and shrill cries meshed in a cacophony of sound. Wagon after wagon streamed in to clog the roadways. Wounded began to literally fill the streets.

Larla was on her knees beside a soldier whose arm was badly shattered. She cut away his sleeve and, gritting her teeth, gently wrapped it in the linen to stop the flow of blood. There was no more she could do, and after a thin smile, she turned to the next soldier, who was little more than a boy.

Other women and men arrived on the scene and she shared her bandage material with them. She couldn't help thinking of the innkeeper's face when he discovered the fate of his sheet. Colonel Somerset would have that added to his bill but Larla knew her grandfather wouldn't turn a hair. Larla recalled her grandfather's adage, "Nothing is too good for a soldier, no matter what his rank." She didn't dare dwell on her grandfather. He'd be in the thickest crush of the battle.

Larla's bright blue eyes were filled with compassion as she tended the wounded. Her normally cream-colored cheeks flushed with the exertion and a generous mouth kept a soothing monologue flowing, reassuring soldiers.

After what seemed like hours, Larla's back began to ache. She stopped for a moment to massage it before moving on to the next man. As she stood there, a wagon rolled alongside her and stopped.

A young private who was grey with fatigue called to her in what almost sounded like a sob. "Ma'am," he pleaded, trying to swallow a lump in his throat, "could you possibly find a bed for Captain Ainsworth? There's no other and I'm afeared he's badly hurt." The boy's lip trembled. "He's one of the best."

Larla went to the back of the wagon and saw the soldier's blood-stained face and soaked bandage on his head. The captain's jacket had been removed and another bandage was wound tightly around his blood-smeared chest. To look at him was to decide he'd bought it, but Larla was made of a stern constitution. She didn't give up easily. She bit her lip as she turned over thoughts in her mind of how she could help him. There were no more rooms available at the inn and this man needed immediate and constant attention.

Drawing a deep breath, Larla told the man, "Drive just down the street to the Hôtel de Bien Ville. If you can carry him into the inn, there's a room he can have."

"God bless," the soldier answered, a suspicious moisture around his eyes. The wagon moved on carefully toward the inn, Larla walking resolutely in its wake.

When they reached the inn the driver got down and gently

lifted the captain out of the wagon. He put an arm under the wounded man's shoulders and tried to get him to his feet.

"Stand to your arms!" commanded the private desperately.

Larla wasn't surprised when the ring of authority in the voice brought an effort from the wounded man to get to his feet.

Larla walked around to the uninjured side, and between them, they got the captain into the inn. Larla was conscious of the man's superior height and breadth.

There was a distinct change in the luxurious entry. The floor was littered with wounded, placed side by side with barely walking space between them. The innkeeper and his staff were busily administering to them.

Larla noticed that she hadn't been the only one to utilize the inn's linens. The sheets adorned many bodies and were taking on a reddish hue.

No one paid them any heed as she directed the private to her room. Between them they placed the captain on her bed. Captain Ainsworth sighed and seemed to lapse into complete unconsciousness.

"If you could help me get his boots . . ." she hesitated momentarily as she took in the wet, stained trousers, ". . . and his breeches off," she finished firmly.

The young private's eyes grew round and color rose in his cheeks. "But, ma'am," he protested. "You're a lady!"

"I'm a good soldier," she retorted. "I've helped with many a wound. I can't let petty things obstruct my helping this poor man." She turned her attention to the captain's head bandage and wrapped a fresh linen around the drying pads.

The private was showing ambivalence. His gaze moved back and forth between the captain and the young lady.

When Larla was finished, she reached for the captain's waistband. That brought the private to life and the boy helped her ease the trousers off, which he set to dry by the fire.

The once white undergarments were now grimy, but it was

the long sinewed legs that took Larla's attention. They were sleekly sculptured and hinted at a deal of strength. A fine covering of dark hair emphasized his masculinity.

She let her eyes wander over the captain's lithe form. His pallor was ghastly, his face drawn with pain. His chest was bare except for a mat of thick hair and the bandage. Neither hid the muscular shoulders that tapered to a narrow waist and hips. The man was a horseman without doubt. Larla found herself imagining the captain in other circumstances without the scars of battle.

"Please try to get Captain Ainsworth doctored up," the private pleaded as he turned to leave.

That brought Larla quickly to the issue at hand. "I'll do my best," she promised as she picked up her pitcher of water and poured some into the large bowl. She moved the candlestick over as she placed the bowl on the stand beside the bed. Her first thoughts were to get rid of the smoke and dirt and make him more comfortable. Then she'd tackle the wounds.

She washed his face carefully, keeping a light touch yet still cleansing the skin. She was not too surprised to find good facial bones, high cheeks, a strong nose that hinted of the aquiline, and sensual lips.

After she finished cleaning the blood from his person, she eased the bandage from his chest, revealing a long saber slash extending from his rib cage to his flank. The cut needed attention.

Her gaze wandered back to his face and she wished he'd open his eyes. She wanted to see their color.

Almost instantly, seemingly in response to her unspoken question, the captain's eyes fluttered open to take quiet stock of her. "Who are you?" he whispered. The low tones came from an educated voice.

Had she spoken the words aloud? "I'm Larla Somerset." Trying to push aside the funny sensation in the pit of her stomach, she assessed the wound, noting it wasn't deep but the blood was welling from the long injury. She frowned, knowing the bleeding must be stopped. "I'll be as gentle as I can," she assured him. "The trouble is there's no doctor available and I think this requires immediate attention." She swallowed her doubts and gave him a forced smile.

Since Captain Ainsworth's eyes had closed and he made no comment, she assumed he'd relapsed into unconsciousness. It was just as well, she thought grimly, as she reached for her sewing kit. She'd put in a few stitches to pull the edges together and then apply a pressure bandage. This wouldn't be the first time she'd set a stitch or two in an emergency.

As she knew from experience that skin was tough to pierce, she picked up her thimble. After threading the needle, she resolutely dug it through the skin. The soldier groaned.

Larla closed her ears to his pain and resolutely pushed the needle through the other side of the cut. Cutting the thread, she made a good square knot and moved down an inch and started the next stitch. She worked quickly, wanting to finish as soon as possible. A thin film of perspiration dotted her forehead and her lips were compressed tightly.

"Are you married?"

The question was such a shock she stopped the needle in midair and looked up into his face. His eyes were still closed but he obviously wasn't unconscious.

"No, nor engaged." She was too busy to dissemble and after wiping her forehead with the back of her arm, she began sewing again.

"That's the best news I've had all day." A deep sigh escaped his broad chest.

Larla didn't understand what significance the fact could have and with a slight shake of her head finished the stitches and began to bind the slash with a strip of clean linen. Her hands trembled a bit as they came in contact with his firm flesh and downy chest hair. The man had a strange effect on her.

"I think I should look at your head." She was willing herself to think of him only as a wounded soldier.

"The whole side of my head feels like it's caved in." He winced as she unwound the bandage.

"I don't know much about head wounds except that they bleed a lot," Larla apologized.

"Is it still bleeding?"

"No, it seems to be stopped."

"Then just put a fresh bandage over it and leave it," recommended the captain.

Larla did as she was bid, all the while wondering if the man was going to die. The thought brought a large lump to her throat.

"Can you find a priest?" the soft-spoken voice asked.

"A priest?" she echoed. Her heart lurched. He wanted to have his last rites before he passed on from this world. Tears clouded her vision. "Lie quietly for a moment and I'll see if one is about." She arranged the bedding about him and patted his hand.

After automatically straightening her riding skirt, she hurried downstairs. Seeing the innkeeper attending to a wounded man by the door, she made her way to him. "Do you know if there's a priest available?" A tiny catch in her voice gave her the innkeeper's full attention.

"You shouldn't be here. This is no place for a lady."

"Rubbish!" she retorted inelegantly. Her eyes were searching amongst the figures who were bending over the wounded.

"If a Spanish priest would be of use, there's one in the back parlor." He nodded toward the archway. "But if you need a French priest, you'll have to go out on the streets."

Larla was not of their faith but she was certain that in an emergency it didn't matter what nationality a priest had. Nodding her thanks she headed for the archway.

Bent over an obviously dying soldier was a short dark man in a brown cassock. He had a round placid face and Larla waited until the man had finished and turned away from the wounded soldier before speaking.

"Father, could you please attend a soldier I've been trying to help? I'm afraid he's dying and he's asked for a priest."

A sad smile crossed the priest's face and he stood up. "Habla usted español?"

"Un poquito." She was fluent in French but had only a few words in Spanish. She repeated her request slowly and added the word "mort," the French word for death.

He nodded, and Larla assumed he must have understood, for he rose to his feet and followed her.

When they entered the room the captain was lying just as she'd left him. She went over to the bed and picked up his hand and stroked it.

"I've found a Spanish priest for you but I'm afraid he doesn't seem to speak much English."

Captain Ainsworth's eyes blinked open and he smiled. The smile completely transformed the pain-ridden face. He was handsome and his dark brown eyes flashed a magnetism that made Larla catch her breath. "I speak fluent Spanish."

The priest moved to his side and the captain broke into a stream of Spanish. The priest stood silent for a moment and the soldier spoke again, an urgency in his voice. Finally the priest nodded and turned to Larla, motioning her to the other side of the bed.

The priest's words were soft and rushed. Larla could catch only an occasional word. He looked back and forth from the captain to Larla, smiling benevolently.

When the priest pulled a piece of paper from the pocket of his cassock, enlightenment came. Captain Ainsworth wanted to leave a will with her as a witness. The priest asked her something and she answered, "Si," thinking she knew what he wanted. She was more than willing to witness the will. It was the least she could do.

Captain Ainsworth squeezed Larla's fingers and watched her intently while the priest began another stream of Spanish. The captain answered him in the same language and then said to Larla, "Please say, 'Si.'"

Larla was close to tears but managed to croak out another "Si." Captain Ainsworth's eyes closed somewhat peacefully. Larla's fingers traced the muscles of his arm, trying to comfort the soldier.

The priest then walked over to the writing table and dipped the pen into the well and scribbled something on the paper and gave it to the captain to sign. With a great effort he shakily signed his name.

Then the paper was given to Larla. It was written in a scrawled Spanish, so she didn't take the time to try to read it, but merely signed below the captain's signature. The "Ainsworth" was quite plain but his first name was almost totally illegible. It started with a *J* and seemed to finish with *y*. She guessed it didn't really matter because it would certainly fill any legal requirements.

The priest gave them what was obviously a blessing and left the room with a measured tread.

As he heard the door close Captain Ainsworth captured her other hand and pulled her closer to him. She was amazed at the strength he had. The insistent pull forced her to sit on the bed. He lifted an arm to her shoulder and lowered her mouth to within inches of his.

His gentle smile would have melted lead and Larla gulped a breath into her airless lungs and tried to return the smile.

"Don't be afraid. Humor a dying man," he whispered as his hands moved to thread her curls. Captain Ainsworth seemed to have the power to bend her will to his.

Larla's lips trembled. She'd never been kissed before, and to see such a strong and obviously educated man brought to the end of his existence couldn't help touching her heart. She'd give him what comfort she could to ease his last hours.

When his insistent lips parted hers, she didn't resist. Soon the feel of his lips and the moistness of his tongue ignited an unknown spark. Waves of delight rippled through her. She had thought that such emotions were not for ladies of quality, but though the feelings were strange, they were not to be ignored.

Pulsing sensations were chasing themselves down her spine while a white heat centered itself in her rib cage and warmed her throbbing breasts.

Sensing her reactions, he bit the edge of her lower lip in a light teasing manner and then returned to ravage the soft depths of her mouth. Larla found herself pulled ever deeper into a spiral of need and desire.

She knew she ought to push him away but couldn't see any real danger in a man who was as badly wounded as the captain. Consequently she let the warmth build into a raging fire.

The captain took her response as a sign of acquiescence to meet his needs. Being a man of indomitable character, he never gave up a skirmish. He saw each challenge through to its completion and had never broken a promise. He gathered his inner resources to make a last effort to reach his goal. His promise to his father would be kept.

His hands caressed her neck and trailed down to her buttons. "I won't hurt you, my darling. Let me make you mine." In an instant her blouse was open, exposing her lacy camisole, and the captain's hands were caressing the exposed twin swellings above the frothy lace.

Larla tried to draw away, the situation clearly beyond her control. She knew she could give him a good push in the right spot and he'd probably pass into unconsciousness but it might also kill him. "Please don't do this to me." Her breath was coming in short gasps and her gaze was caught in the depth of his liquid brown eyes.

"Darling, it's all right. We're safely married and I wouldn't hurt you for the world." The smile broadened and the powerful eyes willed her to give herself into his keeping.

"I don't understand," she breathed in confusion. She tried to sit up but an iron arm kept her at his side.

"Trust me, sweetheart. Comfort me in my last hours." The warm brown eyes were hypnotizing.

Larla was torn. For the first time in her twenty-one years, she found herself unable to think clearly. She prided herself on her instant decisions and ability to summarize any situation accurately, but the captain was a mystery. His voice was suddenly stronger and the strength in the arms around her made a slight shudder shake her. She wasn't certain if it was fear or something else altogether that caused it. "How could you get a priest to marry us on such short notice?"

"You're adorable. On the battlefield any pretense of formality is waived. Come closer, little love, and kiss me," the earthy voice rasped.

Larla shook her head. "I'm not little and certainly not your love." Her pulse began to pound.

"We'll see," he murmured and kissed her into submission. With a swift pull on the drawstring of her skirts and another on her camisole, she lay bared to his piercing gaze. The captain tenderly devoured her with his eyes and hands.

"Oh, please," she breathed heavily, not knowing if she could stop the sequence of events—or if she really wanted to. How could a man at death's door have such strength? A blow to the head would stop his marauding invasion but she couldn't bring herself to attempt it. The rush of blood was still singing in her ears.

"Forgive me, my darling," he whispered softly. "I haven't the strength to take the time to love you as you deserve."

Larla fought the rising panic welling up in her throat. Was she actually married to this overpowering stranger? She hadn't time to do any more thinking as he very gently took possession of her.

CHAPTER 2

Larla opened her eyes slowly, light flooding the room. She turned beneath the tangled covers to determine if Captain Ainsworth was still alive and saw only a slight indentation in the pillow to confirm his presence from the evening before.

Alarmed, she swept the covers back and perused the empty room. All signs of the captain were gone: his trousers that had been drying by the fire, his boots, and his coat. Amazingly, the man had dressed himself and gone. Had he gotten very far?

Picking up her discarded undergarments, she quickly slipped them on and rummaged in the closet for another riding habit. As she ordered her tangled locks, her eyes became riveted on the paper the priest had given her, which had somehow fallen from her pocket.

She reached down and spread the primitive document on the dresser and scanned the Spanish script. She couldn't tell if it was a wedding license or his will. Determinedly she folded it and placed it in the pocket of her skirt and, with her lips in a thin line, made her way downstairs in search of the innkeeper.

The number of soldiers on the floor was very much diminished. Larla speculated that although some were better, many had died. Turning for the kitchen, she encountered the innkeeper carrying several bottles of wine.

"Did you see Captain Ainsworth? The soldier I was tending?" An urgent note crept into her voice.

"I am sorry, mam'selle, but I am so busy that I can not notice anyone in particular."

"He disappeared from my room and I can't locate him. I must know if he's alive." Her anxious blue eyes, fringed with heavy curling black lashes were persuasive.

"Wagons have been going through since dawn. The British Army is transporting all the wounded they feel can withstand the trip to England. There are many who are too seriously wounded to travel." He waved an arm at the soldiers littering his floor.

"Thank you." If Captain Ainsworth were on his feet, would he be deemed well enough to travel? Her grandfather would get to the bottom of this when he came. In the meantime there was more than enough work for her to accomplish.

She frowned suddenly as she thought of the paper in her pocket. She turned back and caught up with the innkeeper. "Do you know anyone who reads Spanish?"

"Oui, mam'selle. My wife is Spanish. Perhaps she could help you." He nodded toward the kitchen door.

Larla looked in the kitchen door and called, "Señora?"

A short plump woman with coal-black hair braided around her head smiled, drying her hands on her apron.

"Please, can you read this for me? A Spanish priest gave it to me. He seems to be helping with the wounded."

"Padre Bartolomeo?" The woman's voice was soft and she took the paper that Larla held out.

"I believe so," she said, thinking that it was the name scrawled on her paper.

The innkeeper's wife read it slowly, her face breaking into a large grin. "Congratulations, Señora Ainsworth. Have no fear. Although it is written in Spanish, it is certainly legal. Padre Bartolomeo has a small mission just down the road."

Taking a deep breath to get her emotions under control, Larla thanked the woman, accepted a tray for breakfast, and made her way back to her room.

Larla sank down into the room's one comfortable chair after placing the tray on the table beside her. It appeared that she had been married to a man she didn't know, consummated the marriage with a rush of emotions she hadn't known existed, and was in some doubt, twelve hours later, if the bridegroom was alive. It had been quite a day, she concluded.

She pursed her lips as she wondered how to approach her grandfather with this tale. Could she forget the episode? Not until she was certain that her monthly tide began as usual.

Normally a young unmarried girl would know nothing of such things, but in the wake of an army, one learned many things prematurely.

Larla drew an exasperated sigh. That was what the dying soldier had wanted—to leave an heir. The man had possibly given his last strength to that purpose.

There was a firm knock on the door and she rose to answer it. She opened it slowly to find her belligerent handmaiden standing there, arms folded in disapproval.

With a shock, Larla realized that she had completely forgotten about the woman.

"Well," snipped Jenny, "I see ye got yerself here all right. Ye don't look as if ye've had any trouble." She picked up the bags and stalked past Larla into the room.

"Humph," she continued. "This don't look a bit like ye." Stalking to the unmade bed, she mumbled about the ways of "the Quality." "I don't know how ye managed to lose me yesterday."

Larla eyed the telltale bed and quickly asked Jenny to fetch the rest of her bags. While the woman was gone she stripped the sheet, rolled it in a ball, and put it by the door.

"Where did you spend the night?" Larla probed when her handmaiden stomped back into the room.

Jenny sniffed. "I was late getting here but I found a space to pitch my tent. Alfred was somewhat reluctant to travel on the road with all the comings and goings-on."

Alfred was Larla's pack donkey that carried all her personal belongings. The donkey was past price in the amount of hardships he would endure, but occasionally the animal balked.

She helped Jenny sort through the packs of clothes and shake and hang them but her mind was turning the inescapable events of the previous evening.

There was no deviousness in Larla. Her grandfather had taught her to face facts and to accept life as it was. The principle had been ingrained in her. Therefore she accepted the trick that fate had played on her and went on with her work.

One of the British doctors had arrived and was attending to the wounded downstairs. Larla could see the man was overworked and dead tired. Jenny busied herself changing a dressing while Larla walked up to the doctor.

"Can I assist you?" she asked in a musical voice. She automatically noted his rank and uniform which proclaimed him a major in the Rifles.

The doctor was kneeling beside a sergeant whose lower left leg was badly shattered. The man was unconscious but groans of pain sounded deep in his chest. The doctor didn't look up.

"Can you assist me while I remove his leg? That's his only chance. I haven't either the instruments or the time to try to save it."

Larla gulped. She could face blood and wounds but to actually remove a man's leg? If it meant saving this brave man's life, she could do it. Straightening her spine, she took a deep breath, and informed him determinedly, "I've never seen it done before, but I can follow orders."

That brought the doctor's head up to see the lovely voice that could speak so positively. When he saw before him a beautiful young lady of obvious quality, he shook his head. "I can't ask this of you. I'll find an older woman or a man." He sounded weary and in some doubt that someone suitable could be found.

"Sir, there isn't anyone else available but Jenny, who acts

as my maid, and I know I can do as well as she." Larla could be just as stubborn as he. "What shall I do first?"

A tired smile lightened the features of the overworked doctor. "See if the kitchen is available. We'll need a well-scrubbed table and some hot water."

Larla had the innkeeper's wife help her clear the table and get it ready. The doctor lifted the patient with practiced ease and deposited him on the waiting table.

The señora, taking one look at the bloody bandage, hurriedly left the room, clearing her throat noisily.

The doctor asked grimly, "Still think you can help me?" There was considerable doubt in his voice.

"You tell me what to do and I'll see that it's done," Larla said with more confidence than she felt. "I've followed this man's army for seven years, and if there's one thing I've learned, it's to obey orders."

The doctor had just finished tying the last of the sutures when a tall grizzled colonel entered the kitchen. The man had a commanding presence despite his receding hairline and full grey side-whiskers. His large frame filled the door as he took in the bespattered scene with frosty eyes. His bushy eyebrows almost met across his nose as he frowned his disapproval.

"What's all this, Larla?" He barked the question as if he were dressing down a raw private.

Recognizing her grandfather's usual tone of voice, Larla didn't turn a hair. "The doctor has just finished saving this soldier's life." Her face was pale and her stomach was a trifle uneasy but she stood her ground firmly. One couldn't afford to show any weakness where the colonel was concerned.

The doctor added approvingly, "This young lady has proved herself a real soldier, sir. I couldn't have managed without her."

The man's words acted like magic. The colonel commended good behavior. "Humph! If your tour of duty is over here, Larla, I need to have speech with you." His eyes challenged the doctor who refused to fall into that trap.

Larla and the doctor exchanged understanding looks and she swept out of the room, her grandfather covering her retreat.

When they reached the privacy of her room he reached down and kissed her briefly on her forehead. "I'm proud of you." This was an accolade coming from him and Larla flushed with pleasure.

He motioned Larla to the chair and stood before her, his hands clasped behind his back and his feet apart as he addressed her.

"We're in the process of mopping up. The carnage is terrible. I've never before in all my service seen so many soldiers lose their lives. There were approximately 124,000 men engaged at Waterloo and we estimate about 60,000 dead." The tough old soldier's usually snapping green eyes were clouded with grief and looked suspiciously wet, but he cleared his throat noisily and regained control of his emotions.

"We're sending all the help we can to the battlefield to bring in any men who are still alive. Unfortunately we have a shortage of doctors for the great number of wounded. All who are able to travel are being sent home where they can get the help they deserve."

This seemed to be Larla's opening. "Grandfather, do you know a Captain Ainsworth? I believe he's in the Guards." Larla folded her hands tightly and waited, small lines of concern showing about her pursed lips.

"Ainsworth?" He cocked his head questioningly at her. "Ainsworth. Hmmm. General Maitland, of the 1st Guard Brigade, has a captain by that name. He's spoken to me of his courage. Is that the soldier you want to know about?" His voice was more stern than usual. His granddaughter was showing unusual interest in a man.

"I believe so." She gathered her courage. "Do you know if he's alive?" She waited tensely. Her grandfather had an unusual memory and if he heard a bit of information, it stayed with him.

"Maitland let me look through the death roles a short while ago, and I believe Ainsworth's name was on it."

Larla slowly sank into the chair, twisting her hands in her lap. She shook her head, wishing she'd misunderstood. The captain's piercing brown eyes and tingling smile was still fresh in her memory.

Seeing her distress the colonel wrinkled his forehead and his grey bushy eyebrows twitched in concern. "Did you know the man?"

Larla raised troubled blue eyes to his green ones. "I married him last night."

The bald statement shook the colonel as a cavalry charge would not. The colonel's mouth compressed into a grim line and his hands clenched into fists behind his back.

Larla smoothed her skirt before concluding sadly, "It seems I am a wife and a widow in a day's time."

CHAPTER 3

Although it was more than four years after the horrible day at Waterloo, Captain Jeremy Ainsworth, more readily known amongst the ton as Lord Marsden, found himself awakened again with the disturbing dream that originated in the wake of the battle.

A beautiful golden-haired witch tended his wounds and rubbed his fevered brow. Then the mists shrouded the scene and only glimpses of a soft pliant figure entwined with his filtered in and out.

Lord Marsden smashed a fist into his other hand. It plagued him not to be able to remember. The face wasn't quite in focus, but the woman called feelings of tenderness in him that no one had ever tapped before.

He wanted to forget the dream and he'd tried, but he hadn't been able to. He had gone so far as to offer for a girl of his acquaintance that was as different from the dream as night was from day. He didn't love her, but he hadn't expected to find a woman to love, only one to bear his children.

Finally deciding that sleep was impossible, he strode down to the stables and saddled Raven, the well-muscled black stallion that carried him when he was in one of his moods.

Jerking on the reins, he kicked the startled stallion into a wicked gallop. Together they raced over the countryside, seeking, searching for an answer to the riddle that plagued his very existence.

Again he went back over the details of the battle. The last thing he remembered was seeing a blinding flash and having a white-hot pain sear his skull. After that the memories faded in and out. He was in a wagon that made his head send out fresh spasms of agony each time it jolted.

Through the mist he saw her wiping his face. He could hear the musical voice talking to him but he couldn't quite make out the words. He had kissed her and she had responded ardently. He remembered stroking her exquisite flesh and then the dream was gone. His dream goddess that tormented his every step, tantalized his every thought—she was always there. Was it real or some figment of his imagination?

The next event that he remembered completely was waking in the hospital and Dr. Guillet telling him that he was a lucky man to be alive. A week. He had lost almost a week from his memory and no matter how he ordered himself to remember, he could not.

Sometime later as he reined in, Miss Marcia Underwood, his recent fiancée, hailed him from across the hedgerow.

"Marsden! How nice of you to think to include me in your early morning ride." Miss Underwood always assumed that the world revolved around her.

Marsden's jaw tightened as he rode toward the gate and opened it for her. He tipped his hat and said all that was proper. He looked upon her with sudden distaste. Her mousey brown hair was suddenly repulsive, her constant smile too sweet, and her entire bearing too, well just too much everything.

Marsden's thoughts returned to the elusive figure in his dreams and a smile softened his countenance. The ways she responded to his ardent advances made him sigh. When would he be able to forget her?

Miss Underwood chatted away, unaware that her prospective bridegroom's attention was far away in a pair of sparkling blue eyes. When she happened to glance at Marsden, his brow was troubled. "Marsden, was it something I said? Would you rather the bridesmaids not wear so bright a color as rose?"

"I beg your pardon, Marcia. I wasn't attending. Tell me again." Marsden's voice was soothing.

"Oh, it was nothing." She pouted prettily. "When we are married will you treat me so shamefully? You haven't been listening to a thing I've said," she scolded him, letting her hand brush down her front, as if to remove some imagined lint, but actually to draw attention to her trim figure.

Marsden caught the gesture, but only a muscle twitched in his cheek in response. For the duration of the ride Marsden paid strict attention to his fiancée and by the time they parted, her smile had been restored.

"By the way, Mama told me that Colonel Somerset recently returned from Scotland with his granddaughter, Larla Ainsworth, Jessamy's widow. Miss Butterworth had it from her butler's sister, who works for Colonel Somerset. Did you know he had married?"

"Yes, I knew. We had a letter from them sometime after Jessamy's death." His expression was bleak as he contemplated his cousin's death. He had been spared but Jessamy hadn't been so lucky. He and his cousin had been inseparable as boys. When Jessamy's parents had died of a chill while the boys were only in short coats, his mother had taken Jessamy in and raised him like a second son.

The news of his death hit his mother especially hard. She was very attached to Jessamy and had strived to make up for the loss of his own parents. Marsden's mother, Lady Worthingdon, wanted an heir to the vast estates that were her son's. She wanted to see children running about the grounds. In short she had pressured Marsden to marry so that she could.

Marsden looked at the retreating figure. How had he let himself be talked into offering for such a shallow girl? She was pretty enough and her portion was assuredly more than respectable but he knew deep down that he had offered for her solely to erase the memories of a pair of deep blue eyes and soft golden curls from his thoughts.

The harebrained idea hadn't worked and now he found

himself stuck with a girl he was beginning to find extremely distasteful.

The clear blue sky overhead and fresh smell of new-mown grass were a perfect background for little John to frolic about. Larla looked on fondly as her three-year-old son played, waiting for Sergeant Tompkins, the colonel's erstwhile batman, to bring up the pony cart for him to have a ride.

Master John, named for his grandfather, began to pull impatiently at his mother's hand. "Mama, are we ready to go now?"

Larla smiled down at the chubby little face covered with eager anticipation. "Yes, sweetheart. We're going now."

Tompkins handed the reins to Larla and then lifted John up to the seat beside his mother. He admonished the little boy to take care of his mother and the tyke nodded gravely.

Larla smiled reminiscingly down at her small son, remembering how John's great-grandfather had accepted his unexpected arrival into the family with surprisingly good grace. When Larla's premonition had proved true, he had sold out and settled with his sister in Scotland for a time so Larla could have her aunt's advice and company while she waited for the event to happen.

Flicking the reins, the old pony moved off and paced sedately toward the woods, where a well-worn track led to the river.

Larla had approved the plan that hadn't brought the three of them home until recently, when he was certain that no one would question Larla's being a widow and the age of her son. Her grandfather had tried to protect Larla and John as best he could. They had lived rather quietly at Aunt Ailsa's but now he felt the boy needed the warmer country air, a pony, and space to grow in and Larla needed to return to the ton to see about acquiring herself another husband. Larla had laughed as her grandfather had told her John needed a father and Larla, well, she needed a man to stir her blood.

Once on the path she stopped the pony. "Would you care for a turn, John?"

The question was superfluous because his eager hands were reaching for the reins. John's excitement was barely contained. He tried so hard to act grown up just as his grandfather had taught him, but sometimes, as now, he couldn't quite hide his natural effervescence.

Between her grandfather and Sergeant Tompkins, they were making a little soldier of him. Larla endorsed their efforts but his nurse was scandalized at their goings-on.

With the ribbons threaded neatly if not expertly between his small fingers, John started the pony docilely down the path. "Nice pony. We go a long way today. Nice pony," chanted John.

Larla watched her son fondly as he pointedly pulled on the reins to turn through the gate. "Mama, I did it. Did you see me?"

"Yes, little man, I did. You accomplished the turn with a nice style."

It was a typical sunny July day. The birds were chirping and the flowers leaned their blossoms to the warmth of the bright sun.

Before they had gone too far, Larla heard the sound of cantering hooves coming toward them and reached to take control of the reins when the horseman came into view. She noted the superb, spirited black stallion with a matched rider astride him.

As the rider perceived the pony cart he checked his horse, slowing the stallion to a walk. Larla assisted her small son to pull up the pony and had to endure his protests.

"I can do it myself," enunciated John clearly.

"You have an excellent driver, ma'am," commented the rider, amusement threading his voice.

Larla took in the military-straight back that sat easily in the saddle. He had a nose that was slightly aquiline and his cheekbones were strong and high. His mouth was generous and at the moment a slight smile curved his lips upward. His chin showed determination but Larla found no fault with it. His riding garb was a superbly fit coat of buckskin with trousers of brown that were molded to his shapely legs and proclaimed, if one was conversant with gentlemen's clothiers, Scott as his tailor.

Larla noted the stylish but plain cut of his clothes and decided that the gentleman had an air for fashion. She thought that his countenance was pleasing, showing more character than elegance, and while the face seemed vaguely familiar, she couldn't quite place it.

In his turn he inspected the golden-haired young lady holding her small son protectively while she seemed to take his measure. He noted the few tendrils of curling hair gently framing an oval face. Her sapphire-blue eyes sparkled with mischief as she stared at him throughout his lengthy appraisal. She was no classic beauty but she was more than pretty. She held her head high as she watched him.

In her forthright manner Larla broke the silence. "This is my son, John. He is, indeed, doing an excellent job of handling the ribbons."

Little John wriggled in his seat, and even though his mother's praise elated him, he was anxious to be off and finish his ride.

"May I be permitted to introduce myself? I am Lord Marsden. You must be Colonel Somerset's granddaughter."

Larla didn't know Lord Marsden, but at once realized why the face seemed familiar. He was a cousin to her dead husband. "I am Mrs. Ainsworth. Colonel Somerset is my grandfather."

Lord Marsden's hand involuntarily tightened on his reins and the powerful stallion began to prance. With a firm hand he brought the animal under control once more. "Mrs. Jessamy Ainsworth?"

The comment struck Larla on her weak point. She wasn't actually certain her husband had been Jessamy but everything pointed to it. Having been taught by a life among soldiers that the best defense is attack, she countered his question. "Why do you ask?"

Lord Marsden's eyes narrowed to black slits for a moment. "My father and mother, Lord and Lady Worthingdon, have recently arrived at Edgehurst for the summer and hearing we might have a relative in the neighborhood, asked me to ride over and extend an invitation for you and your grandfather to attend a small dinner we plan to give on Saturday night next."

"How kind of Lady Worthingdon. We haven't been attending any social functions as yet." Her tone was cool.

John had been looking speculatively at the big black. He dearly loved horses and occasionally, for a special treat, his grandfather would put him up in front when the old man was riding his favorite charger.

"Mama," John called, demanding her attention as he pulled urgently at her gown. "May I ride the big horse?" His large brown eyes raised pleadingly to Lord Marsden.

Seeing Larla about to give the boy a scold Lord Marsden intervened. "I'm on my way to call on the colonel and if you'll permit, Mrs. Ainsworth, he can ride up to the house with me." A warm smile accompanied these words and Larla had a feeling this man liked children.

She hesitated momentarily but it was hard to deny her son this simple pleasure. She could see no harm coming to the boy. "Very well. I'll turn around and follow you back."

Marsden rode to the other side of the cart and reached a strong arm around John, lightly scooping up the small boy and placing him in front of him.

Once there John sat up straight and his deportment was such as would be admired in a much older boy. Lord Marsden smiled down at Larla. "May I compliment you on your son. For his age he is most unusual."

Her heart swelled with pride. John was her life, the center of her universe.

She urged the pony into a trot as she followed behind, when the path narrowed. Mulling over the invitation from Lord and Lady Worthingdon, she acknowledged that it was the first step in recognition of her son's claim to his inheritance. She could assume that the family wanted to look her over and decide if indeed she was Jessamy Ainsworth's widow. Her chin came up. She enjoyed a challenge and if they thought they could maneuver her into renouncing his claim, they had a surprise coming. Her eyes had a martial sparkle that her grandfather would have recognized instantly. It was like a battle cry. Woe betide the man or woman who tried to best her.

Larla watched as Lord Marsden lifted the small boy to his shoulder. He turned to see her coming up the walk and waited for her. John clutched the tall figure with his little arms wrapped securely around his neck. The sight pricked her heart. Her son needed a loving father and nowhere had she seen a man that would fill her strict requirements. A deep sigh welled up within her; that was as much as she allowed for self-pity.

Marsden walked behind her to the side door, following a striking likeness to his dream figure. A prickle of apprehension struck him as he carried the precious little boy and he regarded the little chap closely. He couldn't imagine when Jessamy had married, for he'd been with him the night before Waterloo and Jessamy hadn't mentioned marriage. Something was not quite right about this and whatever it was, he intended to find out.

He lowered the little boy to the ground, grinning amusedly at the youngster.

"Thank you, sir," said John politely, with an almost regal incline to his head. With his duty done, he raced for the stairs where his nurse was waiting.

"Come along, Master John." The woman's voice was severe but her love for the little boy shone plainly in her warm eyes. Taking him by the hand, she led him up the stairs.

Larla tossed her bonnet, gloves, and whip on the side table. Moving over to the ornate bellpull she rang it once.

Within a minute or two their elderly butler, Williams, trod slowly into the room. His hair was thin and white, his eyes a faded blue but his manner was as majestic as it had been years ago. "Yes, madame?"

"Would you ask Colonel Somerset if it's convenient to come to the morning room? Lord Marsden is here."

After giving Lord Marsden a searching glance, he nodded and left the room at the same measured pace he had entered.

Larla ensconced herself in a comfortable corner of a Chippendale sofa and gestured around the room. "Won't you have a seat, Lord Marsden?"

She knew without a doubt why Williams, instead of one of the underlings, had answered the bellpull. Williams wanted to be able to regale the rest of the staff with his opinion of their first morning caller. A tiny smile curved Larla's lips as she thought of the old butler. He had her welfare at heart, just like the rest of her grandfather's servants.

A young man appeared bearing a silver tray with a bottle of wine, a tall flagon of lemonade, and a couple of wine glasses. Larla reached for her lemonade and invited Lord Marsden to help himself to the sherry.

Marsden sipped his wine appreciatively as he covertly studied her. He didn't want to be attracted to her, for she had the golden hair of the girl in his dream. He didn't need anything else to remind him, for the dream interrupted his sleep often enough. But still he was drawn to the girl. She had an unusual presence and a frank way about her that intrigued him.

When the colonel strode into the room, Marsden rose and introduced himself, receiving a curt nod in recognition. The colonel's carriage was as stiff as ever and his manner even more crusty than it had been during his service years. To a lesser man it would have been extremely intimidating but Lord Marsden seemed unaffected.

"You were in the service?" The colonel didn't miss the man's military bearing but he liked everything spelled out satisfactorily.

"Yes, sir. I served in the 1st Guard Brigade under General Maitland."

The colonel humphed a time or two, his bushy eyebrows lowered in concentration as he tested his memory. "You were ordered up to Hougoumont along with the 3rd Guard, weren't you?" There wasn't much he'd forget about those last days of the war. "I don't recall your name but then it's impossible to know every officer in the army." There was a question behind the statement and Lord Marsden took it in his stride.

"I served under my family name, Captain Jeremy Ainsworth. My friends knew my title but we dispensed with that formality."

The colonel's brow cleared. "Ainsworth— You must be a relative of my granddaughter's husband."

Ainsworth! Larla caught her breath as she heard him give his name. Williams had remarked that he thought that Lord Worthingdon was uncle to Jessamy and that Lord Marsden was their son, making him a cousin, but he had neglected to mention that their family name was also Ainsworth.

Larla swallowed and studied Marsden more closely. His features seemed somewhat more full than Jessamy's had been and his bearing more regal. This was a man who was vitally alive and aware of her as a woman. He had that look of appreciation as he gazed over her.

"Jessamy was my cousin. We were said to bear a strong resemblance to each other. He was my only relative and unless you come forward and claim his estates they revert to my father and then to me." That was speaking more plainly than he'd intended but he decided to advance and show a good attack.

Color rose in the old man's cheeks as he looked frostily through Marsden.

"It is my intention to call upon my solicitor and let him ravel the details, but I haven't yet been to London to see to it. Larla insists there is no hurry." He cocked one of his bushy eyebrows at his granddaughter, who instantly raised her chin.

"There'll be time for that later. Grandfather has more than enough means to take care of us." She bestowed on the colonel a warmly loving glance and then gave Marsden a quelling look.

"Perhaps I might be able to facilitate matters. Would you mind showing me your marriage lines?" He wasn't as tactful about this as he'd intended but he had to settle the issue soon because those tantalizing blue eyes were calling to him and he wouldn't permit himself the slightest flirtation until he could be sure she was who she said she was.

Hearing the hint of doubt in his voice Larla hurried from the room. She returned, holding a worn, soiled piece of paper. "If you can read Spanish . . ." her voice trailed off as he reached for the paper.

Opening it gently, he paused before reading it carefully. "During the Peninsular War I spent much time in Spain and learned to speak and read the language as well as any native."

The paper was a certificate of marriage performed by a Spanish priest, Padre Bartolomeo, on June 18, 1815, the day of the Battle of Waterloo. Both the priest's name and Larla's were written plainly but the signature of the bridegroom was somewhat erratic.

With iron control Marsden willed himself to be unaffected outwardly by the signature, but there could be no doubt. The first name was difficult to read but the "Ainsworth" was clear enough. A muscle twitched in his neck. It was the only sign of his shock. He knew he had a blank spot in his memory except for the recurrent dream, but this disclosure was staggering. The signature was his, Jeremy Ainsworth, and this slip of a girl and her charming boy were his wife and son. He suddenly remembered promising himself that he would marry when the first opportunity presented itself during the last hours before the battle.

His thoughts were crashing around in his head, while his outward countenance was quite calm. He couldn't claim his bride at this moment, for he'd recently given in to his family's plea to select a suitable girl and marry. Thank God he hadn't married Marcia Underwood yet, but they were officially engaged. How did a man of honor break an engagement and then calmly announce he was married to another? He must think of Larla and her reputation. If he worked at it, a solution would present itself.

He managed to return the document to Larla and admit that it appeared to be a legal and binding marriage certificate and that he recognized the signature. Calling upon all his vaunted address he managed to extend Lady Worthingdon's invitation to Colonel Somerset and then, in a mental daze, left the house.

Marsden had much to ponder as he rode for home. He was married to the woman who haunted his dreams and he had a son, the finest son anyone could ever have. His spirits soared and then plummeted. He was engaged to another woman. It would take quite some doing to straighten out this toil but he would approach the matter as he would any campaign. Strategy. He must map out his strategy.

CHAPTER 4

Tom Coachman held the pair of matched bays to a steady trot as the Somerset coach bowled toward Edgehurst, while Nurse sat beside him, her arms folded primly across her ample bosom. It was a fine summer morning and he was enjoying the rare privilege of driving some distance.

Colonel Somerset sat upright in the plush traveling coach next to his granddaughter with young John wedged between them. John clutched an old rag doll, of which his great-grandfather mightily disapproved. John had finally received permission to have such feminine frippery when Nurse had the happy idea of dressing the doll as a soldier.

Larla's thoughts kept returning to the tall virile figure who awaited them at Edgehurst. He had been the epitome of fashion with his easy address and assured manner. Larla had been grateful for his kindness to John and he had accepted her claim to be Jessamy's widow without protest. He had recognized the signature, she knew, because she had seen the tightening of his throat and the twitch of a muscle in his neck. It wasn't a big reaction but she had seen it.

Would Lord Marsden introduce her to the other guests as his cousin's wife? For John's sake it was time to start proceedings but up to now she hadn't felt like going through the legal tangle that it entailed.

"See the lieutenant salute?" asked John, enjoying the ride and his beloved doll.

Larla hugged him and dropped a kiss on his forehead. She wanted the best for her son and if it meant having to face a court proceeding and admitting how her marriage came about she'd do it. Of course the ton would probably cut her for such unbecoming behavior but she mentally shrugged away the consequences of such a disclosure.

Thankful that her grandfather had seen fit not only to make her an expert horsewoman and marksman, but also to educate her in mathematics, history, and all the subjects for a young gentleman, she vowed to hold her own in any skirmish that erupted. Knowing that these unwomanly talents wouldn't gain her an appreciation from her peers, she had taken pains to keep them secret since her arrival in Kent.

The huge cast-iron gates of Edgehurst loomed up in front of them and Larla found her breath coming a little faster. The imposing cream-stone structure sat majestically surrounded by gardens and sprawled lazily in several directions. Larla drew a slow deep breath to steady herself, while an inner turmoil raged inside her. What kind of reception would they receive?

As if sensing her thoughts Colonel Somerset turned to her, his stern face relaxing as he took in the deceptive look of fragility. He knew Larla was as tough as shoe leather when she needed to be. Patting her hand, showing an unusual gesture of caring, he growled, "It's time we took this step, m' dear. It will be all right," he assured her easily. He might be retired but he was still a colonel and used to handling situations and men.

Tom pulled the coach up before the big double doors just as a liveried servant ran down the steps to assist them.

Colonel Somerset handed Larla out and then reached for John, who was already trying to negotiate the huge step by himself. He ignored John's efforts and swung him to the ground. Larla grasped his little hand and marched up the steps, her head held high. She wondered what her hosts would say when they discovered they had a small child and his nurse along, but there was no way she'd leave him behind with only servants to watch over him just yet. Her motherly instincts were extremely strong. If they wanted her, they accepted John.

The door was flung open by an elderly butler. Seeing the man, Larla chuckled to herself. Evidently Lord Worthingdon had something in common with her grandfather.

A buxom woman dressed in somber black met them in the large grey stone entry hall with the announcement she was the housekeeper. As she saw little John and his nurse, her face broke out in a smile. "If you'll come with me Mrs. Ainsworth, I'll show you to your room so you may freshen up. Nuncheon will be in about an hour."

The housekeeper then turned to Nurse and directed her to the third floor where the nurseries were located.

Colonel Somerset browsed through the library, taking note of various titles while he waited for his hosts. As he thumbed the pages of an interesting book, Marsden strode in.

"I must beg your pardon, sir, for not being here to greet you as I fully expected to, but Father asked me to step out for a moment and view the new mare that was just delivered from Tattersall's. He thinks she has a touch of colic." Marsden accompanied his explanation with a smile that would charm a marble statue.

The smile made no dent in Colonel Somerset's craggy countenance but Marsden had uttered magic words. There was nothing more important to the old man than his horses. Larla said she sometimes felt that the horses came ahead of her.

Before Colonel Somerset had a chance to reply there was the sound of running feet across the stone floor and John burst into the room, his nurse calling him as she lumbered down the stairs. John stopped in front of Marsden and raised a pair of large brown eyes surprisingly like Marsden's.

"Please, sir, can I see the horse?" He was breathless from his exertions but his exuberance couldn't be subdued.

"You've run away from your nurse again," scolded his

great-grandfather, but a loving smile softened the stricture. "And it's 'may I.'"

Marsden waited with great interest to see what the outcome would be. John was an unusual child and was carving a place for himself in his father's heart.

By this time an agitated Nurse appeared, dropping a curtsey. "I'm that sorry, Colonel. I just turned around and he was gone." She moved forward and grasped John firmly. "Come along, Master John."

John turned obediently but the message in his eyes was plain.

"Would you care to look over the ailing horse?" Marsden directed his question at Colonel Somerset but John answered the question for himself.

"Yes, sir!"

That brought a bark of laughter from his great-grandfather. "Would you mind if we take him along?" His voice was gruff but Marsden could tell he was hiding the affection he had for the little boy.

"I was about to offer, subject to your approval."

It was with great rapport the trio headed for the stables. Colonel Somerset promised Nurse he'd return her charge shortly.

The men adjusted their steps to conform to John's short ones and they conversed knowledgeably about the symptoms of colic and the various remedies. The toddler was straining at the leash but managed to contain himself until they entered the huge stables.

In a stall at the far end of the stable Lord Worthingdon was busily issuing instructions to the grooms.

A stable boy was leading Marsden's newest sorrel stallion, Igor, out to the paddock and was fully occupied with the task, for the fiery stallion was prancing and kicking up his heels.

Eying the magnificent stallion, John trotted toward the animal as fast as his chubby legs would carry him. "Horse! I want to ride the horse!" he called.

Knowing the stallion's propensity for kicking when startled, Marsden raced after the little lad, calling him back.

Colonel Somerset stood at his ease surveying the situation. With a large breath he bellowed, "Attention!"

The stentorian shout not only stopped John in his tracks but also brought various stable hands' heads snapping around to see the source of authority.

When Marsden reached the boy he wanted to pick him up but the youngster stood at attention like an old soldier. The colonel strode up to his grandson, his face stern.

"About-face," he ordered and John turned smartly around, his eyes big with worry. "At ease." The toddler obediently spread his legs and put his hands behind his back but his lower lip was quivering.

"Were the troops ordered to advance?" The question was issued in such a severe tone that Marsden involuntarily flinched.

Wisely John kept his peace. "The punishment can be severe." This proclamation accompanied by a fierce scowl was enough to cause any soldier in his command to blench but John waited to hear the stricture.

John knew his grandfather loved him very much, but even so, a large tear trickled down the chubby cheek.

Seeing the remorse, the colonel relented. "Since you've obeyed orders so well, we'll overlook your lapse."

John brushed away the single tear and a big smile broke across the little face.

"Well, upon my word! I'd never have believed this if I hadn't seen it!" Lord Worthingdon exclaimed as he joined the group.

"Father," Marsden acknowledged, "I'd like you to meet Colonel Somerset. Colonel Somerset, my father, Lord Worthingdon."

The two men exchanged greetings and shook hands. The old colonel noted the resemblance between father and son. Worthingdon kept himself fit and lean, his carriage as straight as it had ever been. His only concessions to his age were greying hair and a few lines in his face.

"I just finished giving instructions to my groom about the new mare. When I heard Colonel Somerset call I nearly stood to attention myself."

That broke the tension and each of them relaxed with a smile.

Lord Worthingdon thrust his hand out to the colonel. He greeted his guests with all due ceremony and finished his apology for not being at the house to meet them, saying, "I'm sure you understand the need to see to a sick horse. One can't be too careful."

The colonel did understand and nodded as he looked over father and son critically. His tough old heart was wrenched for a moment as he thought of his son and how early he'd lost him. He put a hand on his little grandson's shoulder. "May I present my great-grandson, John Ainsworth." The words were filled with pride.

Worthingdon inclined his head in acknowledgement. "Well, there's no doubt in my mind that he's an Ainsworth. He certainly resembles both Jessamy and Jeremy at that age." He cleared his throat. "I don't know why this young rascal of mine hasn't gotten himself married and produced a grandson for me. I'd give a fortune to be able to claim a boy like this for my own." He sighed. "Jeremy has recently gotten himself engaged, so perhaps I won't have to wait too long."

Worthingdon collected himself and led the party through the stable to the stall that housed the new silver-grey mare.

As they trailed after him Marsden clenched his fists into tight balls and took several long deep breaths. It took all the control he could muster to keep silent and not proclaim that this was the longed-for grandson.

Little John was somewhat subdued as they stopped to view the mare. His face showed a wistful look that told his father that the boy would like to see over the stall enclosure.

Marsden bent down and swung the boy to his shoulder so

that his son could see the horse at close range. The youngster eagerly reached out to the velvet muzzle and patted the animal.

"I see he's not afraid of a horse," approved Worthingdon. He was as strongly attached to his horses as the colonel was.

After discussing the merits of the mare, Marsden reminded his father and the colonel that the ladies were probably wondering where they were.

Somewhat reluctantly the party made their way back to the house.

As they entered the morning room, they found Lady Worthingdon and Larla enjoying a comfortable coze. The colonel swiftly concluded that Larla was very much at her ease and unconsciously relaxed his stiff posture.

Lord Worthingdon made the necessary introductions, and while Lady Worthingdon acknowledged them gracefully, her attention was riveted on one small dark-haired boy.

"So this is Jessamy's son." Her fine old faded blue eyes seemed to soften as she took in the small boy. Lady Worthingdon had a full round face and an air of elegance that had probably been great beauty in her youth. A stiff gown of crimson in the prevailing style of high waists adorned her slightly full figure.

John in his best nankins and short coat made a creditable bow and gave his audience a radiant smile. His adult behavior brought an involuntary response.

"Charles," gushed Lady Worthingdon to her husband, "the boy is charming. I'm happy to welcome him into our family." Since this was the claimant to her nephew's estates, it was quite an admission.

Worthingdon smiled and, in doing so, became an older version of Marsden, noted Larla approvingly.

"You should see the boy under military orders. His mother and great-grandfather are to be commended."

Larla stared in silent fascination at father and son, so resembling each other. Marsden's eyes were softer and compelling, but his father's eyes were piercingly alive.

After a slight knock on the door, Nurse slipped in and held out her hand. John gave a deep sigh. He knew that his time had come, and without a word of protest, he walked over to Nurse, bowed to the assembled group, and put his hand in Nurse's. As the door closed they could hear an excited little voice talking about the horse he had petted.

Nuncheon was an informal affair. Only light topics were introduced and it seemed to Larla as if she had been accepted by Lord and Lady Worthingdon without any further proof.

Their son, however, was cut from a different bolt of cloth. One minute he had demanded to see her marriage lines and the next he seemed almost shocked. Had he expected her to be an imposter? She couldn't quite understand the magnitude of his reaction to her marriage lines. She'd put the thought aside for now, but she'd come back to it later.

Declining an offer to rest after lunch, Larla expressed an interest in the horses. She thought she would enjoy seeing the type of horses Marsden kept and wondered if he would be interested in taking her for a ride about the estate.

"Mrs. Ainsworth, you are indefatigable. After the jolting ride you endured this morning, you're ready to set off again."

"You have a very poor opinion of females, sir." Her voice was a little tart. "You have probably forgotten that I've spent a deal of time riding and walking almost every day in the train of the Army. And I assure you that I haven't gotten out of the habit."

Looking at her delicate figure and air of deceptive fragility, it was no wonder he had forgotten that she had lived through what most ladies of his acquaintance would consider a life of extreme hardship. He knew only too well what it was like to be in Wellington's army.

"I suppose you're about to tell me that what you'd really

like to do is try out one of our horses!" he said a trifle sarcastically. She seemed to bring out the rough side of his tongue.

Her face broke into a delighted smile. "Oh, thank you. I'd hoped for that."

Reluctantly he smiled back. "Did you think to bring a riding habit?" He looked askance at her dainty sprig muslin gown nipped in just below the bust in the current style. It was very becoming and sported a twelve-inch flounce at the hem.

Larla looked up at him to see a lurking devil gleaming in his eye. "If you'll give me only ten minutes, my lord, I'll be ready for you."

"Ten minutes, you say? There isn't a lady of my acquaintance that can change her dress in ten minutes." His tone was clearly disdainful.

Larla saw his words as a challenge. "I dare say, but then, you're really not acquainted with me yet, my lord. You would do well to judge me for myself alone, not by the standards you seem to expect." With those words of admonition, she swept out of the room.

Marsden's lips twitched in amusement. Larla was certainly anything but predictable. She would lead him on a merry dance, but he was going to enjoy every minute of the chase.

Within the alloted time Larla wisked herself into the room, a smile dominating her piquant face. A canary habit fit her trim figure admirably and a yellow pill box affair was perched at a rakish tilt on her golden curls.

Marsden made her a leg. "I make you my compliments, Mrs. . . . I'll be deuced if I'll continue to call you so formally. After all we're," he hesitated briefly, "cousins."

Larla had no objections and agreed to first names. "Shall we adjourn to the stables, Jeremy?"

He liked the sound of his name on her lips but the vivacity in her voice made him a little suspect. "Just how well do you ride, Larla?"

She had no false modesty and knew herself to be a superb rider, her authority being the colonel himself. He was a stickler if ever there was one. "I'll contract to ride as well as or better than any other lady of your acquaintance and for that matter better than most men!" She knew the words were inflammatory but she couldn't resist taunting him.

"Anyone who boasts of their talents . . ." he mused pointedly, daring her to flout conventions.

"I'll be delighted to show you, Jeremy! Just let me select a horse." Her eyes sparkled in anticipation.

"I wouldn't miss this for the Regent's entire stable." Since the Prince Regent was well noted for his horses, this was quite a declaration.

This slip of a girl seemed to bring out facets of his personality that he hadn't known existed. She pricked his conscience, she intrigued and perplexed him.

Larla stopped in front of a stall with a spirited sorrel stallion. "I'd like to ride this one." The animal seemed to be the most feisty of the bunch and Larla knew that with the conquest of this horse she would prove to Jeremy her ability to ride.

"Very well, but you ride beside me and I'll set the pace. I want to be able to lift you off Igor if I see that you are having any trouble handling him. Do you understand?"

Oh, she understood his convoluted reasoning all right. This cousin-in-law of hers thought she was a regular looby, wanting to ride an animal beyond her capabilities. She'd show him. The blood pounded in her ears as she strove to keep her quick temper under control. She took several steadying breaths as she waited for Igor to be saddled.

Marsden waited for an answer but none seemed forthcoming. As he'd made his position quite clear, he turned his attention to the high-spirited stallion. He watched uneasily as Igor pranced and bucked while the stable hands placed the unfamiliar saddle on his back.

Larla ignored the animal's playfulness and, lifting the hem of her dress slightly, placed a foot in Marsden's hand. He tossed her up, noting how easily she landed in the saddle.

After placing her knee carefully over the saddle horn, she arranged her dress expertly, her trim ankle only barely showing.

Marsden tried not to stare but found he had to strain. Damn the girl!

He leaped on Raven, who was standing rock still. He'd personally trained the horse and had been through countless battles with the trustworthy steed.

Larla allowed him to lead the way until they were out of sight of the stables. She controlled Igor's pranks easily and Marsden relaxed his supervision. When the opportunity arose, the path widening to a good-size track and Marsden's attention being drawn elsewhere, she eased her reins and gave the sorrel a hard dig in the side.

The Arabian stallion bounded forward and Larla leaned over his neck whispering cries of encouragement, her pale hair streaming behind her.

Marsden was so shocked it took him three full seconds to get Raven into a gallop. He could see at first glance Larla was glorying in the run and cursed her and all females under his breath as she led him a merry chase. The unimpeded view of her streaking along the paths was etched indelibly on his mind. The free-spirited joy that flowed from her riding as one with the horse was a tangible thing.

Marsden's brow wrinkled with line of worry, knowing full well the horse could be almost impossible to stop when he got the bit between his teeth. Igor had unseated many a rider and Marsden was afraid for his termagant wife. Urging Raven to breakneck speed, Marsden finally pulled alongside. Larla reluctantly pulled her horse in and she slowed to a sedate trot. She could see the fury carved in Marsden's face.

"Have you no value for your life? Have you no sense of propriety?"

Larla chuckled aloud. "You're only mad because I didn't obey your orders."

"Let me tell you . . ."

"Yes," invited Larla, "do tell me. Are you now satisfied that I can ride?" A wide demure smile posed innocently across her face.

"I can see that you handle the reins very well for a lady," he admitted ungenerously, when it could be said that she handled the horse far better than most men of his acquaintance. "You will please me by never attempting such a thing again," he admonished her grimly.

Her smile widened and she said sweetly, "I'll try to remember that if I ever wish to please you, but presently the possibility doesn't arise."

Larla waited for a retort, but as they were approaching the stable yard a carriage swung into view. Marsden clamped his jaw shut, biting off a few choice words of advice.

He swung hurriedly off Raven and came over to lift Larla down, taking in her disheveled state. She straightened her skirts and then put a hand to her tangled tresses. As nothing could be done about the disorder, she abandoned the effort, giving a little shrug.

Marsden took her by the elbow and was almost pulling her along, but the party in the carriage headed for them at the side door instead of the front door. The two groups met on the step.

"Good morning, Marcia," Marsden greeted sardonically, staring at his fiancée decked out in cherry muslin trimmed with ribbons. He nodded at the young man with her, "Harold."

The young man stammered his greeting, his broad face reddening at the effort. His new waistcoat of yellow polka dot drew a raised eyebrow from Marsden and he wilted at the seeming censure.

Miss Underwood, holding her parasol at exactly the right angle to protect her complexion against the rays of the sun, was studying Larla, noting her dishevelment. She looked condescendingly down her prominent nose.

"Marcia, may I present Mrs. Ainsworth, my cousin Jessamy's widow. Larla, this is Marcia Underwood . . . my fiancée, and her brother Harold Underwood.''

Larla, who had been taking stock of the fashionable gown and the air of superiority exhibited by the damsel in question, thought that fate had just dealt her a wicked blow. It was difficult to breathe and the blood seemed to freeze in her veins.

The word fiancée seemed to clang around in her head. How could he flirt and challenge her so if he was indeed engaged to Miss Underwood? His affections evidently weren't engaged. Larla eyed the oddly matched pair and came to an instant conclusion. They wouldn't deal well together. Marcia was as cold as yesterday's roast beef.

Marsden moved forward to take his fiancée by the arm. ''To what do we owe the honor of a visit, Marcia? This is quite unexpected.''

She had an overly bright smile plastered on her face. ''Mama said Harold might drive me over so I could speak to you about our marriage plans.''

Marsden's face froze as he stiffly ushered Miss Underwood into the house. Then his penetrating gaze turned to her brother.

''Dash it all! I came down to rusticate for a spell and Mama put the pinch on me,'' he almost whined. Harold was completely under his mother's thumb, that woman holding a tight rein on the purse strings.

''Under the hatches again, Harold? What was it this time? Faro?''

Harold threw him a bespeaking glance and ignored the question.

''If you will excuse me, I'll go freshen up.'' Larla couldn't get away too quickly.

Miss Underwood's evil genius prompted her. ''Ah, yes, you seem to have been in a tussle.'' Her eyes were calculating as she assessed both Marsden and Larla.

Larla's chin came up decidedly, mischief sparkling in her

sparkling blue eyes. She would never flee in the face of battle. "Not exactly," she murmured with a deep sigh, "but I certainly enjoyed the sensations." Looking at Marsden first and then directly at Marcia, she merely waited to see if that proper damsel had a retort. Hearing none, she shrugged her shoulders and made good her escape.

Marcia's face was glowing scarlet in rage, her teeth grinding audibly. The look of pure hatred she sent toward Larla would have withered a lesser woman. With a couple of deep breaths Marcia tried in vain to bring her temper back into control.

"Marcia! You misunderstand. The wind blew her hat away and disarranged her hair. Larla just meant she enjoys being out of doors."

Marcia allowed herself to be talked over. Coolly appraising Marsden's magnificent figure, a thin smile appeared on her lips. "I don't mind a man's little peccadillos," she intoned regally, "but they should be conducted with discretion."

Harold mumbled a sound of protest but she ignored him as she gracefully disposed herself on the sofa, inviting Marsden to sit beside her.

Marsden stared at the woman in disbelief, realizing suddenly he'd engaged himself to a shrew.

He'd been seriously ill when he returned from Waterloo and for months his life seemed to be confined to a bed because of the dizziness. When his body had recovered, he was still sick in spirit. The will to become his former self had temporarily vanished and he'd let his family impose their desires on him. It was just recently that he could put the battles and the terrible losses of life into perspective. The only constant during the entire four years since Waterloo had been the nightmares of the battles and the fantasy dreams of a blond-haired angel.

His face relaxed and he smiled as he thought of his wife and son. He would resolve this stir cake as quickly as possible.

He must have been sleeping when he let his family talk him into this engagement. He and Marcia would have been at each other's throats constantly.

He hadn't been a captain in the British Army for nothing. He understood tactics to a nicety. He'd retreat and attack on another front.

CHAPTER 5

Marsden chose a chair opposite Miss Underwood while she gave her brother a burning look, which that young man rightly interpreted to take himself off. He rose gracefully, brushing off some imagined lint from his sleeve, and mumbled something about looking at the horses.

Miss Underwood sat primly upright, quite confident. Her distressing habit of wanting to run everything and knowing more than anyone else hadn't endeared her to the opposite sex but Marsden hadn't been treated to this side of her as yet.

"I think it's about time we set our wedding date. Mama was asking about it yesterday. It would be best to have it before the little season starts in the fall so we can take in all the routs, balls, and theater parties together." She held up her hand as he began to speak. "I know what you're going to say. It's not much time to get a trousseau together but I've been working on it for some time. I'm certain I can manage. I've reserved St. James, Hanover Square, for the first of September, with your approval. We'll be able to accommodate all our friends."

"My dear, that doesn't suit me at all. I have no desire to go to London to be married. For that matter, I don't care to be married that soon." He eyed his fiancée with faint distaste.

"Marsden! You don't understand." Her foot tapped in vexation. "This is what I want." She spoke as if her word was law and she expected him to fall in completely with her plans.

"Sorry. You know that since I've gotten back home I haven't gone on the town at all. My time in London was in Berkeley Square at the family residence, just to be handy to my doctor. I fear I'm not inclined to the social scene anymore." As he saw how poorly she took that comment he pushed his charge a little farther. "In fact, my dear, I don't know if I'll ever return to the parties and gaieties. They seem so frivolous." His lip twitched as he watched her reaction.

Miss Underwood's eyes almost popped they grew so large. "Marsden," she said in a strangled voice, "please, don't fun with me so. You know this is your life. It's expected of you with your station in life." It was plain to see that she wouldn't welcome a quiet style of living.

"I think being married in our little chapel in the village is as much as I could handle," he responded neutrally, holding back a chuckle.

"What would the Duke of Argle, my grandfather, say to such hole-in-the-corner proceedings?" Miss Underwood was scandalized. Her whole countenance was a picture of mortification.

Marsden was getting ready to deliver a final volley of artillery fire when his mother entered the room. This skirmish was only being postponed.

Lady Worthingdon took in the situation at a glance. A distinct sparkle emanated from her as she saw the engaged couple seeming to be having a disagreement. She kissed her prospective daughter-in-law on the cheek. "How nice to see you. If I'd thought you might brave the heat to come over I'd have invited you to dinner. We're having our niece-in-law and her infant son."

Miss Underwood turned to Lady Worthingdon for support. "How nice! I'd love to make your niece's acquaintance and your dinners are always such a delight. But I don't believe I could make the trip twice in one day. The heat is so exhausting, you know." She sighed deeply. "I just came to talk to Marsden about our wedding but he tells me he isn't up to a social life yet."

Lady Worthingdon didn't bat an eyelash at the remark. "I'm afraid that's true, dear. He does seem to still have some problems with his memory." As Miss Underwood turned to Marsden, his mother gave him a broad wink.

He wasn't certain what to make of it. He hadn't told his mother, or anyone for that matter, about the week missing from his memory and he'd always thought from the way his mother had encouraged him, that she was more than partial to Miss Underwood as a daughter-in-law. It was something to mull over later.

"Marcia, I'll have Worthingdon send one of the grooms over for whatever you might need, and if your mama permits, we'll be glad to have you spend the night." Lady Worthingdon was the epitome of a gracious hostess.

Harold strolled in and greeted Lady Worthingdon with grave courtesy before turning to Marsden in great animation. "You've a fine bit of horseflesh in your stables. Several I'd like to throw a leg over."

"I'm sure you're welcome. We were just discussing having you and Lady Marcia stay for dinner. Would you care to join us or have you already made plans?"

Things were dull at Laurel Court and Harold seized upon the opportunity to be away from his overbearing mother. "I'd be happy to stay."

Considering the matter settled, Lady Worthingdon excused herself to make the necessary arrangements. She had a secret smile as she gave her requests to the servants. Her son was finally beginning to take an interest in his life. "It shouldn't take too long before Jeremy realizes what type of girl Marcia Underwood is," she chuckled to herself. Her ploy to make him do something, anything, had worked admirably. "And to have a darling niece like Larla and her son thrown into the pot at the same time is just what the doctor ordered. I only hope Jeremy will see Larla's worth," she added fervently in an undertone as she made her way to the servant's hall.

Dinner proceeded smoothly, as all Lady Worthingdon's affairs did. She steered conversations into neutral channels and solicited opinions on current events. The pace was quick and lighthearted.

Larla responded as if she were accustomed to moving in the finest circles, and Miss Underwood, keeping an eagle eye on her to see if she was gauche or committed a faux pas, was doomed to disappointment.

Harold, finding himself next to Larla, regaled her with his funniest stories. Larla, as was dictated by polite society, divided her time between Harold on her right and Lord Worthingdon on her left.

Marsden watched the scene disapprovingly from across the table. He seemed to be jealous of the attention Larla was receiving. His comments to Miss Underwood were short and almost curt.

Lady Worthingdon watched the byplay interestedly. A little smile curved her generous lips and a light danced in her faded blue eyes. Life promised to be exciting and she was in a position to enjoy it to the utmost.

Correctly she withdrew the ladies to one of the drawing rooms while the men were left to their port. As they seated themselves in the blue salon with its Aubusson carpet and graceful Chippendale furniture, she launched the topic of fashion into the conversation.

When the topic moved to fall gowns, Miss Underwood had been suppressed as long as she could stand. "Dear Lady Worthingdon, I have decided that September is a good month for our wedding and came over specially to talk to Marsden about it." She hesitated a moment, casting a look at Larla that should have frozen her into immobility.

Larla merely smiled back nonchalantly and settled herself comfortably into the large wing-backed chair. "There is something to be said for September weddings," she granted easily.

"Something Marsden said led me to believe that he's not enjoying the best of health. Can you tell me what seems to be wrong?"

"As he doesn't like to bother me with any problem, I can't really tell you, my dear. However, lately I have noticed a change in his behavior . . ." Lady Worthingdon let the words trail away suggestively. Actually the change seemed to be for the better as soon as he met Larla, and for the moment it certainly was a problem.

Miss Underwood had frowned at these words but Larla's countenance became a study in smiles. Larla seemed to have gained an ally in Lady Worthingdon and wondered just what the redoubtable soul was up to. Larla knew for a fact that Marsden had no problems.

Lord Worthingdon announced as the men trailed in, "Our son convinced us that we shouldn't linger over our port tonight but should get back to the ladies."

"How delightful! Now we can all have a comfortable talk." Lady Worthingdon eyed her son speculatively, giving him a special smile.

Harold inquired of the group, "Did you hear that there is going to be horse racing at the village fair next week? How about you Marsden? Your black can probably outrun anything on four legs."

"I'd forgotten all about the fair." Seeing the astonished look on Harold's face, Marsden added quickly, "I've had other things to occupy my mind." Taking in the disapproving glare on Miss Underwood's face and the anticipatory light in Larla's, he exclaimed, "The very thing. Larla will get a chance to meet some of our neighbors and there will be lots of fripperies to buy."

Lady Worthingdon picked up her cue. "What a wonderful excuse to have a small house-party. Why don't we plan on all of you coming down next week, say Friday, and spending a long weekend. We'll all go together to the fair and even take in the horse races."

Colonel Somerset had been very quiet up to now chiefly because he'd had a long day and been fed extremely well.

His head had been nodding for several minutes but as soon as he heard the words "horse race" he became alert.

Watching him rub his hands in anticipation, Larla knew Lady Worthingdon had one guest she could count on. Larla was conscious of a little warmth flushing her face. She would be glad to see more of her cousin.

"We'll be happy, my lady, to be of your party," boomed the colonel.

Lady Worthingdon's gaze passed on to Larla. "I'd be most happy, ma'am, but would you mind having John? I don't like to leave him with the servants."

"That darling boy is welcome here anytime. I'd like nothing better than to claim him for my own." Her gaze moved on to Miss Underwood. "How about you Marcia? Will you join us?"

"Yes, of course." A country fair was not her idea of entertainment, but she wasn't about to be left out. "But surely a fair isn't a place for a little boy?" she disapproved with acerbity.

Larla's mouth compressed in anger as she carefully worded her answer. "Fairs seem to be just made for little boys. Marsden, don't you agree?" She turned to Marsden with a slight deference.

"Oh, I agree wholeheartedly." His lips twitched amusedly as he watched Larla best Miss Underwood in a duel of words. He turned to his father. "Do you remember taking me when I was still in short coats and I struck out to see the horses on my own?"

Lord and Lady Worthingdon exchanged warm looks. "I well remember, son. I almost gave you three of my best right then," he laughed, waving his large hand.

"My dear Charles, you never put a finger on him. Marcia, would you invite your papa and mama to join us? I'll send a note home with you."

"Thank you, Lady Worthingdon, but knowing Mama I'm afraid she may not come."

For the evening entertainment Miss Underwood was persuaded to sing. With a becoming hesitation she went to the piano. Miss Underwood was gifted with a dramatic soprano voice, but often made the mistake of trying to sing arias that were beyond her preparation.

Marsden stood propped against the Adam mantle, in a coat of lavender superfine nicely molded to his splendid physique, his arms folded and an expression of extreme boredom marring his features.

He almost winced as Miss Underwood trilled her way through a difficult passage in the last song in her repertoire.

Larla watched Marsden from across the room, his tedium pleasing her secretly. He was very pleasant to the eye and she grinned at him and nodded almost imperceptibly when he glanced in her direction. He flashed her a brilliant smile in return.

Miss Underwood, seeing his smile, mistook its cause and finished her song with an air of triumph. "Do you sing, Mrs. Ainsworth?" she asked condescendingly, smoothing her stylish gown of striped amber sarsnet.

"I don't claim to be in your class," Larla demurred. She let eyes fall to the floor to hide her delight in the request.

"But you mustn't judge yourself too harshly," Miss Underwood cooed, thinking to cause an unfavorable comparison between the two of them.

"Would you consider favoring us with a song, Larla?" Marsden requested gently.

Lady Worthingdon added her support. "I would so love to hear you, dear. You have such a musical speaking voice."

"Very well, but I hope you won't be disappointed," sighed Larla and seated herself at the piano. Soon she was lost in the simple country ballad, singing in a light, lyric soprano voice, accompanying herself with a simple harmony. Larla's light voice thoroughly contrasted with the heaviness of Miss Underwood's. Larla's tones rang clear and free while she concentrated on the message of the song. Larla hadn't had the opportunity that Miss Underwood had to refine her gift, but she did possess a fine instrument.

Miss Underwood's look was sullen at best, her lip curling in displeasure.

When Larla was done, Marsden strode over to the piano and helped her up. "The voice is beautiful," he murmured, "just like its owner."

Larla flushed becomingly, while Miss Underwood turned slightly pale. The scene wasn't unfolding at all as Miss Underwood had planned. Her fingers curled in her palm and she strove to turn the attention back to herself. "Very nice," she intoned coolly.

Lord Worthingdon nodded his approval. "Delightful, my dear. I could listen to several more."

Larla looked at him apologetically. "I'm afraid my real talents lie in other directions."

"Oh, painting and embroidery perhaps?" inquired Miss Underwood with faint skepticism, as she pressed her charge.

"No, riding and shooting. I've had a deal of experience in both." Larla's eyes danced as she spoke.

"Oh, then you hunt?" Miss Underwood returned genially, knowing she had the best seat in the county.

"No, I've never had the pleasure, but I'll guarantee I can cover any ground and be on my mount at the finish," she stated simply.

"By Jove!" exclaimed Lord Worthingdon. "I'll be glad to mount you anytime. You must join us when we begin the hunt. As for shooting, we'll be happy to include you in the fall when we begin pheasant season."

"I'd be delighted to accompany you and let you judge my skill yourself." She shifted her focus to return Miss Underwood's exchange of fire. "Do you shoot, Lady Marcia?"

A slight shudder passed over the delicate features. "No, my father doesn't consider it a fitting pastime for ladies."

Before Larla could make a suitable retort, her grandfather

stood up. "Larla, my dear, I'm tired. Come walk with me upstairs."

Acknowledging the temporary cease-fire order, Larla rose and placed her hand on her grandfather's arm, bidding the assembled company a good-night.

Marsden sported a broad smile as he acknowledged the salutation.

Miss Underwood merely inclined her head and turned to Marsden imploringly. Marsden winked at Larla over his fiancée's head.

Larla grinned as she ascended the stairs. Colonel Somerset patted his granddaughter's hand consolingly. "You'll have to polish up your company manners," he adjured her as they reached the upper hall. "It's easier to ignore such rudeness. Show your worth by your deeds, my dear."

This was sound advice from a man of experience and Larla listened. "I can't understand why she's taken me in such violent dislike, but I never was one to run from a confrontation," she warned.

The old colonel managed a frosty smile. "The woman is plainly jealous of you. You have far more to offer a man than she has and she's clever enough to see it. After all, she hasn't married Marsden yet and you remember the old adage, 'There's many a slip between the cup and the lip.' "

"Grandfather, you're an old darling!" Larla beamed at him.

He snorted, but looked quite pleased. "Strategy, my dear," he murmured encouragingly.

"I've a week to gather my forces and make my battle plans. I've learned a thing or two in this man's army." With that sally she whirled into her bedchamber, smiling thoughtfully.

The colonel chuckled, seeing many skirmishes ahead. He knew that look in his granddaughter's eye. She wouldn't give up any battle without a fight. Weighing the competitors, he murmured to himself, "I'll put my blunt on Larla."

The next few weeks promised to be the most entertaining

in a long time and he would watch the strategies and tactics with a practiced eye. Marsden had yet to find out about her mettle. The old man snorted with laughter. Marsden would need a fast horse to keep pace with his granddaughter's antics, but if anyone could he seemed just the man to do it.

CHAPTER 6

John eagerly jumped down from the carriage. "Is it time to go to the fair yet, Mama?"

"No, little man, tomorrow is the day. Maybe today Lord Marsden will let you look at the horses again." Larla's voice softly soothed her son and she walked him up the steps to Edgehurst.

Larla's eyes sparkled as she anticipated renewing her acquaintance with Marsden. He was the first man since Waterloo to make her heart flutter. He was arrogant, domineering, and forthright, but he was also gentle, teasing, and stirred her senses. Was ever a man so contradictory?

They sat down seven to dinner, the colonel, Larla, Lord and Lady Worthingdon, Marsden, Miss Underwood, and Harold.

At Lady Worthingdon's inquiry, Miss Underwood responded, "Mama couldn't think of traveling the five miles in this heat."

Larla lifted an eyebrow in question at Marsden. As she thought of the entire days of marches she had endured in the army, a faint smile crossed her rosy lips.

There was a distinct answering twinkle in his eyes. He seemed to know just what she was thinking.

The more she saw of Marsden, the more she was certain that the two of them were well matched. Life would never be easy, but it wouldn't be dull either. The first problem to surmount was to remove Miss Underwood from the scene. The best way to do that, she decided thoughtfully, was to find her a more acceptable mate, one who would enjoy her strict up-bringing. That would be a definite challenge.

After dinner the ladies gathered in the drawing room while the men lingered over their port. Miss Underwood droned on, full of knowledge of the local museums and exhibits, extolling the virtues of the Elgin Marbles.

Larla managed to keep a smile pinned on as she listened to the prosing voice, but her mind was far away, planning a campaign that would considerably change the course of her life. It was strange how interesting life had become since Marsden had stormed into her world. A warmth stole up her middle and radiated outward as she thought of her attraction to her well-formed, decidedly male cousin.

She'd need to do some serious socializing if she were to come up with an eligible candidate for Miss Underwood's hand. However, any goal worth having was worth working for, and she'd set her mind and her heart on this one. She would set to work to organize an evening of entertainment at Somerset Place.

The gentlemen seemed to be in remarkably good spirits, having downed more than one bottle of wine when they joined the ladies. Larla smiled shyly at Marsden when he quizzed her visually. The feeling of attachment strengthened each time he came near.

"Would it suit you ladies," asked Lord Worthingdon genially, "if we leave about nine in the morning? That will give us enough time to peruse the booths before the horse races in the afternoon. We can have lunch at the fair. They always have lashings of good food. We can take our own wine and eat al fresco style. We'll be home in good time for Yves to fix us a sumptuous dinner."

It was generally agreed the plan was a sound one and after a time of lighthearted speculation on the outcome of the next day's races, the assembled group broke up.

The colonel and Lord Worthingdon went off to the library while Miss Underwood hurried upstairs after Lady Worthingdon, hoping to gain her support in pinning Marsden to a date. Harold trailed behind.

Marsden took Larla's hand. "Well, cousin, are you ready to call it a night or can I interest you in a moonlight stroll through the gardens?"

Larla looked at Marsden speculatively. "Just cousinly interest in my welfare, Jeremy?"

"Oh, at the very least, Larla."

Marsden took her arm and led her out through the french doors. The almost full moon and colored lanterns gave the garden a fairyland appearance that delighted Larla.

"I would like to open Somerset Place with a card party or an evening of entertainment. Which do you think would be best, Jeremy? My idea is to invite the neighbors to socialize and get to know us."

"Card parties go over rather well with the older set and if there were a little dancing for the younger generation, well, the party would almost be a guaranteed success."

"Are you saying that you would enjoy dancing, Jeremy?"

"Only if I may dance with you," he responded warmly, a faint light of admiration gleaming in his eyes.

"Why, Jeremy, I believe you're flirting with me, and you an engaged man." She let her salvo begin the duel.

"Larla, darling, you have the most unruly tongue."

"Are you telling me you're not flirting with me? Horsefeathers! And here I thought we were making progress."

"Termagant, someone certainly needs to take you in hand and I believe I'm just the man to do it." The warmth of his tone belied the brashness of his words.

"I'm waiting, Your Lordship." Her eyes sparkled with mischief. "When do the lessons begin?"

"Now," he growled quietly, drawing her into his arms. He covered her soft mouth with his, quelling her resistance. The kiss began as a demonstration of mastery but graduated rapidly to a study of gentleness and seduction.

"I . . ." Larla began, dazed by the magnetism of his lips and the sensuality of his rugged chest.

"Darling, I will teach you to be silent yet," he mused before kissing her breathless again.

Sensation upon sensation crashed about Larla's head and washed its way down through her unresisting body. Her breath caught in her throat and she found herself making little mewing sounds. When he released her suddenly, she took a steadying breath before asking with confusion, "What about Miss Underwood?"

"Have faith, my darling. It will all work out in the end." He tweaked her nose playfully before leading her back to the house.

As he escorted Larla to the foot of the stairs, she had much to think about. Jeremy hadn't said that he was breaking his engagement, but that seemed to be the context of his remarks.

She floated up the stairs on a cloud and promised herself that she would work harder at finding Miss Underwood a man worthy of her lofty self.

The assembled party set out early the next morning, the ladies riding in an open carriage while the gentlemen rode.

Miss Underwood, holding her parasol stiffly, commented on the brightness of the sun. Larla shrugged. She didn't own a parasol and didn't really feel the need. The brim of her fashionable poke bonnet with saffron flowers and ribbons sufficed. The confection matched the saffron walking dress trimmed with the same daisies.

Marsden directed the way and the conversation between the men, covering the fine points of the various horses racing during the afternoon.

The fair was in full progress, jugglers tossing their plates and balls high into the air, vendors calling their wares, and children whooping at the antics of the clowns.

Marsden saw the look of adoration on little John's face as

he neared the carriage. "Larla, may I take John up before me?"

At the question John's arms reached up without waiting for approval. He knew his mama couldn't be so poor-spirited as to refuse him this treat. At Larla's nod, he reached down and scooped up his small son, swinging the infant into the saddle in front of him.

"You're spoiling him dreadfully," Larla commented complacently.

Miss Underwood added her oar. "There's no need, Marsden, to make yourself uncomfortable." Her lips pressed firmly together.

"Surely that's my business," he returned in a deceptively gentle tone.

Miss Underwood blanched at the stricture and turned away to find something else to complain about.

Lady Worthingdon listened to this exchange with a deal of satisfaction, a bemused smile transforming her for a moment into the girl of her youth. She nodded to herself in approval of the conduct of her son.

While the men took their mounts to the grove, which was set aside for stabling the horses for the day, the ladies strolled down the lines of booths. Embroidery, fancy candles, ribbons, flowers, preserves, and many more items tempted them.

Larla moved forward to a booth presided over by an elderly woman. An appetizing array of aromatic pastries wafted along to Larla's nose. Turning to see if Lady Worthingdon would like to have one of the delicacies too, Larla bumped into a very solid young man.

"Lady Wor— Oh, I beg your pardon. I'm afraid I wasn't watching where I was going." She smiled winningly at the gentleman of some twenty-five or twenty-six years.

He responded gallantly. "I'm sure it was my fault. I was concentrating on the delectable pastries," he said in a gravelly tone. It was evident from his portly frame that he en-

joyed his food. Tearing his gaze from the rich spread, he
assessed Larla with an expert eye, deciding she was a cut
above the average damsel.

"May I introduce myself? I am Broome," he stated with
due pomp and a formal bow.

Larla wondered if she were supposed to recognize the
name. "I'm Larla Ainsworth, here with Lady Worthingdon."

As the rest of the ladies continued down the row of booths,
Lady Worthingdon recognized the gentleman with Larla and
made her way to them. "We didn't expect to see you here,
Broome. I thought you still in Paris," Lady Worthingdon observed dryly.

Broome again bowed and made a suitable reply.

Miss Underwood gave him the nearest thing to a smile.
Larla noted it was an unaccustomed exercise and it set her to
thinking. Her glance returned to Broome who was talking
animatedly about his visit to Paris and his impressions of the
Louvre, the palace of Versailles and the Place de la Concorde.

Larla caught Lady Worthingdon's eye and they silently
agreed that Broome was a little too much, too much everything. They listened and observed as Miss Underwood hung
on his every word, adding her thoughts to his discourse.

The glimmer of an idea began to form and her smile grew
as she thought of the possibilities.

Lord Worthingdon found them at that moment and Larla
shelved her thoughts for a while.

"The races begin at one, so we'll stroll about until you
ladies are ready to eat." Recognizing Lord Broome, he
greeted him casually and introduced the colonel and Marsden to him.

Having found a kindred spirit, Broome placed his arm at
Miss Underwood's disposal and as they made their way along
the booths, Larla saw the first signs of animation on her face.
She mentally applauded her plans.

As the men headed for a stall showing various kinds of
tack, a thin elderly dark-skinned woman dressed in a colorful

skirt and peasant blouse approached Larla. Large gold earrings dangled from her ears.

"Pretty lady, I tell your fortune? Cross my palm with silver and I tell your future."

Larla hesitated. This was a new experience for her. She had been around bands of gypsies when they were in France but no one had ever suggested giving her a glimpse into the future. "Nonsense," exclaimed Miss Underwood disparagingly, "it's nothing but a pack of lies. Come, we don't want anything to do with her."

The other men were involved in studying the various saddles and bridles, but Marsden stayed close to Larla, his eyes twinkling at Miss Underwood's comment. He waited to see how she'd take the censure.

Larla took a deep breath and answered brightly, "I'd love to hear my fortune." She opened her reticule to find the necessary piece of silver, but Marsden was already tossing the gypsy a coin, the size of the piece opening the gypsy's eyes in appreciation.

The old woman took Larla's hand and peered at it assessingly. "You are a one-man woman. I see a tall dark man in your past, your husband, I believe. You will be faithful to him until death. You have a great surprise coming soon and I see great happiness in store for you." She turned a knowing look at Marsden and gave him a toothy grin.

Larla's first reaction was disappointment. If she believed the gypsy, she'd never have another husband, and she had only one night in her past. She looked up to see Marsden staring at her, a peculiar expression showing on his handsome face.

Marsden was having trouble holding himself in check. He gazed down at Larla with a particularly soft smile and turned Larla's knees to jelly.

Lady Worthingdon was plainly disappointed and as the gypsy asked her if she could tell her fortune, she replied, "No, thank you, I'm afraid I know my future and have all I want in life"—she gave Marsden a mischievous glance—"except my son to be married and present me with a dozen grandchildren!"

This announcement brought an appreciative grin from Marsden, but Miss Underwood bridled immediately.

"I'm sure I know my duty to present my husband with an heir but a dozen . . ." Words failed her.

Marsden took his cue and opened fire. "You must understand, Miss Underwood, that I am looking forward to a very large family." He overemphasized the "large."

With the look of acute pain on Miss Underwood's outraged face, it was all Larla could do to keep from laughing out loud. She turned away to keep her brilliant smile to herself, but not before Marsden winked conspiratorially.

Lord Broome heard the exchange in quiet disapproval as he joined the group. He looked at Marsden with faint distaste. "I believe that such personal matters could better be discussed more privately." He offered his arm to Miss Underwood and led her away.

"Lord Broome," Miss Underwood gushed, "thank you for taking me away from that . . ." She shuddered delicately.

"Quite all right, my dear. Gently bred ladies shouldn't be subjected to such treatment."

Marsden tucked Larla's arm in his, and with a more than warm look, he escorted her through the congested aisles.

"You are very nice to me, cousin." Larla's eyes twinkled at him, her thoughts centering on how comfortable she was with him.

"Jeremy, please. I find it difficult to think of you as a cousin."

Larla's back stiffened and she stopped to search his face. "You think I'm not really your cousin's widow? My solicitor in London, I'm certain, will have no difficulty in confirming my claim."

"Hold on, little spitfire. I didn't mean anything of the sort.

I . . . just prefer to hear my name on your lips." He ground his teeth in audible frustration.

Larla wrinkled an eyebrow at him. He was flirting with her as if he had a right to. He was outrageous but intriguing, decisive yet gentle, and more man than any woman could ask for. Was the gypsy's word prophetic? Did her plan have a chance? Marsden's words reminded her that she would need to make a trip to London and take care of the legalities of turning Jessamy's estates over to her son.

"You have forcibly put me in mind that I've been terribly neglectful in not ensuring John's inheritance. I believe that next week, if Grandfather feels up to it, I'll go see Litchfield and put the matter in train."

His face tightened for a moment before he was laughing down at her. "Why don't you ask the one who can help you most? I'd be glad to assist you."

"How can you help?" She watched him assessingly, ready to utilize any information he let slip.

"Why not let me drive you to London and we'll tackle both your solicitor and our family man. I'm sure that if I verify the signature you'll have no problem." If she wouldn't go with him he'd have to beat her to London and cue his solicitor, he mumbled to himself.

"Very well, if you'd like to drive me, I accept gratefully." She paused for a moment. "I suppose I should bring along my maid, for even though I'm a widow, the ton would look down on arriving in London without a chaperon."

He grinned engagingly. "I didn't know you had a maid. I've never seen evidence of one."

Larla giggled. "Oh, I have one, but not the kind you're used to. I inherited her from my days in the army. I couldn't turn her off and she does look after me. She's an excellent watchdog." Larla peeked up at him from under her delicate lashes.

"Now you have my curiosity up. I can hardly wait to make her acquaintance."

"You may be sorry because she'll see that you toe the line."

When she perceived his look of astonishment, she laughed outright. "Not that I expect you to get out of line, I'm just giving you an insight into her character."

Lord Broome approached them. "Miss Underwood is desirous of partaking of some refreshment and I find myself sharp-set."

Larla had to turn away to hide her amusement. The man looked able to go a month without eating, living off the fat of the land so to speak. Her shoulders bounced at her direction of thought. She couldn't look at Marsden for fear her amusement would completely engulf her.

Lady Worthingdon gathered up her party expertly and herded them to a small grove with wooden tables and benches placed for the convenience of patrons. She dispatched the men to purchase the food.

"I hope someone remembers to buy a few Maid of Honors." The thought of the delicious pastry with jam and cake filling made Larla's mouth water.

Lady Worthingdon gave her an indulgent look. "I'm certain Broome won't miss a trick."

Miss Underwood missed the statement's dry humor. "Of course, Lord Broome will know exactly what to bring us. He's a very thoughtful and knowledgeable young man," she uttered in her most prim manner.

Hearing her champion Lord Broome, Larla began weaving her plans in earnest. In one of Shakespeare's plays someone told the hero that the heroine was in love with him and then told the heroine that the hero was in love with her. The outrageous attempt at matchmaking had resulted in marriage. Larla decided she wasn't enough of a scholar to remember which play it was, but the idea seemed to have possibilities.

Lady Worthingdon, seeing how the wind was blowing, decided to give Fate a nudge. "I'm worried about Marsden," she announced, her face suitably grave.

Larla stared at her hostess. She could see nothing wrong with Marsden. If anything he was almost too perfect, except for his disagreeable habit of wanting to take charge of everyone. He could try, she mused coolly, but he wouldn't succeed with her. She meant to make her own decisions.

Miss Underwood picked up the hint Lady Worthingdon had thrown out. "You don't mean he's having another bout of that trouble he had when he came home from Waterloo?" A deep frown marred the white skin of her forehead.

"I really couldn't say." Lady Worthingdon confided reluctantly. "He doesn't talk about it, but I find him doing such odd things." She could see her information had clouded Miss Underwood's countenance.

Miss Underwood's lips tightened to a straight line as she seemed to weigh the statement for possibilities.

"We mustn't let such disagreeable thoughts mar our day. I see an empty trestle table over there we can commandeer." The older woman led the way, her air lighthearted as she saw how her comments were received.

Larla felt that there was something behind her hostess's words, but she couldn't make out what that astute lady had in mind. Larla gathered up her courage, and as she sat down she remarked to Miss Underwood, "Lord Broome is certainly an attractive man, isn't he?"

Lady Worthingdon gave Larla a quizzing look. Larla's face only hinted at her mischievous thoughts.

Miss Underwood replied sincerely, unaware of the undercurrents. "He certainly is, such a refined mind and so knowledgeable."

The ladies turned to observe the return of the gentlemen, laden with various delicacies. Larla's eyes moved from approving Marsden to assessing Broome. Miss Underwood seemed to be studying Marsden with a gimlet eye, while Lady Worthingdon watched interestedly the varying reactions on all the characters in the forthcoming drama.

Larla beckoned Broome with a dazzling smile, indicating

that he should sit beside her. He managed a formal bow before he set his large assortment of food down and settled his portly frame on the bench beside Larla.

Marsden scowled fiercely, his eyebrows almost joining across the bridge of his nose. His teeth almost audibly gnashed as he saw Broome seemingly fawn over Larla. He turned his attention quickly to his fiancée and took a place beside her.

Conversation dwindled while delighted diners consumed the concoctions and confections. Larla scanned the assemblage while she savored one of the Maid of Honors. "Where is Mr. Underwood?"

"He toddled off with a few cronies," Colonel Somerset answered nonchalantly as he selected another meat pie.

"You're missing him?" snarled Marsden, leaning across the table.

Miss Underwood was plainly shocked at the tone he used. It had been her experience in the past that Marsden was always so subdued and refined.

"I automatically keep track of a party I'm with. I guess it's because I'm so used to looking after my son." She cast a loving glance at the little boy seated between Lord and Lady Worthingdon, who were busily plying him with various pastries.

"Umph." It was a dissatisfied grunt. Marsden was in a quandary. He was plainly jealous of any man who paid Larla attention. Upon introspection he discovered that in addition to wanting to acknowledge his son, who was everything a doting father could wish for, he wanted the mother with a force as fierce as it was astonishing. In all his days he'd never experienced anything akin to this. He had been prepared to accept Larla as his wife, even without recollection of the events that had transpired at Waterloo, but now he realized that his need for her was desperate, consuming, and explosive.

He let his mind wander back once more to the events that

had made her his. He was riding for Hougoumont and mentally promising himself to marry the first presentable woman he saw to try to ensure the succession. Then he was in the thick of the battle. Prince Jerome had led the French in and attacked the outpost of Hougoumont. They had been bloodily repulsed by the Hanoverians, Nassauers, and units of the Brigade of Guards.

There was a cacophony of shouts, a discharge of carbines, and bullets were dropping as thick as hailstones about them. Man after man fell but the British never gave up. He remembered the saber cut he took in his chest but he disregarded it until something exploded in his head. His last thought was that he was dying and he had failed his father.

His memories were sketchy from that point until he woke up in the Sorbonne in Paris. He remembered only the compassionate blue eyes and silky blond curls. He had been told the famous Dr. Guillet had removed a shell fragment from his skull and he had been unconscious for a long period. After the successful surgery he had slowly regained full use of his senses.

The entire scene didn't carry a clue how he had found and married Larla or why she didn't recognize him. His instincts must have been working, however, for he had found she was a prize. The problem of the immediate future seemed to be how to get Miss Underwood to cry off so that he could convince Larla to remarry him. It would take some intricate strategies to bring it about, but he hadn't wasted his years of service.

CHAPTER 7

After finishing their nuncheon the gentlemen escorted the ladies to the carriage, which had been pulled into line near the finish. Lady Worthingdon chatted easily to her young charges, a light note of anticipation creeping into her voice. They watched various preliminary attractions, a dancing bear being the highlight.

Marsden led the way to the stabling area. Lord Broome stood off to one side holding a scented handkerchief to his nose and sniffing deeply, while the old gentlemen shared a knowing smile. Each rider saw to his gear and discussed strategies for the six-furlong race with his grooms. It would be third on the agenda.

The first race was for two-year-olds and won easily by a big bay horse that was the pride of a local merchant. Shouts of encouragement and approval filled the air. The second race was for fillies only and the clamor was just as deafening.

At the call for the third race Lord Worthingdon, the colonel, and Marsden swung into their saddles and rode up to the starting line. Both the colonel's mount and Lord Worthingdon's pranced and skitted away from onlookers. Marsden's Raven stood at attention like the seasoned campaigner he was.

Marsden seemed to be scanning the lineup critically, memorizing each detail of the opposition, when his gaze fell upon a weasel-faced man on a showy bay.

The man's shifty eyes were on the colonel's horse Warrior and his attention was riveted on the colonel's iron control of his mount. Marsden's jaw clenched and he sat a little straighter in the saddle, seeming to be poised for instant action.

The local greengrocer cleared his throat in anticipation of his importance in starting the race. When he judged the racing field in approximate line, he dropped the flag signaling the start.

The horses lunged forward, muscles bunched, and men leaned low over their mounts. Marsden held Raven in with a firm hand, watching the jockeying for first place between the colonel and the weasel-faced man from a length behind. Just then as the colonel looked to the other side to assess the competition, the weasel-faced man jerked his bay in front of Warrior, knocking the horse off his pace and almost unseating the colonel. The colonel held his seat gallantly and gave Warrior encouragement to regain lost ground as others flashed by.

Marsden growled under his breath, keeping pace behind the leader before calling in his best military yell, "Charge!" Raven needed no further urging to close in on the bay.

The weasel-faced man had a triumphant grin on his face as he streaked toward the finish line until he discerned the pounding hoofbeats moving up rapidly beside him. Marsden was leaning low over Raven, keeping a sharp eye on the man astride the bay. Horse and rider seemed one as they moved in seeming slow motion pulling ahead of the leader inch by inch. Raven was bred for endurance over a long campaign but gave a good account of himself winning by head and shoulders.

The finish line was a cacophony of sound as cheering, screaming, and shouting whizzed by in an indistinct blur. Marsden reined in and turned to face the man. "If you ever break the racing code again, I'll personally break every bone in your body!"

"Don't know what cher talkin' about," was the surly reply. The man's lip was curled in anger.

"Ask anyone if Marsden's word is good. I have eyes everywhere." This was accompanied by Marsden's fiercest military stare to disobedient troops.

The man finally cowered under its power and disappeared into the throng of people and animals.

The colonel reined in beside him, having tied with Worthingdon for third place. The old man was fuming. "Did you see what the blackguard did to me? I'd like to teach him some manners!"

"I saw. You didn't have a fair chance to beat Raven." He paused a moment and then added, "I doubt we'll see any more trouble from that miserable piece of mouse bait today."

Worthingdon had ridden up in time to hear this masterly setdown and smiled warmly at his son. "I thought we should take action against the fellow but I see you have already taken charge of it." A wealth of pride filled his voice.

The ladies awaited their return with varying emotions. Lady Worthingdon smiled indulgently, Miss Underwood sat primly, while Larla brimmed with a mixture of pride and anger.

Larla smiled broadly at Marsden as he rode up. "Marsden, I'm so pleased for Raven but what are you going to do about the scoundrel that ruined Warrior's race?"

Lord and Lady Worthingdon exchanged looks of affection before turning to their son.

"That little matter has been dealt with. I seriously doubt there will be any more difficulty along that line."

The tone of his voice told Larla all she needed to know. He had taken care of the problem quite well. Larla turned to her grandfather. "I'm so sorry Warrior lost but I'd like to be bet that if we raced Raven and Warrior again with me up, Warrior could win easily. After all, Grandfather, you must weigh thirteen stone and that's a disadvantage."

A rakish sparkle colored Marsden's eyes as he questioned, "Would you like to race me at Edgehurst? You'll have the advantage in weight but I fancy I'll have the advantage in experience."

"Done!" Larla agreed happily.

Before anything more could be said, Miss Underwood threw her oar in. "I must say that I couldn't undertake such a course." She shuddered delicately. "So unladylike."

Marsden turned to face the virago, seemingly determined to give her an ear-turning that she'd remember for years to come.

Larla put a gentle hand on his arm. "Marsden," she begged softly.

He gazed down at the bright blue eyes and winked at her before sending the conversation in a new direction.

Miss Underwood found herself at a loss. Marsden was her third attempt to get herself a husband, the other two having slipped off the line. Her mother had counseled her to hold Marsden at all costs. She eyed her fiancé suspiciously.

Lord Broome moved over to speak to her. Miss Underwood focused her attention upon him and basked in his approval. He patted her hand reassuringly.

Larla almost at the same instant became aware that John wasn't in the carriage. She searched the crowd. There was no sign of him. "I've lost John." It was a flat statement. There were no hysterics but she rose with determination to step down to go in search of him.

Marsden dismounted quickly and was there to pluck her out of the carriage. He noted her coolness, her composure, and smiled at her reassuringly.

Miss Underwood seemed about to swoon, her eyes glazing and her breathing becoming irregular. "The gypsies must have kidnapped him," she moaned. Lord Broome frantically fanned her, but Marsden completely ignored her.

The colonel knew his great-grandson. "It's not like the scamp to run off. He'll be hereabouts and have a good explanation."

The men tied their horses to the back of the carriage and spread out to hunt for the little boy. Marsden stayed with

Larla. "There's no use running off half-cocked. Where do you think he might head?"

"I'll thank you to know I don't go off half-cocked, as you express yourself. I go fully loaded and watch out if I'm hunting for bear," she sallied, twinkling.

Marsden chuckled. "Are you telling me you have actually hunted large animals?"

"I'd like to wager that I can shoot as well as you," she returned, flashing him an impudent smile.

"We're going to have an interesting time, horse racing and shooting. Do you have any other talents?"

She turned a provocative glance to him. "I've many other accomplishments."

"Ah, now you've succeeded in whetting my curiosity." He casually placed an arm around her small waist.

Her back stiffened. "I'm afraid you've misconstrued my meaning." Her large blue eyes glowed fire.

"I beg your pardon," he apologized with a grin. "It was only a cousinly gesture. I thought you might need the support. Most of the ladies of my acquaintance would swoon over the possibility of their son being kidnapped."

"Rubbish! I'm not a parlor or weak-minded female. I'll find my own son." Larla stalked off in the direction of the gypsy encampment.

"After you, my lady," ribbed Marsden after the fact.

As they approached the caravan they saw the large-wheeled wagons, which were painted in gay colors and drawn in a semicircle. A large fire was presided over by several older women who were stirring and testing something in a large kettle slung above it. Each gypsy had on the traditional costume with bright materials and bangles.

An older man moved toward them with an aura of power. It wasn't his height, for he certainly wasn't tall, but he gave the impression of great strength of body and mind. He focused black eyes directly on them.

"What may I do for you?" he inquired in a neutral tone, his hands together in a sign of subservience.

Larla wasn't fooled by the somewhat humble demeanor. She could feel the leashed power ready for action if called upon.

Marsden introduced himself and Larla. "Mrs. Ainsworth's son has wandered off and it seemed possible he might make for your camp. Have you seen a precocious three-year-old? He has dark hair and dark eyes." He frowned slightly as he thought of his precious son being lost.

Heavy black brows met in the center of a broad forehead. "Are you accusing my people of taking the lad?" There was a distinct threat in his voice.

Before Marsden could reply, Larla cut in. "Assuredly not. I have made the acquaintance of many of your people while I was in France. I know you are much maligned. Do you happen to know a chief by the name of Ramano? I was able to do him a slight service and he told me if I ever needed help from any other gypsy clan all I had to do was shake your hand like this."

She paused as she extended her hand and gave the secret greeting.

The gypsy's face cleared instantly into a broad smile. "Come everyone! We have honored guests."

Men, women, and children approached from all angles while Marsden raised an eyebrow at Larla. "There's no end to your talents," he murmured into her ear.

Larla grinned mischievously at him while she waited for the gypsies to gather.

As soon as the group was assembled the chief spoke. "We are pleased to welcome Mrs. Ainsworth and Lord Marsden." There were appropriate murmurs. "Has anyone seen a small boy with dark hair and eyes?"

A youngster about ten answered. "I saw Johan with a small boy down by the horses."

"Very good. If you will please come with me . . ." He

turned to Larla and Marsden and dismissed the others with a wave of his hand. He led them to the back of the camp where a line was strung between two large oaks, with numerous horses tethered to it. Nearby on the back of a small gelding was John, his heels dug in the horse's flanks, his eyes shining with excitement. A gypsy boy of about fourteen was letting him ride in circles around him.

John called excitedly as he saw his mama and Marsden approach. "Mama, see I can ride the big horse all by myself."

The gypsy chief flashed a smile at Larla. "Your son is going to be a horseman."

"You can be certain of that," added Marsden. "I intend to take care of it."

Larla was delighted with her son, merely observing Marsden for a split second before turning back to her pride and joy.

Marsden picked John off the horse and held him tightly for a moment. "Did you see me, Lord Marsden?" the youngster asked.

"Oh, yes, we saw you but perhaps you can explain how you happened to get here." Marsden queried sternly.

The gypsy boy looked up at Marsden with alarm. Marsden reached into his pocket and flicked the lad a gold piece. "We appreciate the good care you took of our boy."

Larla's back began to tingle. Our boy? Was it anger or anticipation that made it so? Marsden might not have realized he'd said it but she certainly hadn't missed the implication. She'd file it away for future reference in her campaign plans.

The chief seemed satisfied with the outcome and ushered his guests back to the campfire.

Larla held her hand out again. "Now I am in your debt. Please remember that if I may be of any service to you, you only need let me know." She flashed him her famous heart-melting smile.

The chief bowed gracefully over her hand. "It was nothing. We are glad to have been of service."

Larla turned to her small son. "Now perhaps we can hear your excuse from being off your post."

John seemed puzzled. "Why, Mama, I wasn't on duty. No one said. I thought I was dismissed." He sounded injured.

At the tone the chief's mouth twitched in amusement. "I believe you have the makings of a good soldier here as well as a horseman."

John looked at the chief with interest. "I'm only a private now but I'm going to be a general," he confided engagingly.

Marsden was struggling hard not to laugh while Larla gave him a scorching glare. John was right. No one had thought to tell the youngster when they sat watching the race that he was not to leave the carriage. The fault was hers.

"Very well. You have a good defense. I'll present your case to the colonel." Her eyes shone warmly with love as she watched her small son securely held in Marsden's arms.

John nodded contentedly. "Now we'll be all right," he announced, exactly as the troops had said when they saw Wellington in their midst.

After a few minutes of cordial farewells, they started their way back to the carriage. They met the colonel and Lord Worthingdon striding toward them.

"What have you to say for yourself, young man?" The colonel's tone would have had most of his troops shaking in their respective boots.

John was entirely unaffected by either the ferocious frown or the freezing tone. He held his arms out to his grandfather, who took him and held him close for a moment.

"Now tell me, why did you leave your post?"

"I wasn't on duty. No one told me." He repeated his defense.

Larla nodded. "The officer in charge was negligent," she grinned at him.

"Humph, humph," the colonel grunted, but his features softened as he released the small boy.

Lord Worthingdon looked on with what could only be envy.

As they came to the carriage Lady Worthingdon's face relaxed visibly. "I'm so happy he's safe."

Miss Underwood puffed up her cheeks and straightened her bonnet purposefully before tossing in her advice. "I see you found him. I hope you've given him something to remember this by. He's inconvenienced all of us." She looked at Broome for support.

Broome smiled at her and patted her hand. "He must be taught his place."

"I'll thank you to be a little less busy about affairs that are none of your business!" thundered Marsden with unaccustomed rudeness.

Miss Underwood gasped, looking for all the world like a drowning fish, while Lord Broome turned a violent shade of crimson. There was an awkward moment of silence while the members of the party pretended to study anything but the scene in front of them.

Larla jumped into the breach, saying, "I saw an organ-grinder and a monkey on our way back here and I'm sure John would like to give the monkey a penny or two. While you gentlemen watch the rest of the races I'll entertain my son."

"I think I'd like to find a shady spot and have a cold drink," said Lady Worthingdon with resolution. "Marcia, perhaps you'd like to join me?"

That austere young woman bowed her head in acknowledgement. Lord Broome volunteered hurriedly, seeming to want to be away from the cause of his discomfort. "I'd be happy to escort you ladies and procure a drink for you."

Miss Underwood beamed her appreciation at him and accepted his arm graciously.

Larla watched Broome and Miss Underwood covertly as she made her way down the aisles. Her smile grew as she considered the possibilities. She felt she need have no scruples concerning the plan she was about to embark upon. Everyone would be pleased with the result.

Larla and John soon found the organ-grinder in the midst of a large congregation of children. When John saw the little monkey with his tiny velvet cap and feather he jumped up and down in his excitement. Larla smiled indulgently at her precious son and clasped his hand tightly.

"Remember, you are not to desert me no matter what takes your interest," Larla admonished her young son earnestly.

He nodded solemnly. "Mama, may I have a penny?" He raised his large dark eyes to hers in an expression that reminded Larla of a poor, undernourished destitute child.

She chuckled inwardly. Her son was up to every trick in the book to gain his own way. She opened her reticule and pulled out the required coin.

"Ho, monkey!" he called and secured the grinder's attention by waving his penny. The man seemed to whisper to the animal and the little creature scampered over to John, bypassing several children who were standing watching. The monkey doffed his cap and his tiny hands grasped the coin. He sat for a moment on John's shoulder and John gasped his delight. Then he raced back to his master and danced for the group to the accompaniment of the little organ.

The children clapped wildly. John pulled at his mother's skirt. He wanted to repeat the performance. Larla indulgently reached for another coin and gave it to John.

John was about to call to the monkey again when he noticed a ragged boy at his shoulder. The lad was a little older than he and watched the monkey with great yearning. The tattered child gave no hint of bitterness for his plight, only a weighty sorrow filled his eyes. John was generous to a fault. He extended his penny to the urchin.

The boy hesitated for a moment, studying John then his mother. When Larla made no comment, the lad took the penny and began waving it over his head. The monkey quickly made his way over and ran up the youngster's arm. He squirmed and shouted with joy. John seemed to get as much fun just watching as the urchin did from holding the creature.

Larla drew a deep breath of pride. Whatever it had cost her to have had such a fiasco of a marriage, it had been well worth the loss to have such a reward as John.

She had just reached down for another penny to give John when she saw Harold with his head down, kicking the dust as he walked.

"Harold, we've been wondering where you disappeared to." Had he run into some trouble?

At the sound of her voice Harold looked up and forced a smile on his face. "I met a couple of my friends down here. They're great guns." His voice rose enthusiastically. "They know everything that's going on and . . ." The words trailed off.

Keeping an eye on John, Larla put her hand on Harold's arm. "If you're in trouble please let me help you. I've noticed that you haven't been in high spirits for some time and I've a great deal of experience in helping young men. It isn't the horse races is it?"

He gazed at her with troubled eyes and seemed to mentally shake himself. "No, I haven't been interested in the races today and there's nothing you can do about my problem. Besides you're a girl and very little older than I am."

Larla chuckled. "I know, but I've been raised around young army officers and I've seen the kind of trouble they get into." She bent closer. "Tell me, what is it? Women, wine, or money?"

Harold was taken aback at her question. Nice young ladies weren't supposed to know about men's peccadilloes. "I'm not in the petticoat line," he muttered dejectedly.

"And you're obviously not inebriated so it has to be money." Larla reassured him. "We'll find a place at Edge-

hurst where we can talk privately. I'm sure I can help you."
Her eye kept wandering to John.

"I don't know why you should," he grunted with a surly
edge to his voice.

"Because I like you and I like to help people. We'll be
going back to Edgehurst soon and I'll manage a time."

He pressed her hand, raising himself from his dejection
momentarily. "Thank you. I still don't know that you can do
anything but I'm honored that you want to help me."

Larla gathered up her small son and walked through the
throng to the carriage. Her mind was busily planning how to
wrest the information from Harold. He wasn't positive yet
that he should confide in her. She would win him over, and
then she would help him.

CHAPTER 8

As Marsden strolled into the gold salon at Edgehurst, Miss Underwood arose and placed her arm on his. "Marsden, I feel we should talk." Her tone was deceptively meek but her lips were compressed firmly.

He turned to the family gathering. "If you'll please excuse us." He ushered her down the hall to one of the small sitting rooms.

Larla leaned forward to speak softly to Mr. Underwood. "It's such a lovely evening. I'd like a breath of air."

"I'd be glad to," he stammered somewhat incoherently, his face turning a bright shade of red.

With the younger members of the party dispersed Lady Worthingdon commented, "I'm sorry Lord Broome was unable to join us. He'd have made a fourth for bridge."

"His mama doesn't often let him off the leash," was Lord Worthingdon's outspoken reply.

Turning to the colonel, Lady Worthingdon explained, "His father died when he was quite young and he succeeded early to his father's dignities. He is Lady Broome's only child so perhaps she is overprotective of him."

"It'll be a miracle if he ever finds a wife that suits his mama," Lord Worthingdon commented.

Lady Worthingdon smiled enigmatically and made no reply. Her eyes were brimming with merriment.

It was a warm evening with a hint of a breeze. The light from the windows shed a faint glow in the garden on the hedges and flowers.

Larla, when she deemed they were out of earshot of the

house, turned to the young man. "Now let's have it!" She spoke briskly in much the manner she'd addressed erring young lieutenants. "I'm sure if you share your problem you'll find it's not such a big thing."

"You don't know! There's more to this tangle than I'd like to tell." Harold's face was etched with anguish.

"Just start at the beginning. You can trust me. I won't tell a soul. It was the first lesson my grandfather taught me about soldiering—how to keep a secret," Larla prodded him patiently.

He lifted his shoulders in a shrug that seemed to decide the issue. "I ran into a couple of friends who had also been sent down from Oxford. I can tell you we've shared a lark or two. There was the time we picked up the big toy spider and put it in the headmaster's study. He went crashing out the window in his hurry to get away." He started to chuckle like a child in short coats. Seeing the amused expression on Larla's face he decided she was a great gun and unburdened himself of the rest of the story.

"Bootle had heard there was to be a good cockfight today during the fair. It was kept quiet, only a select few men were told. I was extremely lucky to be included. I can see a horse race most anytime but a cockfight . . ." He stopped for a moment to see how Larla was taking news of a cockfight.

She merely encouraged him to go on.

"It was in that big barn past the gypsy camp. I had some money I could put up and I won on the first fight. Then maybe I got overconfident. I plunged on the second and lost. I was going to quit but a friend of Bootle's came in. He's an older man and really knows his way around town. He said you had to keep playing to win and so I did. I kept losing and found I had dropped three hundred pounds." He paused to assess Larla's reaction to this last disclosure.

Larla asked in a reasonable tone, "How did you plan to pay?"

Mr. Underwood hesitated for a moment and dug his hands

deep into his pockets. "Bootle's friend, Beaufort, lent it to me on the spot. I'm to pay him back next week or sooner if I get up to London."

"That was quite handy," she observed dryly. "And where will you raise the three hundred pounds?" she asked interestedly.

His frown disappeared and a mischievous smile tugged at his lips. "M' father won't advance me any more until next quarter day but I'm willing to bet that Marsden will help me out."

Larla's eyes softened and her lips parted as he mentioned Marsden. "If that's the case why are you so down pin?" she puzzled.

He hung his head and kicked at the turf. "Beaufort wanted some kind of pledge that I'd pay him and I let him hold my grandfather's watch. It's an old thing that is usually put away. It's to be mine someday but the thing is covered with gems and looks a fright. It's nothing I'd ordinarily carry but my own watch is at Rundell and Bridges being repaired and so I borrowed Grandfather's. Beaufort took it, but I've an uneasy feeling I might not get it back. He mentioned something about interest. I just don't feel that I can burden Marsden with that."

Larla nodded. The man thought that he was dealing with a green stripling lad too ashamed to tell his elders of his mistake. Not many lads would confess such a story.

Larla looked Harold straight in the eye. "The first thing to do is to offer Beaufort his three hundred pounds and ask for the watch. If he refuses, come to me. I believe I can see a way to get it back." Her brisk tone and manner were encouraging.

Mr. Underwood took her hands in his and raised them to his lips. "You are truly an angel."

From somewhere behind them a twig snapped. "I can't call inviting an assignation in the garden with a mere boy angelic!" ground out an outraged Marsden.

Larla jumped in shock but recovered quickly, making a small motion with her hand for Harold to go away, before turning to face Marsden, a militant light in her eye.

Underwood merely swallowed and looked from Larla's calm face to Marsden's furious one. He couldn't seem to break the tension between the two, so with a quick "If you'll excuse me . . ." he was gone.

Marsden's brow cleared but it was an ominous voice that offered to see Larla safely inside.

"I thought you were busy planning your wedding with Marcia," Larla baited him.

"You little vixen. You'd try a patron saint." Jerking her to him he kissed her violently until she became pliable in his arms. Then he set her back a pace and looked her over minutely, with grim satisfaction, noting her bruised lips, flushed cheeks, and rapid breathing.

Larla saw no words of apology coming and took refuge in a stinging retort. "My, now you're compromising me and engaged to another. What a pickle you're in." Having fired her heaviest weapon, she retreated to the house, aware that behind her she'd left an absolutely livid Marsden.

A satisfied smile touched her lips as she returned to the gathering, making the older members of the party grin appreciatively. Marcia was nowhere in evidence.

As Larla sat down to breakfast, Marsden treated her in the friendly manner he'd always used. There was nothing to be gained from surveying his countenance. It was bland and held an air of innocence. Larla was not to be taken in by such tactics.

Lord Worthingdon greeted his guests as he joined the group. "When are we to have this famous horse race?"

"Anytime is fine with me," Larla replied gayly.

"Would after breakfast suit you, son?" Lord Worthingdon inquired. "I'll order the horses saddled while we change our clothes."

"Yes, I'm itching to clear the air," Marsden mocked, his eye firmly on Larla.

Lord Worthingdon turned to Larla.

"That's agreeable to me but I'd like to see what course we are to run," she replied calmly, knowing it was a circular track because she'd inquired at the stable the previous day.

The colonel smiled at his granddaughter and nodded his approval of her strategy.

"We have a track just beyond the kitchen gardens, near the stables. You'll have plenty of time to look it over before we start this famous race."

Lady Worthingdon seemed to note the arrangements with satisfaction but Miss Underwood had no comment and kept her head down. She seemed unusually quiet this morning.

Within minutes the party had reassembled in the back parlor, anticipation running high.

Marsden was a fine figure of manhood in his molded buckskins, while Larla was smartly attired in a leaf-colored habit. The skirt had extra fullness, while the jacket fit like a glove to her curves and was closed with pearl fasteners. Boots of soft kid encased her feet and a small derby with flowing green gauze veil completed the stylish outfit.

The party chatted amiably as they wandered to the stable area.

As Warrior was led out of the stable behind Raven, Marsden noticed that the saddle was not a lady's. Before he could protest, Larla walked forward smiling and patted the stallion on the nose. Larla spoke a few words to the groom, who bowed with a grin and stepped back.

She turned the stirrup at an angle to make it easier to mount and swung up gracefully into the saddle, the divided skirt falling into place on each side. She looked down provocatively at Marsden, as if waiting for him to make some comment.

Marsden bit his lip to keep from smiling and turned to see his fiancée's reaction.

Marcia gasped when she saw Larla mount the horse astride. It was a thing not done by most ladies, being a trait only a select few of the rich and very dashing could get away with. She clamped her mouth shut in a disapproving line, struggling to keep from saying something of censure.

Marsden mounted and maneuvered Raven beside Warrior, commending her attire with a gracefully turned phrase.

"Let's walk around the track before we start so Warrior will know what's expected of him," Larla requested prettily, not knowing how to take his gallantry after the previous evening.

Marsden saluted her with his whip. "You're not going to let me have the least advantage," he complained pointedly.

"Why should I? You're a lot bigger and stronger than I. In that respect I don't have a chance."

Marsden looked at her sharply and paused for a moment before he spoke. "If you're referring to last night, I know that it wasn't my overpowering you that made you respond to me so sweetly."

Larla didn't have a good answer for that sally and so contented herself with urging Warrior forward to hide her blush.

At the completion of the circle Larla saw that chairs had been set out for Lady Worthingdon and Miss Underwood but the men were crowding the fence.

"I'll start you," called Lord Worthingdon as he produced a large white linen square. "On the count of three I'll drop my handkerchief."

Both Marsden and Larla raised their crops to their hats in a salute and waited the signal. As before, Raven stood like a rock while Warrior was more nervous. He seemed to feel Larla's tension.

Larla watched Lord Worthingdon closely. As soon as she heard him start to count, she eyed his closed hand. The moment his fingers opened her mount leaped forward, gaining a distinct advantage over Marsden.

Marsden closed the two lengths slowly, almost leisurely,

observing Larla's considerable skill. She rode like a centaur. Larla glanced over to Raven and noted that the horse was galloping easily beside her. Marsden wasn't pushing to take the lead. She smiled triumphantly. She had hoped to lure Marsden into just such a position. Warrior was noted for his strong finishes and the horse always pulled past the fastest horses on the turns. It was his part of the race.

Larla's laugh tinkled on the flying wind. Intently she leaned forward and whispered in Warrior's ear. It might not have been what she said. It could have been some hidden leg-command, no one could tell, but on the instant the old war-horse was lengthening his stride to a thunderous pace. The ladies were aghast and could only stare fascinatedly as first Larla and then Marsden streaked down the last few feet of the backstretch into the far turn.

Lord Worthingdon crowed, "Jolly good show."

The colonel smiled contentedly and replied in his most dry tone, "I believe they're well matched."

Worthingdon's head snapped sharply toward the colonel, a look of puzzlement on his face. A second later a bright smile changed his whole countenance as he caught the gist of the double entendre. "I believe you might just be right, my friend."

Both men turned to view the finish of this most unusual race.

Marsden grimly pushed Raven to the limit. Raven was a tried and true war-horse that could endure days on end of battles and fatigues. However at a short distance the horse was at a slight disadvantage and Marsden hadn't seen the finish of the colonel's race. That was the first mistake. The second had been to underestimate Larla's campaign strategy.

Larla was in her element, glorying in the thrill of winning. She didn't take time to glance over her shoulder. The finish line was too close. She was rounding the turn into the home stretch. Urging Warrior on, she stayed low and crooned her words of encouragement.

Larla loved the big horse. He was fast for the short distance and durable for the long. On a day's trek Raven might have the advantage but here today, the race was hers. Marsden wouldn't underestimate her again, she concluded with a wonderful feeling of satisfaction.

By the time Larla approached the finish line she could see the entire party cheering and waving. Even her grandfather was leaning at the rail with a dazzling smile.

The only exception was a subdued Miss Underwood. That damsel sat disapprovingly ramrod straight, her arms folded primly on one of the lawn chairs that had been brought out for her use. Her face was set in stern lines that could have made the most hardened youngster tremble.

The cheers dissolved to whoops of laughter and congratulations as Larla crossed the finish line a length ahead of Marsden. Larla took the compliments graciously.

"I could easily believe that you are an even better rider than my son," Lady Worthingdon told her delightedly. "It does him a deal of good not to be toadied and deferred to," she added confidingly.

"I doubt it will happen again, Lady Worthingdon. Today, I was just lucky." Larla held her hostess's eyes with understanding.

Marsden made his way to Larla, catching the last of her words. "Today's riding included no luck, my dear. It involved consummate skill and a great deal of strategy. I make you my compliments." He bowed with a flourish. "The loser claims his consolation prize."

With no more warning than that, Marsden pulled Larla into his arms and planted a burning kiss on her lips. When sputters and coughs could be heard in the background, Marsden looked up to see Miss Underwood's face positively mortified. He laughed gleefully. Bowing again he excused himself and chortled, "My fiancée is jealous."

With several long strides he was at Miss Underwood's side and smothered her with the same hot and demanding kiss he'd bestowed upon Larla. Miss Underwood began to struggle and push him away desperately.

When Marsden finally released her, she endeavored to maintain what was left of her prim demeanor. She straightened her bonnet and smoothed her dress before pressing her hands to her hot cheeks.

Lord Worthingdon opened his mouth to protest but his lady put a detaining hand on his arm. When Worthingdon encountered a language only a long and happily married man might interpret, he nodded and fell silent.

Miss Underwood finally controlled her ragged breathing. "Well, I have never in my life been a party to such, such . . . decadence."

Marsden's lips twitched. "You must know I'm a man of strong passions, Marcia." He leaned forward and growled for her ears alone, "You already know I'm planning a large family and I can hardly wait to get started."

Miss Underwood's color paled from flaming red to ashen white. She started to tremble. With a great deal of resolution she stuck up her chin and marched away from the party, her back stiffened, looking neither right nor left.

Larla was struck by the absurdity of the situation. To her it was hilarious that Marsden could have such a devastating effect on her, while his poor fiancée was plainly terrified of his touch. Marsden seemed to be utilizing every weapon in his arsenal to get rid of his fiancée and Larla had confirmed in her mind that his fiancée was unwanted but a man of principle could not cry off. It could be done only by the female involved and Larla meant to help the poor soul.

Larla hoped that Marsden had finally realized that he couldn't be even reasonably happy with such an immature goose. The more she thought about the stricken look on Miss Underwood's face and her reaction, the more she chuckled as she strolled back to the house.

Marsden put his arm around her and growled fiercely, "What is it that's struck you funny?"

Larla's eyes twinkled merrily. "Why should I tell you and give away my secrets for free?"

"And what fee do you wish?" he challenged her.

"Why, for you to acknowledge my superior horsemanship, of course. What other wish could I have," she asked boldly.

"Caught me unprepared, didn't you?" he murmured seductively.

"I believe in utilizing all available assets," she sallied easily, a lively laughter brimming in her lovely face.

"It seems I didn't do my reconnaissance work well," he drawled, twinkling.

"No one's perfect, my lord," she demurred.

"I'll come about when we take a hand on the pistol range. I won't underestimate you again, Larla." He said her name as a caress.

The older set seemed content to observe Marsden and Larla and the easy comradery they shared as they made their way back.

CHAPTER 9

The following week saw Larla comfortably ensconced in Marsden's curricle, having accepted his invitation to present her at his solicitor's office. Larla watched the checkerboard of green move by as Marsden tooled the matched bays toward London. She had agreed readily with Marsden when he had suggested it was too beautiful a morning to be closed in. The curricle was much more comfortable for the short journey.

The baggage carriage followed more sedately on its deep-swung leather hinges, carrying Jenny and Marsden's valet. Larla smiled as she thought back over Jenny's strictures about not letting Marsden drive out of Jenny's line of vision and Marsden's shocked reaction to the no-nonsense female.

Marsden had listened meekly as Jenny had given him his orders, later turning a sardonic glance at Larla and questioning, "Is she always this brusk?"

When Larla gave him an affirmative reply, he laughed. "A regular sergeant, I'll bet. It seems you were well guarded upon your travels with the army."

Larla looked at him piercingly. Had he guessed about her marriage? That incident was the only time she had lost Jenny for an entire night. "Jenny has always had my interests at heart."

Soon they approached the red cobblestones on the outskirts of the city and Marsden tightened his rein and slowed his team. "Larla, I've arranged for you to stay at Grillon's Hotel. It is the customary place for unaccompanied ladies to stay."

He silenced her question with a nod. "I'll be staying at the family residence in Berkeley Square. I wouldn't hurt your reputation for the world and for you to be seen staying in my company wouldn't do."

Larla held her tongue. That arrangement suited her fine. She had two errands to accomplish that she'd rather Marsden didn't get wind of—retrieving Harold's pledge because he hadn't been able to make the man turn it over and her plan to ensnare Broome for Miss Underwood.

They pulled up in front of the prestigious hostelry with all due ceremony. Marsden tossed the reins to a waiting lackey and helped Larla from the carriage. Ushering her into the plush interior, he murmured reassuringly, "Everything will turn out fine."

Jenny followed in their wake, directing hotel employees which trunks and valises to bring in. Her concise orders to the hotel staff commanded instant respect.

The waiting clerk pushed the register toward Larla, speaking a few courteous words of welcome. Larla wrote "Mrs. J. Ainsworth" in a firm hand and received a key to her room.

Marsden watched as Larla and Jenny followed the uniformed figure to the grand stair. He went out whistling with a jaunty bounce to his step.

"Jenny, I want you to inquire at the desk and see if Lady Broome is registered here. I have some business to attend to with her." Larla made the statement offhandedly.

Jenny looked quizzically at her mistress. "Yer up to something, missy, and I want to know what it is."

"Jenny, you wound me. What could I be up to with a lady I've never met?"

Jenny merely humphed.

Marsden and Larla were ushered into the senior Mr. Nevel's private office with great respect. Mr. Nevel was an elderly man, tall and thin but with surprisingly straight shoulders and carriage. Larla concluded that the man had seen service in his younger years. His sparse white hair and bushy eyebrows detracted from a pair of knowing brown eyes.

Mr. Nevel was the Ainsworth solicitor and handled all transactions for the entire family. He rose at their entrance and placed a chair for Larla. Sitting down behind his desk after greeting his guest he inquired politely, "How may I serve you?"

"I am the widow of Jessamy Ainsworth and I'm here to prove my claim to his estates for our son, John."

At that Mr. Nevel's eyebrows shot up into his receding hairline and he turned to Marsden for confirmation.

"There is no doubt in my mind that young John Ainsworth should have Jessamy's estates." Marsden's voice was cool, matter-of-fact.

Larla gave him a warm smile, which he returned with interest.

Mr. Nevel discreetly assessed the couple in front of him.

Larla opened her reticule and carefully removed a dirty piece of paper which she silently presented to Mr. Nevel.

He opened it and then adjusted his pince-nez glasses as if to see better. As his eyes rested on the signature at the bottom of the page, his glasses almost fell off his nose and his eyes grew round. With an obvious effort he removed his glasses and wiped them on a clean linen while he stared at Marsden silently.

Marsden locked glances with the older man. "You can testify to the signature, I'm sure."

"I'd recognize the signature anywhere," he returned evenly. "I'm prepared to go on record as saying that this is a legal wedding instrument and is properly signed." His voice had a hint of iron in it as he stared intently at his lifelong client.

"Thank you. That's just what we wanted to know. You don't mind seeing to it then, that all Jessamy's properties are placed in the name of John Ainsworth with his mother as guardian." Marsden's voice was just as strong.

Larla looked first to Marsden and then to the solicitor. There were undercurrents here that she couldn't quite understand. She was missing some element of the conversation but what it was, she didn't know.

"That can be arranged without trouble. However, Marsden, shouldn't some provision be made for the . . . widow?" Mr. Nevel questioned sharply.

"How remiss of me. Naturally some of the income must be paid to Mrs. Ainsworth," Marsden responded smoothly.

"Thank you both but that isn't at all necessary. My grandfather sees to all I need. Our estates can more than afford to keep me comfortable." Larla's chin inched up a fraction.

Both men exchanged significant glances, as if to weigh some issue between them.

Mr. Nevel implored, "It's only proper that you should receive a share. If you consult your own solicitor, he'll corroborate that. I should hate to have him think we treated you shabbily." He turned to Marsden for confirmation.

Marsden nodded almost imperceptibly, the two men reaching a silent agreement that the matter would be settled satisfactorily between the solicitors.

"Thank you, no. I'll speak to Mr. Litchfield and if necessary he can get in touch with you."

Larla rose to leave, carefully tucking her marriage lines away in her reticule.

Marsden leaned over the desk and picked up a pen. "You forgot to have me attest to Jessamy's signature." He wrote swiftly while Larla finished closing her reticule and smoothed her gown.

The sharp-eyed solicitor read the few scrawled words and smiled gratifyingly. Turning to Larla, he spoke warmly, "I'll see to your interests, ma'am. It's been a pleasure to meet you."

Marsden took her arm and escorted her from the room after the courtesies were paid. Larla was so busy congratulating herself on crossing that hurdle that she missed the sad shake of the solicitor's head and Marsden's conspiratorial wink and a silent message that passed between the men.

James was waiting with the curricle and Marsden assisted Larla up before taking the reins. The servant jumped up behind as Marsden gave the fresh team the office to start.

Litchfield's office was similar to Mr. Nevel's with the exception of a large print of Wellington on the wall.

"It looks as if Mr. Litchfield is an admirer of the Duke." He stared at the painting thoughtfully.

"Can you imagine my grandfather having any other kind of solicitor?" She grinned at him.

Mr. Litchfield was a man of some sixty years and although he had good carriage there was nothing about him to suggest he was an old soldier. He greeted Larla like a lost relative.

"Larla Somerset! How attractive you've grown. Come sit down and tell me how you're faring and what your grandfather is up to these days."

Larla quickly introduced Marsden. "Lord Marsden is now my cousin-in-law."

He acknowledged the younger man politely and turned back to Larla. "I take it you've not come to see me on a social visit."

Larla flushed a little. "I'm afraid I've neglected all our old friends. I've been staying in the country." She folded her hands nervously in her lap. "I have a story to tell you."

At those words Marsden's entire body seemed to tense. He quit breathing as he waited for the next words.

"I married a very fine man at Waterloo. He was gravely wounded and died of his injuries." She swallowed hard and gripped her hands tightly. "I did all I could to help him, even sewing up a gash in his side, but it wasn't enough." Her voice trembled as she spoke and her hands clenched nervously in her lap. "The man I married was Jessamy Ainsworth, Lord Marsden's cousin. I have my marriage lines here." She opened her reticule and passed the worn document to Mr. Litchfield.

He examined it carefully. "This appears to be legal. Is there any question about it?" He turned to Marsden assessingly.

"No, I have accepted Mrs. Ainsworth's claim in front of my solicitor, the senior Mr. Nevel. He has set in train the legal procedures to claim all the estates and money he had held for Jessamy for John Ainsworth, Larla's son."

"Good. Then all you need of me is to get in touch with your man and see that all the details are taken care of satisfactorily."

Larla smiled charmingly at the older man. "Thank you, Mr. Litchfield, for all your help. You have always looked after my family's interests well."

Marsden stood up to leave and said stiffly, "There will be no problem about Mrs. Ainsworth's claim."

Mr. Litchfield allowed himself a slight smile. "I have a duty to my client, but it's just a matter of form to get in touch with Mr. Nevel."

Marsden seemed to be mulling something around in his mind. He turned to Larla and suggested slyly, "Perhaps Mr. Litchfield would like to know where your wedding took place."

"We can go into that later if I find it necessary," parried the solicitor as he saw Larla begin to squirm.

Larla took a steadying breath. "Oh, I don't mind telling you. It was at the Hôtel de Bien Ville in Brussels."

Marsden's shoulders sagged momentarily. He shook his head. The name meant nothing to him.

Mr. Litchfield came around his desk and took Larla's small hand in his. "Remember me to your grandfather and ask him when he's going to come up to London to see me." He patted her hand paternally. "If you find you need me don't hesitate to send me a message. I promise to take good care of you as I've done for your grandfather over the years."

With an exchange of bows Marsden escorted Larla out. He was frowning when they reached the street.

Larla's eyes softened as she noted the wrinkles on his forehead. He seemed to be worried about her not accepting a portion of the money. Maybe he would confide in her. "Is there something troubling you, Marsden?"

He smiled at her question. "Not a thing. The world is upside-down, I've lost my mind and I feel like Little Bo Peep." He signaled James, who instantly drew the curricle up to the curb.

"I had no idea you knew fairy tales." She was hugely entertained by what she thought was his funning.

"Darling, I've been living in one for sometime now. Ever since I met you, as a matter of fact."

Larla considered his statement. The impact was frightening and she latched on to something she could handle. "How did you know my name means 'darling' in Hindi?"

"I didn't until you told me just now, but it's a perfect name for you." He lifted her to the seat and then tossed James a coin and said, "I believe I need a new pair of driving gloves. I'll meet you at Berkeley Square."

James bowed gravely, giving his master a pained expression.

Larla giggled. Marsden no more needed driving gloves than she did today. The man was flirting with her and she found she enjoyed it immensely. Larla blushed rosily as she tried to restore her equanimity. "I was born in India and my grandfather took one look at me when I was born and called me Larla. I remember my mother telling me about it and how she laughed." She was silent for a moment. "My parents were so happy. They loved army life. Then came cholera sweeping the country . . ." her voice broke as she remembered the shattering event of her childhood.

Marsden reached over and placed a large warm hand over hers. "They were happy and they were together." A wealth of understanding warmed his words.

This man made her want to curl up on his shoulder and let him protect her from the world. She shook herself mentally.

That couldn't happen just yet, for she had other things to accomplish first. Making an effort to redirect her thoughts, she commented, "Where is St. James Street? I've heard all the famous men's clubs reside there. Could we drive past?"

Marsden almost choked in his surprise. "That's impossible," he sputtered. "Ladies do not go there." He risked a burning glance at Larla, who was sitting with an amazingly innocent smile on her face.

"Oh, you mean only light-skirts are welcome," she surmised accurately, her eyes full of mischief, peeking at him from under sooty lashes.

"Larla!" he thundered. "Hasn't your grandfather taught you anything?"

"But of course. I can ride, shoot—"

"Stop your blathering! You know well what I meant."

Fury raged within him and Larla waited to see if it would explode. "Temper, temper," she admonished him. When he turned to stare at her, she merely broadened her smile. "Better mind your horses."

His hands slackened their grip on the reins and the horses broke into a canter. Marsden turned his attention to his team, growling at her.

This made her chuckle aloud. "Oh, Marsden. I know you're not that starched. You can't hoax me."

A sheepish grin appeared. "Possibly, but I refuse to let you make a terrible faux pas that would turn the ton against you."

She shrugged the stricture off and turned her mind to the problem of Lord Broome.

Marsden roused her from her deep concentration by saying, "I thought we'd stop at a little sidewalk café on Piccadilly for lunch. Then I'll drive you back to Grillon's or you might prefer a little shopping. I have an appointment to see Joseph Hume."

"Isn't he a member of Parliament?"

"Yes, and at present he is fighting against flogging and imprisonment for debts."

"Are you trying to assist him?"

"I have some ideas of my own. I want to do something for our disabled soldiers. Many of them are starving because they can't find work."

"Isn't there an old soldier's home in Chelsea?"

"The Royal Hospital was founded by Charles II but it is always full, with a long waiting list. The pensioners wear uniforms, dark blue greatcoats in winter and scarlet frock coats in summer. The trouble is we need more places like that."

"I applaud your idea. I hope Hume supports you."

Marsden threw her a tender smile.

Larla deliberately fluttered her eyelashes provocatively at him. "There is something I'd like to do this afternoon if it's acceptable."

"If it is within the realm of possibility, your wish is my command." He threw her an inquisitive glance, waiting for her to give him her request.

Trying to maintain an innocent air, she looked down demurely before flashing him a little-girl smile that would melt the most hardened of hearts. "I'd like to drive your team."

He opened his mouth to deny her ability to hold his team, when he seemed to reconsider. "I suppose that with me beside you there's not much chance of you getting into trouble."

"Such kind words in approbation of my driving skills. Why thank you, Marsden," she chimed sweetly.

Marsden chortled and handed her the reins.

Larla took the team in hand firmly. When a group of urchins ran into the street in front of them, Larla swung the team expertly out of the way.

Marsden sat with his arms folded, giving her a nod of approval. He let his attention wander as he saw that she was more than capable of handling the spirited horses.

Larla was watching the names of the streets carefully. Suddenly she saw it. Glancing quickly at Marsden, she could see he was busy waving to a gentleman across the flagstones. With a flick of the whip and a deft pull on the reins, she had the team turned and bowling swiftly down St. James Street.

For one shocked instant Marsden gaped at Larla, who was smiling innocently at him. Then he furiously grabbed the reins from her and tried to slow the team to a more sedate pace.

Grinding his teeth, he speedily pulled the team to a brisk trot. Then turning back to Larla, he growled menacingly, "What the devil is the meaning of this?"

"Tisk, tisk, your language, Marsden," she needled him mischievously. "That must be White's. There's the famous bow window."

"Don't look!" he commanded forcefully. "Watch the team and nothing else."

Larla was smiling broadly, completely disregarding Marsden's strictures. She saw several men lounging in wing-backed chairs within the club turn to take her measure.

Marsden swore under his breath and kept his team to the pace. It was impossible to turn around on the crowded street. "Now, young lady, just how do you think you're going to explain this behavior? If you think that the Patronesses of Almack's will give you a voucher, you're beside the bridge."

"Pooh! That's easy. I'll just say that your horses got away with you." Larla wasn't a bit repentant. She was in fine fettle.

Marsden's face mirrored several emotions and turned bright red before he was able to speak. "My horses got away with me? And me a member of the Four-in-Hand Club?" He shook his head distractedly, finally catching the humor of it and bit back a grin. "Termagant!" When he could take his eyes from the road, he found Larla giggling and finally, in a release of air, let out a bark of laughter.

"I don't know what I'm going to do with you," he murmured bemusedly when he could catch his breath.

"You'll work it out in time, I'm certain," Larla replied

cheerily. She folded her hands in her lap and treated him to her innocent smile.

"You must have realized that every man in White's is going to think you're my new—" He bit the words off.

"Mistress? Chère amie? How very interesting. Do you change them often?" she asked conversationally.

He snorted. "You unprincipled brat! It's time someone took you in hand!"

Her laughter tinkled the air. "Are you applying for the position?"

"What I'd like to apply is my hand to your very enticing posterior!"

"Why Marsden! How shocking." She was enjoying herself hugely.

Several minutes later they were pulling up to the Grillon's. "I think we've had enough excitement for one day. Would you care to join me for lunch in the dining room?"

"I'd be delighted, my lord."

"Don't try to flummer me, my girl. I'm up to your game and I play for keeps," he retorted.

"Oh, I hope so," Larla whispered under her breath.

CHAPTER 10

Larla was munching a piece of Stilton when she saw Lord Broome enter the dining room in the wake of a rather large-bosomed older woman. Larla had no doubt that this was the overprotective mama.

Broome's shoulders slumped and he followed in the woman's commanding wake. Lady Broome gazed about the room regally before the maitre d' escorted her to a window table. Her high-waisted gown of puce taffeta swished as she walked.

Larla's sympathies were aroused for the young man so plainly miserable. His corpulent figure was encased in a grey waistcoat and white smallclothes, but he looked far from fashionable.

Marsden breathed in her ear, "Lady Broome rules her son with an iron hand."

Larla nodded. Her brain was already refining the daring plan she'd concocted. Her eyes began to dance and her lips twitched in amusement.

"You look as if you had a little mischief up your sleeve," Marsden commented drily.

"Now how can you say such a thing?" Larla queried. "My intentions are pure as the driven snow."

"The snow probably has the devil's pitchfork in it," he parried.

"You wound me," she sighed dramatically before spoiling it with a giggle.

Marsden chuckled at her, causing other diners to glance in their direction. Lady Broome raised her lorgnette and gave Marsden a baleful look that almost convulsed Larla. Marsden inclined his head politely, while Larla was hard-pressed to keep a respectable smile.

As Lady Broome returned her attention to her son, Larla looked from them to Marsden and back, trying to decide how best to seize her opportunity, when Fate decided to help her.

Marsden pulled out his watch. "I didn't realize the time. I must leave now if I'm to be at Hume's punctually." He smiled ruefully at Larla. "I'll leave the coach and James with you so you can shop to your heart's content. Just ask at the desk and one of the men will see it's brought round."

He stood reluctantly. "I'll see you for dinner. I have something special in mind."

Larla took a bite of trifle, being careful to appear to be enjoying the dish.

Marsden's eyes were warm as they rested on her. "Do you mind being left? I see you're not finished but if you'd rather not be here alone, I'll escort you to your room."

"After the rugged life I've led I think I can be trusted to see myself safely back to my room," she conceded drily.

"At this point I'm not sure about anything," he growled, before bowing and striding from the room.

Marsden had barely left when Lord Broome rose. He bowed stiffly to Larla. "Mrs. Ainsworth, my mother would be pleased to meet you. Would you join us at our table?"

Lord Broome introduced Larla with great formality. "Mother, I'd like you to meet Mrs. Ainsworth. Mrs. Ainsworth, my mother, Lady Broome."

That formidable lady held a frosty smile. "Won't you please join us. The waiter will bring over your tea."

Larla thought this was more of a command than a request but nodded her agreement and sat down. The waiter brought Larla's things and two large plates of roast beef to the Broomes. Seeing the pile of food, Larla had to suppress a giggle. There was no doubt why mother and son had such ample proportions.

After attacking a slice of beef, Lady Broome directed her

attention to Larla. "What's this I hear about your being the widow of Jessamy Ainsworth and having his son?" she asked bluntly.

Larla kept her poise. She had parried worse questions in her years in the trail of the army. "It's true. John and I have lived a very secluded life for several years but now I've decided it's time to meet my obligations. I'm here in London to have both the Ainsworth and the Somerset solicitors take care of it." Larla wondered if the woman was just a busybody or if she had some special interest.

Seeing no reaction, Larla continued. "Lord Marsden has acknowledged the claim and so has his solicitor. I don't anticipate any problems." Would that be enough information to satisfy the woman? Larla knew the fastest way to have the ton learn of her arrival would be for one of the gossips to spread it about. Larla would make good use of the woman in return for giving her what she wanted.

Lady Broome nodded absently, seeming to be lost in thought while she studied Larla. Lord Broome was applying himself assiduously to his plate.

"How long have you been a widow, Mrs. Ainsworth?" the matron queried pointedly.

Larla was shocked by the question but didn't let it ruffle her answer. "For about three years." Plainly the woman was nosing around for a suitable marriage candidate for her precious son.

Larla took a sip of her tea and decided to begin her first skirmish in her war for Marsden. "Lady Broome, you have such a popular son," she stated baldly.

Lord Broome raised startled eyes. He paused in his eating, his fork suspended in midair. Then he shook his head slightly as if deciding that he hadn't heard correctly.

Lady Broome's eyes narrowed. "Are you telling me that some woman is trying to snare my son?"

"Certainly not." Larla opened her eyes wide and tried to look as ingenuous as possible. "It's just that I've noticed how everyone around him is so interested in his opinions." Here she surreptitiously crossed her fingers. Larla seemed to consider for a moment. "Take Miss Underwood, for example. She literally hangs on Lord Broome's every word."

Now she had their undivided attention. Lord Broome dabbed his lips with his napkin and actually smiled.

Lady Broome went so far as to put down her cutlery. "You must be mistaken. That is, if you mean Marcia Underwood, granddaughter of the Duke of Denley." She waited grimly for Larla's reply.

"Oh, is she a duke's granddaughter? I didn't know. She is very learned and she seems to appreciate Lord Broome's mind. I've been listening to her tell how much she admires you." Here she crossed fingers on both hands. Surely it was all right to stretch the truth in a good cause?

Lady Broome's eyes became very calculating. "As she is engaged to your cousin-in-law, this is difficult to comprehend."

"That's true, but I've a feeling she's regretting it and doesn't know quite how to cry off. I'm afraid that Marsden is too rackety for her." Silently she offered up a prayer that Marsden would forgive her for this if he heard of it.

Larla took a final sip of her tea and stood up. She didn't want to overdo it. Nor did she want Lady Broome to decide to throw her matchmaking skills in Larla's direction.

She'd accomplished phase one of her mission. On to phase two. "I meant to send a note round to you inviting you to Somerset Place Friday next, but since we've met I thought I'd deliver it in person. I'm having a small party to meet our neighbors. I'd like it very much if you both could come. I'm planning on Lord and Lady Worthingdon, Marsden, the Underwoods, and a few cronies of my grandfather's. I can promise you an excellent dinner. Our chef is superb."

Lord Broome looked to his mother for her decision and as she regally nodded her head, he smiled at Larla. "We'll be happy to come. We're in London only on a visit to our medical man."

"Are you ill?" Larla asked solicitously.

"No, but Mother's health is precarious and we feel it necessary to keep in touch."

Larla had heard how Lady Broome had convenient attacks if her son showed any interest in a female. Marcia might just be the solution to several problems.

"You're very wise," she responded gravely, holding a rising laugh in. As she left, after making her excuses, she heard Broome calling the waiter. Larla chuckled. Her chef was going to have a challenge he hadn't had since they arrived at Somerset Place.

When she opened the door to her room she found Jenny examining her wardrobe. The maid was talking to herself and Larla ignored the small stream of complaints.

"Jenny, I would like you to do something for me. Go down to the desk and see if anyone there can give you Henry Beaufort's address."

Jenny snorted. "First Lady Broome, now this. What next? Asking for a gentleman's lodgings, indeed." The maid didn't wait for an answer, she just stomped off, muttering imprecations.

Larla took out one of the plainest gowns in the armoire and after donning it quickly, went to her dressing table. She opened a drawer, pulling out a wicked-looking derringer that fit in her hand like a glove, and hefted the small double-barreled pistol a time or two, her lips pursed as she analyzed her plan.

As her grandfather had said when he'd presented the weapon to her it was useless unless it was always loaded. Nevertheless she checked the load and was satisfied it hadn't been tampered with. Picking up her reticule, she placed the derringer carefully in it. She'd just finished when Jenny returned.

"The clerk didn't know but a gentleman standing near

heard my request and said that the man resides at 110 Albermarle Street. It's not too far from here.'' She stood waiting for Larla's reaction, taking in the reticule waiting on the dresser and a large straw hat next to it. There was nothing wrong with Jenny's reasoning powers even though she'd not had the advantages of an education. Coupled with Larla's request she knew that mischief was afoot.

"We're going to make a call on a gentleman who is unlawfully holding a watch that belongs to Harold Underwood.''

"And just why didn't Mr. Underwood collect it himself?'' Jenny's arms were crossed, her stance wide-set and her lips firmly compressed.

"He tried but it seems Mr. Beaufort is reluctant to part with the watch and Harold doesn't want anyone to know about his loss.'' Larla picked up the straw bonnet and placed it carefully on her head, working with it until it suited her, sitting at a decidedly rakish tilt.

As she did so Jenny reached over and, seemingly suspicious, picked up Larla's reticule. She nodded as she felt the weight of it but kept her mouth shut. Setting it down again she made her way to the tall armoire that stood against one wall and searched inside until she found her old heavy cloak. With her back to Larla she carefully removed an old army pistol and placed it in the deep pocket of her skirt. She patted the bulge, smoothing the lines of her skirt, and adjusted her apron accordingly.

The old woman muttered under her breath, "I may not shoot as well as the mistress, but there's many a man that wished he could shoot as well as Jenny Bailey.''

Larla ignored the low tones, already knowing that Jenny wasn't pleased at the prospect of visiting a gentleman's residence.

"I don't suppose there's any use of my suggesting you ask Lord Marsden to help you?'' Jenny asked grimly.

"Why should I involve him? I promised Harold I'd tell no one about this coil.''

Jenny rolled her eyes heavenward. "Now I'm no one?" Her tone gave her away. She was plainly delighted that Larla took her into her confidence while refusing Lord Marsden the privilege. "Shall I have the carriage brought around?"

"No, there's no use advertising where we're going and with Marsden's crest on the panel everyone in the street could make a good guess who was calling on Beaufort. We'll start out to walk and hire the first cabbie we see."

Jenny threw up her hands. "Now we're to be in the hands of some driver we know nothing about." Her disapproval was strong but she knew better than to make any more comments. Larla could easily tell Jenny to stay at the hotel.

Larla picked up her reticule, pulled on her gloves and left the room, Jenny following dutifully behind.

They started the walk toward Bond Street and soon Jenny was able to attract the attention of a driver waiting for a fare for his hackney cab.

Larla got in while Jenny gave the man the direction and added he'd be expected to wait for them. Jenny told the man an extra coin would be offered upon completion of the return trip.

The cabbie nodded gratefully and his horse looked able to use any extra that would be coming.

The trip was relatively short but the tension between Larla and Jenny grew. When the cab stopped Larla commanded, "Wait for me for five minutes and then come. I want an element of surprise on my side."

Jenny looked mutinous but thought better of it. "Very well. Five minutes it is," she barked waspishly, consulting the small watch pinned to her shirtwaist. As Larla mounted the steps and raised the knocker, Jenny watched and listened alertly.

Beaufort himself opened the door, looking quite astonished to find a beautiful young girl on his doorstep. "Come in my dear," he invited leeringly. He viewed the rented cab and mumbled absently to himself, a secret smile forming on his lips.

Larla's lips thinned at the endearment but she allowed herself to be led into the drawing room.

"This is such an unexpected pleasure." His eyes feasted on her delicate figure. He noted the deceptively plain lines of the gown.

Larla stopped his speculation. "I'm afraid you're not going to think so before I leave." Her voice was firm, almost regretful.

His lip curled disdainfully at her remark but she ignored it. "I've come to retrieve Harold Underwood's pledge and watch," she announced calmly. "I have the three hundred pounds in my reticule and am willing to trade it."

He laughed sadistically, snorting in amusement. "Just why do you think I'd settle for that today when I wouldn't make that bargain with Harold yesterday. The watch is in lieu of payment for the interest due me."

Larla's shoulders squared as she faced him, determination written in every line of her body. "We both know he is underage and is not legally liable for such a debt and I have the distinct feeling that Bow Street would like to have word of this affair. Give it to me and we'll forget the whole thing."

He assessed her again and Larla could see that man was up to no good. "Well, if he wants the watch so badly I'll give it to you in place of those diamond earbobs you're wearing, the three hundred pounds, and a little of your time. I never look a gift horse in the mouth."

Larla mentally castigated herself. She'd forgotten she was wearing the earrings, but it didn't matter. She had the upper hand here, though he didn't know it yet.

Beaufort opened a drawer in the rosewood desk nearby and produced the jeweled watch and note. "Come and get them, my dear."

Larla had casually opened her reticule and grasped her derringer firmly while he was busy in the drawer. Pointing it directly at Beaufort she requested gently, "Give me the watch and the pledge."

Beaufort was visibly shaken. "Now, now, my dear, someone could get hurt. Those are a menace in the hands of someone unskilled." The man took a step toward her, gaining courage. "You couldn't hit the side of a barn door. Better give it to me before you hurt yourself."

"Stand where you are and put the watch on the table. I assure you I'm no novice with this weapon."

Beaufort took another menacing step toward Larla. She sighed and calmly squeezed the trigger. Beaufort screamed and clapped his hand over his ear. He looked in horror at his fingers which were covered with blood. Rage consumed him as he realized Larla had blown away a small portion of his ear.

"I told you I hit where I aim and the next shot won't just graze your ear." Larla's voice crackled her determination.

The door opened and Beaufort looked up to see another woman with a pistol, this one a large model being steadied over the woman's sturdy arm and aimed squarely at him.

"Stand where you are! One more step and this pistol will make short work of you." Jenny stood her ground.

"I see my reinforcements have arrived. My maid can shoot as well as I," she informed him casually.

Beaufort seemed to slump and pushed the watch and note across the desk.

Larla moved carefully to retrieve them, keeping out of Jenny's line of fire. Larla threw the bills down on the desk, taking care they scattered, before whisking herself from the room as Jenny covered her retreat.

Both sank back against the worn seat and then Larla started to laugh as the driver put his horses to the trot.

"Did you see his face? I think he was afraid I'd blown his entire ear off instead of barely grazing it."

Jenny shook her head. "And what did you plan to do if he attacked you? You'd have had to kill him and that would have been a messy affair."

Larla sighed. "You sound just like Grandfather. I planned my battle carefully and held my troops in reserve. It was just a matter of timing and it went like clockwork."

"That may be but I've a strong notion that your grandfather won't laugh when he hears about this."

"You're not to tell him." Larla called to the cabbie. "Please drop us off in Bond Street." Larla had asked Harold Underwood to meet her for tea at the Ritz at four, so they had best get their shopping done in a hurry.

Marsden would have been amazed, surmised Larla, as they moved from shop to shop making purchases in a rapid style previously unknown to the establishments, to see her campaign strategy while buying additions to her wardrobe.

After sending Jenny and the mountains of packages back to Grillon's, Larla allowed Mr. Underwood to seat her in the famous mirrored tearoom filled with potted ferns and greenery. She was happy to accomplish her mission to extricate Harold from his folly. She hoped that he had learned his lesson.

After the waiter had served them a sumptuous assortment of small sandwiches, cakes, and pastries, Larla leaned across the table. "Open your hand," she whispered.

When Harold extended it, she dropped the jeweled watch and note into it. Harold's eyes grew round. "Mrs. Ainsworth, how ever did you get this?" he asked in astonishment, looking from the timepiece to Larla.

She shrugged nonchalantly. "I just requested it, reminded the man that you are under age and told him that if he didn't make the trade, I'd go to the law and he'd not even get the principal back."

"I don't know what to say. I can't believe that you did it. I know I didn't give you Beaufort's address . . ." his words trailed off with a sigh of inadequacy.

"Don't refine too much on the matter. I just hope that you learned a valuable lesson."

"You can be certain of that," he vowed. "I still have to

return the watch to my grandfather and bring you the money Marsden loaned me. Mrs. Ainsworth, I wish you hadn't gone to see that fellow. I can see now that the fellow will stop at nothing to have his way," he said with a troubled heart.

CHAPTER 11

Larla stode into her room at Grillon's smiling. She was glad that Harold had seemed so repentant. She only wished that he had confided the whole to Marsden. Jenny was busy shaking out new gowns and hanging them in the armoire.

Larla opened the lids of the three hat boxes strewn about the bed amongst the many other packages and picked up a pale green bonnet trimmed with a profusion of ribbons. She had just tied the ribbons under her ear, when a peremptory knock was heard at the door.

Jenny opened the door to a Marsden resplendent in fawn waistcoat and pantaloons, with cream smallclothes, a beaver top hat, and shining Hessian boots. Larla saw the glint directed at her and felt a rush of warmth. This man had the power to draw emotions from her that she hadn't known existed. She smiled as he bowed.

"You are beautiful beyond words in that green confection," he greeted her appreciatively.

"I'm happy you approve. You can see I've been shopping."

"I must say you've had a busy afternoon," he commented cryptically, surveying the mountains of boxes and packages.

Larla directed a sharp look at him. Was he hinting that he knew of her activities? How could he? She'd planned her siege carefully, not been detected, and she thought she'd thrown up a plausible smoke screen with the number of packages she'd purchased. No, she decided quickly, he couldn't know.

"Did you, by chance, purchase something suitable for a night at the theater?" he inquired casually.

"The theater?" she asked delightedly. "I'd be most happy to accept, if this is an invitation, my lord," she teased, twinkling.

"It is, and I know you'll agree that the new play featuring Kean is worthy of your regard. It's playing at the Lyceum Theatre in Wellington Street, off the Strand. The Lyceum was the first theater to install the new gas lighting system and makes the evening so much more enjoyable," he informed her. "I've invited a couple of friends of mine to join us."

"Will I know them?" She tilted her head coquettishly. "It has been ages since I've seen a new play. What time should I be ready?" Her eyes shown with anticipation of the projected treat.

He merely grinned and said, "Wait and see. If it's agreeable to you, we'll have an early dinner here. Could you be ready by six?" he asked doubtfully. That was slightly less than an hour away.

"You forget you're speaking to an old campaigner. I'll undertake to be ready in twenty minutes if you say so."

"I wish I might see it," he mused with a grin.

"You will," she confided engagingly. "There are considerable facets about me you haven't seen yet."

"I shall undertake to rectify the oversight immediately, say in twenty minutes." With that he was gone.

Larla trilled a note of laughter before launching herself at the armoire. Jenny worked deftly along with her mistress to pull the necessary garments from their places.

Marsden seated Larla solicitously at a choice table in the corner which was surrounded by greenery. Larla opened her menu to give it careful study.

Marsden caressed her with his eyes and Larla could feel their heat through the card at her fingertips.

She knew herself to be turned out in prime style in the sea-green gauze gown that hinted at a fairylike appearance, but he always seemed to put her at a disadvantage. Her hair was piled high on her head with a few curling tendrils teasing her ears, and when she looked up she found Marsden staring at them in fascination. Her diamond earbobs and single diamond pendant completed the vision of loveliness and Marsden seemed charmed with the effect, but his inspection made her giddy.

"The roast prime rib is always very good," he suggested.

Larla grimaced as she thought of the Broomes' consumption of that particular dish at nuncheon. "I believe I'd rather have the poisson de beurre. One can never go wrong with fish in England." She'd also had a substantial tea and fish wasn't too filling.

Marsden gave the waiter the order and then sat back comfortably, stretching his legs and enjoying the companion sitting prettily across from him.

Larla decided attack was the best strategy for her planned house party and launched her first volley at Marsden.

"Jeremy, I'm having a small weekend party at Somerset Place Friday next and I'd like you to come along with Lord and Lady Worthingdon. I plan on Miss Underwood and family and a few of my grandfather's friends."

"Larla, I wouldn't miss it for anything and I believe that my parents are free." He seemed to find something amusing about the invitation.

Larla casually announced that she had already invited Lord Broome and his mama. "They have an interest in our new chef," she added mischievously.

Marsden didn't disappoint her. "Broome! Now why the devil would you want that prosy bore?" he inquired suspiciously.

"He's a very interesting man," she replied with a straight face.

"Interesting?" He quirked an eyebrow at her, noting the dancing eyes. "You, my darling, are up to some mischief and I have no doubt I'll be called upon to play a part in it."

She deliberately fluttered her long lashes at him provocatively before spoiling the effect by a wide grin. "I guess that you'll have to wait and see, won't you?"

"You don't propose to put me out of my suspense, then?" he prompted her encouragingly.

"I like surprises and I venture that you might just like this one too." Larla was glorying in his rapt attention, the air almost electric about them as they traded gazes.

"I might come up with one or two surprises of my own," he warned her, letting his masculine appraisal of her crackle the atmosphere.

"I said that I like surprises," she conceded graciously, still grinning.

He took a healthy swallow of his wine and abruptly changed the subject. "I promised to remedy my ignorance of such a lovely damsel. Could you be persuaded to tell me how you happened to meet my cousin? I was with Jessamy the night before the battle and he never mentioned the possibility of being married. When each of us made out our wills, he assuredly would have mentioned a fiancée." He idly turned the stem of the glass in his fingers while intently watching her reaction.

Larla was plainly startled at the change of topics. Before answering she tossed several facts about in her head. Jeremy had acknowledged her claim, even recognizing the signature. He was showing several signs of a man trying to fix his interest and he seemed sincere. The strange thing of it was that Larla wanted to confide in him and lay her problems at his feet.

She took a steadying breath before beginning. "As we hadn't made an announcement of the engagement, that's understandable," she improvised rapidly, knowing she couldn't endanger John. "We were married after the battle."

Marsden digested the fact for a moment, visibly shaken. "I'm sorry that you didn't have longer together," he consoled.

"I can't see that it matters how long we had together," she puzzled. What was his purpose? "His wounds seemed serious and I thought he was about to die." She paused for a moment as she recalled that fateful day. "He wanted so badly to be married, I couldn't refuse him." Her voice trailed away sadly.

Marsden stared blankly to the window, seemingly trying to see the picture. When his glance returned to Larla, his eyes softened. "There's more to the story than that, darling, but I won't press you for the details. You'll tell me in your own good time," he whispered confidently.

Larla nodded. Someday perhaps she could share the tale with him.

"There are many places in London I'd like to share with you. Are you able to stay for another day?"

Larla smiled regretfully. "I'm afraid I must get back to Somerset Place. I've a party to arrange and a small son who misses his mama terribly when I'm gone."

"I look forward to your party and your surprise."

Larla wondered if he would look forward when he knew just what the surprise was. There was certain to be some sort of a scene, if she had any understanding of Marcia Underwood.

Marsden entertained her with such humorous stories about himself and his cousin when they were small that Larla didn't notice the time slip away.

Marsden's friends stood up to greet them as they entered the Ainsworths' box near the front of the stage.

"Sarah and Will, I'd like you to meet my cousin, Larla Ainsworth. Larla, Sarah and William Talgarth, particular friends of mine."

After seating the ladies together in the middle of the box, the gentlemen took their places beside them. Larla smiled at Mrs. Talgarth, who obviously adored her husband. Within a very short time Larla discovered that her new friend shared interests with her, both riding and an animated interest in politics. It seemed that Mr. Talgarth was a member of the House.

Just before the lights went down, Larla discovered she was being stared at by a dark-haired man in the box across the way. Upon closer inspection she discovered it to be Beaufort.

"Who is that man, Larla? He seems to have an uncommon interest in you?" questioned Sarah.

Marsden looked sharply about to determine where and who the impertinent soul was. His eyes narrowed as he recognized the notorious moneylender. He turned to Larla, who looked somewhat flustered.

"I thought possibly the man might be staring at me, but it seems to be you he's looking very unhappy with," he deduced correctly. "What is that man to you?" he asked probingly.

"I'm afraid that I did something to aggravate him," she evaded, looking to where the man's periwig completely covered his ears. That small fact caused her lips to turn up slightly.

Marsden maintained a thoughtful facade for a moment. "Tell me about it," he commanded.

Larla shook her head. The couple on their right seemed interested and Marsden noted their silence. "Another time then," he said reluctantly.

As the lights dimmed Larla could still see a determined line about his mouth that told her plainly the subject was not closed.

During the intermission the gentlemen went off to procure some refreshments. Sarah turned to Larla and begged, "Tell me. Who was that man?"

Larla smiled ruefully. "He's someone that I dislike excessively and I'm afraid I let him know it." It was as much as she was willing to part with.

Sarah grimaced. "The man seems to want to strangle you, if his looks can be interpreted correctly. It must have been quite a scene."

Larla grinned. "Oh, it was. It was."

"My husband says that there's no one in the world he'd liefer go to in a fix than Marsden. If you're afraid, why don't you confide in him. Marsden has never turned down a friend in need, according to Will."

Larla nodded as their escorts returned. "I wish I were able to, but in this instance, it's not my story to tell," she whispered back.

As she expected, Marsden probed deeply into the affair on the drive back to Grillons. Larla couldn't in honor tell him what the problem was. She had promised Harold Underwood that she wouldn't divulge his secret and she meant to keep her promise. That was something her grandfather had taught her early and she wouldn't forget.

Marsden gave it one last try. "Larla, darling. That man is a notorious moneylender. His reputation is very bad. I'm afraid of what he might do if you've crossed him inadvertently." He waited.

"It certainly wasn't inadvertent, and you're right I did cross him, but it's not my story to divulge." She looked up at Marsden with soulful eyes. "I'm so sorry, Jeremy, but I promised."

"Darling, you're playing games with me," he admonished her impatiently.

"Games?" she inquired, struck with the injustice of his comment.

"Yes, but this isn't the time or place for them. I promise you we'll get to them later." His eyes twinkled their guarantee. "I only want to protect you."

"I know and I appreciate all your efforts on my behalf."

He seemed sorry to let the evening slip away. As they

pulled up to the hostelry Marsden said, "Would eleven o'clock suit you to be ready to leave in the morning?"

She nodded her agreement and ascended the stair lost in thought, wondering about Harold and if he had returned the watch to the Duke of Denley.

Early the next morning as Marsden was tying his intricate neckcloth the butler announced Mr. Underwood was downstairs, extremely desirous of seeing him. Marsden directed that he be sent up and went back to lowering his chin slowly as he gently pushed the folds of the white linen. His valet stood by reverently with several spares if his lordship's first efforts should fail.

Harold stepped quietly into the room, fascinated as he watched the delicate creases being made. This pattern was called the Mathematical and took most gentlemen several tries to achieve a respectable effect. Not so this morning for Marsden.

"There, I believe that will do," he told his valet, who bowed and left the room, taking the extra cravats.

"Now, Harold, what may I do for you?"

Harold hemmed and hawed for a moment, shuffling his feet, making several false starts.

Marsden bade him sit down and pulled up a chair beside him. "Tell me about it," he encouraged the young man, who was evidently having a difficult time finding words to express himself. Marsden knew that the lad wouldn't have sought him out this early if he hadn't something important on his mind.

"Do you remember when I asked you to lend me the three hundred pounds last week?" Harold looked forlorn.

"I remember," Marsden agreed dutifully.

"Well, it was to pay back a debt I owed to Beaufort." He looked up to see how Marsden was taking his disclosure so far.

A muscle jumped in Marsden's neck, but that was the only

outward sign of his tenseness. "Go on," he replied neutrally, the name bringing his every faculty to alertness.

"When I went to pay it back, he refused to give me the watch I'd given him for security so I walked away without settling the debt." Harold now had sweat on the top of his lip.

"I see," said Marsden noncommittally.

"Somehow Larla had the story from me. I'm not sure how she did it, but I certainly didn't expect her to take care of it." His eyes were considerably troubled. "Anyway she retrieved both the watch and the pledge from Beaufort. I don't know what to do, but I feel that the scoundrel may try something. I would never have told her if I had any idea that she would go herself."

"What?" Marsden ejaculated. "She said she went herself?"

"That's what she said," he apologized.

He stood up and patted Harold on the back. "You should have come to me with the whole in the first place, but I can see you've grown a deal through the experience. Don't worry any more about it. You've done the right thing and I'll take care of it from here." A martial light emanated from Marsden's dark eyes.

Harold shook his hand and mumbled his gratitude, handing Marsden the wad of bills before departing speedily.

Marsden rubbed his chin in concentration. "The abominable chit!" He would delight in settling this business now that he knew what it was about.

CHAPTER 12

Marsden was late, Larla noted, glancing at the clock in the hotel lobby, and it was unlike him. Jenny was clucking in the background, having loaded the baggage coach some twenty minutes before.

As the clock chimed twelve, Larla was relieved to see Marsden stride in. "I beg your pardon," he apologized profusely, "but I had some urgent business to attend to."

He had a mysterious air of satisfaction about him and Larla wondered what had caused it. As they made their way through the cobbled streets Larla realized that Marsden wasn't wearing his driving gloves and upon closer inspection saw that his knuckles were somewhat swollen and bruised.

She didn't have to wonder what had caused the injury. She'd seen enough of them in the army to recognize when a man had engaged in a bout of fisticuffs. The ranks had been full of feisty Irishmen who loved a good fight every now and then.

"Did you hurt him badly?" she asked quietly.

His head snapped around. An amused eyebrow quirked at her. "Aren't you jumping to conclusions, Larla?"

She straightened militantly and fixed a determined eye on him. "You know perfectly well what I'm speaking about. Those knuckles didn't just happen to look like you planted a facer on someone."

"Tisk, tisk. Boxing cant on the lips of a lady? Larla, really. I must beg you to mind your manners," he riposted with a grin.

Larla was certain that Marsden had been to see Beaufort,

but had he known about the watch and Harold's pledge? "Was it Beaufort?" she asked hesitantly. She had to be certain.

"Are there any others that I must settle with, Larla?" he asked in a grave tone.

"Not that I know of," she laughed. "Just tell me one thing. "Did Beaufort tell you the whole?"

Marsden allowed himself a small chuckle, remembering the scene with Beaufort quite vividly. "Harold confessed his part in the tale and begged my forgiveness. I fancy that he's a reformed character." He touched her cheek tenderly. "Now I'd like to hear your version of the story."

"I'm sorry that I couldn't confide in you last night, but you see I had promised Harold I wouldn't tell." She peeked at him from under veiled lashes. "I've known that something was bothering Harold since the fair. Somehow I got him to trust me with his problem. I advised him to come to you. When he refused to give you the whole of it, I told him to offer the money to Beaufort and try to redeem both the watch and the note. I also asked him to let me know if Beaufort refused to part with the watch. He thought by not giving me the money, I wouldn't try to extricate him from his coil, but I'm made of sterner stuff." She threw him a sassy grin.

"I'm beginning to understand that fact," he agreed willingly.

"So I planned my strategy and executed my plan," she murmured depreciatingly.

Engrossed in their conversation about Beaufort and their respective encounters with the villain, they barely noticed the fields and villages slipping by.

"And just how did you manage that feat?" Marsden's eyes held a rueful admiration.

"I merely told him that Harold was a minor and that under the law he couldn't even collect the interest and he'd do well to settle for his principal back. I added as a clincher that Bow Street probably would like to have word of him."

"Let me understand this correctly: you drove the coach to Beaufort's where anyone could see the crest on the panel?" he questioned with deceptive quiet.

"I did no such thing. I have a little sense," she said indignantly, her eyes flashing their contempt for such deplorable tactics.

"Very little," he assented readily.

"I hired a hackney carriage and took Jenny with me," she flashed back.

"With Jenny along you couldn't get into too much trouble," he sighed in relief.

"I left her in the cab," she retorted spiritedly.

"You tackled the cur alone?" he roared, thunderstruck.

The unaccustomed noise startled the team and Marsden was fully occupied with his horses for several moments while he pulled his temper back together.

"I did and when he refused to trade, saying he'd settle for my earrings and some of my time, I took out my derringer. I warned him I'd shoot him if he didn't comply, but the man had to be shown," she said with relish.

"You mean you shot him?" he queried disbelievingly, trying to stifle a laugh.

"In the ear," she grinned.

"You should have aimed better," he growled when he thought of the blackguard's behavior.

"I hit him where I aimed. I had no intention of doing much more than scaring him." She waited while he digested this and then continued. "I had arranged to have the reinforcements arrive on cue, and Jenny burst into the room, brandishing her wicked-looking pistol. She looked as though she'd enjoy putting a hole or two through Beaufort."

With that, Marsden threw back his head and roared with laughter. Larla chuckled with him. "It must have been quite a sight."

"You should have seen his face! He couldn't believe that it was actually happening to him. Jenny kept him in her sights while I made the trade and we made a hasty retreat." She knew her grandfather would have been proud of her determination. "Now it's your turn to answer a few questions. Did you really knock him down?"

"Bloodthirsty little thing, aren't you?" he quizzed her mockingly.

"Well?" she demanded impatiently.

"As a matter of fact I did make it a point to see him this morning and impress upon him that a change of climate would be good for his health. He objected and I had to, shall we say, change his mind."

Larla knew that he wouldn't disclose any more but was certain that Beaufort had taken the worst of the exchange. It was a delicious feeling to know that Marsden had settled the account and that the man wouldn't be around to bother others.

"I believe that I'd like to see your pistol and your marksmanship today," said Marsden as they turned into the carriage drive at Somerset Place. "Would you and your grandfather consider coming to dinner so we might test your skill on our range?"

"Why certainly, Jeremy. Just let Jenny get my things unpacked and I'll be most happy to accommodate you, if John is invited." Her face sparkled her delight.

"John is always welcome at Edgehurst, Larla, just as you are." He searched her face intently.

"Thank you," she breathed raggedly, swallowing a sudden lump in her throat.

He handed her down from the curricle, holding her just a fraction too long. Larla shivered under his probing gaze. Then the spell was broken as Jenny joined them, carrying one of the portmanteaus and directing a footman to see to the others.

After obtaining the colonel's agreement to the projected

dinner and contest, Marsden took his leave, giving Larla's hand a tight squeeze.

John rushed up the steps at Edgehurst to greet Marsden, "Papa!" The little figure threw himself into Marsden's arms excitedly. "Are you going to shoot with Mama?"

Marsden chuckled his happiness at the accolade. The youngster didn't know that Marsden was actually his father, but he seemed to recognize that his mother spent a lot of time with him.

"Yes, John, I certainly am. I want to make sure your mama can handle a gun properly." He repressed a grin as he spoke, knowing he'd get some reaction to the inflammatory statement.

The colonel, who was ascending the steps at a more sedate pace with Larla, snorted at Marsden's remark. "Taught her myself," he barked impatiently.

"Yes, Jeremy, and he had to be a very patient teacher. I could never do anything correctly for the first few times. I was probably his worst pupil," she teased laughingly.

"Nonsense," replied the colonel, "she's a fine shot. "You'd do well not to underestimate her."

Marsden looked questioningly at the colonel before glancing down at his lovely wife. "I have promised myself not to be surprised at anything she does. She's a remarkable woman."

Lord and Lady Worthingdon met them in the gold salon while Marsden went to fetch the pistol case.

"How nice of you to come all this way so that we might share in the fun," said Lady Worthingdon graciously.

"I wouldn't want to deprive you unnecessarily, ma'am," grinned Larla.

"Do you intend to beat him again?" mused Lady Worthingdon in a hushed tone, seeing that the men were engaged greeting one another.

"I certainly shall do my best," she said earnestly.

"You do him so much good, dear. He's finally begun to

laugh again since you've come home." She looked fondly at Larla. "You mark my words. Things have a way of turning out for the best," she said assuringly.

"But sometimes Fate needs a bit of a helping hand," returned Larla mildly.

"Just so," agreed Lady Worthingdon.

Lord Worthingdon shook the colonel's hand. "Glad to have you, George."

"I'm delighted to witness this event, Charles," returned the colonel enthusiastically.

"It's been some time since Jeremy has been so interested in shooting. I am glad to see him returning to an active life and I believe that your Larla has stirred him up, I must say, for the better."

"Larla's quite a woman, Charles. Completely up to Marsden's weight. It wouldn't hurt my feelings in the slightest to see a change in the direction of the wind," he said in a sly aside, "if you get my meaning."

Lord Worthingdon nodded with a smile. "We're quite taken with her."

"Shall we adjourn to the target butts?" Lord Worthingdon asked, turning to the ladies as Marsden strode in.

Both the colonel and Marsden carried gun cases, while Larla and Lady Worthingdon followed, each taking one of John's hands.

One of the footmen placed a table convenient to the firing line, and the boxes containing the powder, patches, and pistols were placed on it.

"Would you care to be first, Larla?" asked Marsden deferentially.

"I don't mind," replied Larla offhandedly. She picked up her double-barreled derringer, checking the load, and aimed it carefully at the target, squeezing the trigger easily. Both shots found the outer rim of the center circle.

Marsden's eyebrow shot up considerably. "Admirable shooting," he acknowledged. Picking up one of his pair of duelling pistols, he drew down on the target and fired and hit the center of the bullseye.

"Jolly good," exclaimed the colonel.

"Righto," added Lord Worthingdon.

Larla didn't say anything, but stood with a small smile.

Marsden turned to her and inquired, "Would you mind trying one of mine?" He gestured to the box.

"I'd be honored." She took the proffered weapon from the case and checked its load and balance. Pointing it at the target she pulled the trigger slowly. She barely missed Marsden's mark.

"Would you like to try my derringer, Jeremy? I warn you it throws slightly high and to the right."

Marsden picked up the small gun and placed powder and patch, then rammed the balls into place. Heeding Larla's warning he adjusted his aim and fired the weapon. He marked one of the outer rings of the target. "You're right, it throws considerably to the right. I don't know how you shoot so well with such a poor choice of weapons."

"Would you like to have the contest with your pistols?" she asked merrily.

"Certainly," he agreed gravely. "I never say no to you," he added in a whisper for her ears alone.

"Best out of five?" Larla's face was flushed.

"How about best out of ten?" Marsden countered.

"Fine with me." Catching sight of her grandfather's wink, she grinned in response.

John held Lady Worthingdon's hand tightly, whispering throughout the match. It was clear he wasn't the least bit frightened by the loud reports.

"Well, darling," concluded Marsden with a triumphant grin, "I make it nine out of ten for me to your eight."

"I concede you the better shot, Jeremy," she agreed easily, staring bemusedly into his magnetic eyes, "but one day you must test my skill at chess. I should think that there are several contests still to be played." Larla's face sparkled with challenge.

"Oh, to be sure. There are many more yet to come," Marsden acknowledged. "I'm available most anytime. Perhaps we'll find a time at Somerset Place this weekend?"

The colonel and Lord Worthingdon exchanged knowing looks. "We'll be delighted to provide an audience to any contest you set up. We've had a delightful afternoon, Jeremy and Larla," Lord Worthingdon informed them jovially.

Marsden took Larla's arm and led the way back to the house. "I believe there are a few contests we'll leave them out of," he murmured teasingly.

CHAPTER 13

Larla made her way downstairs to the kitchen immediately upon leaving her bedchamber, knowing that the temperamental chef would be having trouble with the kitchen maids hired for the party's duration. Jean Claude was waving his arms about in a stream of French entirely unintelligible to the three kitchen maids. The women looked harassed as each vied with the other to gather ingredients for various dishes. The result was complete chaos with frustration being the order of the day.

Larla stepped in and sniffed the air, the aroma of fresh bread and rolls permeating the basement regions. "Jean Claude, it smells heavenly," she complimented sincerely. "Would it be possible for you to speak in English to these girls? They are not so gifted in languages as you," she said diplomatically. "I believe that they are very desirous of following your most exacting commands if they could only understand them."

The Frenchman rolled his eyes heavenward but nodded his agreement.

"I came down to see if there is anything you wished to consult me about before my guests arrive this afternoon. I know I may count on you and your staff to produce superlative meals for my first party."

"Madame, it shall be magnifique." He kissed his fingers in a Gallic gesture. "Merci. I shall not disappoint you. Your breakfast is ready if you are, madame," he said deferentially, executing a deep bow.

Larla smiled and left him issuing commands about the

preparation of pastries and her morning repast. When things got hectic in the kitchen Jean Claude would invariably revert to his ancestry and begin a constant monologue of voluble French.

As she reached the small dining room to sit down to await her breakfast, Marsden swung jauntily into the room. She looked past him to see if Williams was behind him.

"I told your butler I'd announce myself."

"Is this your surprise for the day? I didn't expect guests until nuncheon." She cocked her head saucily at him. "Didn't your cook have breakfast for you?"

"I wasn't hungry for food," he said offhandedly with an appreciative leer.

Larla felt the blush rise upward to engulf her face. This man was completely cutting up her peace of mind. She found that her thoughts were constantly reverting to the masculine figure now tantalizing her vision. "Won't you join me for a little breakfast. Your first choice doesn't seem to be on the menu," she returned pertly.

Marsden leaned back with a bark of laughter. "How prettily you reprimand me."

The maid brought another place setting while a couple of footmen brought in toast, scrambled eggs, grilled potatoes, and rashers of bacon.

Marsden scooped himself a healthy serving of each, much to Larla's delight. He maintained a stream of small talk of local events and happenings, while making Larla feel that the subjects weren't at all what he had on his mind.

She knew herself to be beyond prudence where he was concerned, and she felt her partiality to his company must be noticed.

"Has the colonel come down yet?"

"Grandfather? He's no slugabed. I would imagine he's busy inspecting the horses." Her eyes twinkled. "I believe he wishes to show off his stable to Lord Worthingdon," she confided.

"My father will enjoy that. Much of his life is spent around his horses. Most country gentlemen seem to share an interest in horses."

"I have met only one notable exception." She dimpled merrily.

"Ah, yes. Lord Broome. You shouldn't have any trouble entertaining him, but I'm afraid that your chef may find his hands full," Marsden grinned.

Larla acquiesced with a giggle.

"I suppose that the preparations will keep you so busy that you don't have time to show me about this morning," he bantered easily.

"What a campaigner must you think me!" she retorted, stung. "I am completely at liberty. I plan in advance." A secret smile lit her face as she thought of exactly how much she had planned.

"Then how about giving me a quick tour of the estate. We could take the pony cart and John could have a treat driving."

She flashed him a brilliant smile. "The very thing. I'll ring for his nurse and see if he's had his breakfast." She yanked one of the ornate bellpulls on the wall.

Several minutes later the nurse entered the room and bobbed a curtsey. "Yes, mum?"

"I'm taking John for a ride. Will you bring him to me as soon as he's ready?" Larla always had a kind smile for her servants. She had found long ago that her servants fell over themselves to do her bidding when she included a little graciousness in her requests.

"I'll bring him right away," she responded with another bob and hurriedly left the room.

"This is extremely nice of you, Jeremy, to bother with a small boy. You may be bored to death." She threw out the hidden question.

"Not with your son, darling," he retorted amusedly. "I've

never seen such an intelligent lad." The tone was distinctly proud.

A short time later they were trotting toward the home wood where John was to have the professed treat. The youngster bounced eagerly on the seat, awaiting his turn with great anticipation.

Larla handed the reins to her son tenderly, a special softness in her eyes as she watched him. After a few minutes of intense concentration, John looked up at his mother and Marsden grinning.

"See, Papa, how I can drive," he exclaimed proudly.

"John," Larla began to remonstrate the small boy.

Marsden covered her hand with his and shook his head. It was clear he was pleased with the title. He looked searchingly into her eyes, as if trying to decide something, but Larla couldn't think what it might be.

"A toothy morsel for gossip at my own party," Larla murmured, torn between his complaisance and her fear of scandal concerning John. "That's the second time he's done that."

"I think you worry yourself unnecessarily. Don't you follow the adage, 'Children are to be seen and not heard'?" His lips twitched as he surveyed her countenance.

"I plan to bring John down to meet our guests and let him greet them. Then he'll be taken back to the nursery for his own dinner and play until bedtime." She chewed her lip reflectively. "I'll instruct him in advance to call every gentleman 'my lord,' and every lady 'my lady.' "

"I knew you'd find a way to control the situation. I could even arrange to be absent for the big moment, if you'd like," he offered jestingly.

Larla stared at him in silent fascination. He had come just short of making a declaration of his intentions to her, but he hadn't seemed to make any progress to detach Marcia. This party ought to do the trick if she had her way.

Soon it was time to return to the house. Marsden covered

two tiny hands with his large ones. "This is how we turn the horse correctly, John," he instructed quietly.

Larla had a suspicious moistness in her eyes as she beheld the lesson. Marsden seemed completely at his ease with her precious son. She swallowed a lump that arose in her throat and mentally reviewed her campaign strategy to unite Marcia and Lord Broome.

When they strolled into the great hall, John saw his nurse and started to scamper for her. Suddenly he stopped and walked back to stand directly in front of Marsden.

"Papa, I love you," the little boy declared gravely, before running to his nurse.

It was sometime later when the house guests began to arrive. General Hathaway and his wife, who lived at Hathaway Court, a few miles distant, were the first to enter the crimson salon. Upon seeing his old friend asleep in a large Chippendale chair, he motioned the butler not to announce them.

The old jokester stealthily moved to stand in front of the dozing colonel while his wife stepped aside and merely shook her head. The general held up his hand and motioned the party to silence.

Larla's eyes were on Marsden as he watched the proceedings from a place by the finely worked wood mantle. Marsden had a rueful grin, standing at his ease.

"Stand to your arms!" roared the general, a huge grin engulfing his face. The stentorian shout could have awakened the dead.

The colonel jumped up out of his chair, his hand reaching for his nonexistent weapons. As he perceived the general's guffaws and his friend slapping him on the back, he smiled and laughed in return. "You old dog! Up to your old tricks again, I see."

General Hathaway chortled merrily, as did Major Denton and Colonel Rothchild, who had just arrived upon the scene. "Remember the time . . ." and the men were off reminiscing about old times.

Mrs. Denton greeted the general's wife with a chuckle. "It seems they're never too old to make a joke."

Larla's eyes were still glued to Marsden. She had seen this particular joke played too many times in the past by both old friends to pay them much mind, but Marsden's reaction was alarming.

Marsden's face had completely drained of color. He raked a hand through his carefully arranged locks, destroying the style à la Brutus that had taken his man a full twenty minutes to accomplish. At first Larla thought he was in pain but seconds later he seemed to have recovered.

She moved quietly over to speak to him as the others enjoyed their joking. "Marsden, is something troubling you?" She searched his face. "May I help?"

"Larla, darling, I've just remembered what happened to me in that first week after I was shot," his tone was remorseful, and he turned pain-filled eyes to hers.

"Did the general's roar bring your memory back? How much better you must feel not to have an empty place in your memory." She patted his arm reassuringly.

"You don't understand," he whispered desperately. His gaze was exceedingly tender and he stroked her hair.

Larla merely stared at him in confusion. "I'll try, Jeremy."

There wasn't time for more, for Williams was announcing Lord and Lady Worthingdon and the Underwoods. Soon Lord Broome and his mama, along with several others, joined the assembled group.

After a substantial tea Larla escorted each of her guests to the rooms that had been prepared. She purposely had put Marcia Underwood at the end of the south wing so Miss Underwood would be the last guest to her room.

Upon opening the door to the lovely room in rose and cranberry damask, Larla motioned her guest to a chair and sat down opposite her. "How fortunate you are Miss Underwood, engaged to one man and have another almost falling over your feet." Larla tried to put the proper degree of envy in her voice.

Marcia's mouth opened to repudiate such a statement when she apparently reconsidered. "Oh?"

"Haven't you noticed how attentive Lord Broome is to you? I have remarked upon it several times. He has only the most complimentary things to say about you, Miss Underwood. Could you tell me your secret?" Larla's eyes were all innocence.

"I'm sure I don't know what you mean," stammered Miss Underwood, blushing faintly.

"Even Lady Broome has noticed it," Larla added, if not quite truthfully. The woman would be paying strict attention to Marcia in the future, Larla consoled herself.

Miss Underwood seemed thoughtful for a moment before offering a few words of encouragement to Larla. "Don't be too down pin, Mrs. Ainsworth. Lord Broome much admires a high moral tone. When you have learned town ways, I'm certain your time will come," she murmured condescendingly, as if Broome were the biggest plum on the marriage mart.

With that Larla stood and made her escape before she succumbed to a fit of laughter that was threatening to explode. She hadn't dreamed in her wildest fantasies that her opening salvo would be so well received.

Dinner was an unqualified success. Jean Claude had outdone himself, every dish not only delicious but also extremely appealing to the eye. Lady Broome waded through the many courses like a starving peasant and her son kept pace admirably.

Marcia, seated beside Broome, was unusually animated. Marsden merely picked at his food, spending most of his time glaring across the table at Harold, who was conversing happily with Larla.

Lady Worthingdon missed none of the byplay. She said in

an aside to her spouse, "I believe that we'll be vastly entertained this weekend." She sparkled her approval.

Miss Underwood, noting the gathering frown on her fiancé's face, asked quietly, "Is something wrong, Marsden?"

"No!" he snarled back rudely.

Marcia's eyes snapped her disapproval and turned to Lord
Broome on her other side.

"Tell me, Miss Underwood, what is your opinion of the
sauce on the asparagus?" Broome droned, apparently unaware of the disputation.

Marcia took her cue gratefully and tasted the delicacy. She
enlightened him as to her opinion, while Broome busily
made great inroads on his plate. "I must say, Lord Broome, it
is an honor to see a man do justice to his meal." She accompanied this statement with an admiring look.

Broome swallowed hastily, almost choking.

"Are you all right?" she inquired solicitously.

"Thank you. So considerate, so much the lady. I applaud
your superior mind, Miss Underwood. Always showing the
proper tone to an assembly."

Marcia flushed slightly at the compliment.

Larla noted the growing preoccupation of her two guests
with a deal of satisfaction. Marsden, although he might not
know it, was doing an admirable job with the rear guard. He
was keeping his fiancée slightly off balance with his constant
changes in behavior, Larla applauded silently. A quick glance
at Lady Worthingdon told her that Marsden's mother was
extremely needle-witted and might be called upon to add her
inspiration in an emergency.

After dinner Larla led the ladies to the drawing room,
while the gentlemen remained to enjoy their port. At other
times Larla might be bored by this rigid custom, but tonight
she planned to make another foray into the opposing strong-
hold.

Larla took a seat on the vacant couch and directed conversation through local gossip and a few political debates, before trying to venture into her latest scheme.

It was Lady Worthingdon that fired the opening guns, much to Larla's amazement.

"My dear Lady Broome, I must compliment you on your son. His manners are so genteel, such as must please the most exacting companions, and so knowledgeable . . ." she let the sentence dangle.

Lady Broome's bosom seemed to swell to alarming proportions, while Lady Worthingdon maintained a company smile. Larla was fascinated by the exchange between the two women.

"Thank you, Lady Worthingdon," she acknowledged graciously. "It's such a pity that I've not been— That is, Broome has not been able to find a suitable wife. It is my dearest dream that he marry and have an heir. So far there has been no one that appeals." She sighed deeply and fingered her long rope of pearls.

Mrs. Hathaway and Mrs. Denton grinned understandingly at each other.

Mrs. Underwood took up the battle cry unknowingly. "Excellent lineage and a good dowry are essential." She gazed dotingly on her daughter, who at her mother's praise of her most noted virtues had modestly cast her eyes downward.

Lady Worthingdon's eyes were twinkling with mirth. "Broome is worthy of anyone, I daresay, even a duke's daughter."

Larla watched Lady Broome for her reaction to the volley thrown out by Lady Worthingdon. Broome's mama seemed to consider the idea for a second before letting her gaze fall to Miss Underwood.

Larla picked up the attack immediately. "Tell me, Miss Underwood, didn't you mention visiting the Louvre in the spring?"

Miss Underwood, grateful for a topic that she could warm

to, began to expound on the virtues of the museum situated in the heart of Paris.

During her discourse the door opened to admit the gentlemen, but Larla saw that Lady Broome had heard enough to recognize a kindred spirit for her son.

Denton and Rothchild strolled in arm in arm, each making a gesture of acknowledgement to the ladies.

"What are we going to do about Sir Robert Peel?" Lord Worthingdon was asking.

"As Home Secretary, he has a deal of influence but his opposition to Reform must be squashed." Marsden's voice rang through the drawing room as he allowed the colonel to precede him. Perceiving Larla, he strode directly to the love seat and sat down beside her, turning his back to his fiancée.

Mrs. Underwood's thin cheeks grew a mottled crimson, while her daughter's mouth formed an angry line at the slight.

Larla began to question Marsden quickly about the issue at hand when he murmured under his breath, "Not now, darling."

Larla heaved a resigned sigh and turned to hear what Major Denton was saying about the Reform. The heated argument subsided for a moment as the colonel addressed a comment to the ladies about the coming card party.

Miss Underwood, seemingly stricken by her fiancé's rudeness, sent her mother a distinct silent appeal but that woman merely closed her eyes for a second and gave a slight shake of her head. As a result, Miss Underwood's hands clenched tightly in her lap.

Lord Broome hadn't missed the direct cut Marsden had given his fiancée and made his way to her, pulling up a chair so as to sit near her. He spoke in low tones, and although Larla couldn't hear what was being said, it was apparent that he restored Miss Underwood's good humor and considerably eased the tension.

Things couldn't be working out better, thought Larla as

she peeked at the two from under her heavy lashes. Her eyes danced their mischief as she began to chart her next step.

Marsden was intrigued by the emotions that flitted across Larla's visage. "Tell me," he coaxed.

Her eyes widened innocently. "What would you have me say?" she parried quickly.

"I want you to confide your mischief to me, my darling. I know you're up to something. I can see it in your eyes," he concluded with an appreciative grin.

"I might have something to share tomorrow. Will you join me in a nice gallop after breakfast?"

Marsden nodded his assent before his attention was reclaimed by his father who wanted him to reinforce an opinion on the state of the policies of the Home Secretary.

Soon it was time for the ladies to retire upstairs to finish their preparations for the evening cards and dancing. Larla marshaled her forces about her, checking with various staff members to see that everything was in readiness for the rest of the guests to arrive. The trays of refreshments were beautifully arranged, the carpets in the ballroom rolled back, the chandeliers shining, and flowers fragrantly permeating the air.

Larla, dressed in a resplendent gown of melon organza draped with lace and clusters of flowers, stood graciously beside her grandfather in his dress regimentals and greeted the new arrivals with a pleasing touch of deference.

"It's a pleasure to have you." Larla eyed the Talgarths with some envy. "I'm so glad that you could come." They seemed to be so much in love and happy in each other's company.

The colonel directed the older members to the front salons, where the furniture had been removed to accommodate a number of card tables. Others made their way to the ballroom, where the orchestra was entertaining until the dancing began later.

The atmosphere was informal and the rooms were filled with chatter and occasional laughter. Larla moved among the groups, seeing that no one was left without a companion of some sort. The colonel stood back and silently applauded her efforts.

General Hathaway walked up behind him and murmured, "Very pretty manners, George. She'd make a delightful political hostess," he surmised shrewdly.

"Amen," granted the colonel complacently. After chatting with his cronies for a few more minutes, Colonel Somerset beckoned to Marsden. "I'd like to deputize you to help open the dancing with Larla, if you have no objections."

Marsden said all that was proper and made his way leisurely through the rooms in search of Larla. Upon seeing her across several card tables, he drew her to him with a questioning nod and a wink. As she passed, she spoke a kind word to each guest, leaving behind an impression of a great lady.

Marsden smiled tenderly down at her. "Do you think it's about time to start the dancing?" he queried.

Larla acquiesced gracefully and let him escort her to the ballroom. The colonel was there before them and alerted the musicians.

With a bit of fanfare, the dancing was announced and Marsden swept Larla into his arms. After watching for a few minutes, other couples joined them and soon the floor was filled with couples.

Lord Broome moved importantly through the crowd to gain Miss Underwood's side and begged her hand for a dance.

"Why, Lord Broome, I'd be most happy to accompany you," Miss Underwood gushed with sugary sweetness.

"Too kind," protested Broome with a superior smile.

Officers in Wellington's army were well versed in the fine art of dancing and even the colonel and his cronies made the rounds so that each lady had several partners to skillfully take her about the floor.

Larla's hand was much sought after and she adroitly made each partner value his dance with her highly. She bestowed her most gracious smiles upon all who danced with her and succeeded in making an angry frown about Marsden's lips. Larla noted the exact moment when Marsden sought his fiancée's hand to dance the waltz.

Larla knew better than to indulge herself, even at a country dance in her own home. She had yet to be approved by the Patronesses at Almack's and to dance the waltz before she had done so would be considered terribly fast. So Larla merely stood beside her grandfather and grinned knowingly at Marsden and Miss Underwood twirling about the dance floor.

It was apparent that Miss Underwood was protesting Marsden's cavalier treatment of her and thereby not doing herself any good.

Larla was quite pleased at the progress being made and her smile was radiant. The scene in front of her was as good as any play she had seen and certainly more interesting.

Here was Lord Broome looking like a puppy who had just had a bone stolen from him and was waiting intently for his chance to snatch it back. Determination was etched on his normally placid face.

Marsden was glaring at her glacially while Miss Underwood droned on, seemingly unaware of the direction of her fiancé's gaze. Larla smiled gayly at the couple and made her way purposefully to Lord Broome.

"Lord Broome, I don't believe that I've had the opportunity to compliment you on your dancing. So refined and graceful." She waited for the expected invitation, and Broome didn't disappoint her.

"Why, thank you, Mrs. Ainsworth. Would you care to allow me to be your partner for the next dance? I don't quite approve of the waltz. It seems a little fast," he confided condescendingly.

"I do believe that you're right. I shouldn't like to see you waltzing. It would spoil your image." Larla was hard-pressed not to grin.

As Larla let Broome partner her for the country dance, she peeked at Marsden and Miss Underwood to see that he had almost jerked Miss Underwood to the floor in silent frustration.

General Hathaway begged for the honor of Larla's hand for a turn on the dance floor, and Larla accepted prettily. "You dance delightfully, my dear."

Larla grinned. "With Grandfather to teach me, how could I dare do anything else?"

The general roared with laughter, causing several guests to stare at the couple so obviously enjoying themselves.

His eyes twinkled as he caught Marsden's look of potent anger. "I believe that you have your work cut out for you there, young lady," he chimed merrily, nodding toward Marsden.

Larla turned to see the object of his interest and her eyes locked with Marsden's for an uncomfortable moment before she turned back to the general. "I do believe that you speak the truth, General Hathaway."

Just before the end of the evening Marsden claimed Larla for a second dance. "I believe this one is mine," he growled to a young lieutenant who was ready to take her out onto the floor.

"I'm sorry, Lieutenant Wynchbold. I'd forgotten that I promised Lord Marsden," she apologized prettily.

Marsden swept her into his arms and looked down at her possessively.

"That wasn't very well done of you, Jeremy," Larla remonstrated lightly.

"That puppy," snorted Marsden, "can find someone else for his amusement. You're about to become very busy."

"Oh?" queried Larla interestedly.

CHAPTER 14

A vision of loveliness in her newest habit of crimson velvet, Larla made her way to the stables. Marsden noted the way the material clung to her trim figure as she walked. He approved the stylish curl of a short ostrich plume on her shako and the matching gauze that floated out behind as she walked. Her matching crimson boots were of kid and completed the stylish outfit procured that busy afternoon on Bond Street.

Larla moved with assured grace, knowing the riding costume was all the rage and, from the look that Marsden was giving her, was more than worth the price that had sadly diminished the contents of her purse.

A stable boy had just finished saddling Igor and brought the high-spirited stallion into the courtyard. As Larla approached, Marsden moved forward, taking her hands in his and pressing them warmly, commenting on the delightful picture she made.

Larla flushed warmly, a becoming pink staining her cheeks. She laughed gayly. "Shall we go?" she asked hurriedly, itching to be off.

Marsden tossed her lightly into Star's saddle before being fully occupied with Igor as he mounted the frisky stallion. For a few seconds he let the horse work out the kinks as he kicked, stretched, and bucked a bit.

Larla admired the consummate horsemanship that brought the stallion under control. Marsden had just the right degree of tension on the reins and spoke soothingly to the animal. He worked the horse until he was satisfied with its performance. Then he smiled at Larla and led the way from the courtyard.

As the two moved off, Tompkins strode up double time from the house, tipping his hat. "If it's all right with you, missy, I plan to take Master John out with a leading rein this morning. He has done so well in the ring, I think it's time for him to advance."

"As long as I know you're with him, Sergeant, I won't worry," Larla returned with a smile. The old man had called her missy since she was in leading strings and she rather liked the endearment.

The old soldier saluted and, with a brisk about-face, marched into the stables, calling orders to the stable hands.

Marsden's conversation was confined to simple pleasantries for the first leg of the ride. He seemed content with the delight of the ride and the day. Larla didn't seem to mind, her face wreathed in a happy expression that told all she was enjoying herself.

Igor chafed at the bit, itching for a good run. When an open field was reached, Marsden turned to a grinning Larla and asked, "Would you care to let the horses kick up their heels a bit?"

Larla nodded, but was already lengthening her stride and let her mare have its head. Her delicate face flushed with pleasure and the gauze veil attached to her shako flew on the breeze while the plume bounced daintily.

Star kept pace with the bounding stallion, which Marsden had well under control. Stride for stride they raced across the meadow.

Hooves pounded the earth, clumps of damp earth sprayed behind, and the fields seemed to flash by as the riders enjoyed the morning gallop. The sun beat down on the sparkling dew and perked up the heads of sleeping flowers.

Soon they approached the path that skirted the home wood and they reined in slowly, content to let the horses pick their way through the tall grass.

"Now Igor will mind his manners." Marsden patted the horse's neck. "He just needs to get the kinks out first."

Larla agreed complacently, a sparkle lighting her face. Everything was going just as she had planned.

As they walked the horses along the path, Marsden perceived it and queried, "Now tell me what you're up to, Larla. I have the distinct feeling that I won't like it and I'd just as soon be prepared."

Larla's face became a study in concentration. She pursed her lips and nibbled distractedly at them. Her plan to convince Miss Underwood to cry off depended upon Marsden's genuine rage when he discovered the scene that Larla had set.

She smiled slyly. It was just about time for Williams to suggest to Broome that Miss Underwood might care to see the gardens. Larla didn't think that it would take much to induce Marsden to walk with her in the garden after their ride and discover the two in a hopefully compromising position.

She peeked at him coquettishly from under fluttering lashes. "What do you think of a gentleman who woos a woman that's engaged to another?" She let the question hang on the air for only a second before asking, "You wouldn't call him out would you?" That was the only drawback in her campaign strategy that she could see.

"Just what are you getting at, my sassy little baggage?" He reached over and tweaked her nose with a raised eyebrow, studying her anxious expression.

"I guess that I'm asking if a gentleman found . . ." she struggled to maintain her composure, ". . . his fiancée in a compromising situation would he be in honor bound to call the man out?" The words came out in a rush, a slight frown marring her usually sunny countenance.

Marsden knew Larla too well to assume that this was a rhetorical question and considered it carefully. "He's not bound, but in some cases he might if his affections were engaged. Otherwise he might just allow himself the privilege of flying into a rage. By the time he was done," said Marsden grimly, warming to the subject, "his fiancée would know that she would never be left alone but always have a chaperon to watch over her while he was gone and that her movements would be very much curtailed."

Larla bit her cheeks to hold in a grin as she thought of how Miss Underwood might react to the coming scene. If Larla were any judge at all, and she believed that she was, Miss Underwood would rise to the occasion nicely and react with furious indignation.

If Larla could contrive to be several steps ahead of Marsden and exclaim in shock, it just might answer. No one besides the four of them need ever know the whole of the situation. Marsden wouldn't question Larla's shock or her word. It would be left to Broome to try to explain. The more Marsden pushed him, she surmised, the more Miss Underwood would bristle.

"A terrible fate, I'm sure," Larla observed drily, thinking that if she stiffened her resolve everything would come out satisfactorily for all involved. She needn't actually lie. All she need do would be to cry and tell Marsden not to look. The mischievous twinkle in her eyes glinted in anticipation.

"Your time is coming, my meddling little vixen," he apprised her with determination.

"I believe you may be right, my lord," she murmured consolingly.

Although he questioned her closely, he could gain no more information. Larla used every feminine wile she possessed to divert his attention and change the direction of conversation.

Marsden had much food for thought as they continued up the path. His gaze kept wandering to the figure of innocence chatting gayly beside him.

Jenny, with Master John in hand, marched down the steps and to the stable. The little lad skipped merrily. A militant angle held her chin up as she confronted the old sergeant. "Now see here you take good care of this youngster," she admonished him as she might one of the under maids. It was a running battle between the two.

Tompkins' brows drew together in a frown. "I always tend to my business. See that you tend to your own," he advised her at his most crushing. Reaching for the lad, he swung him to his shoulder, giving Jenny a curt nod before disappearing into the stables.

Jenny humphed a couple of times before turning on her heel, muttering to herself about the animadversions of the man's character.

A cob had been saddled for Tompkins and a sleek pony of indeterminate age for John. He let the lad mount himself before swinging into his saddle. The groom respectfully handed the leading rein to the sergeant and the sergeant led John out into the stable yard. "We'll be heading for the home wood and the stream. There's several places there a boy might like to play," he advised the head groom, who merely grunted his acknowledgement.

"Are we going for a real ride, Sergeant?" asked John excitedly.

The old man permitted a softening of his harsh features. The boy was a favorite with all the staff and had won their hearts long since.

"That we are, Master John. That we are. There's a couple places that you might like to see," said the old man with a wink. "How'd you like a trot?"

John was already urging his little pony to a faster pace, his chubby little hands intent on keeping control, just as he'd been taught.

The old man gazed fondly down at the happy child beside him and let the boy ride on a slack rein, making him feel he was in control. "Dig in with your knees," he admonished gently, seeing the youngster beginning to bobble in the saddle.

John was a natural rider and obeyed instructions absolutely. His military training had taught him to obey first and ask questions second.

After a nice canter, which rocked the pony like a wood horse, John barraged his mentor with questions. The old soldier answered each one with precision and patience, teaching his young pupil every facet of riding that he could impart.

"We'll cut off here and head for the stream," announced the sergeant as they came to a trail into the wood. "There's a spot here, I fancy you might enjoy. If we approach quietly, we may see some trout," he advised.

John's eyes sparkled in anticipation and he pressed his lips together in an effort to be still. After dismounting, they crept up to the babbling water and tiptoed to the edge.

"See," whispered the old man, pointing to the shadow under a rock. John nodded and watched in silent fascination for a few seconds. Soon the cob and pony were pushing to get a drink and the old man nodded.

John led his pony to the stream bank and watched as the water rippled around the animal's nose as it drank.

A slight noise brought the sergeant's head snapping up. With a quick lunge he tossed John in the saddle, unsnapped the leading rein, and turned the pony for home. "Hold still," he whispered urgently.

Three unkempt figures burst through the trees brandishing clubs and yelling wildly. It was a terrifying sight for a little boy, but he obeyed his orders, keeping a good hold of his reins.

"What do you want?" the sergeant growled authoritatively. He hadn't served in His Majesty's Army for nothing. He eyed the men discouragingly, noting each detail of their dirty, hungry appearance.

"We want money," snarled one that had an arm missing at the elbow, while the others nodded.

"We have none," replied the trusty servant calmly, surveying the men intently as they advanced slowly from the deeper wood. Out of the side of his mouth he whispered, "Hold tight, John."

"Then we'll take th' boy and keep 'im until you bring us a thousand pounds," barked another. They began to fan out to surround the twosome.

Tompkins didn't hesitate. He slapped the pony a violent blow on the hindquarters with the leading rein and yelled over his shoulder after the retreating figure, "Head for home, boy!" The pony was flying down the path at a dead run, leaving a cloud of dust behind. John seemed to have a tight hold, for he was sitting straight in the saddle, the sergeant thought in grim satisfaction.

The sergeant turned back to the men as they lunged at him. "Attention!" he roared thunderously at the nondescript figures, his face a study in scowls.

He wasn't too surprised to see all three straighten up resembling what they had once been, His Majesty's troops. "Name and rank," he barked ferociously.

"Bill Wilson, corporal, served under General Lord Hill of the II Corps, 1st Infantry Division." The man spoke with an amount of pride.

"Bert Green, private, the same." Bitterness tinged the words of the one-armed man and he watched Tompkins warily.

"Bob Somer, private, the same," the third man replied defeatedly, his shoulders beginning to sag.

The sergeant's face strangely softened. "So you men served together and fought at Waterloo? I know the death toll in Lord Hill's command was high. You were lucky to live to tell of it."

"Lucky? To come home to find no work, no means of feeding ourselves or our families?" cried Somer unbelievingly.

"We'd have been better off dead," spit out Green, waving his stump to emphasize his words. He seemed undecided for an instant before growling, "We've lost the boy but we still 'ave you. Mayhap somun will pay t' get you back." Desperation clouded the man's face.

"I can be of use to you," the old man admitted readily, "but not that way. If you're honest about wanting to work I'm certain my master will see you get it. He never turns an old soldier away. Follow the path down to the stables. Tell anyone there that Sergeant Tompkins sent you and wait for me. I have to find his lordship's grandson first." He gave the men a curt nod and mounted his cob, unconcerned for his safety. He considered the sorry trio and admonished them, "Make yourselves presentable and then come along."

He gave the horse a sharp kick in the flank that sent it galloping down the trail, leaving the three men staring thoughtfully after him.

CHAPTER 15

Larla was laughing at the picture Marsden described as he told of one of his military exploits, thoroughly caught up in the tale, when Marsden jerked Igor to a sudden stop.

In the distance a small figure could be seen clinging valiantly to a terrified galloping pony. It took less than a second for Marsden to swing his horse in the direction of the runaway and urge him into a full-scale charge. Larla wasn't far behind.

John had two hands full of mane, along with the reins, and was desperately hanging on for dear life. The sergeant had told him to hold on and he was, fiercely. "Home, pony," the little voice told his steed. "We get help."

Marsden rode in a wide circle around the little pony, which was heaving and blowing, and eased alongside. "Pull up on the reins, John," he commanded gently. He watched his son obey and soon was pleased to see the pony stop. "Well done, son. You'll make a real soldier."

Marsden dismounted and snatched his precious child from the quieting pony. He was hugging the boy possessively when Larla reached him.

"I stopped him, Mama. I did it myself. No one helped me," John announced proudly.

Larla's eyes were misty with love and relief as she beheld her small son with his arms tightly wound around Marsden's neck, and Marsden didn't seem to mind the discomfort a whit. She knew Marsden's gesture to let John stop the pony would save him from fright and it had been done masterfully, without John's realizing anything was amiss. Marsden had slowed his mount, turning the pony back toward Larla by putting Igor to head him gently. Marsden was in complete control of the situation without her small son's being aware of it.

After assuring herself that her son was indeed fine, she asked in a troubled voice, "John, why were you racing on your own? Where is Sergeant Tompkins?"

"He's back with some bad men who wanted money," said the little voice which was beginning to tremble. "He hit my pony. Told me to go home. Mama, the sergeant needs help." He raised large brown eyes to his mama, pleading for her understanding.

Larla took John and hugged and squeezed him until he squirmed. Marsden glanced back toward the wood uneasily, his indecision showing plainly.

Larla responded gravely to her small son, "Don't worry about the sergeant. He's proven himself against worse situations time and again. He'll be fine, John." Her eyes turned to Marsden. "Right now I'm concerned about getting John back to safety and I'd feel much better if you'd come with us." She accompanied the request with a tremulous smile.

Marsden bent down to John. "How'd you like a ride on my horse? It's not a treat for babies. Only big boys can ride him."

The cherubic face grinned happily at him. "Yes, Papa." Marsden shouted with laughter, hugging the boy again.

"Could you lead the pony, darling?"

Larla nodded her assent, her voice beyond words at the touching sight of her small son reposing so comfortably in Marsden's arms. She couldn't remonstrate with her son on his use of the title even if she wanted to, for the words wouldn't come past the lump in her throat. If her scheme worked, Marsden might claim the title legally.

Larla swept onto Star without assistance and threw him a provocative glance, daring him to censure her.

"Madam Independence," he grinned, handing her the

pony's rein, then swinging up into the saddle behind his son. With his arms about the boy, he started home.

Before they'd gone too far, the grizzled old man came tearing down the path as fast as the short legs of the cob would go. He drew in with an audible sigh.

"Thank God the young master be safe," he gasped, winded from his efforts to urge the horse to more speed.

"He did very well. A credit to your teaching," Larla commended him.

"Where are these vagrants?" growled Marsden. "How did you escape?"

"They're not bad men, Your Lordship. Just old soldiers who've fell on hard times. They can't find work and are hungry." The old man's eyes strayed lovingly to the child.

"So they just let you go?" The question was cool.

"Not exactly. I told them that the colonel would find them work." His chin came up defiantly, as if he were waiting to be told differently.

Marsden's countenance softened slowly to a slight smile. "Providence has thrown me a challenge right in my own backyard. Now I'll have a chance to practice what I preach." He winked at Larla.

The sergeant's countenance relaxed somewhat and the old man nodded his approval. He took the reins of the pony from Larla, giving her a broad smile.

"The men agreed to come to the stables. They seemed eager enough so I expect they'll arrive shortly after us." Tompkins fell in line behind what looked like a perfect family morning-ride.

It was a quiet party that rode into the stable yard. The old soldier was off his horse first and reached for John. For a moment he merely held the lad close, his old eyes showing a suspicion of moisture. When he set John on the ground his tone was gruff.

"I be pleased to see you've learnt your lesson well." He

stood tall and straight, snapping a very military salute to the small boy.

The child answered in kind and then turned to his mama. He watched Marsden, who had a funny smile on his face, lift his mama down slowly from the horse. She had a funny smile too. He asked the sergeant why.

The old man ruffled the boy's hair affectionately. "They be in love," replied the sergeant, quite gratified by the sight.

John seemed to consider the idea for a moment then turned to his mother. "Did you see, Mama? I'm only a private and the sergeant saluted me!" There were no signs of the ordeal he'd just been through, only a proud but tired smile.

Larla and Marsden beamed impartially at the child and old man before exchanging knowing glances. John's shoulders began to sag and his eyes clouded as they walked through the stable yard. The excitement of the day took its toll.

Marsden scooped his son up into his arms. "I'll carry him if you have no objection?" Marsden curled the sleepy head on his shoulder and stroked the hair from his face.

"Thank you, Papa," mumbled a yawning voice.

Larla's heart grew warm at the sight, her face softening as she beheld Marsden's tenderness. With a deep breath, she straightened her spine and lifted her chin a fraction. Her resolve to play this farce to its conclusion was unchanged as she watched Marsden steadily. "Would you care to take a turn in the garden? We have some lovely blooms at this time of year."

Marsden turned to Tompkins. "Call the colonel and me when the men arrive," he admonished.

"Yes sir," was the prompt reply, given as though to his commanding officer.

Larla chatted easily, keeping the conversation light and her eye ahead to the fountain court. There in the shelter of the tall hedges with wrought-iron benches she expected to find the would-be lovers. It was the most likely spot in the garden for conversation. She crossed her fingers, hoping that Williams had been able to give her guests the required gentle shove.

Smiling ruefully, she thought of the scene with Williams. The old butler had known that something was in the wind, but he couldn't quite say so. Larla had prevailed upon him because she knew that the faithful retainer could be counted upon to do his part and if Broome and Miss Underwood would perform their parts as expected, all would be well.

Marsden's gaze wandered to his companion and saw a decided sparkle of mischief. His eyes narrowed thoughtfully and he gazed about him to see if there were any distractions or surprises ahead. The small boy in his arms stirred restlessly.

Larla led the way leisurely to the south gate, which meant passing beneath the nursery windows. Entrants to the fountain court had to move through in single file at that entrance.

The sound of water rushing and spraying gave a sense of serenity, while effectively blotting out any possible conversation being overheard within the court. Lush roses of cream, jonquil, and deep crimson gave a variety to the verdant foliage.

John's nurse must have been at the window, surmised Larla, as that good woman came bearing down upon them. "I'll take him, Mrs. Ainsworth," she said lovingly, grasping for the precious bundle.

"He's had quite a deal of excitement this morning, and I believe he needs some rest," Larla explained.

"Very good, mum," she said and, after bobbing a quick curtsey, she was gone.

Asking Marsden a question about Hume to distract him, Larla took a deep breath and walked quickly up to the gate that opened into the fountain court. Blood pounded in her veins as she walked through the hedge archway into the court.

Her countenance relaxed for an instant, taking in the figures of Broome and Miss Underwood with hands entwined conversing on one of the benches. She stopped dramatically, her arms flailing behind her to halt Marsden's progress through the entrance way. "Oooooh!" she moaned in simulated horror.

In the twinkling of a second she was pushing Marsden back out the gate. "Marsden, I wouldn't have had this happen for the world. I'm certain there's a logical explanation. Please don't call Broome out," she begged loudly in a rush.

Marsden's lip curled sardonically. Setting Larla aside, he strode into the court. Larla moved quietly behind him, biting a telltale smile.

"So!" he roared contemptuously, "you've been trifling with my fiancée." The disdainful look had been known to make the most seasoned troops cower.

Broome had jumped up aghast at Larla's words and he began to tremble at Marsden's. His speech was garbled and he stuttered his excuses to deaf ears.

"And you, Marcia, are to blame for leading the poor man on," Marsden continued with a scornful sneer. "When we are married I swear never to leave you to your own devices. I believe you are in need of a constant chaperon. Keeping you barefoot and pregnant may help curb your loose ways." He growled the last, his eyebrows concealing his eyes in a severe frown.

"Why don't you speak for yourself, Marsden," retorted Miss Underwood, stung by the unjustness of his remarks. "We thought you must have gone for the day with your . . . cousin," she finished maliciously.

"You want to know where I've been?" he thundered in a blighting tone. "I've been rescuing my son from kidnappers!" He stressed the words with a measured emphasis.

At the horrified expression on his fiancée's face, he moved in to deliver his final volley. "Yes, I said, *'my son!'* "

While Miss Underwood might have been said to feel a

profound shock to the extent of feeling faint, Larla stood stock-still in amazement.

Broome took a handkerchief from his pocket and began fanning Miss Underwood, whose eyes were beginning to roll. He turned a malevolent look upon Marsden. "She's far too good for the likes of you. She deserves better."

Marsden, with a hint of a sardonic smile, agreed casually, "You're probably right."

Larla had taken a few seconds to register the magnitude of Marsden's announcement and began to laugh until the tears cascaded down her cheeks. "Marsden, how dare you," she gasped between fits of merriment.

Broome's cheeks puffed up like a pouter pigeon. "Upon my word, I've never heard of anything so brazen." He fanned Miss Underwood harder, his face all consideration as he turned to comfort her.

"I've taken more than a lady should have to bear," choked a revolted Miss Underwood. Her delicate constitution had been subjected to more atrocities than could be expected of one so carefully nurtured. "It's too much," she sobbed with a tremulous sigh, pulling the diamond from her finger and flinging it at Marsden. "Marsden, I'm sorry. We should not suit," she informed him with a shudder. "Broome, take me away from here," she begged the portly gentleman supporting her.

Broome threw Marsden a scathing look. "If it weren't for Mrs. Ainsworth, I'd call you to account," he threatened with a deal of bluster.

"You could always try," Marsden acknowledged wryly, sounding quite benevolent despite the provocation.

Miss Underwood determined to get the last word in. "I wish you joy of him, Mrs. Ainsworth." She looked from one grinning face to the other. "You deserve each other," she spit out scathingly. Turning on her heel, she leaned on Broome for support to escape the garden.

Marsden chuckled. "I certainly hope so," he said hopefully.

Larla was gasping, trying desperately to stop laughing, but to no avail. In her wildest dreams, she hadn't foreseen such a finish to the scene. "I must say, Jeremy, that was a masterful ploy to rid yourself of an unwanted fiancée. That line would never have occurred to me." She wiped her eyes on a serviceable handkerchief.

Marsden was watching her appreciatively with a rueful smile. He took her hands in his and raised one to his lips. "Praise the Lord, it's done. I was afraid there for a moment that in spite of the provocation, she'd stand firm."

"You needn't applaud just yet, my lord. You've just ruined my reputation," she lectured him with mock severity. "And just what are your intentions now?" An insolent grin accompanied the ironic question.

"Why the honorable thing, of course. Marry you." His tone was cavalier.

Larla wasn't satisfied with his casual way for settling the situation. She wanted a declaration of his esteem and she intended to make him announce it. "I believe my credit is good enough to carry me through this when I explain you were merely funning."

"You abominable little minx. You know very well that I have intended to marry you from the beginning. I hinted at the fact several times and you understood quite well that a gentleman must wait for a lady to cry off the engagement."

"You certainly took your time about it," she retorted pertly and fluttered her eyelashes at him in feminine appreciation of his powerful form.

"I seem to remember distinctly telling you that someone needed to take you in hand, my girl, and you have just met your match."

"Fustation," she grinned, daring him to try.

He crushed her to him and administered a ruthless kiss that tingled and tangled her insides.

Larla was left in no doubt of his passions nor his ability to bring her under his thumb. The kiss had suddenly turned tender and questing, begging her for her participation. Larla felt her knees begin to buckle as the onslaught continued and she stepped back in breathless awe.

He merely clucked his tongue. "Wait until we're alone," he said warningly and glanced toward the upper windows of the house.

"Is that statement supposed to mean something, my lord?" she needled him engagingly, recovering herself.

"Yes, you mannerless brat. It means that you are going to be my wife in every sense of the word and that you are going to learn to obey me when I give you a command."

"This I've got to see," she murmured appreciatively, biting off a huge grin.

"Come along, my charming minx. You engineered this denouement and you're going to stand by and take some of the responsibility for this campaign."

"You mean to tell me that I don't get to have a gentlemanly proposal where you get down on your knees?" she asked incredulously.

He ground his teeth in frustration. "It's your own fault. You can't tell me that you didn't orchestrate this entire scene. I know you better than that. You'll just have to settle for what you can get, my unrepentant baggage." His eyes spit fire as he gazed down into her questioning face.

Taking her by the hand, he pulled her along to the side door.

"Well, if that's the way of it, I guess it will have to do." She sighed disgustedly but ruined the effect entirely by letting a smile crack the corners of her pose.

"We'll get the rough ground covered first," he adjured her curtly.

"I'd like to bet that your former fiancée is staging a regular

Cheltenham tragedy," she commented offhandedly. Larla was in high spirits and nothing could dampen them.

"We'll take it in stride, my misbegotten little strategist." He put a comforting arm about her shoulders and flicked her nose.

CHAPTER 16

In the drawing room, Miss Underwood was quietly sobbing, her mother wiping her face with lavender water while Broome chafed her hands. Trying to compose herself, she made several disjointed beginnings. Finally she gave up the attempt and drew several deep breaths.

Lady Broome clucked her disapproval of the events, but it could be told at a glance that neither Miss Underwood nor her son was the object of her censure. Her countenance was rigid as she scanned the other occupants of the room.

Lady Worthingdon repressed a smile as she commiserated, "My dear, how dreadful for you. I fear you are right to give him back his ring. He must have more problems than we knew."

Lord Worthingdon snorted but said nothing as he took an elbow in the side. He compressed his lips and glared at his wife, who returned the most bland of looks.

Somewhat calmer, Miss Underwood raised her face to give the assembled group a watery smile. "I must apologize for creating such a scene." Her eyes were red and puffy from her exertion, but she spoke evenly. She struggled to sit up and tried to order her disheveled appearance.

Lady Broome nodded at such proper sentiments. "Such a credit to you, Mrs. Underwood. Any mother should be proud to have your daughter for her son." She gave the stricken mother her most ingratiating smile.

Mrs. Underwood, every inch a duke's daughter, replied loftily, "Thank you, Lady Broome. I perceive that we have much in common." She then turned a disdainful eye to Lord and Lady Worthingdon. "I believe that my daughter is very well out of such a ramshackle entanglement."

Lady Worthingdon's eyes were dancing her delight, but she was able to maintain a stern composure. "I understand your sentiments completely." The observation was given in the most neutral of tones.

Lord Worthingdon shook his head in disbelief. His hands were thrust hurriedly into his pockets and he seemed to be counting rosettes in the plaster molding.

Mrs. Underwood considered the situation carefully. It was clear that she sensed that there was more to the affair than was being told, but she couldn't quite catch the essence of it. After allowing herself a glance at Broome's solicitous attention and his mama's approval of his actions, her face began to clear and she permitted herself a faint thin smile. "You have my condolences, Lady Worthingdon," she said condescendingly.

The colonel surveyed the scene from the doorway, pulling on his ear distractedly. An expression of disgust crossed his craggy features as he heard of Marsden's supposed problem. Being a man of action, he wheeled around with an about-face and strode off in the direction of the side door, the quickest way to the garden.

Larla and Marsden were met by a smoldering scowl from an obviously irate colonel. His arms were folded, his stance wide as he intercepted them.

"Grandfather, John and Sergeant Tompkins were accosted by kidnappers in the woods," Larla proclaimed baldly, sensing that attack was the best defense.

Marsden intervened quickly, sensing the heavy tension. "We have some destitute soldiers in the home wood. Mistakenly they thought to hold John for ransom but the sergeant saw to it that John got away."

The colonel's eyebrows jumped up into his receding hairline as Marsden spoke. "Is the boy safe?" He fired the question at Larla like a missile.

Larla placed her hand comfortingly on her grandfather's arm. "He's upstairs with his nurse. He followed his orders explicitly and rode his pony in a wild gallop across the fields, staying in the saddle and stopping by himself. He was a real trooper."

Colonel Somerset coughed and humphed several times. The thought of his only grandson being in the hands of kidnappers almost overcame him. "The boy might have been killed." He shook his head before adding, "I'll send some men out to look for them."

"Leave it to the sergeant," Marsden advised coolly. "He's convinced these old soldiers are not bad fellows and is having them come in to the stables. He feels that we can do something for them."

There was silence for a moment while the colonel considered the statement. Then he nodded his acknowledgement. "There's no work for many of them and the government is providing for only a very few. Charity begins at home and in this case I guess I can at least have a word with them." His brows were knitted together in a frown.

He then seemed to recall the business at hand. He glared intently at his granddaughter. "Now, madame, perhaps you'll be good enough to come into the drawing room and see if you can explain this muddled story Marcia Underwood is babbling about."

Larla slid a scorching glance at Marsden. Her grandfather's use of the word 'madame' assured her that there was dangerous ground ahead. "Marsden ought to have that honor," she allowed politely.

Marsden's eyes twinkled at her, before turning to the colonel. "I'll be most happy to, sir."

Colonel Somerset quirked an eyebrow at Marsden but said nothing. Turning back to the drawing room, he stifled a sudden smile. Larla and Marsden marched silently behind.

Upon their entrance a sudden hush fell upon the party and

they looked like a scene from Madame Tussaud's. All eyes were fastened on Marsden and Larla.

Marsden held Larla's hand tightly and took a decidedly military stance. "I must apologize to all of you," he addressed the group formally. "Miss Underwood and I have agreed we do not suit. For my part that makes the news I have to share with you somewhat easier to impart. As most of you know, I lost my memory for a while after the battle of Waterloo. Some events have only just returned to me." He grasped Larla's hand.

His next words had the effect of an artillery shell exploding into the drawing room.

"I must be grateful to my wife, Larla," he said quietly, "for being so patient, waiting for me to recover my lost time." He gave her a bracing smile.

The gasps were readily audible. A buzz of sound erupted and the guests voiced their incredulity. Eyes grew wide and heads shook, while Lady Worthingdon just sat back and smiled benevolently.

"You see, Larla knew that she married Jeremy Ainsworth in Brussels but thought I had died of my injuries. It was only J. Ainsworth that was listed on the death rolls and Larla didn't know about Jessamy at that time. When she returned here she was amazed to find I was alive and that the man on the death rolls was Jessamy. Hearing of my loss of memory and seeing that I didn't recognize her, she felt it best not to say anything in case the shock should damage my mind." He paused to take a breath and squeeze Larla's hand.

"I regained my memory suddenly yesterday and didn't quite know how best to approach the situation until Marcia, courageously, sensing that something was wrong, took it upon herself to decide that we should not suit." He gazed kindly upon his ex-fiancée. "I have used her disgracefully, and I beg her pardon. I hope that she will be justly rewarded for her perception and consideration in this matter." He gave her a slight bow.

"Larla and I have unraveled details of our marriage and you may all wish us happy." Marsden sounded quite pleased with himself.

Colonel Somerset strode forward and enveloped his granddaughter in a hearty embrace. "I'm very proud of you, my dear. He's a fine man."

Lady Worthingdon took Larla's hands. "We're delighted to welcome you as a daughter instead of a niece. We couldn't be happier. To be able to claim both you and John for our own . . ." Her voice broke on the last and she wiped a tear unceremoniously from her cheek.

Lord Worthingdon clasped his son's hand and thumped him on the back. A warm look of approval passed from father to son.

Amid the host of subsequent congratulations, Marsden raised his hand. "Under the circumstances, I would like to invite all of you to the Edgehurst chapel tomorrow to hear Larla and me reaffirm our marriage vows," invited Marsden smugly. "We feel it best to have an English record with John listed as my son. Now if you'll excuse us, my wife and I have much catching up to do." Marsden executed a distinguished bow to the assemblage and dragged a bemused Larla from the room.

For several moments silence reigned supreme, astonished guests staring as they tried to comprehend Marsden's bald disclosure.

Williams calmly walked in at his most dignified, filling the void caused by the gaping mouths, and announced in stately tones, "Nuncheon is served."

Lord Broome observed himself to be the only one ready to make a move toward the dining room and, feeling the need to bestir himself, took Marcia's hand and gently raised her from the sofa. "Dearest Miss Underwood, you have borne much these last days. You have earned a high place of honor for your forbearance in this matter and I would count it a privilege to escort you to the table." Lord Broome offered his arm.

"With the greatest of pleasure, my lord," beamed Miss Underwood, her eyes showing more animation and significant signs of recovery.

Broome patted her hand consolingly as he drew her toward the dining room and awarded her his most interested smile.

In the book room at the back of the house, Larla had recovered her wits and proceeded to rake her new spouse over the coals. "Marsden! How dare you say that we will reaffirm our vows tomorrow? I can't possibly have a dress to wear in that amount of time. It's unthinkable, unfeasible, and decidedly unreasonable. I won't do it." She stomped her foot vexatiously.

Marsden watched his fuming wife appreciatively, a tolerant smile hovering about his lips. It was clear that he was enjoying her temper.

"Don't you dare laugh at me," she fumed hotly.

"I wouldn't think of it," he returned with a glib smile. "You are just about the same size as my mother was when she was married to my father. Her wedding gown is of pure silk, trimmed with seed pearls and will probably fit you admirably."

Larla eyed him in disgust. Didn't he know that she wanted to pick her own dress? When she had married before, it had been a hole-in-the-corner affair. She vowed to have more this time and visualized a wedding with all the trimmings and decorations.

"I ought to take you across my knee and paddle some sense into you, but alas, I fear it is a task beyond my limitations," he teased lovingly.

A complete set of emotions flitted across her face as she struggled to make a reply. "You'll never get me to agree to your suit that way, my lord," she finally retorted cheerfully.

Marsden countered with an amused chuckle. "Ah, the light

begins to dawn," he concluded knowingly. "I should have known better than to think I could claim you without any more trouble than this."

When she turned a questioning gaze upon him, he touched her cheek with his finger and brought a becoming color to her face.

"Will you do me the honor to become my wife," he began huskily, "wretched and abominable girl that you are?"

"Yes, Jeremy, I will," she laughed readily, "but only to save you from boredom. You seem to have led a singularly uneventful life for the past few years. I plan to change that," she informed him impishly.

"Oh, ho," he answered meditatively. "I foresee some very interesting times ahead." He took her into his arms and stared down at her affectionately.

"Most assuredly," she interjected heatedly, "and you might even enjoy some of them but you aren't out of the woods yet." She looked at him consideringly. "Even if I like the dress, it will probably take some alterations and cleaning. Just what do you have to say about that?" She waited coolly for his answer.

"I took the precaution of having my mother's maid clean and press the dress earlier in the week. And if that doesn't suit you, I also requested Miss Clairemonde of Bond Street herself to attend to you within the hour upon receiving my message. I gave her what I thought to be your size and you may depend upon it that she will bring something suitable to the occasion. Surely you will be able to find something to your liking."

Larla let her head rest upon his chest and gurgled for a moment before raising mischievous eyes to Marsden. "Oh, I have," she assured him with a grin, drawing her palms down his chest over his superbly fitted buckskin riding coat.

CHAPTER 17

Larla followed her son enchantingly down the aisle. John was an ensign in miniature, wearing the familiar dress regimentals. Larla deduced that Jenny must have seized an old uniform belonging to the colonel and ripped and cut until she'd accomplished her goal.

Larla's eyes strayed to the perfect specimen of manhood waiting her at the front of the chapel. His eyes were fastened upon her, extending to her alone a special smile that softened his sharp features.

The profusion of flowers and decorations in the small chapel gave Larla's heart a warm glow as she thought of Lady Worthingdon's insistence to take care of the details. Her new mother-in-law had surpassed herself.

As she reached the chaplain, she became aware of the magnificence of Marsden's molded coat of bath superfine suiting in pale blue, snowy white waistcoat, and matching small-clothes. His virile form was handsomely encased in the stylish garments and made Larla very aware of his person. He had limited his jewelry to one watch fob and his family signet ring, but the resultant effect was one of quiet elegance.

The wedding gown procured from Miss Clairemonde was a lovely creation in daffodil satin nipped in under the bust with a row of yellow roses and trimmed with contrasting leaf-colored ribbons. Marsden hadn't thought about Larla's superior height when he'd offered his mother's gown. This was just as well. Larla had enjoyed choosing this one of her own and had delighted in the arrangement of flowers for her hair in lieu of the traditional veil. She had placed the small bouquet at the back by the cascading golden ringlets.

Larla was recalled from her wanderings as Marsden grasped her hand and the ceremony began. She made her responses in a clear voice and Marsden answered with firm husky tones.

Their eyes beheld only each other and the small congregation watched in silent approbation of the simple ceremony. Marsden kissed her thoroughly, while Larla seemed to melt into his embrace.

After gazing down at her tenderly, Marsden took her arm and the couple led the bridal party to the dining room for the elegant dinner that had been prepared. The Broomes and Underwoods were conspicuously absent.

Little John skipped alongside his mama, his excitement barely contained. "Are you really my papa now?" He cast an adoring plea to Marsden.

"Absolutely, John. You are my son and heir," he assured John quietly.

The serious note in his voice caused Larla to look at him sharply. There were still many questions to be answered. She hadn't had time to voice them before with all the bustle to get ready for the ceremony. She knew that Marsden had greased the wheels exceedingly with a large sum to Miss Clairemonde and several others, but she had still not had a spare moment to puzzle out the actualities of her first marriage and if Marsden was in reality her first husband.

Whatever the result, she was satisfied, for with the English ceremony, there could be no doubt. She allowed herself to be diverted as Marsden filled her plate with an assortment of delicious dishes.

John had picked and chosen his meal with infinite care, she noted with approval. The small boy ate his meal with the perfect assemblance of a gentleman and responded to questions with very candid answers.

Larla held her breath as Mrs. Hathaway asked him, "Do you like your new papa?"

"Yes, my lady," he responded politely. "Did you know he's my very own?"

Mrs. Hathaway laughed delightedly and Larla sighed her relief. Soon she signaled his nurse, who was hovering at the door and John bid the guests a good-night.

Major Denton, another old friend of the colonel's, asked as soon as they had reconvened in the drawing room, "Just how do you plan to announce this marriage to the ton?"

Larla turned to her new husband. "Yes, please, tell us, Jeremy. I'd like to know how you plan to solve this predicament."

Marsden grinned wryly. "That's simple. It's already taken care of. Remember, we told Lady Broome."

"What's that to say to anything?" asked Mrs. Hathaway, seemingly at a loss.

"I'm afraid I don't quite understand," added Larla, thinking that some sort of announcement in the paper had to be made.

Lady Worthingdon started to laugh, while her husband permitted himself a broad smile. "Larla my dear," she explained jovially, "you probably haven't had a chance to really take Lady Broome's measure as yet. She prides herself on having the reputation of one who always has the latest news about town. By this time all of London has been apprised of your whirlwind romance. You won't need to say a word. And by Marsden convincing everyone that Marcia perceived the problem and courageously cried off, she'll not look too foolish." She paused a moment, giving Larla a heartwarming smile. "I believe a small notice in the London *Gazette* announcing an At Home for Lord and Lady Marsden, after you return from your honeymoon, would be sufficient for the formalities."

"Unexceptional," the colonel approved.

"Honeymoon?" queried Larla dangerously, turning to Marsden with fiery eyes. "We—"

"Quite right and it's about time we had a discussion about that and several other important points," interrupted Marsden determinedly. "If you'll all excuse us . . ." he asked politely, pulling Larla from her chair. With a firm arm around her, he whisked her quickly from the room.

Larla heard her grandfather conclude contentedly, "Now there's an excellent commander. Knows just how to handle his troops and when to beat a hasty retreat."

A general laugh followed and Larla turned an incensed glare at Marsden as they walked down the spacious corridors. "And just what do you propose now?" she requested icily. He hadn't consulted her about the arrangements or even let her say good night or good bye.

"Why to beat you into submission, of course," he whispered wickedly, a devilish smile glinting at her. He placed an arm about her waist and gave her a quick hug, leading her up the stone stairs to his suite in the far wing.

Larla tried valiantly to look furious, but the humor of his outrageous remark overcame her better judgment and she chuckled at him. "I don't know what to make of you, Jeremy. Just when I believe I have your measure, you add a new element to the battle."

"Must we always have a battle?" he questioned beguilingly, giving her a full measure of his magnetizing gaze as he guided her into his suite.

"I'm certainly willing to open negotiations for a truce," she suggested amiably, swallowing a lump that seemed to be forming in her throat. Her pulse was already elevating.

"Not a lasting peaceful settlement?" he persisted carefully, his eyes branding her with their touch.

"What are you willing to offer?" she interrogated closely.

"How about a honeymoon in Paris and several trips to Monsieur Worth?" He waited expectantly as he named the famous designer.

"A promising beginning, but what would John be doing while we're off galavanting?" A telltale smile lurked at the corners of her mouth.

"John will be quite busy visiting his indulgent grandparents and having his great-grandfather riding over at every whiff and turn."

"I believe I could accept those terms for a temporary cease of hostilities if I were certain your affections are engaged," she probed carefully.

"My darling, it's been midsummer moon with me ever since I met you at Somerset Place and since I regained my memory, I've hardly been able to contain myself." He tenderly brushed the hair back from her face and sealed her lips with his.

Gently he teased her lips with his moist tongue, begging admittance. His hands traced the feminine curve of her hips and pulled her more securely against him.

Larla heard a pleading whimper and realized it was her own. Drawing a deep breath, she stepped back. There were still some questions that needed answering.

She tossed her head to one side and slanted him an inquisitive gaze. "Just what do you mean 'midsummer moon'?"

"It's an old expression. It means someone who's not quite right in the head. Like me—almost out of my mind with love for you and didn't know how to claim you," he explained fondly.

He branded Larla's neck with hot kisses that made her blood begin to pulse. One hand caressed the back of her neck while the other crept down her spine. Larla's world narrowed and the room faded.

With a great effort she clutched at his shoulders, trying to keep from falling over the precipice into the abyss of his virile lovemaking. She swallowed the lump forming in her throat. "You have yet to explain to me why you encouraged Grandfather to take over your plan for an old soldiers' retreat."

Marsden smiled at her caressingly and swung her lightly into his arms, depositing her on the large poster bed with deep blue hangings. Easing himself to her side, he kissed the tip of her nose and lightly tickled it with his tongue. "Your grandfather needs a purpose in life. If we take John away, where he sees him only a day or so a week, he's going to be a very lonely man." The intense brown eyes showed a deep compassion as he spoke.

"Your logic cannot be faulted, Jeremy," she breathed in his ear, nibbling it sensuously.

"I have enough land and funds to care for several sons. We have no need of the land that will be yours some day. I plan to help your grandfather build the cottages and he'll administer the plan with the sergeant's help. I've set aside considerable assets to finance the project. I'm certain that your grandfather will find enough for the men to do between your estates and ours. Now could we return to setting the terms of our contract?"

"Admirable strategy, my lord," she teased him lovingly, "but you've neglected an important point."

"And what could that be, my love?" He stared appealingly at her parted lips.

Larla found the need to wet them under the heat of his gaze. "You have yet to convince me that you actually are my husband. How do I know you regained your memory and that John is indeed your child? If he's not, he's not heir to the title and I'd as soon we untangled the legalities now."

"You're rushing your fences, darling. I'm coming to that detail." His fingers deftly released the myriad small buttons at the back of her gown, while quieting her questioning with his lips. Ardently he sought the warm moistness of her mouth. Assiduously he surveyed each recess and staked his claim possessively.

Larla found her hands unconsciously undoing the buttons on his vest and then moved to his shirtfront. Marsden sat up with a burning desire raging fiercely in his eyes and silently removed his coat, vest, and shirt. Larla's hands splayed over the furry chest.

Marsden smiled tenderly down at her and moved one hand to a scar not quite hidden by the curling hair. Larla's senses began to spin as she traced its puckers. No surgeon had stitched that gash. Larla raised startled eyes to his.

"Jeremy, you wretch!" she squeaked, rolling off the bed in heated indignation. Her gown fell to a heap around her ankles, but she merely kicked it aside and planted both hands firmly on her hips. "You knew all this time and didn't tell me?" Her anger threatened to overcome her and her breasts strained at the confinement of her thin chemise.

Marsden grinned appreciatively at the sight. "Now, sweetheart, you did claim to be Jessamy's wife and I wasn't certain that you'd want me back." He leaped up to encircle her in his arms, but she stepped back behind a chair.

"Go on," she invited him grimly.

"I thought that if I kept throwing criticisms at Marcia and showed her I'm a man of violent passions, I could get her to cry off. Then I would have time to court you as you deserved to be courted. I hadn't counted on Marcia standing fast for so long. As a gentleman how could I announce to my fiancée I'm already married? I was truly thankful when Broome appeared on the scene and for some reason became interested in Marcia."

Larla allowed herself a slight smile and inclined her head regally. "You're welcome."

"I should have figured that you were at the root of that venture." His eyes held a twinkle of admiration.

"I'm interested in the rest of this most original tale," she informed him dangerously.

"I had tried every trick I could think of to divest myself of a disagreeable fiancée, including telling her we wouldn't entertain, I preferred the quiet life, and that I expected her to give me a dozen children." He sighed exasperatedly, then made a quick lunge for her, but she scampered to the writing table. He advanced slowly.

"I'm well aware of that," she snickered. "Just when did your memory return?" she pressed suspiciously.

"I regained my memory two short days ago, when General Hathaway hollered 'Stand to your arms.'" He shook his head as he started around the table, Larla backing away from him.

"I was so ashamed of my conduct, it was almost too much to bear. Can you forgive me?" His eyes stared into hers and when she nodded, a smile lightened the lines of tension in his face. "My only excuse is that I promised my father I would marry and beget him an heir before I died. Even in my unconscious state, I discerned quality when I saw it," he added musingly.

Larla paused for a moment in indecision, just long enough for Marsden to grab for her across the table. She whirled away to the far side of the room, Marsden close on her heels. She waited behind an oversized wing-backed chair. "And are you going to do better by me this time?" she challenged him wickedly.

"Larla, darling, you can push a man only so far," he warned her threateningly.

"Oh?" Larla taunted him deliberately, stepping out from behind the chair, provocatively swinging her hips and casting him a silent invitation from under fluttering lashes.

Marsden watched the little dance of female provocativeness with a burning hunger, which grew rapidly. "Congratulations, darling, you just passed the limit," he drawled, grinning, and masterfully swept her into his arms.

He dropped her gently on the bed and covered her length with his own. "This is where you belong, my charming but elusive wife, and I intend to see that you uphold your part of the treaty."

"And just what is my part, Jeremy?" she murmured inquir-

po

ingly. "You haven't gotten to that part of the negotiations yet."

"I want your promise that you'll work beside me," he bargained cunningly.

"That's easily given," she agreed recklessly.

"Good. We'll begin our work tonight," he directed, a deal of satisfaction in his tone.

"Work? Tonight?" She couldn't quite understand his meaning.

"Certainly," he grinned wolfishly. "I remember telling Marcia distinctly in your presence that I'm a man of intense passions and that I intend to have a dozen children. Right now, I'd like to begin work on it." He followed the words with a kiss designed to stamp out further argument.

Breathlessly Larla snuggled against him and whispered, "I'll help you." She ran her fingernails lightly down his chest.

"That's it, darling. I knew I could gentle you," he concluded with a growl of male dominance.

"The cease-fire lasts only until dawn," Larla informed him with a beguiling smile. "Tomorrow's another day."

Historical Dictionary
of Thailand

by
May Kyi Win
Harold E. Smith

Asian Historical Dictionaries, No. 18

The Scarecrow Press, Inc.
Lanham, Md., & London

959.3
MAY

3 1257 01136 9997

SCARECROW PRESS, INC.

Published in the United States of America
by Scarecrow Press, Inc.
4720 Boston Way
Lanham, Maryland 20706

4 Pleydell Gardens, Folkestone
Kent CT20 2DN, England

British Cataloguing-in-Publication Information Available

Library of Congress Cataloging-in-Publication Data

May Kyi Win and Smith, Harold E.
Historical dictionary of Thailand / by May Kyi Win and Harold E. Smith.
p. cm. — (Asian historical dictionaries ; no. 18)
Includes bibliographical references.
1. Thailand—Dictionaries. I. Smith, Harold Eugene, 1916–   . II. Title
III. Series.
DS563.5M3   1995   959.3'003—dc20   95-24597   CIP

ISBN 0-8108-3064-7 (cloth : alk. paper)

⊖™ The paper used in this publication meets the minimum requirements of
American National Standard for Information Sciences—Permanence of
Paper for Printed Library Materials, ANSI Z39.48–1984.
Manufactured in the United States of America.

CONTENTS

EDITOR'S FOREWORD   vii

PREFACE   ix

ACKNOWLEDGMENTS   xi

ABBREVIATIONS   xiii

MAPS   xvi

CHRONOLOGY OF EVENTS   xix

INTRODUCTION   xli

THE DICTIONARY   1

BIBLIOGRAPHY   197

    Introduction   197

1. GENERAL

A. Bibliographies   202
B. Statistics   205
C. Description and Travel   208
D. Guidebooks and Directories   209
E. Biographies   211

2. HISTORY

A. General   212
B. To 1782   214
C. 1782-20th Century   215

3. POLITICS AND GOVERNMENT

A. General	218
B. Government and Administration	220
C. Constitution and Law	222
D. Armed Forces	223
E. International Relations	
1. General	224
2. With China	226
3. With Great Britain	226
4. With Japan	227
5. With the United States	228
6. With Others	228
F. Insurgency	230
G. Refugees	230

4. ECONOMY

A. General	231
B. Agriculture and Land Policy	233
C. Finance and Banking	236
D. Industry and Trade	238
E. Development	241

5. SOCIETY

A. Population	244
B. Anthropology and Archaeology	247
C. Chinese	249
D. Muslims	251
E. Ethnic Groups	254
F. Education	256
G. Philosophy and Religion	257
H. Sociology and Social Conditions	261
I. Women	264
J. Drugs and Public Health	268

WITHDRAWN

6. CULTURE

A. Art and Architecture	269
B. Customs and Festivals	272
C. Music and Dance	275
D. Language and Literature	276

7. JOURNALS AND NEWSPAPERS

A. Thai Journals and Newspapers	280
B. Foreign Journals	281

APPENDICES

1.	Kings of Ayutthaya, Thonburi and Bangkok	283
2.	Kings of Sukhothai	285
3.	Rulers of Lan Na or Chiang Mai	285
4.	Population of Thailand by Province and Enumeration Region	287
5.	Population of Thailand, 1910-1992	290
6.	Expenditure on Gross Domestic Product	291
7.	Gross Domestic Product by Industrial Origin	292
8.	Parties and Number of Seats for the Elections of 1983-1992	293
9.	Elections Since 1932	294
10.	A Chronology of Coups d'Etat in Modern Thailand	295
11.	Prime Ministers, 1932-94	296

ABOUT THE AUTHORS	297

EDITOR'S FOREWORD

Thailand, in many ways, is similar to most other countries in Southeast Asia. It boasts a dynamic economy, an upgraded educational system, gradual improvement in governance and rapid modernization. It also shares some of the drawbacks, including social problems and pollution. Still, in other ways it remains quite different. It was the only country to avoid colonization and thus has a stronger sense of nationhood and deep cultural roots. It is also nearest to Indochina and Burma, a disadvantage during the communist threat, an advantage now as these countries also try to clamber onto the bandwagon.

Thailand, with its similarities and uniqueness, its advantages and drawbacks, presents a very varied picture which is often hard to grasp. Yet, the authors of the *Historical Dictionary of Thailand* have managed to cover an amazing number of aspects: history and culture, economy and society, politics and religion. They have also focused on many of the leading personalities, whether politicians, educators, writers, kings or military men. To this can be added major cities and provinces, political parties and ethnic groups. Together with a handy chronology and a selective, but quite comprehensive bibliography, this is an extremely useful introduction to an extremely interesting country.

As the reader will quickly notice, the authors know the country well. May Kyi Win, who speaks and reads Thai and is a longtime observer, is presently the Curator of the Donn V. Hart Southeast Asia Collection of Founders Memorial Library at Northern Illinois University. Harold E. Smith, who was twice a visiting professor at Thai universities, is presently professor emeritus of the Department of Sociology at Northern Illinois University. He is also the author of numerous articles and chapters on Thailand as well as the initial *Historical and Cultural Dictionary of Thailand* (Scarecrow, 1976). This new book takes a big step further.

Jon Woronoff
Series Editor

PREFACE

Interest in Thailand by Westerners and others grew rapidly after World War II. Today, Thailand continues its longtime role as a leader in Southeast Asian affairs. With its current booming economy, it has a significant role in international trade. During the colonial period and later when communism threatened, Thailand remained a stable and independent nation.

In this volume, we have attempted to provide some glimpses of Thailand's long history since the 13th century. Biographical sketches, including those of the kings who were revered leaders of the Thai people, are presented. Many significant events are briefly chronicled in a focus on domestic affairs of this important nation in Southeast Asia. The impact upon Thailand of neighboring countries and the Western nations, France, Great Britain and the United States, are also treated. The treatment is necessarily brief and has been prepared primarily for the use of the general reader. A fuller history would require numerous large volumes. Scholars are offered more detail in the selected bibliography.

Biographical entries in this book are by first name because the Thai refers to one another by first names rather than by surnames. Family names began to be used in 1916. Cross-references are provided by the use of the abbreviation (q.v.), see, see also and the listing of related entries.

The name "Thailand" became official in 1939. Since the late 18th century, the nation was called "Siam"; but an alternative name for the nation before 1939 was the name of the capital city, Ayutthaya, which was also the name of the country for more than three centuries. The form "Thai" is used to refer to people who speak a particular language which belongs to the Tai-language family. We have tried to avoid confusion between "Thai" and "Tai" by including with the word "Tai" the word "language." For instance, one of the Tai language words that appears frequently is "wat," which in British translation is the "Buddhist temple compound."

all

No precise standard exists for the romanization of the Tai-language script. In this work, the authors have employed what they consider a generally used romanization of Tai-words and expressions. We have been guided by romanization of Tai utilized by the Thai government and the United States Library of Congress. An important limitation of these methods of transliteration in the absence of tones, which are essential in the pronunciation of Tai-words. In this dictionary, most romanized Tai words appear in italics, beside the English equivalent.

A Chronology of Events in Thailand appears before the dictionary itself. This can be a handy reference or a kind of framework for those who wish to explore specific time periods of Thai history.

May Kyi Win and Harold E. Smith
Northern Illinois University
DeKalb, Illinois, U.S.A.

ACKNOWLEDGMENTS

We wish to thank Suphat Sotthitada for sending materials from Bangkok and Dr. Chaiwat Roongrungsee, Prasert Bhandhachat, Damrong Wathana, Walapa Thayinda, A. Bond Woodruff, Grant Allan Olson, Linda Groat and Janet Engstrom for their aid and guidance. We also thank the series editor, Jon Woronoff, for his helpful editorial suggestions and Richard P. Vaupel, for his skillful drawing of maps according to our specifications. We are especially grateful for the use of the Donn V. Hart Southeast Asia Collection at Northern Illinois University Libraries. We appreciate the editorial aid of Ruth Engelmann and Ruth Rhoads. Finally, we wish to express our special gratitude to Rhea Valleau Smith, the coauthor's wife, whose daily encouragement and assistance made our task less burdensome.

ABBREVIATIONS

AID	Agency for International Development
AIT	Asian Institute of Technology
APEC	Asia-Pacific Economic Cooperations
ASEAN	Association of Southeast Asian Nations
ASEAN-CCI	ASEAN Chamber of Commerce and Industry
ASPAC	Asian and Pacific Council
BAAC	Bank of Agriculture and Agricultural Cooperatives
BIBF	Bangkok International Banking Facility
BOI	Board of Investment
CPM	Communist Party of Malaysia
CPT	Communist Party of Thailand
ECAFE	Economic Commission for Asia and the Far East
ESCAP	Economic and Social Commission for Asia and the Pacific
ETA	Expressway and Rapid Transit Authority of Thailand
ETO	Express Transportation Organization of Thailand
FAO	Food and Agriculture Organization
FDA	Food and Drug Association
FTI	Federation of Thai Industries
GDP	Gross Domestic Product
IAEA	International Atomic Energy Agency
IBRD	International Bank for Reconstruction and Development (World Bank)
ICAO	International Civil Aviation Organization
IDA	International Development Association
IFCT	Industrial Finance Corporation of Thailand
ILO	International Labour Organisation
IMF	International Monetary Fund
ISAS	Institute of Southeast Asian Studies
ITU	International Telecommunications Union
JPPCC	Joint Public and Private Sector Consultative Committees
JSS	Journal of the Siam Society
MOE	Ministry of Education
MOF	Marketing Organization of Farmers

MOI	Ministry of Industry
MOI	Ministry of the Interior
MOT	Mass Communication Organization of Thailand
MRTA	Metropolitan Rapid Transit Authority
MUA	Ministry of University Affairs
NEC	National Education Council
NESDB	National Economic and Social Development Board
NIDA	National Institute of Development Administration
NSO	National Statistical Office
OSS	Office of Strategic Services
OUP	Oxford University Press
PAT	Petroleum Authority of Thailand
PAT	Port Authority of Thailand
PROP	Principal Regional Office for Asia and the Pacific (UNESCO)
RFD	Royal Forest Department
RIT	Rajamangala Institute of Technology
RTG	Royal Thai Government
SEACEN	Southeast Asian Central Bank Group
SEAMEO	Southeast Asian Ministers of Education Organization
SEAMES	Southeast Asian Ministers of Education Secretariat
SEATO	Southeast Asia Treaty Organization
SET	Stock Exchange of Thailand
SLORC	State Law and Order Restoration Council
SUPPORT	Supplementary Occupations and Related Techniques Foundation
TAC	Thai Airways International Corporation
TAT	Tourism Authority of Thailand
TBA	Thai Bankers Association
TCC	Thai Chamber of Commerce
TISI	Thai Industrial Standards Institute
TISTR	Thailand Institute of Scientific and Technological Research
TMD	Thai Meteorological Department
TOT	Telephone Organization of Thailand

TOT	Tourist Organization of Thailand
TPI	Thai Petro-Chemical Industry
UN	United Nations
UNEP	United Nations Environmental Program
UNESCO	United Nations Educational, Scientific and Cultural Organization
UNICEF	United Nations Children's Fund
UNIFEM	United Nations Development Fund for Women
UPU	Universal Postal Union
USAID	United States Agency for International Development
USOM	United States Operations Mission
WHO	World Health Organization
WMO	World Meteorological Organization
VOPT	Voice of the People of Thailand

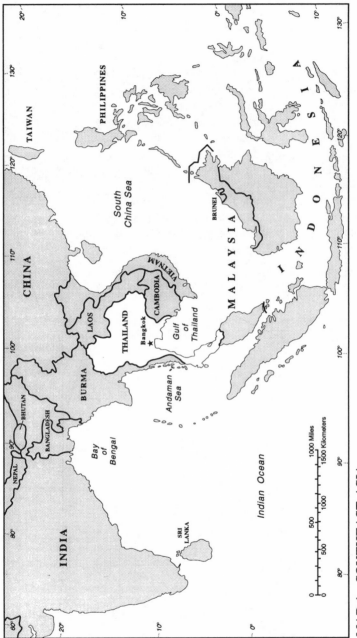

MAP 1. SOUTHEAST ASIA

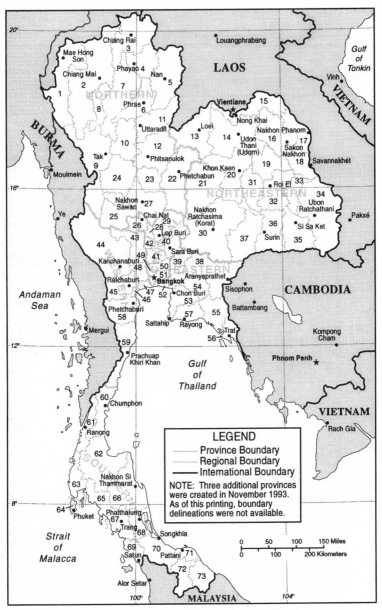

Chiang Rai
3
Mae Hong
Son
Chiang Mai
2
1
NORTHERN
Phayao 4
7
Nan
5
Phrae 6
8
11
Uttaradit
10
12
Tak 9
Phitsanulok
24
23
22
Phetchabun
21
Nakhon
Sawan 27
25
Chai Nat
26
28
29
Lop Buri
43
42
40
30
44
49
41
39
38
Kanchanaburi
48
50
Sara Buri
Ratchaburi
51 Bangkok
45
47
54
46
52
Chon Buri
Phetchaburi
53
58
57
55
Sattahip
Rayong
56 Trat
59
Prachuap
Khiri Khan
60
Chumphon
61
Ranong
62
63
Nakhon Si
Thammarat
65
66
64
Phuket
67 Phatthalung
Trang
68 Songkhla
69
70
Satun
Pattani 71
72
73
Alor Setar

Louangphrabang

LAOS

Gulf
of
Tonkin

Vinh

VIETNAM

Vientiane 15
Nong Khai
Loei
13
14
Udon
Thani
(Udorn)
Nakhon Phanom
16
17
Sakon
Nakhon
18
Savannakhét
Khon Kaen
20
19
31
Roi Et
33
34
32
Ubon
Ratchathani
Pakxé
Nakhon
Ratchasima
(Korat)
36
Si Sa Ket
35
37
Surin

EASTERN

Aranyaprathet
Sisophon

CAMBODIA

Battambang

Kompong
Cham

Phnom Penh ★

VIETNAM

Rach Gia

BURMA

Moulmein

Ye

Andaman
Sea

Mergui

Gulf
of
Thailand

SOUTHERN

Strait
of
Malacca

MALAYSIA

LEGEND
.... Province Boundary
Regional Boundary
━━━ International Boundary
NOTE: Three additional provinces
were created in November 1993.
As of this printing, boundary
delineations were not available.

0   50   100   150 Miles
0   100   200 Kilometers

20°

16°

12°

8°

100°

104°

MAP 2. REGIONS AND PROVINCES OF THAILAND
(Key to province names listed on next page)

Provices

(Listed Numerically)

1. Mae Hong Son
2. Chiang Mai
3. Chiang Rai
4. Phayao
5. Nan
6. Phrae
7. Lampang
8. Lamphun
9. Tak
10. Sukhothai
11. Uttaradit
12. Phitsanulok
13. Loei
14. Udon Thani
15. Nong Khai
16. Sakon Nakhon
17. Nakhon Phanom
18. Mukdahan
19. Kalasin
20. Khon Kaen
21. Chaiyaphum
22. Phetchabun
23. Phichit
24. Kamphaeng Phet
25. Uthai Thani
26. Chai Nat
27. Nakhon Sawan
28. Sing Buri
29. Lop Buri
30. Nakhon Ratchasima
31. Maha Sarakham
32. Roi Et
33. Yasothon
34. Ubon Ratchathani
35. Si Sa Ket
36. Surin
37. Buri Ram
38. Prachin Buri
39. Nakhon Nayok
40. Sara Buri
41. Phra Nakhon Si Ayutthaya
42. Ang Thong
43. Suphan Buri
44. Kanchanaburi
45. Ratchaburi
46. Samut Songkhram
47. Samut Sakhon
48. Nakhon Pathom
49. Nonthaburi
50. Pathum Thani
51. Bangkok
52. Samut Prakan
53. Chon Buri
54. Chachoengsao
55. Chanthaburi
56. Trat
57. Rayong
58. Phetchaburi
59. Prachuap Khiri Khan
60. Chumphon
61. Ranong
62. Surat Thani
63. Phangnga
64. Phuket
65. Krabi
66. Nakhon Si Thammarat
67. Trang
68. Phatthalung
69. Satun
70. Songkhla
71. Pattani
72. Yala
73. Narathiwat

Provices

(Listed Alphabetically)

Ang Thong (42)
Bangkok (51)
Buri Ram (37)
Chachoengsao (54)
Chai Nat (26)
Chaiyaphum (21)
Chanthaburi (55)
Chiang Mai (2)
Chiang Rai (3)
Chon Buri (53)
Chumphon (60)
Kalasin (19)
Kamphaeng Phet (24)
Kanchanaburi (44)
Khon Kaen (20)
Krabi (65)
Lampang (7)
Lamphun (8)
Loei (13)
Lop Buri (29)
Mae Hong Son (1)
Maha Sarakham (31)
Mukdahan (18)
Nakhon Nayok (39)
Nakhon Pathom (48)
Nakhon Phanom (17)
Nakhon Ratchasima (30)
Nakhon Sawan (27)
Nakhon Si Thammarat (66)
Nan (5)
Narathiwat (73)
Nong Khai (15)
Nonthaburi (49)
Pathum Thani (50)
Pattani (71)
Phangnga (63)
Phatthalung (68)
Phayao (4)
Phetchabun (22)
Phetchaburi (58)
Phichit (23)
Phitsanulok (12)
Phra Nakhon Si Ayutthaya (41)
Phrae (6)
Phuket (64)
Prachin Buri (38)
Prachuap Khiri Khan (59)
Ranong (61)
Ratchaburi (45)
Rayong (57)
Roi Et (32)
Sakon Nakhon (16)
Samut Prakan (52)
Samut Sakhon (47)
Samut Songkhram (46)
Sara Buri (40)
Satun (69)
Sing Buri (28)
Si Sa Ket (35)
Songkhla (70)
Sukhothai (10)
Suphan Buri (43)
Surat Thani (62)
Surin (36)
Tak (9)
Trang (67)
Trat (56)
Ubon Ratchathani (34)
Udon Thani (14)
Uthai Thani (25)
Uttaradit (11)
Yala (72)
Yasothon (33)

CHRONOLOGY OF EVENTS

4,000 BC	Prehistoric settlements at Ban Kao, NonNok Tha, Ban Chiang and other Southeast Asian sites.
3,000 BC	Cast bronze technology used in settled communities in the Mekong River region.
500 BC	Peoples of the Tai-language family present in northern Southeast Asia and in South China.
500-800 AD	Slow spread of Tai-language peoples south and west of their area of origin.
800-1000	Dvaravati, a Mon civilization, occupied what is now central and western Thailand.
800-1200	Mon centers fall successively under domination of the Khmer Kingdom of Angkor. Chiang Saen, Phayao, Nakhon Si Thammarat and other small principalities established with kings or chieftains of the Tai language family.
1238	First independent Thai principality, Sukhothai, established in 1238 by Sri Indraditya after defeat of Khmer garrison.
✓ 1259	Lan Na Kingdom established by Mangrai in northern Thailand. Capital, Chiang Mai, built in 1296.
1275	King Ramkhamhaeng built the Sukhothai Kingdom into a great power. His stone inscription was first use of Tai-language alphabet.
1300s	High-quality glazed ceramics produced commercially at Sukhothai and other towns.

1317-1355	Lan Na experienced four decades mostly as vassal state of Mongols.
1350-1569	Ayutthaya City State, founded in 1350 by U Thong (Ramathibodi I), asserted suzerainty over smaller states in area. For two centuries, kingdom ruled by 18 kings of two dynasties.
1355-1526	Golden Age of politically strong Lan Na Kingdom. It developed culturally with Ceylonese Buddhist influence. Lan Na ruled by six famous kings during this period.
1378	Suhkothai Kingdom succombed and made part of Ayutthaya.
1448-1488	Trailok, King of Ayutthaya, is famous for innovations in civil and military administration.
1454	Civil and military officials given limited titles to land in Ayutthaya.
1511	Portugese from Malacca, the first Europeans, established embassy in Ayutthaya.
1525	The Pali Chronicle, Jinakalamali, completed in Lan Na Kingdom.
1526-1558	Decline of Lan Na Kingdom under seven weak kings. Became a vassal to Burma in 1558.
1548-1569	Chakkraphat of Ayutthaya successfully defended his kingdom from Burmese attacks. Next king, Mahin, failed and Ayutthaya was occupied by Burmese in 1569.
1558-1776	Lan Na dominated by Burmese who used it as a base for attacks on Ayutthaya and Lan Xang.

1569-1584	Ayutthaya Kingdom under Burmese suzerainty, Maha Thammaracha was vassal king.
1570-1577	Cambodian forces captured territory and removed population during six invasions of Ayutthaya.
1584-1590	Independent Thai state Ayutthaya restored and ruled by King Naresuan the Great. Two invasions of Burma by Naresuan.
1592	Burmese invasion repulsed at Nong Sarai when Naresuan killed Burmese Crown Prince.
1600s	Siam (or Sayam) became accepted name of present Thailand among Westerners. Asian and European traders and Christian missionaries made significant impact on Siam's art, sculpture and architecture.
1605	Dutch traders arrived in Ayutthaya. Trading company established in 1613.
1612	British traders arrived in Ayutthaya. East India Company opened trading posts there, in Chiang Mai and Pattani.
1629-1656	Prasat Thong became King of Ayutthaya.
1634	Japanese embassy opened in Ayutthaya.
1656-1688	Period of preeminence of Kingdom of Ayutthaya (Siam) under King Narai the Great. International trade expanded during his reign.
1662	Louis XIV, King of France, sent ambassador and missionaries to Siam.
1680	French East India Company opened office in Siam's capital.

1686	King Narai signed Treaty of Alliance with France. French garrisons established.
1688-1703	Phetracha became King of Siam and arranged ouster of foreign troops and missionaries.
1733-1757	King Borommakot strengthened Buddhism and governmental administration.
1767	Ayutthaya, Siamese city of a million persons, destroyed by Burmese army. Population and treasure moved to Burma. City burned.
1767-1782	Resurgent Siamese Kingdom established under King Taksin. Rival kings and chiefs at Phimai, Fang, Phitsanulok, Lan Na, Nakhon Si Thammarat, and Champassak became vassals.
1776-1933	Lan Na Kingdom's capital, Chiang Mai, became vassal state of Siam, with Kavila and his descendants as rulers.
1779	Siam conquered Vientiane and Emerald Buddha acquired.
1782-1808	Rama I (Yot Fa), famous general, became Siamese king in 1782 and built new capital, Bangkok.
1785	Massive five-army Burmese invasion defeated by Siamese.
1787	Rama I directed completion of definitive text of Buddhist scriptures, Tipitaka.
1787, 1793	Siamese invasions of Burma failed.

1797	*Ramakian*, a Siamese version of the Hindu famous epic, *Ramayana*, translated and set to verse.
1797, 1802	Burmese invasions of Lan Na defeated with aid of Siamese.
1805	Three Seals Law Code, a reformulation of previous laws, promulgated by Rama I.
1809-1824	Siam ruled by King Rama II (Loetla), known for his literary works.
1824-1851	Siamese King Rama III (Nangklao) strengthened Buddhism and signed 1826 Burney Treaty with Great Britain.
1833	Presbyterian and Baptist Missions founded. Dan Bradley, M.D., practiced medicine in Siam.
1836	First school with instruction in Siamese and British opened by American missionaries.
1844	July 4. First Tai-language newspaper published by Dan Bradley.
1851-1868	King Mongkut, a scholar of Latin, English and other subjects, arranged friendly relations with European states, avoided colonization of Siam, modernized Siam and hired European advisors.
1856	"Siam" used as name of the nation for first time by King Mongkut in Bowring Treaty of Commerce and Friendship with Great Britain. United States and nine Western nations secured similar treaties, permitting extraterritoriality.
1857	*The Royal Gazette*, first periodical in the Siamese language, founded.

1862-1867	Anna Leonowens of Great Britain taught King Mongkut's son Chulalongkorn and others.
1867	Cambodian provinces of Siam placed under French protection by treaty.
1868-1910	Under King Chulalongkorn, Siam's independence strengthened after territorial concessions to France and Great Britain. Postal and telegraph facilities were constructed. Young Siamese studied in Europe.
1871	First modern Siamese school opened in the Royal Palace.
1874	Anti-slavery Act was proclaimed.
1882	Siamese embassy established in Europe.
1884	First government school for common people established in Bangkok. Wachirayan Library in Bangkok founded.
1885	Siamese embassy established in United States.
1887	Department of Education established by King Chulalongkorn. Japan established first foreign embassy in Bangkok.
1888, 1893	Siam transferred northeast Laos and whole east bank of Mekong to France.
1892	Belgian Rolin-Jaequemyns employed by King Chulalongkorn as advisor. System of government ministries and provincial administration established. Budget system and regular audit created.
1893	"Paknam" incident gave France concessions.

1896	Siam recognized French protectorate in Cambodia. Franco-British agreement recognized Kingdom of Siam.
1897	Siam and Britain agreement excluded third powers from the peninsula. Siam's building of canal across Kra Isthmus forbidden. Nation's first railroad completed between Bangkok and Ayutthaya.
1897-1899	Siamese embassies established in Russia and Japan.
1902	King Chulalongkorn decreed the Sangha Law of Buddhism. Provided for lay supervisors of monastic property.
1904	February. Siam ceded to France Sayaboury and part of Champassak. 1986 Anglo-French Convention that defined French and British spheres of influence in Southeast Asia was confirmed.
1905	Bangkok City Library established.
1907	Siam ceded Cambodian provinces of Battambang, Siem Reap, and Sisophon to France.
1908	Law on Constitution of Courts promulgated.
1909	Provinces of Kedah, Kelantan, Perak, and Trenganu ceded to Britain.
1910-1925	Reign of King Vajiravudh, a writer and poet, promoted Thai nationalism.
1916	Chulalongkorn founded the first state University of Medicine, Civil Service and Engineering, which combined in one unit

previous schools. King Vajiravudh ordered Siamese to adopt surnames. Siamese military force sent to Europe to aid allies in World War I.

1920-1926   Treaties with Western nations gave Siam autonomy and abrogated previous extraterritoriality.

1920s   Imported novels and films circulated widely in Siam.

1921   Compulsory education through fourth grade proclaimed. State railway extended north to Chiang Mai.

1923   Metric system adopted.

1925-1926   February 1925 and August 1926. Border questions with France resolved. Franco-Siamese High Commission on Mekong River questions created.

1925-1935   Prajadhipok became king. Dealt with government finances in disarray and impact of the Great Depression. Attempted to introduce a constitution.

1927   Prince Bhumibol Adulyadej born in Massachusetts, U.S. Son of Prince Mahidol of Songkhla.

1932   Absolute Thai monarchy changed to constitutional one in a bloodless coup led by European educated military officers and civil servants.

                 August. Manoprakornnitithada named first prime minister of Siam.

1933-1938	Phahonyothin served as prime minister.
1933	Lan Na became the northern Siamese provinces of Chiang Mai, Nan, Chiang Rai, Mae Hong Son, Lamphun, Lampang, and Tak.
	October. Bloody rebellion to restore the monarchy, led by Prince Bowaradet, fails.
	November. First Siamese government election gave both men and women the right to vote. Founding of Fine Arts School, later named Silpakorn University.
1934	Thammasat University was founded.
1935	King Prajadhipok abdicated Thai throne succeeded by Ananda Mahidol.
1937	Treaties of friendship and commerce were concluded with Western nations. Siam recovered sovereignty lost in previous treaties.
1938-1944	Phibunsongkhram named prime minister, marking political ascendancy of military.
1939	The nation's name changed to "Thailand." Western calendar adopted.
1940-1941	December 1940 to January 1941, Thailand at war with France on eastern border. Treaty of Tokyo restored Thailand's territories west of Mekong River.
1941-1944	December. Prime Minister Phibun permitted Japanese army to occupy Thailand during military campaigns. Pridi Phanomyong led an underground movement against Japanese.

1942	January. Thailand declared war against U.S. and Great Britain. Bank of Thailand was established. Pridi appointed to Regency Council.
1942-1943	1943 Treaty in Tokyo restored to Thailand Shan area of Burma and four Malay states lost to Britain in 1909.
1943	Two state universities founded, Kasetsart for Agriculture and Silpakorn for Fine Arts.
	October 25. Japanese opened bridge over Kwai River. Many Allied and other prisoners died during its construction.
1943-1944	Thailand suffered wartime shortages, inflation, bombings, lack of imports and inability to export.
1944	July. Prime Minister Phibun forced to resign. Khuang Aphaiwong and four other civilians served brief terms as prime minister until 1948.
1945	September. Pridi Phanomyong, as regent, repudiated all Phibun's agreements with Japanese.
	December. Anglo-Thai Peace Treaty restored to Britain four Malay states and Shan region in Burma.
1946	June. Prince Bhumibol Adulyadej made king after death of Ananda.
1946-1947	Thailand signed peace treaties with Australia and The Netherlands. Thailand returned to France Mekong territories acquired in 1941.

Thailand and China signed treaty of friendship and commerce. Thailand joined United Nations.

1947   November. Army and police harass and arrest "leftist" students and politicians.

1948   April. Phibunsongkhram returned as prime minister backed by new political elite. Phibun imposed restrictions on Chinese citizens. Thai-Malay leaders arrested and Malay language schools closed. Islamic and Malay organizations banned.

1949   Pridi Phanomyong forced into exile after failed coup against Phibun.

1950   Beginning of U.S. annual economic and military aid to Thailand of $10 to $100 million.

        May 5. King Bhumibol Adulyadej's coronation ceremonies at Grand Palace.

1951   June. Manhattan Rebellion against Prime Minister Phibunsongkhram failed. Armed clashes caused over 300 casualties. National Scheme of Education proclaimed. Both private and government schools permitted.

1952   Thammasat University became new name of previous University of Moral and Political Science (1933) and Law School (1897).

1954   College of Education, Prasarnmit, with seven branch campuses created. Southeast Asia Treaty Organization (SEATO) created.

1955   June 14. Commercial television broadcasting commenced. United Nations regional headquarters established in Bangkok for ESCAP, FAO, UNICEF and other agencies.

	King Bhumibol Adulyadej's 22-day visit to northeast provinces to build societal unity.
1956-1957	Prince Wan Waithayakorn served as president of United Nations General Assembly.
1957	25th century of Thai Buddhist Era.
1957-1963	Sarit Thanarat became prime minister after coup; ruled with martial law; national development emphasized.
1959	Thai Airways International established as state enterprise.
1960	National Scheme of Education extended compulsory education from four to seven years, established secondary schools and universities. Secret agreement with U.S. provided defense of Thailand.
1961	First Five-Year National Economic Plan adopted. Led to stronger Thai economy. Inauguration of American Field Service study abroad for Thai students.
	April. United States military center for intelligence reporting established at Bangkok airport.
1962	Rusk-Thanat agreement confirmed U.S. protective alliance for Thailand.
1963-1973	Thanom Kittikachorn named prime minister. Emphasized social and economic development to combat rural discontent and widespread insurgency.

1963-1964	United States military intelligence centers established at Ubon Ratchathani and Udorn Thani.
1964	Chiang Mai University founded. First of 12 state universities in the provinces.
1964-1979	Period of economic unrest and insurgency in northeast, northern and southern areas. Communist party active.
1965-1966	Three U.S. military installations established in Udorn Thani and Khorat.
1965-1968	U.S. waged air war against North Vietnam from Thailand bases. U.S. Rest and Rehabilitation Centers established at Bangkok.
1966	July. Thai Air Force and Navy joined U.S. and engaged in war operations. Bank for Agriculture and Cooperatives established. National Institute of Development Administration founded for only graduate studies.
1966-1967	Thai army units sent to Laos and South Vietnam in Vietnam War.
1967	Association of Southeast Asian Nations (ASEAN) established. The Minerals Act authorized state ownership and management of all minerals on or under the land surface.
1969	University of Medical Sciences renamed Mahidol University. Private colleges authorized to grant degrees.
1971	Ramkamhaeng University established. First unlimited student admissions.

1971-1973	Thailand under martial law, ruled by National Executive Council. Thanom Kittikachorn elected prime minister.
1973	October 14. Student-led uprising. Prime Minister Thanom and two others forced into exile.
1973-1977	Four-year period of civilian prime ministers: Sanya Dharmasakti, Seni Pramot and Kukrit Pramot served.
1974	Securities Exchange Market established in Bangkok.
	December. Fifteen-year ban on China trade lifted.
1975	March. Thailand normalized diplomatic relations with China.
	August. Pathet-Lao took control of Laos. Refugees fled to Thailand.
	November. Thailand closed border with Laos temporarily. Military forces of U.S. evacuated from Thailand.
1976	October. Police and right-wing mob attacked students at Thammasat University. Many deaths and injuries. Thousands fled to countryside. Thanin Kraivichien installed as prime minister.
1977	After military coup, Kriangsak Chomanan became prime minister for three years. Investment Promotion Act passed by Assembly to secure foreign and domestic capital. The Ground Water Act empowered governmental

	control of ground water development and management.
1978	Start of a period of high growth with Gross Domestic Product growing by 7 to 9 percent a year until early 1990s. Airport at Chiang Mai authorized for international traffic.
1979	January and April. Thai and Lao prime ministers exchanged visits and communiqués. Labor Court established. Vietnam invaded Cambodia. Refugees flooded eastern Thailand.
1980s	Natural gas discovered in Gulf of Thailand and oil found in southeast Thailand.
1980	Return of 3,000 intellectuals, who fled to countryside after 1976 right-wing repression. General Prem Tinsulanonda selected prime minister by House of Representatives.
1980-1982	Thousands of Cambodian and Laotian refugees expelled from Thailand. Many migrated abroad.
1983	First International Gem Fair held in Bangkok.
1987	Celebration of King Bhumibol's 60th birthday.
1987-1988	Thai military officers held a series of meetings with officials in Burma to improve relations.
	December 1987 to February 1988. Ban Rom Conflict, a border battle between Thai and Laotian armies, ended in cease-fire.
1988	July. National election held. General Chatchai Choonhavan became prime minister. Seen as advancement of democracy.

August. Celebration of King Bhumibol as the longest reigning Thai monarch.

September. Burmese students became refugees in Thailand after Rangoon's military coup. United States pressured Thailand to enforce copyright laws.

November. Thailand and Laos established a joint committee to demarcate common border after repeated clashes. Agreement reached to repatriate to Laos 80,000 Laotian refugees in Thailand.

1988-1989   Thai foreign minister conferred with Vietnamese and Cambodian officials to promote a cease-fire in Cambodia and establishment of an international peace-keeping force.

1989   January/February. UN requested Thais to end alleged forced repatriation of Burmese students.

April. Thailand evacuated 10,000 Thai construction workers declared illegal by Singapore.

June. Thai industrial output rose to a new high. Santo Asoke defrocked. Accused of rebelling against Buddhist authorities. To improve relations and for logging contracts, Thai military leaders conferred with Burmese in Rangoon.

November. Thai ban on export sales of strategic items to Laos was lifted. Thailand promoted improved relations with Laos, Cambodia, Vietnam and Burma to increase trade.

December. Thai and Malaysian officials persuaded Communist party of Malaysia to abandon armed struggle.

1990   January. General Chamlong Srimuang re-elected mayor of Bangkok.

February. Bangkok's port workers staged four-day strike.
July. Thailand's first major social security legislation enacted.

August. Typhoon Gay struck southern Thailand. Extensive property damage and death of 450 people.

September. Peace conference on Cambodia failed in Bangkok.

October. Thailand denied recognition of or aid to new refugees from Burma.

1991   February. General Sundhara Kongsompong led bloodless coup. Prime Minister Chatchai arrested. National Assembly dissolved and martial law declared.

March 2. Anand Panyarchun named interim prime minister.

March. Agreement with Laos on border disputes and economic cooperation. New east coast seaport opened at Laem Chabang.

October 1991 and January 1992. Rapprochement between Thailand and Vietnam.

November. Repatriation of the 300,000 Cambodian refugees in Thailand began.

1992

January. Value added tax (VAT) implemented.

February. Thailand and Laos agreed to cooperate in developing tourism.

March 8. Collision of ferry and oil tanker killed 95 persons in Gulf of Thailand.

March. Pro-military parties won a majority in election. General Suchinda Kraprayoon named prime minister. Thai and Burmese troops clashed on border.

April 1. Minimum daily wage of 115 baht ($4.60) established for Bangkok, adjacent provinces and Phuket.

April 30. Cambodian Refugee Camp was closed following a massive repatriation program. Those refusing repatriation became illegal immigrants.

May. Securities and Exchange Commission created to regulate capital markets.

May 17-21. Pro-democracy protest led to military crackdown. Prime Minister General Suchinda forced to resign.

June 10. Anand Panyarchun reappointed interim prime minister.

June. Law passed requiring prime minister be an elected member of House of Representatives.

September. Pro-democracy parties won in national election. Chuan Leekpai named prime minister. Thai Airways International placed under civilian control.

November 2. Establishment of the fund of baht 1.3 million for Quality of Life Improvement. This enables programs for low income persons in Bangkok and other urban areas of Thailand.

1993   March 20. United States and Thailand resumed cooperation in military defense and security following a two-year break.

March 24. Approval obtained for appointment of women as assistant district officers.

May 10. World's worst doll factory fire killed 188 workers and injured 488 others.

June 20. Phra Nyanasamvara, supreme patriarch, made his first visit to China.

June 24. Two million dollars in aid for Thai military training in U.S. resumed.

July 15. King Bhumibol Adulyadej gave four million baht ($160,000) to the Bangkok metropolis.

August 29. Prime Minister Chuan Leekpai conferred in Beijing with Chinese Prime Minister Li Peng to strengthen bilateral relations.

August to December. Dry weather and drought affected central and northeast Thailand.

September. Thousands of Burmese refugees permitted to obtain work permits in Thailand.

September 20. The government led by Prime Minister Chuan Leekpai removed the Social Action party from the coalition.

September, October. Thais and Malaysians conferred to end terrorists violence on border.

October 16. Vietnamese Communist party chief sought naturalization of the 40,000 Vietnamese in Thailand.

1994   January. "Traffic Crisis '94" campaign started.

February. First communication satellite, "Thaicom 1," started operating.

February-March. Most critical drought in 30 years.

March. Government launched the Bangkok International Banking Facility (BIBF).

April. "Thai-Lao Friendship Bridge" over the Mekong River opened. King visited Vientiane, Laos (his first trip to a foreign country since 1962).

May. First AIDS Relief Coordination Center was set up in Chiang Mai. Cabinet approved a bill to replace the Anti-Trade Women and Children Act of 1928.

"June 9, 1994-June 9, 1996 Reforestation Campaign" launched.

July. "Bus Lovers' Club" was established to promote the use of public buses. The Bangkok Metropolitan Administration opened the first waste water treatment plant to ease water-pollution in the Chao Phya River.

August 10. Labour and Social Welfare Ministry authorized to allow illegal Burmese immigrants to work in Thailand, but conditions apply.

September. The logo "Original Quality Rice from Thailand," was adopted to enhance the quality of genuine Thai rice in the world market. Thailand initiated a new medical treatment program using satellite communication, known as Telemedicine project and designed to improve medical services in rural areas. The Cabinet approved the new anti-prostitution draft bill, which would replace the existing anti-prostitution act in use for more than 30 years.

November. Thai exports exceeded the one trillion baht ($40 billion).

1995

January. The ASEAN (which includes Thailand and seven other Southeast Asian nations) launched the Environment Year.

February. The government endorsed a tax reform package to bring the average import duty down from 30.24% to 17.01% by 1997. The Cabinet approved the Royal Thai Air Force to buy a radar-equipped automatic air defence system from the US to cover the south as the region should have security facilities comparable to such neighbors as Malaysia.

February 17-26. Board of Investment's massive trade fair held at Laem Chabang deep sea port in Chon Buri Province.

March 16. Thailand signed an agreement for long term purchase of electricity from the Nam Thuen II hydro power project in Laos.

March 29. Thailand and Cambodia signed two agreements to promote and protect investments and tourism and help brighten the climate for trade and investment cooperation.

April 3. Thailand's first ultra-high frequency television station was approved by the government.

April 5. Thailand, Laos, Cambodia and Vietnam, the four riparian countries of the lower Mekong basin, supported by the United Nations Development program, signed an agreement to cooperate in the use of the river.

May. Several major schools in Bangkok changed their hours to ease inner city traffic congestion. A constitution amendment was approved that extends voting rights to those 18 years and older.

May 16. The Charles Lindbergh and Anne Morrow Lindbergh Foundation in New York awarded Queen Sirikit the 1995 Lindbergh Award, for her educational and humanitarian efforts on behalf of the people in Thailand and other countries.

May 19. The *Bangkok Post* was elected to the United Nations Environment Programme's Global 500 Roll of Honour for advancing the cause of conservation and environmental protection.

INTRODUCTION

Overview

The Kingdom of Thailand, formerly Siam, is located on the central part of the Southeast Asia mainland. Its capital is Bangkok. The countries on its borders include Burma, north and west, Laos, east, Cambodia, southeast, and Malaysia, south. The country appears in outline like the side view of an elephant's head. The trunk corresponds with a long peninsula in the south which constitutes the western border of the Gulf of Thailand. The rest of the country corresponds to the elephant's head. In area, Thailand is only 514,000 square kilometers (200,000 square miles) or slightly smaller than France.

Geographically, there are four principal regions. In north Thailand is a series of high mountains. One range of these extends southward along the Burmese border. Four prominent rivers constitute the headwaters for Thailand's dominant river, the Chao Phraya. Terrain in the north makes possible shifting cultivation in the uplands and wet-rice farming in the valley lowlands. The Central Plain, known for its fertile alluvial soils, is the heartland of Thailand. The very important Chao Phraya River, which drains into the Gulf of Thailand, is the most prominent feature. The river, together with a complex network of canals and two lesser rivers, sustains an agricultural economy and provides waterways for moving people and goods. At the southern edge of this region is the Bangkok metropolis and surrounding cities. It is the nation's center of business, commerce, industry, foreign trade and tourism.

The northeast is mostly a plateau with rolling low hills and lakes and has only fair soils. Rainfall, while seasonal, supports cattle production, rice and other agricultural crops. Small rivers there drain into the Mekong River which forms the principal eastern boundary. Mountains constitute the western and southern boundaries. In south Thailand, a north-south mountain range is the backbone of the long peninsular shape. There are narrow coastal plains, chiefly on the eastern side. The south is mostly forested and large rivers are noticeably absent.

Thailand has a tropical climate. The southern and eastern coastal areas of the Gulf of Thailand resemble a tropical rain forest. There is little seasonal variation in rainfall, which is 2,300 to 2,500 millimeters (90 to 100 inches) annually. North Thailand, the Central Plain and the northeast regions have a tropical savanna climate with marked wet and dry seasons, and rainfall amounting to about half that of south Thailand. The wet season starts in April or May and continues through October. Typically, the rains are accompanied by a drop in temperature which averages between 24 and 29 degrees C (75 to 85 degrees F). Temperatures in north Thailand show greater variation and average 16 degrees C (60 degrees F) in the cooler part of the year. The cooler temperatures are replaced by a hot season from late February through May.

The People

In 1994, Thailand's population was estimated to be approximately 60 million. The annual growth rate was 1.6 percent, which is down from the 3.0 percent rate of 25 years ago. About one-half of the population is under 20 years of age.

The people of Thailand are predominantly descendants of a Tai language group that predates historical records. Approximately 85 percent of today's population are called the "Thai." They consist of the Central Thai, the Kham Muang or northern Thai, the Thai-Lao of the northeast and the Pak-Thai of south Thailand. Non-Thai minority ethnic groups include the Karen, Khmer, Hmong, Mon, Mien, Lahu, Akha and Lisu. The most numerous immigrants, coming to Thailand for hundreds of years, have been the Chinese who are very largely assimilated. The Thai-Malay are the largest unassimilated minority. These non-Thai groups, while retaining their distinctive languages, also learn standard Thai which is taught in the schools and is the official language of the nation.

About 15 percent of the Thai people live in metropolitan Bangkok. This city, the nation's capital, is the predominant center for business and for most other activities. It is also the seat of the national government. There are six other large cities, each of which has a population of over 100,000. The three largest of these are Nonthaburi (pop. 265,000 est.), Nakhon Ratchasima (pop. 203,000 est.) and Chiang Mai (pop. 200,000 est.). About two-thirds of the Thai people dwell in agricultural villages. The contrasts in living conditions between large urban centers and rural villages are very great. The national government of Thailand and the Constitutional Era is discussed later.

Buddhism is the religion of more than 90 percent of the Thai people, though many spirits of an earlier period have been incorporated into religious practices. Significant events are marked by appropriate rituals in which the Buddhist clergy participate. Making merit and following the Buddha's teachings is more evident in the rural villages than in the cities. Much of rural community life is centered on the local Buddhist temple-compound called the *wat*. The largest non-Buddhist minority are Muslims. There are very small populations of Christians, Hindus and other religions.

Natural Resources

Until recently, Thailand has had an abundance of land suitable for agriculture, amounting to roughly two-thirds of the country's total area. At present, however, there is a growing pressure for access to cultivable land. In the past 25 years, rapid cutting in the woodlands has greatly diminished Thailand's extensive forests of hardwoods and softwoods. Thailand is located within the metalliferous belt of Southeast Asia. This natural resource has assured the country a wide variety of mineral deposits. Rainfall in Thailand is normally plentiful, but the short wet season in the northeast is typically followed by periods of drought. The burgeoning population of Thailand and the requirements of wet-rice agriculture have created the necessity for water storage and effective water management.

The Economy

In large part, Thailand has a rapidly developing market economy. Capitalism is mostly private, but the infrastructure has been well supported by the government. A role for state enterprises continues, though their importance has decreased. Today, industrial output accounts for at least 70 percent of the total export earnings, agriculture and fishing provide the remainder of the exports. Twenty-five years ago, agriculture and fishing were leaders in exports. Even so, almost two-thirds of Thailand's labor force is engaged in agriculture, forestry and fishing. Rice growing occupies most cultivated land. Other export crops are cassava, sugar cane, pineapple, maize and rubber. The number of farmers without access to land has greatly increased and presents a serious problem.

Tourism is the leader in generating foreign exchange earnings in Thailand. Manufactured products yield the second largest amount in foreign exchange. In the past decade, industrial output has grown rapidly; the leading export items are textiles and garments, computers and parts, gems and jewelry. Since the value of imports generally exceeds the value of its exports, Thailand has had repeated trade deficits. The major imports are machinery and transport equipment, chemicals and petroleum. Prior to World War II, most Thai commercial activities were in the hands of Chinese and Sino-Thai merchants. In recent decades, however, ethnic Thais have become active in business affairs.

Thailand is a lower middle income country according to the World Bank. In all of South and Southeast Asia, only India and Indonesia, with much larger populations compared to Thailand, have a larger gross domestic product. Since the 1960s, foreign private investment has been both encouraged and aided. The Japanese and Americans have been the leaders in foreign investment in Thailand. The Thai economy is gradually changing from one dependent on cheap labor and abundant resources to one that is increasingly dependent on imported capital goods and advanced technology.

History

The origins of the Thai nation are shrouded in prehistory. Findings of archaeologists indicate there were human settlements in Southeast Asia as early as 4,000 years ago. A Tai-language tribal group was thought to have first emerged in the northeastern part of Southeast Asia. This area is believed to be a prehistoric center of wet-rice cultivation. Members of this tribal group, who possessed rice growing skills, gradually developed their own distinct language. Today, the Tai language family is represented by the Shan of Burma, Tai Dam of Vietnam, Tai Lao of Laos and several segments of the people of Thailand who have distinctive languages. These early peoples, including the previous Mon, Lawa and other indigenous peoples, migrated west and south following river valleys where they had access to water. Gradually, settlements based on rice growing developed. From these early settlers, the ancestors of the Thai people adopted important cultural elements. In time, these settlement-communities coalesced into small principalities headed by a military chief. The region that is now Thailand was previously one with a Mon-Lawa culture, known as the Dvaravati civilization. It developed in central Southeast Asia in the 6th century and had already adopted Theravada Buddhism of the Pagan Kingdom in Burma.

EARLY KINGDOMS (1238-1378)

In many cases, those we now call the Thai asserted leadership of the military-agricultural principalities. Eventually, there was conflict with the Khmer rulers who had become established in Southeast Asia from the 10th century. In the 12th century, two independent Thai kingdoms emerged in the northern part of what today is Thailand. The Sukhothai Kingdom was founded in 1238 and the Lan Na Kingdom in 1296. In the former, Ramkhamhaeng (reigned 1279-1317) is remembered as a paternalistic king in whose reign the Thai alphabet was designed. The Lan Na Kingdom experienced periods of both stability and instability and became a vassal of Burma from 1558 to 1774.

[318 (margin note)

THE AYUTTHAYA ERA (1350-1767)

In the 14th century, the new Thai Kingdom of Ayutthaya was established by Ramathibodi (reigned 1350-1369). The capital city, Ayutthaya, was established along the Chao Phraya River about 120 kilometers (75 miles) north of the Gulf of Thailand. By the 15th century, this Kingdom or City State of Ayutthaya had defeated the Khmer forces of Angkor and was the strongest power in Southeast Asia. The Sukhothai Kingdom was overcome and incorporated into that of Ayutthaya. Borommatrailokanat, King of Ayutthaya (reigned 1448-1488), is known for creating a central government organization with both civil and military administrations.

Contacts with European powers for purposes of trade developed in the 16th century. The name Siam began to be used by Europeans to refer to the Kingdom of Ayutthaya. By this time, Burma had become powerful and in 1569 captured the Siamese capital, making it a vassal state. Burmese suzerainty ended about 15 years later under the brilliant military leader Naresuan, who restored the kingdom's independence. He later became King Naresuan (reigned 1590-1605). In the 17th century, under King Narai (reigned 1656-1688), trade flourished especially with the Dutch and British, and diplomacy blossomed with France. Siam's battles with Vietnam for control of Cambodia continued into the 18th century. Meanwhile, Burma used three armies to attack, capture and destroy Ayutthaya in 1767.

THE BANGKOK ERA (1767-1932)

King Taksin (reigned 1767-1782) and his generals led Siamese forces in restoring and unifying the kingdom after the catastrophic loss to the Burmese in 1767. By expelling the Burmese forces from Lan Na in 1774, that kingdom was added to Siam as a vassal state. Yot Fa, a very able Siamese general, became King Rama I (reigned 1782-1809), and established Bangkok as his capital. The royal Chakri dynasty which he initiated, continues today. With great energy, Rama I rebuilt the economy and society. He also restored Siamese art, literature and architecture, and strengthened Buddhism. Together with his successors, Rama II and Rama III, a revitalized stature and stability was brought to Siam. The territories and population were enlarged to include portions of what today are Laos, Cambodia and Malaysia.

In the second half of the 19th century, Britain and France were acquiring colonies in Asia. The successful Siamese response to this threat was a credit to the remarkable skill of the next three Chakri kings and their advisors. As a result, Siam was not colonized by a foreign power. Trade treaties negotiated under King Mongkut (reigned 1851-1868) opened Siam to international trade, but at the price of reduced income from trade and the intrusion of foreign consular courts. King Chulalongkorn (reigned 1868-1910) yielded Siamese territories to the French and British in order to preserve his country's independence. During his reign, needed changes were made in the legal system and modern methods were introduced into the administration of government.

CONSTITUTIONAL ERA (1932-)

A coup d'etat in 1932 changed the Siamese monarchy from an absolute to a limited one. This significant change reflected the thinking of the Siamese who had been educated in Europe. Bhumibol Adulyadej is the present king of Thailand and the 9th monarch of the Chakri dynasty. His coronation ceremony was in 1950. As king he symbolizes the unity of the nation and enjoys a revered status. The constitution defines the king as the titular head of state. Political power is wielded primarily by the prime minister and his cabinet. One of the prominent governmental regimes of this era was that of Prime Minister Phibunsongkhram who obtained the office twice following coups that he led. In promoting Thai nationalism, Phibun initiated the name change from Siam to Thailand in 1939. The Japanese occupied Thailand (1941-1944) which brought about the end of Phibun's first term of office. Pridi Phanomyong, a short-term prime minister, was the principal author of Thailand's first constitution. Sarit Thanarat, an army commander, was prime minister (1957-1963) and promoted major economic development and rural education. He governed successfully as a paternalistic authoritarian.

Politics and the government have generally been in the control of a succession of military cliques. Their control and the frequent coups have long been a controversial issue, but it came to a head in October 1973, when Prime Minister Thanom Kittikachorn was deposed following a violent student-led uprising. A constitution was demanded that would permit democracy in government. During the period 1960-1975, when communism seemed to be expanding in Asia, the United States agreed to assist Thailand. A large amount of economic and military aid was provided. In turn, the United States was permitted to conduct aerial warfare against Vietnam from bases in Thailand.

Considerable political stability existed in Thailand during the long tenure of Prime Minister Prem Tinsulanonda (1980-1988). He was given a prestigious award by King Bhumibol Adulyadej. May 1992 brought another popular and bloody uprising in Bangkok that toppled Prime Minister Suchinda Kraprayoon. Subsequently in 1992, a new law was enacted that requires the prime minister to be an elected representative to the National Assembly. Lack of this provision was the major factor in the opposition to Prime Minister

Suchinda.   There has been a gradual increase in support of democratic institutions in Thailand.   Three elements make for a promising outlook for Thailand. These are Buddhism, pride in the Thai culture and a high regard for the unifying role of the Thai monarchy.

THE DICTIONARY

- A -

เจ้า อาวาส

ABBOT (CHAO AWAT). The head monk of a temple compound *(wat)* (q.v.). His appointment is made at a higher level of the Buddhist monkhood *(sangha)* (q.v.), of which he is a part. He has administrative, custodial, clerical and possibly disciplinary tasks. He selects subordinates, supervises instruction and is responsible for the functioning of the temple in accordance with approved procedures. Buddhism and temple activities have a major role in village life. Thus, the abbot is often a key community leader in village affairs such as road repair, water improvement and agricultural development. Abbots are appointed largely on the basis of their seniority and popularity with laymen and other Buddhist monks (q.v.). Abbots are also found in higher levels of the Buddhist monkhood, and serve as religious administrators of a district (q.v.), province (q.v.) or region (q.v.). These positions correspond with levels of governmental units.

อาจารย์

ACHARN. The title or name for a person employed as a teacher, who holds a bachelor's or advanced degree. According to Thai tradition, teachers are regarded with deference, courtesy and respect. The title may be used similarly for those who possess recognized talent or knowledge or those who engage in public service, which is greatly respected and admired. For example, Buddhist monks, who are unusually knowledgeable, are often addressed as *acharn*.

AGRICULTURAL TECHNOLOGY. Compared to traditional rice (q.v.) farming in small paddies using transplants, rice agriculture (q.v.) in the Central Plain (q.v.) has been largely mechanized. Tractors have replaced water buffalo for power to till the soil. Mechanical pumps have replaced the manual pumps to bring in water. Government irrigation (q.v.) dams and distribution systems are in operation for hundreds of thousands of hectares (1 to 3 million acres), especially in the lower Central Plain. Rice farmers have adopted varieties with high yields and early maturation, which permits double cropping. Fertilizers and herbicides are

1

used also. Increased use of irrigation, new rice varieties and double cropping is characteristic of rice production in northern Thailand as well.

In response to demands, market gardeners near Bangkok (q.v.) and in some areas of northern Thailand are producing a variety of vegetables and fruits. Emphasis on vegetables and fruits is accompanied by the requisite new technology. In northeastern Thailand (q.v.), traditional farming methods are still widely in use.

AGRICULTURE. Approximately two-thirds of the population of Thailand are engaged in farming. In the past two decades, Thai agriculture has shown impressive expansion. It has responded to population growth and to the demand for exports (q.v.). By the early 1980s, nearly all the arable land had been occupied except in the south. Future growth in agriculture must come from improved technology and more intensive cultivation. The main types of agriculture found are cash crops, livestock, poultry and rice (q.v.) grown for subsistence. Small farms of from 2.5 to 7 hectares (6 to 17 acres) is the general pattern of farm operation. Farmers mostly own some land, but usually rent additional land. However, in the cash crop areas of the Central Plain (q.v.) tenancy predominates.

Rice production in Thailand takes up more land than all other crops combined. However, due to market demand, cassava (q.v.), sugar cane, maize, kenaf, coconuts (q.v.), cotton, pineapples and rubber (q.v.) are important crops. Together with rice and fisheries, these crops are major producers of foreign exchange. Livestock production includes poultry and eggs, dairy, buffalo and beef. The proportion that agricultural and livestock products contribute to Gross Domestic Product has been declining. It amounts to approximately 15 percent. This is only a relative decline and reflects the rapid expansion of other sectors of the economy. Total agricultural production continues to increase. (See AGRICULTURAL TECHNOLOGY; LAND TENURE AND TENANCY.)

ALCOHOLIC BEVERAGES. There are several alcoholic beverages native to Thailand that are brewed completely or largely from rice (q.v.). One of these is a whiskey generally called *mekong*. *Hlao khao* is a rice wine that varies in strength according to when and where it is produced. It is very popular with the working classes. Singha beer commands at least 80 percent of the Thai beer market and is well known abroad. Those who can afford the high price drink imported liquors.

ALMS ROUNDS (BINTHABAT). The early morning walk of Buddhist monks (q.v.). In this way the people have an opportunity to give the monks food in a bowl carried for this purpose. Merit (q.v.) is conferred on the donor by the monk's acceptance of the alms. In order for the monks to spend the main part of their time studying the Buddhist scriptures (q.v.), they are not permitted to work for compensation.

AMBHORN (JAYAPANI) MEESOOK, KHUNYING (1920-   ). Daughter of Luang Tong and Tamtong Jayapani Archvicharsarn, she was born in Bangkok (q.v.). Khunying Ambhorn is the first Thai woman to receive a Ph.D. degree in comparative education from Harvard University. She held several senior posts in the Thai Ministry of Education and has contributed professionally in many areas of social development. In 1985, she received an honorary Ph.D. degree in social administration from Thammasat University. In 1992, the UN Food and Agriculture Organization awarded her the Certificate of Merit in recognition of her exceptional services to the needy and the underprivileged. She also received several decorations from King Bhumibol Adulyadej (q.v.). She is married and has three daughters and one son.

AMPHA BHADRANAWIK (1921-   ). The first woman ambassador of Thailand. She joined the Foreign Ministry in 1944. She began her career as third secretary of the royal Thai Embassy in Washington, D.C. In 1967, she became first secretary of the Royal Thai Embassy in Bonn and rose to the post of counsellor and chargé d'affaires, which is a special grade for civil servants. In 1977, she was appointed ambassador to Sri Lanka. During her tenure in Colombo, she was elected president of the Colombo Plan Council for Technical Cooperation in South and Southeast Asia.

AMPHOE. See DISTRICT.

ANAND PANYARACHUN (1932-   ). Business executive, foreign affairs officer, interim prime minister. Anand was educated in Thailand and Britain. He served in the Ministry of Foreign Affairs, 1955-1992, mostly as the Thai representative to the United Nations and as ambassador to Canada and the United States. In business Anand has been chairman of the Saha-Union Corporation, Union Securities Company, Univest Development Company, Pan Asia Footwear Company and Star Block Company. He has also served on the board of directors of several other companies.

Anand's political leadership was recognized at the time of the February 1991 government political crisis. He was named interim prime minister on March 2. Fifteen months later, in June 1992, when another political crisis occurred, he was again called to be interim prime minister until a new election could be held. In both cases, he put together a team of capable cabinet officers and his administrations were seen as quite effective. While he was a highly regarded political leader, he avoided membership in a political party.

ANAT ARBHABHIRAMA (1938-   ). Educator and engineering researcher.   Anat earned a civil engineering degree at Chulalongkorn University. In the United States, he completed a Ph.D. in civil engineering. Anat has been a teacher, researcher and occasional administrator at the Asian Institute of Technology (AIT) in Bangkok (q.v.) since 1966. He advanced to the rank of professor at AIT in 1975. Water resources engineering has been Anat's principal research interest. He has also served for short periods in the cabinets of two prime ministers and on a number of governmental committees dealing with water resources. He was honored as "Outstanding Researcher of the Year" in 1987. He has published numerous articles and papers on water resources and hydraulics.

ANCIENT CITY. The name of a huge outdoor museum at Bang Po which depicts Thailand's history and life-style of the past in a majestic and unique manner. The approximately 75 structures required more than ten years to build at a cost of over 200 million baht (q.v.) ($10 million). The 90 hectares (215 acres) site is located 30 kilometers (19 miles) south of Bangkok (q.v.). The structures at the Ancient City are not only a tourist attraction, they are also a visual reminder to the Thai people of the glory and splendor of the history of their country. Construction of the Ancient City was supervised personally by Lek Wiripun.

ANGKOR. Angkor is the name of an ancient kingdom and its capital which is generally called the Khmer Kingdom. Extensive monumental remains of that kingdom are in what is now Cambodia (q.v.) near the city of Siem Reap. The most famous of these monuments is Angkor Wat (q.v.). In the 13th century, when Angkor was a great city, the Khmer Kingdom controlled the territories of present-day Thailand, Laos (q.v.), Burma (q.v.) and the Malay Peninsula (q.v.). In wars with the Siamese Kingdom of Ayutthaya (q.v.), in the late 14th and early 15th centuries, the Khmer gave up part of their western territory and moved their capital east to Phnom Penh. The city of Angkor was abandoned and became lost in the jungle. It was rediscovered by a French archaeologist in 1861.

ANGKOR WAT. The most famous and extensive of the Khmer (q.v.) temple monuments located near Siem Reap in western Cambodia. It was built in the 12th century by the Khmer King Suryavarman II who ruled from 1113 to 1150. It served as a temple in which he was worshiped as the god Vishnu during his life, and where at his death he was entombed and embodied as Vishnu. The Angkor Wat shrine was for Suryavarman II a Hindu shrine and a microcosm in stone of Khmer cosmology. The central temple represented Mount Meru, the pivot of the world where the gods lived. This Khmer cosmology was of Hindu origin as was the cosmology of Siam (q.v.) and other Southeast Asian kingdoms of the time.

ANIMISM, THAI. Animistic beliefs are convictions of truth based on emotional response to the universe without differentiation between persons and things. The Thai peoples (q.v.), who were animists prior to becoming Buddhists, have retained these beliefs.

In rural areas, and for some city residents, they are an important part of the religious practice that includes propitiation of a variety of spirits. (See PHI CULT.)

ANUMAN RAJADHON (1888-1969). One of Thailand's greatest writers who also had a distinguished career in government service. His writings under the pen name "Sathira Kose" were widely acclaimed; his interests included history, ethnology, philology and archaeology. He authored numerous scholarly publications. Awarded the honorary degree, Doctor of Literature, by Chulalongkorn University, he served on the faculty of Chulalongkorn University in the Fine Arts Department, where he was director-general. He also served in the National Culture Institute and was chairman of the Royal Institute.

ARCHITECTURE. Examples of traditional Thai architecture are readily found in any Buddhist temple compound *(wat)* (q.v.) and at royal palaces, where religious and royal buildings, rectangular in pattern, are constructed in wood. The accentuated sloping roofs were covered with glazed tile in color. The superimposed layers or step-like progression of these roofs are probably the result of additions to the main portion of the building, or protection from sun and rain. At both ends of the ridge of each roof of the religious or royal buildings there is a horn like finial, called *cho fa*, which somewhat resembles a swan's tail. It appears that the *cho fa* is a modification of the horned-mask that can be seen at the end of the roof line of buildings found in Indonesia and parts of the Pacific, where this feature is used for magical or animistic purposes.

Reinforced concrete structures and architectural styles adapted from the West came into wide use in the 20th century, especially in urban areas. High-rise buildings, e.g., hotels and condominiums, dominate the landscape of Bangkok (q.v.) and are prominent in other cities. Efforts to harmonize traditional Thai and modern Western architecture are continuing. (See BOT; CHEDI; MONDOP; PRANG; STUPA; WIHAN.)

ASALHA BUCHA. See BUDDHIST MONKHOOD DAY.

ASIAN AND PACIFIC COUNCIL (ASPAC). A group of nations during the 1960s which cooperated in mutual assistance to safeguard their independence from the communist threat and to develop their respective economies. Thailand was a member, along with Australia, Japan, Malaysia, New Zealand, South Korea, South Vietnam, the Philippines, and Taiwan.

ASSOCIATION OF SOUTHEAST ASIAN NATIONS (ASEAN). An organization, formed in 1967 consisting of Thailand as well as Brunei, Indonesia, Malaysia, the Philippines, and Singapore. Thailand was active in the founding of this association which is intended to promote cooperation in the fields of food production, commerce and industry, civil aviation (q.v.), tourism (q.v.), communications, meteorology, shipping, etc.

ASTROLOGY. The harmony desired between the individual and the cosmos is still sought through the use of astrology in Thai society. The day and hour of many important occasions, such as house warmings, marriages and cremations, are seldom set without consulting an astrologer or a Buddhist monk (q.v.) who will make lunar calculations to ensure an auspicious date. Lucky and unlucky dates vary according to the year, month and birthday of each person. In November, March and July, Tuesday is considered an unlucky day on which to start an important undertaking. Certain specific dates, such as the 13th, 14th and 15th of every lunar month, are lucky or auspicious. Most religious ceremonies are held on the 8th and 15th days of the waxing moon. While belief in astrology is declining, elements of it persist. (See COSMOLOGY.)

AYUTTHAYA (AYUDHAYA), KINGDOM OF. A famous and powerful kingdom of the Tai speaking people. Its capital, Ayutthaya, was situated on the Chao Phraya River (q.v.) in what today is central Thailand (q.v.). The kingdom was founded in 1350 by Ramathibodi I (q.v.) who was the first king (reigned 1350-1969). He firmly established the Buddhist religion (q.v.), compiled a law code and tried to enlarge and unify the kingdom. Within 100 years, Ayutthaya was the strongest power in Southeast Asia. It included a number of partially autonomous areas ruled by relatives of the king who owed him allegiance.

From the Angkor Kingdom (q.v.) concepts of the role of the monarch were adopted. These included notions of the king as (1) having universal power, (2) being a god, and (3) being lord of the land. A special court language called *ratchasap* (q.v.) was developed to be used in conversations with or about royal family members. Agriculture, especially wet-rice (q.v.) production, flourished. Surplus rice was sold abroad and Ayutthaya became a center of economic activity. In the 16th and 17th centuries, contacts with Western nations occurred and focused chiefly on trade.

A major threat to the security of Ayutthaya was the rising power of Burma (q.v.) during the 16th to 18th centuries. In a two-year invasion, Burmese forces in 1767 captured Ayutthaya and its treasures, after which the city was burned and left in ruins. During its more than 400 years of existence, the kingdom had a succession of 33 rulers. Some of the more famous kings were Ramathibodi I (q.v.), Borommatrailokanat (q.v.), Chakraphat (q.v.), Naresuan (q.v.) and Narai (q.v.). (See KINGSHIOP; MONARCHY.)

- B -

BAHT. The monetary unit of the Thai currency is the baht. In a much earlier period, the unit was named the tical. The value of the baht was tied to a selected basket of foreign currencies in 1984. The exchange rate in 1994 was approximately U.S. $1 = 25 baht.

BALANCE OF PAYMENTS. In recent years, the excess of annual merchandise imports over exports (q.v.) has varied between $2 billion and $7 billion. During the same period, the value of services exported and other transfers annually has exceeded service imports varying from 10 percent to 33 percent. Thus, a positive balance of payments has been maintained. For the early 1990s, Thai international reserves increased and were chiefly in foreign exchange.

BAMBOO. Various species of bamboo are found in Thailand. The plant may be low and climbing or, more commonly, tall and tree-like. The stalks are round, jointed and hollow. In many places bamboo is used as wood for construction, furniture, utensils, fiber, fuel, paper and innumerable small articles. Bamboo sprouts are eaten as a vegetable, and the grain of some species is also utilized for food.

BAN. The traditional name for a grouping of families and individuals, their adjacent places of residence in a given locality and a ritual community centered on a Buddhist temple compound *(wat)* (q.v.) or other religious structure, which contains a shrine dedicated to venerated spirits. Mutual cooperation in religious practices enhances the villagers sense of belonging to a moral as well as a social community. In central Thailand, instead of *ban*, the term *bang* is sometimes used. For example, Bang Kla is the name of a small municipality just east of Bangkok (q.v.), which is located on the Bang Pakong River. Bang Kla was previously a village, whose growth in population changed its status to municipality. But the word *ban* also means house. To overcome this ambiguity, the central government uses the term *muban* (q.v.) to refer to a so-called village administrative unit. However, the *muban* does not necessarily coincide with the village as a ritual community. For each *muban* a headman is typically elected. His role in village life is defined in terms of government concerns rather than according to village interests. Above the *muban* is the *tambon* which is the name of an administrative unit for several (sometimes ten to 15) adjacent *muban*. The headman or leader of a *tambon* is called a *kamnan* (q.v.) and receives a small monthly salary.

BAN CHIANG. Name of a village and archaeological complex in northeastern Thailand where there have been prehistoric finds of great importance. There is evidence of rice (q.v.) production, forging of bronze implements and a distinctive pottery dating back as early as 3000 BC. If the dating of these finds is fully confirmed, the Khorat Plateau could be the first rice producing area in Asia. In addition, the discovery of bronze production at Ban Chiang challenges the previous traditional view that the invention of bronze occurred only once and that was supposedly in the Middle East about 2800 BC.

BAN KEO. An important archaeological site in Kanchana Buri Province. Signs of prehistoric dwellings were sighted by Mr. Van Heekeren, a Dutch prisoner of World War II, who was forced to work on the Kwai River Railway. In 1961, a Thai-Danish expedition conducted systematic research here. Skeletons, fine pottery, animal bones and various objects dating from 2000 BC (Neolithic period) indicated that the settlement belonged to the Lung Shan civilization originating in north China.

BAN KON YANG. A large village of Karen (q.v.) hill people in Lamphun Province. This mountain group is one of the most advanced. The dress of both men and women, their craft products, and the design and decoration of their houses attract many tourists.

BAN MEO. A village and community development center in Phitsanulok Province which was established to encourage the settlement of the Meo (q.v.) hill tribes (q.v.).

BANGKOK (KRUNG THEP). The largest city and capital of Thailand. This former village became prominent in 1782 when it was chosen by King Rama I (q.v.) as the site of his capital. It is the seat of the national government. The Bangkok metropolitan area is the center of international travel, tourism (q.v.), industrial production, foreign trade, transportation, location of government ministries and agencies, the press, radio (q.v.), television (q.v.), publishing (q.v.), banking and insurance, and the headquarters of the labor unions (q.v.).

The development of Bangkok economically has been due in large part to the Chinese (q.v.) who migrated to Thailand by the hundreds of thousands during the 100 years prior to World War II. They became the retailers, traders, bankers and investors and still are the most prominent group of persons in Thai economic life. Today, with its United Nations (q.v.) agencies, a prosperous economy, and an active group of foreign embassies, Bangkok may be seen as a world capital.

The maze of canals crisscrossing the city initially have gradually been paved over for streets. However, the loss of the canals as drains accentuates travel problems during the annual floods. The national airport, Don Muang (q.v.), is Bangkok's only airport which must handle both domestic and international air traffic. Construction of express highways is unable to cope with the increase in city motor vehicle traffic. As much as 80 percent of the country's automobiles are in the Bangkok area. The city's congestion and air pollution is a serious problem. In a sense, Bangkok is a paradox since the old is retained and the new is accepted. The more than 200 Buddhist religious temple compounds *(wat)* (q.v.) having a traditional Thai architecture (q.v.) vie for attention with tall modern hotels, office buildings, condominiums, futuristic cinemas and modern shopping centers.

BANGKOK METROPOLIS. A special unit of government, created in 1971 to combine Bangkok (q.v.) and the Province of Thonburi, which is located on the opposite (west) bank of the Chao Phraya River (q.v.). This large unit has a population in excess of 6 million. Since 1975, the city metropolitan government includes a governor (q.v.), four deputy governors and a 41-person assembly, all elected by popular vote. Bangkok in population is approximately 25 times the size of the next largest city of the nation. In some ways, Bangkok is a "Thailand" that is both separate and largely dominant over the rest of the country. Unique tasks of government led to the creation of the Bangkok Metropolis. Bangkok has reflected a mixed economy with both state enterprises and successful private entrepreneurs. However, the metropolitan area is confronted with needs such as improvements in the water system, sewage disposal and health care.

BANKS. See FINANCIAL SYSTEM.

BANYAN TREE. An East Indian fig tree, whose branches send out adventitious roots to the ground, sometimes causing the tree to spread out over a wide area. In Thailand, as in the rest of Southeast Asia, the banyan tree is considered a sacred tree as it is the usual abode of spirits. A well-known grove of banyan trees is located near Pimai (q.v.).

BARNHARN SILPA-ARCHA (1932-   ).   Thailand's 21st prime minister, after his Thai Nation party won the most seats in the general election in July, 1995. Barnharn, known as one of the consummate deal makers in Thai politics, was born in the central province of Supan Buri. Having made his fortune in the construction business, he entered politics in 1974 and two years later, won his first seat in parliament. In 1991, he became an interior minister in the national administration. When the Thai army staged a coup, alleging widespread corruption, Barnharn and other key members of the government were accused of wrong doing. His assets were seized as were those of unusually wealthy individuals. Later, a commitee appointed by the military, stated that there was insufficient evidence and ordered the assets returned.   Barnharn remains highly popular in his home town province of Supan Buri. He is praised for building good roads and schools, many of which are named after him, as well as hospitals and other services. He has pledged to improve Bangkok's traffic problems, to promote Thailand's growth as a regional trade and communications center, to further political reform and to encourage distribution of wealth.

BAYINNAUNG. King of Burma (1551-1581) who led the Burmese conquest of Siam (q.v.) in 1569. That Bayinnaung was a strong monarch is indicated by his success in unifying, through military conquest, the former city states of Pegu, Arakan and Ava in Burma together with the former Mon (q.v.) Kingdom and Shan States. Following his military success in the north, his suzerainty was extended over the Lan Na Kingdom (q.v.). From all of these territories, Bayinnaung was able to assemble a huge army for an invasion of central Siam (q.v.). In 1568, he led an assault against the Kingdom of Ayutthaya (q.v.). It ended in the defeat of the Siamese (q.v.) forces under the weak King Mahin and the capture of and sacking of Ayutthaya, the capital, in 1569. Mahathammaracha (q.v.), who as governor of Phitsanulok had assisted the king in Burma in his campaigns, was installed as the vassal king of Thailand. In 1574, Bayinnaung was successful also in capturing Vientiane, the Kingdom of Lan Xang. (See NARESUAN.)

BETEL (MAAG). A masticatory made from slices of betel palm seeds usually spread on a betel pepper leaf together with other flavorings, particularly lime paste. Betel, a mild narcotic, is chewed widely throughout Asia and Oceania, especially by older women. Chewing betel has been extremely popular from the Sukhothai period to the 19th century. Habitual chewing results in red-stained lips, darkened teeth, distorted jaws and constant ejections of red spittle by the betel chewer. Chewers claim that it alleviates hunger, cures stomach problems and preserves the teeth. The habit was officially banned in Thailand in 1945.

BHIKKHU. See BUDDHIST MONK.

BHUMIBOL ADULYADEJ. Present king of Thailand (1946-). A grandson of King Chulalongkorn (q.v.), he was born in 1927 in Massachusetts, where his father, Prince Mahidol of Songkhla (1884-1929), was studying medicine at Harvard. He became king upon the death of Ananda Mahidol, his older brother, in 1946. He continued his studies in Switzerland and was crowned king in an official ceremony in May 1950. A week earlier, he married Mom Rajawongse Sirikit (q.v.). She was officially named queen on the day of the coronation. The principal residence of the royal family is at Chitra La Da Palace in Bangkok (q.v.). The royal couple have four offsprings. Their only son is Crown Prince Vajiralongkorn (q.v.). They have three daughters, Princess Ubolratana (q.v.), Crown Princess Siridhorn (q.v.) and Princess Chulabhorn (q.v.).

To advise him in his official duties, the king looks to the Privy Council (q.v.) and for day-to-day affairs he relies on His Majesty's Private Secretariat and on the Office of the Royal Household. The king does not have authority to issue decrees or to veto actions of the Thai National Assembly (q.v.). However, he does occasionally have indirect influence since all matters of governmental administration are done in the name of the king. Similarly, all draft laws are submitted to the king before promulgation. Among his other duties are presiding at state ceremonies and formal functions. He dispatches and receives envoys to and from friendly nations. At graduation ceremonies, he presents university diplomas, or swords to graduates of military academies. He also invests all officers of the Armed Forces who attain the rank of general or its equivalent.

The king is popular with the Thai people. He, Queen Sirikit and others of the royal family have a reputation for their concern for victims of natural disasters, the poor people, and policemen/soldiers injured while performing their regular duties. King Bhumibol has pioneered in contacts with the Thai population in the provinces and in helping them to feel they are part of the nation. These contacts are facilitated by the royal family's use of official residences in five upcountry provinces. Bhumibol has initiated hundreds of development projects relative to plants, animals and water control in widely scattered places in Thailand.

The king has on occasion played an important role in times of crisis and political instability. During the October 14, 1973 student-led uprising (q.v.), the king met with both student and government leaders. He participated in securing new government leadership. Later, support of the monarchy (q.v.) in crises in 1976, 1981 and 1992 made a difference. Regard for the monarchy had declined by the close of the reign of King Prajadhipok (Rama VII) (q.v.). Under Bhumibol, the present king, the Thai monarch has again become a source of national pride, a symbol of national unity and a central pillar of the nation.

Among the king's hobbies and skills are his achievements in music. He plays the piano and at least five other musical instruments (q.v.). He has composed songs and ballads which are widely played and sung in Thailand. On the 42nd anniversary of the king's coronation, he received the title of King Bhumibol Adulyadej the Great at a ceremony conducted by the prime minister. This honor was bestowed previously on Rama I (q.v.) and Chulalongkorn (Rama V) (q.v.).

BILAUKTAUNG RANGE. A mountain range 500 to 1,500 meters (1,600 to 4,900 feet) high along the boundary between southwestern Thailand and southeastern lower Burma.

BINTHABAT. See ALMS ROUNDS.

BODHISATTVA. One destined to become Buddha (q.v.); a person who has achieved enlightenment but defers achieving nirvana (q.v.) in order to help others achieve it.

BORDERS, NATIONAL. Thailand has a perimeter of approximately 4,500 kilometers (2,800 miles) which borders on four countries. It also has 2,000 kilometers (1,250 miles) of coast line on the Gulf of Thailand (Gulf of Siam), the Andaman Sea and the Strait of Malacca. The longest borders are with Burma (q.v.) on the west and north, and Laos (q.v.) in the northeast. Thailand also shares borders with Cambodia (q.v.) on the southeast and with Malaysia (q.v.) in the south. The nation's boundaries are not well marked except for a short stretch of the western border with Burma, marked by the Salween River, and about 900 kilometers (560 miles) of the northeastern border with Laos, defined by the Mekong River (q.v.). Boundary lines are generally respected by the population although certain mountain groups along the border in northern Thailand and the Lao people along the Mekong River in the northeast (q.v.) pay little attention to border-crossing formalities.

BOROMMAKOT. King of Ayutthaya (reigned 1733-1758). Borommakot came to the throne after a successful battle with the sons of the previous king. The Kingdom of Ayutthaya (q.v.) was strong and prosperous during most of his 25- year reign. As king, he increased the number of departments handling governmental affairs. This reduced the chances that any one department head would have enough power to seize the throne. Borommakot won acclaim for (1) his support of Buddhism (q.v.), (2) better control over territories which today are part of Cambodia, and (3) renewed cooperative relations with Burma (q.v.). However, Burma, under a new king, invaded the Kingdom of Ayutthaya five years after Borommakot's death.

BOROMMATRAILOKANAT. King of Ayutthaya (reigned 1431 1488), also known as Trailok. He was an important monarch in the history of his nation. On assuming the kingship (q.v.),

Ayutthaya (q.v.) had expanded the kingdom's territories considerably which called for improvement in administration. Trailok fashioned new laws which delineated a very complex hierarchical society. These laws specified the place and position of every individual. They also divided the governmental administration into civil or the Mahatthai (q.v.) and military or the Kalahom (q.v.). Under each were various subdivisions. For each unit, functions were specified so that all persons in the nation were attached to a department for compulsory labor service.

Government officials in Trailok's reign received no salary. To provide an income for them and to regulate the system of land tenure, he instituted the *sakdi na* (q.v.) which established a system for all able-bodied men to provide labor for each unit of government. These laws of Trailok, while modified, guided the nation's government officials for nearly four centuries. War with King Tilokaracha (q.v.) of Lan Na (q.v.) occupied Trailok throughout his reign.

BOT (UBOSOT). The most important building in the temple compound *(wat)* (q.v.). In this building, situated within a consecrated area, the monks assemble for ordination (q.v.) and other religious rites as well as for disciplinary affairs peculiar to the Buddhist monastic order. (See BUDDHISM; BUDDHIST MONK.)

BOWARADET REBELLION. In October 1933, one year after the Revolution of 1932 (q.v.), which ended the absolute monarchy (q.v.) in Thailand, a counter-revolution occurred. It was led by General Prince Bowaradet and some retired Thai army officers, who sought to restore the power of the monarchy. Military forces led by General Prince Bowaradet advanced on Bangkok (q.v.) from the north, but they were defeated by other forces led by Captain Phibunsongkhram (q.v.). The rebellion was one of the most violent events in modern Thai history. The defeat of the Bowaradet rebellion meant a consolidation of power by those who promoted the Revolution of 1932.

BOWRING, SIR JOHN (1792-1872). British author, editor and statesman. While governor of Hong Kong, he was appointed envoy to Siam (q.v.). When in Bangkok (q.v.), he negotiated with King Mongkut (q.v.) who was aware of Britain's lack of tolerance for defiance. This was shown by the successful British wars with Burma and with China in the Opium Wars. (See BOWRING TREATY.)

BOWRING TREATY. A treaty of Friendship and Commerce executed by Great Britain and Thailand in April 1855, which contained terms favorable to Great Britain. King Mongkut (q.v.) and Sir John Bowring (q.v.) were the chief negotiators. For the first time, Thailand granted major extraterritorial privileges to a foreign power. British subjects were exempted from the jurisdiction of Siamese (q.v.) authorities. They were also given privileges of trade, residence, property ownership and travel. The Bowring Treaty was the forerunner of similar treaties concluded with 12 other Western trading nations within the following 15 years.

BRAHMANISM. The name for certain Indian religio-cultural patterns adopted by Thai kings in the Ayutthaya (q.v.) period. Brahmanic influences on the Thai monarchy (q.v.) resulted in large part from the capture of Khmer (q.v.) prisoners of war, including artisans and high officials. The concept of the king as *deva raja* or god-king was adopted in the 15th century by kings of Ayutthaya. While the idea apparently came from Cambodia, it was already widespread in Southeast Asia at that time. The *deva raja* concept made the Thai king an object of cult conducted by royal Brahmans, who became officials in the king's retinue. In the Bangkok period (since 1782), the concept declined in favor of other kingship (q.v.) concepts. Other Brahmanic religious patterns found in Thai culture include ghosts, spirits and gods of various ranks.

BRIDGE ON THE RIVER KWAI. The notorious railway bridge in Kanchana Buri Province which was built as a link between Bangkok (q.v.) and Burma by the forced labor of Allied prisoners and foreign slaves during World War II. The work was harshly supervised by the Japanese military forces which had taken over Thailand. Thousands of prisoners and slaves who died in the effort are interred in Kanchana Buri War Cemetery (q.v.) on the outskirts of Kanchana Buri City. The story of this event has been depicted in both literature and film.

BUDDHA. The name attached to Siddhartha Gautama, a native of southern Nepal (ca. 563-483 BC), and leader of a movement which founded Buddhism (q.v.). Following a period of asceticism, penance and meditation in the Indian jungle, Gautama claimed he had found peace in the truth of life's unreality and in the necessity of causing the cessation of the desire to live. Gautama asserted that he became Buddha, the Enlightened One. For 45 years he taught and preached as he traveled and developed an order of monks among his followers.

BUDDHA GAYA. The place where the Buddha (q.v.) received enlightenment, located in Bihar, India. There is a temple and the bo tree under which Buddha is said to have received enlightenment.

BUDDHA IMAGES. Numbering in the millions, images of the Buddha (q.v.) appear in all sizes throughout Thailand as objects of veneration and worship in homes, temple compounds *(wat)* (q.v.), schools, offices and numerous other places. They are borne in processions, used as talismans and pendants. They are made of bronze or other metal amalgams and occasionally of stone. Small images may be of gold, silver, brass, crystal or glass. During the reign of King Rama III, it was decided that 40 different postures of the Buddha could be recognized. Images have been cast of each of these postures and are now kept in the museum room of Wat Phra Keo (q.v.). Generally, the "enlightenment" posture is reflected in Buddha images. In this posture, the Buddha sits cross-legged with the left hand open on the lap and the right hand resting on the right knee with fingers turned downward. The best known large golden image of the Buddha is one dating from the Sukhothai period enshrined at Wat Trimit (q.v.) in Bangkok (q.v.). It weighs approximately five metric tons. (See SCULPTURE, RELIGIOUS.)

BUDDHADASA BHIKKU (1906-1993). A widely admired and respected theologian. The Suan Mokh Meditation Center near Chaiya in Surat Thani Province of southern Thailand was developed under his leadership. The Center grew to 50 or more monks (q.v.) in residence. Buddhadasa has been a critic of those Thai Buddhists who use religion for personal and worldly benefit. For example, the Buddhist emphasis is on "merit making" or preoccupation with the externals of religious rituals and ceremonies in order to better oneself in the world. Buddhadasa taught that the foregoing was not only useless, but led one away from genuine religious practice. These criticisms have resulted in making him a controversial figure. (See MERIT-DEMERIT.)

Buddhadasa has offered a comprehensive and influential interpretation of Theravada Buddhism (q.v.) for today's devotees. The originality of his thought system has been seen as stemming from a profound understanding of Buddhist concepts. Buddhadasa's teachings have been collected and published in almost 50 volumes that include his lectures as well as his written work. Only a few of these writings have been translated into English. However, one that became available in 1971 is *Toward the Truth.*

BUDDHISM. A major world religion founded by Siddhartha Gautama, who after a period as an ascetic declared that he had achieved "enlightenment" and that he was Buddha (q.v.). He died in 483 BC. The year of his enlightenment, 543 BC, was the official beginning of the Buddhist Era (BE). There are two main divisions of Buddhist teaching and thought. Thai Buddhism exemplifies the Hinayana or Theravada school. Its scriptures are the Pali (q.v.) Canon sometimes called the Narrow Way of Salvation or The Way of the Elders. Nirvana (q.v.) is possible only for the few who withdraw and devote themselves wholly to religious matters. The existence of a god or an individual soul is denied. Theravada Buddhism is also followed in Burma, Laos, Cambodia and Sri Lanka. A second school--Mahayana Buddhism--uses the Sanskrit (q.v.) interpretation of Buddha's teachings, and is sometimes called the Broad Way of Salvation. It holds that all laymen as well as ascetics have an equal chance of gaining nirvana and that there are pure souls in paradise and numerous successions of Buddha. Mahayana Buddhism is followed in China (q.v.), Japan, Nepal, Korea, Vietnam and by many Chinese in Thailand.

Propagation of Buddhism depends on a monastic system. In Thailand this is the Buddhist monkhood called *sangha* (q.v.) in which traditionally all men were to spend at least one rainy season retreat (q.v.) in studying the scriptures and living the life of an ascetic. The Thai government cooperates with the Buddhist monkhood providing financial assistance, protection and concessions to traveling monks, and promotes monastic education and aids in Buddhist teaching in the Thai schools. The literature and mural art of Thailand have drawn heavily on various tales from the life of Buddha. Laymen are also active in the propagation of Buddhism through the Buddhist Association and the Young Buddhist Association (q.v.).

Some of the ways that Thai Buddhism has departed from Gautama Buddha's teaching include (1) Regard for the Buddha as God or a messenger of God which implies a belief in God or that Buddha was a god who still lives. The offering of prayers to Buddha reflect such attitudes--all of which are a repudiation of the Buddhist catechism. (2) The widespread retention in Thai religion of spirit worship and animism (q.v.) as evidenced in spirit shrines everywhere, and clerical sprinkling of holy or lustral water. (3) Almost universal emphasis on fun-loving and pleasure-seeking activities by the Thai people who value that which makes them happy or *sanuk* (q.v.). This is the opposite of Gautama Buddha's injunction to extirpate all longing for happiness. (4) The recent efforts in Thailand to develop a sense of nationality and political individuality. In fact, the nation's leaders are looking to Buddhism and the Buddhist monkhood as allies in developing the country's resources, in improving living standards and the well-being of the Thai people. But these are things from which Gautama Buddha taught people to free themselves. Buddhism is the predominant religion in Thailand. It is reported that 94 percent of the population profess to be Buddhists. (See DHARMA; ETHICS OF THAI BUDDHISM; KARMA; MERIT-DEMERIT; PRECEPTS; THREE FUNDAMENTAL PRINCIPLES; THREE GEMS; WHEEL OF THE LAW.)

BUDDHIST ALL SAINTS DAY (MAKHA BUCHA). Buddhist All Saints Day commemorates the miracles which occurred just prior to the death of the Buddha (q.v.). At that time Buddha gave an assembly of 1,250 disciples the many rules (Patimokkha [q.v.]) which Buddhist monks (q.v.) are expected to follow. Celebration of this event, which is also a national holiday, occurs on the day of the full moon in the third lunar month. Merit-making (q.v.) activities include releasing caged birds, burning incense and an evening procession around the chapel *(bot)* (q.v.) in the Buddhist temple compound *(wat)* (q.v.) with devotees carrying lighted candles. The anniversary of the founding of the Thai Buddhist Association is also celebrated on this day.

BUDDHIST LENT (KHAO PHANSA or KHAO VASSA). The three-month period starting the day after the full moon of the eighth month, when many young Thai males temporarily enter the temple compound *(wat)* (q.v.). During this time, they engage in intensive religious activities and become familiar with the ascetic life of a Buddhist monk (q.v.). This experience has been regarded traditionally as a type of desired maturation. The first day of Lent is a national holiday and is accompanied by much merit-making by the Buddhist laity. Buddhist Lent is also referred to as the "Rainy Season Retreat (q.v.)."

BUDDHIST MONK (BHIKKHU). A man who renounces at least temporarily the ordinary world and accepts an ascetic role of self-denial, discipline and study of the scriptures of Buddhism (q.v.). The first step in becoming a monk is the rite of ordination (q.v.), which typically occurs in June or July prior to Buddhist Lent (q.v.). Most Thai men who complete the ordination ceremony expect to be monks for the three month period of Buddhist Lent or for a shorter period. Other men see the role of monk as a career and remain in that status for one or a few years or for a lifetime. Becoming a Buddhist monk *(bhikkhu)* or novice *(nen)* (q.v.), is the most meritorious act of renunciation because merit (q.v.) is accumulated not only by the monk or novice but also by his father, mother, sponsor (if any) and others who assist in his ordination ceremony. Traditionally, all Thai males were expected to assume this ascetic role for at

least one Rainy Season Retreat (q.v.). Today, less than half of
the Thai males fulfill this religious obligation. In the urban areas
of Thailand and in southern Thailand, there is a pattern whereby
young men become monks for a short period of time, usually two
weeks. In northern Thailand, most become ordained as novices
(nen), while elsewhere most new ordainees are monks.

Monks and novices learn and recite regularly the rules
regulating their behavior (patimokkha [q.v.]). In principle, monks
are not parish priests but monastics who live a life of self-denial
and discipline, who study the Buddhist scriptures (q.v.) and who
are responsible for the property and rites of the Buddhist
monkhood. Their duty to the laity is primarily that of imparting
knowledge of the *dharma* (q.v.) or the teaching of Buddhism.
The monkhood is also one of the Three Gems (q.v.) to which the
laity can go for spiritual betterment. Next to the king, monks are
the most honored and respected persons in Thai society.

While the monk's ascetic and monastic roles are emphasized
in Buddha's (q.v.) teachings, his pastoral service role is important
also. It is the latter which brings respect, prestige and continued
material support of the laity. The monk is not permitted to work
for compensation. Rather, he obtains food from daily alms
rounds (q.v.) and food plus other materials from the numerous
merit-making ceremonies that occur at the temple compound
(wat) (q.v.) where he centers his life. At the same time, the laity
need the monks in order to receive merit (q.v.) and to live in
accordance with the precepts of Buddhism. Both monks and
novices play a major role in the religious life as well as the
secular life of the community. They help to preserve social
stability by their example of patience and serenity. They may
give counsel in answer to various inquiries, act as arbiters in
personal quarrels or provide safekeeping for villagers' savings.
Many of the larger temple compounds offer *dharma* courses and
other studies for the monks, who advance in status upon
completing their exams successfully. The rank of the monk is
indicated on his decorated fan of red or gold cloth.

Today, some monks act as moral mentors, psychological
counselors, personal and social advisors. These progressive
monks are named "development monks" *(phra pattana)*. They
also undertake community work, such as the construction of

roads, digging of wells, and setting up of cooperative programs and day-care centers. They also set up credit unions to encourage saving among villagers, particularly among school-aged children and youth. In addition they give advice on agricultural problems and domestic issues, such as gambling and alcoholism. They play a leading role in the development of community programs in the poorer areas of the country. Laymen show their respect for monks by addressing them as *phra* (q.v.), or holy one. (See BUDDHISM; BUDDHIST LENT; KATHIN; NEO-BUDDHISM.)

BUDDHIST MONKHOOD (SANGHA). The Thai national order of Buddhist monks (q.v.), or Buddhist monkhood, which also includes novices (q.v.) as junior members. The membership is estimated to include 250,000 during the Rainy Season Retreat (q.v.), when many young men enter the organization for a period of up to three months. Others join for one or a few years while still others make the *sangha* their life career. The organizational basis of Thai Buddhism (q.v.) is the *sangha* whose members have the task of preserving the *dharma* (q.v.) through study, teaching and pastoral services to the laity. The member monks and novices are enabled to carry out religious duties and affairs as a result of the material support provided by laymen who, in exchange for their alms (q.v.), receive merit (q.v.) which is highly valued. The *sangha* has a hierarchical structure which closely parallels that of the civil government and maintains supervision and discipline of the members. The supreme patriarch (q.v.) or head of the *sangha*, appointed by the king, is assisted by a number of councils composed of high-ranking monks. (See ABBOT; SUPREME PATRIARCH.)

BUDDHIST MONKHOOD DAY (ASALHA BUCHA). Buddhist Monkhood Day commemorates the Buddha's (q.v.) sermon to his first five disciples. It is celebrated at the full moon of the eighth lunar month. This holy day was established in 1958 by the Buddhist monkhood *(sangha)* (q.v.) and adds significance to Buddhist Lent (q.v.) which commences the following day. The celebration includes chants by the monks (q.v.) and a sermon.

BUDDHIST SCRIPTURES (TIPITAKA). The three baskets of the law of Theravada Buddhism (q.v.), written in Pali (q.v.) and arranged in three parts or *tipitaka*. It consists of the rules and regulations for the conduct of Buddhist monks (q.v.), discourses and sermons supposedly of the Buddha (q.v.), and supplementary explanatory treatises. (See BUDDHISM.)

BUDDHIST TEMPLE COMPOUND (WAT). Buddhist religious center consisting of a small or large complex of buildings. Buddhist monks (q.v.) are typically present, in which case the center could be called a monastery. There are more than 17,000 Buddhist temple compounds in Thailand, and their importance for religious and community activities is very great. Among the buildings in the temple compound, the temple *(bot)* (q.v.) for the use of the monks is the most important, next is the people's temple *(wihan)* (q.v.). These two structures are similar in architectural design. If a temple compound contains a celebrated Buddha image (q.v.), it will be located in the temple used by the monks. On an altar in the people's temple, there will be any number of Buddha images. The temple compound may include one or more *sala* which are rest houses of simple construction. They are used for visiting, local meetings and as places to sleep overnight.

The village temple compound is typically the first place in the village to have indoor plumbing, a television set and various other amenities, if they are available at all. Thus, the temple compound is frequently a window on Thai society beyond the village. Temple facilities are often a contribution by wealthy patrons from urban centers whose gifts are a convenient way for the giver to make merit (q.v.). Many larger temple compounds have a library *(ho trai)* for housing the books and manuscripts used in Buddhist studies. Nearly all temple compounds have one or more religious monuments. Besides its use for religious services and events, the temple compound is the site for fairs, festivals, marriages, funerals and other public events. Other functions found within the temple compound include counseling, providing a news center, safe keeping of funds and caring for the aged or sick. Supervision of the temple compound is in the hands of the chief monk abbot (q.v.). He is assisted by other monks and lay leaders. (See BOT; BUDDHIST MONK; CHEDI; KAMMAKAN WAT; WIHAN.)

BUNGBANGFAI. See ROCKET FESTIVAL.

BUNNAG FAMILY. Several immigrants and their descendants who were economic and political leaders in the Siamese (q.v.) royal government. They served from the 1600s well into the 20th century. Two Persians, Shiekh Ahmad and his brother, took Siamese (q.v.) wives. The former was appointed by the king of Siam (q.v.) to be in charge of the agency that dealt with Muslim traders. In time, he rose to head one of the major government ministries. With Ahmad's commercial skills, the king was better able to exploit the income potential of foreign trade. Sheikh Ahmad's son and his subsequent descendants, as well as the descendants of Ahmad's brother, continued in strategic government roles. The Bunnag name was taken in the early 19th century when one of the above descendants, Mahasena (Bunnag) had a mother who was the queen's sister. He controlled a major government ministry as did his son Dit Bunnag. Dit's son Suriyawong (q.v.) was a powerful official in Siam from 1851 to 1883, in the reigns of King Mongkut (q.v.) and King Chulalongkorn (q.v.). Another of Dit's sons, Kham Bunnag, was also a high government official, a diplomat and historian.

BUPPHA NIMMANHEIMIN (pseudonym DOKMAI SOT). The leading Siamese (q.v.) novelist of the pre-World War II period. Buppha was the author of 11 novels and numerous short stories. A central concern of Buppha was the moral choices that Siamese people face due to the conflict of their traditional values with those of the West. This theme was especially prominent in her novel *Her Enemy*, which appeared in 1929. One critic referred to Buppha's novels as containing religious discourses in disguise.

BURMA, RELATIONS WITH. Historically, the relations between Burma and Thailand involved more conflict than cooperation. Burma established diplomatic relations with Thailand on August 24, 1948. Since the Indochina crisis following the Vietnamese invasion of Cambodia (q.v.) in 1978, both countries improved their relations for domestic and regional security. Political tensions between the two countries are caused by the various dissident groups living along both sides of the Thai-Burmese border. Conflicts in the economic areas are related to the problems of smuggling Thai goods, drug trafficking in the Golden Triangle (q.v.), illegal immigration, and fisheries. On September 18, 1988 the Burmese military crackdown of mass demonstrations forced thousands of dissident students to flee as refugees to areas along the Thai border controlled by ethnic rebels. A Foreign Investment Law decreed on November 30, 1988 granted timber and fishing concessions to Thai firms and opened border trade with China (q.v.) and Thailand. In April 1993, the Thai Cabinet agreed to open 14 temporary border crossings to facilitate importation of logs from Burma. The opening of trade and border crossings has facilitated the rise in trafficking of Burmese men, women and children, with the same routes used to transport people as used to transport drugs and goods. Thai generals have maintained close links with Rangoon since Burma's State Law and Order Restoration Council (SLORC) took power in 1988. (See BAYINNAUNG; HSINBYUSHIN; LAN NA; MYANMAR; NARESUAN; TAKSIN.)

BUSINESS ASSOCIATIONS: THEIR POLITICAL ROLE. A marked increase in the number and importance of business associations is a significant recent development in Thailand. In promoting their collective interests, business organizations are now active politically and have contributed to the economic development (q.v.) of the nation. Since the mid-1970s, Chambers of Commerce (q.v.) grew from four to 72 while Trade Associations (q.v.) increased from 75 to more than 175. Also new are Organizations that Represent Business as a Whole (q.v.), Employers Associations and Foreign Chambers of Commerce (q.v.). Cooperation between government and business is becoming institutionalized through the Joint Public and Private Sector Consultative Committees (JPPCCs [q.v.]).

The large number and strength of business associations is indicative of a gradual change in Thai political institutions. Perhaps it is no longer correct to characterize the Thai governmental system (q.v.) as controlled by a military-bureaucratic elite. The autonomous and effective business organizations are able to initiate, modify or prevent policy introductions in the National Assembly (q.v.). Another indication of this change is the inclusion of business representatives on numerous government committees. Some elected members of the Assembly and some cabinet (q.v.) officers come with a background in business also.

- C -

CABINET. See COUNCIL OF MINISTERS.

CAMBODIA, RELATIONS WITH. The small Southeast Asian nation of Cambodia, on Thailand's eastern border, has had a history closely linked to that of Thailand. One of the earliest human settlements developed in what today is Cambodia and the ancient Khmer Kingdom of Angkor (q.v.) was centered there. Prior to 1860, for most of a century, portions of what is present-day Cambodia were a part of Siam (q.v.) and the Cambodia of that time was a vassal of Siam paying tribute. When, in the 1860s, Cambodia became a colony of France, Siam was forced by French military pressure to give up areas it previously claimed.

Cambodia has been and continues to be an important trading partner of Thailand, although there were interruptions in periods of political instability and civil war. Internal conflict in Cambodia and the Communist takeover in 1975 caused Thailand to strengthen its eastern military defenses. Thailand faced additional threats associated with the Vietnamese invasion and subjugation of Cambodia in 1979. Both events brought about a massive inflow of refugees (q.v.) to Thailand. During 1980-1982, thousands of refugees from Laos (q.v.) and Cambodia were expelled. Factional violence in Cambodia in the late 1980s brought another wave of refugees which the United Nations helped to care for. In 1988-1990 Thai government officials arranged conferences in an attempt to bring about a peaceful settlement among the Cambodian political factions. Finally, in November 1991, an agreement between Thailand, Cambodia and the United Nations provided for repatriation of more than 300,000 refugees.

CASSAVA. A starchy root crop cultivated mainly in southeastern Thailand and also in parts of the northeast (q.v.). The tuber roots when boiled are eaten as a vegetable. Cassava is used domestically and in foreign countries in the refined forms of flour, meal, tapioca and tapioca products. Cassava has been important as an export crop since the 1950s and export demand has increased. Total exports (q.v.) recently have been second only to that of Brazil. European countries are a major market.

CATHOLICISM. In Thailand, adherents of the Roman Catholic faith together with other Christians represent less than one percent of the population. Catholicism was first introduced in Thailand in 1606 by missionaries from Portugal. The number of Catholic adherents is estimated to be 240,000 which is about 75 percent of all Thai Christians. They are found chiefly in Bangkok (q.v.) and northern Thailand. The Catholic congregations are administered by two archdioceses and eight dioceses. There is an active Catholic Association in Thailand, a number of Catholic operated hospitals, and more than 100 parochial elementary and/or secondary schools.

CENTRAL PLAIN. The region of Thailand consisting of the alluvial plain of the Chao Phraya River (q.v.), its tributaries and a surrounding piedmont belt. The central Plain was originally the principal area of settlement of Tai-language (q.v.) speakers, later known as the central Thai, who have been in control of all or part of the area since the 13th century. The central Plain contains fertile soils and the nation's main concentration of agriculture (q.v.). The large lowlands are overlaid with fertile silt deposited by flooding from the Chao Phraya and the lesser Meklong (q.v.) and Bang Pakong Rivers. The delta plain north of Bangkok (q.v.) is intensively cultivated chiefly for rice (q.v.) but for other grain crops as well.

The Bangkok metropolis (q.v.), which includes Chon Buri, and is the nation's capital and the largest urban area, is on the central Plain. Other important cities include Ayutthaya (q.v.),

Chon Buri (q.v.), Lop Buri (q.v.), Nakhon Sawan, Nakhon Pathom and Ratcha Buri. The Chao Phraya River is a much used waterway for commerce. It supplements the extensive network of air, land and rail transportation. There are deep water ports near Bangkok and the mouth of the river.

CERAMICS. Siamese (q.v.) ceramics appear to be characterized in three somewhat interrelated groupings: (1) Pottery in the Lop Buri (q.v.) area which developed between the 11th and 14th centuries. These ceramics exhibit Cambodian influence. (2) Pottery and dishes of fired clay known as the Sukhothai (q.v.) type found at Si Satchanalai (q.v.), formerly known as Sawankhalok, which has been in celebrated ruins since the 15th century. This label describes everything from richly glazed and single-colored pottery known as Celadon to a variety of hand-painted ceramics. Potters at this site produced an enormous range of ceramics for 14th and 15th century export to Indonesia, the Philippines and elsewhere. The Sukhothai type of ceramics is similar to that made in China (q.v.) previously. (3) Chiang Mai wares which resemble the Sukhothai style and which were initially produced by potters forcibly removed from Si Satchanalai in the late 15th century. Their descendants still produce this style with modifications at Chiang Mai (q.v.). Examples of each of these styles are preserved in either the National Museum (q.v.) in Bangkok (q.v.), the National Museum in Ayutthaya (q.v.) or in private collections. Prehistoric evidences of early pottery have been discovered in the Ban Chiang (q.v.) area of northeast Thailand.

CEREMONIES AND FESTIVALS. Ceremonies and festivals in Thailand can be summed up in three principal categories: (1) religious festivals (q.v.), which are connected with the practice of Buddhism (q.v.) and are dated by the lunar calendar; (2) national holidays, which follow the Western calendar; and (3) other festivals and events. Three of the latter, which are celebrated throughout the nation, are Songkran (q.v.) in April, Kathin (q.v.) in October and Loy Kratong (q.v.) in November. Four festivals popular in specific areas are the Chiang Mai Flower Festival (q.v.) in February, the Royal Plowing Ceremony in May (q.v.), the Rocket Festival (q.v.) also in May or June, and the Surin Elephant Roundup (q.v.) in November. In addition, there are many fairs across the country, some of which include beauty contests and commercial activities. Information and exact dates for ceremonies, festivals and fairs can be obtained from the Tourist Organization of Thailand (TOT) and the *Bangkok Post* newspaper.

CHAKRAPHAT. King of Ayutthaya (reigned 1548-1569). He spent a large part of his reign in wars with Burma (q.v.). That kingdom had become unified, first under King Tabengshweti and later under his brother King Bayinnaung (q.v.). The armies of Burma were defeated during their first invasion. During the second they besieged Ayutthaya (q.v.) and forced Chakraphat to give them four white elephants. Chakraphat died during the third campaign, whereupon his son Mahin became king. Seven months later, in 1569, the Burmese captured Ayutthaya.

CHAKRI DYNASTY. The name Chakri designates the hereditary line of kings of Siam (q.v.) since 1782. His majesty, King Bhumibol Adulyadej (q.v.) is the current monarch and the ninth of this dynasty. The first three Chakri kings have been identified with the name Rama. For subsequent Chakri kings, other names have been used. The founder of the line, Rama I (q.v.) (also Yotfa), who reigned from 1782-1809, was the chief commander of the army (Chakri) prior to his elevation to the royal throne. There was no eligible heir at the time of the previous king's death. The rebuilding of the kingdom commenced by the previous king, Taksin (q.v.), was effectively broadened and continued by Rama I following the 1767 fall and destruction of Ayutthaya (q.v.). Rama II (also Loetla), who was a poet, reigned from 1809-1824 and is known mostly for development of artistic culture and Buddhist renewal. King Rama III (also Nang Klao), who reigned during 1824-1851, expanded the territory of Siam and outdid his predecessors in promoting Buddhism (q.v.). The fourth Chakri monarch, Mongkut (q.v.), reigned from 1851-1868 and was well versed in Western civilization and languages when he assumed the throne of Siam. He promoted foreign trade and contacts with the West.

Chulalongkorn (q.v.) (reigned 1868-1910) continued the modernization of Siam begun by King Mongkut. He was also a leader in domestic reforms and in devising foreign policies that were crucial in saving Siam from becoming the colony of either France or Britain. Vajiravudh (q.v.) (reigned 1910-1925) promoted nationalism and education. With the aid of assistants, he secured improvements in treaties relating to extraterritoriality and tariff autonomy with Western powers. When Prajadhipok (q.v.) (reigned 1925-1935) ascended the throne, Siamese (q.v.) regard for the monarchy (q.v.) was at a low ebb. Prajadhipok agreed under pressure to end the absolute monarchy in Siam in 1932. It was replaced by a constitutional form of government. He abdicated the throne in 1935.

Since the events of 1932, the Thai king serves as head of state and as a unifying force in the kingdom, but with no legislative or executive power. Ananda Mahidol (reigned 1935-1946) died mysteriously at the age of 21. However, under the ninth and present king, Bhumibol Adulyadej (q.v.) (reigned 1946-), the prestige and influence of the Thai monarchy has greatly increased. He has restored the throne to a position of high esteem.

CHAKRI MEMORIAL DAY. A national holiday celebrated on April 6 with ceremonies to mark the founding of the Chakri dynasty (q.v.) of kings in 1892 by Rama I (q.v.). King Bhumibol Adulyadej (q.v.), who is ninth in succession in the royal line, provides leadership in the activities. He is assisted by the queen, others of the royal family, the prime minister, and other government officials in ceremonies which are held principally in Bangkok (q.v.).

CHALOOD NIMSAMER (1929-). Famous sculptor, painter and known for printmaking. Chalood has been recognized as an heir of Silpa Bhirsari (q.v.). He studied at Silpakorn University in Thailand as well as art schools in Rome and New York. For his work in several fields of art, Chalood has consistently been considered an integrative artist. He has been widely honored for having won three times at the kingdom's National Art Exhibition. Among his students are several well-known Thai artists.

CHAMADEVI, QUEEN. A royal daughter of the King of Lop Buri (q.v.) in the 7th century AD. She was asked to rule the northern Kingdom of Hariphunchai, now Lamphun Province. She was a warrior and defeated the enemy from South India. When peace came, she made Buddhism (q.v.) a state religion and codified a secular body of law for her people, ordered the Buddhist scriptures (q.v.) revised by highly learned Buddhist monks (q.v.), and built several historic temples. Her statue stands in Lamphun Province.

CHAMBERS OF COMMERCE. In the early 20th century, the Chinese Chamber of Commerce represented a wide array of businesses in Bangkok. However, in the 1980s, the Thai Chamber of Commerce (TCC) took a leading role. It included provincial chambers of commerce as members which grew to 72 by 1986. The TCC, with a staff of more than 70 in the early 1990s, had representatives on at least 56 government committees and subcommittees. Along with the Board of Trade, the TCC is in the forefront as a representative of business interests in both Bangkok (q.v.) and the provinces (q.v.).

CHAMLONG SRIMUANG. Army officer, politician, governor. A former active-duty army major general, Chamlong gained prominence as a party leader who was elected governor (q.v.) of the Bangkok metropolis (q.v.) in 1985. City improvements during his administration enabled him to win reelection in 1990 by a landslide vote. Later, he was elected to the House of Representatives (q.v.) as a member of the Palang Dharma party. Chamlong gained considerable notoriety in the 1992 Pro-democracy Demonstrations (q.v.) in Bangkok (q.v.) against Prime Minister Suchinda Kraprayoon (q.v.). He led the popular demonstrations and demands for Suchinda's resignation. After his arrest, incarceration and hunger strike, he was freed by action of King Bhumibol (q.v.). Following the September 1992 national election, Chamlong and his Palang Dharma party became part of the ruling coalition.

CHANGWAT. See PROVINCE.

CHAO AWAT. See ABBOT.

CHAO PHRAYA (CHAO PHRA). Traditional title given to the holder of the highest rank in the civil government under the now defunct *sakdi na* (q.v.) system. Also the name of the main river in Thailand.

CHAO PHRAYA RIVER. The principal river of Thailand, located in the midst of the central Plain (q.v.). It provides water for some 10 million rai (400,000 acres) of agricultural land. It drains southward from headwaters in the mountains of northern Thailand and empties into the Gulf of Thailand where it forms a large delta. The Chao Phraya dwarfs all other Thai rivers and is sometimes referred to simply as "the river." The smaller Suphan River, located about 75 kilometers (47 miles) west of and parallel to the Chao Phraya, is considered a distributor since the two rivers share headwaters. From the place where three northern rivers join to form the Chao Phraya to the Gulf of Thailand is about 400 kilometers (250 miles). All except the very largest ships are able to go up the Chao Phraya River to the city of Bangkok (q.v.), which is about 30 kilometers (19 miles) from the river's mouth. Barges and boats provide year-round transportation over nearly the whole length of the Chao Phraya River. However, technological development in modern Thailand has changed the river. It has gradually lost its significance as a means of transportation. Population growth and a lack of city planning has turned the river into a sewer, receiving polluted water from towns and factories. (See RIVERINE COMMERCE.)

CHAO THI (PHRA PHUM). A Thai expression meaning Lord of the Land or Place. Traditionally in central Thailand, the landowner constructed a miniature house, a spirit house, which is then perched on a post at about eye level, near the family dwelling. It is regarded as the shrine of the guardian spirit *(chao thi)*. Food offerings are made to the *chao thi* on the anniversary of his installation in the spirit house, New Year's day, and other special occasions. The spirit is told of projected trips by members of the family, and of births and deaths. Its help is sought during illness and misfortune.

The villagers of the northeastern and northern regions do not have *chao thi* or *phra phum* shrines in their house compounds, but they typically have a community spirit house where the spirits of the founders of the village are honored annually in the sixth lunar month. (See PHI CULT.)

CHART THAI. See THAI NATION PARTY.

CHATCHAI CHOONHAVAN. Politician, prime minister (1988-1991), army general, foreign affairs officer. Chatchai was educated in Thailand and graduated from the Royal Thai Military Academy. In the army, he advanced rapidly to the rank of general. Chatchai retired from the army in 1974 to enter politics and was elected to the House of Representatives (q.v.) in 1975. As a civilian, he served with distinction as deputy foreign minister during the Indochina War. In the 1988 national election, Chatchai served as leader of the Thai National (Chart Thai) party. He became prime minister as leader of a six-party coalition and the first elected prime minister since 1976.

During Chatchai's two-and-a-half years in office, the Thai economy was booming. Politically, there were charges of corruption among high officials in the Chatchai administration and increased attention to the disparity of incomes which disadvantaged the less privileged groups.

While Chatchai was a clever tactician and a coalition builder, he did not project strong leadership. Challenges from the military members of the National Assembly (q.v.) came to a head in February 1991 when, in a bloodless coup led by General Suchinda Kraprayoon (q.v.), Chatchai was removed as prime minister.

CHATTRA. The nine-tiered royal umbrella. It appears over the royal throne when the king presides at formal ceremonies as head of state, at the opening of the National Assembly (q.v.), when receiving foreign envoys at the Chakri Throne Hall in the Grand Palace (q.v.) and for religious ceremonies at the Royal Chapel in Wat Phra Keo (q.v.).

CHEDI (STUPA). The most venerated religious structure for Thai Buddhists. Dome-like in appearance, it consists of a drum-like base, a bell-shaped dome topped by a circular colonnade or tapered pinnacle which rests on a square seat. Originally, the *chedi* enshrined relics of the Buddha (q.v.). Later, it housed relics of holy men or kings and finally has become a religious symbol as the cross is for Christians. It may be referred to as *phra chedi* to indicate veneration. The *chedi* is found in Thailand in a variety of forms and sizes. (See also STUPA.)

CHEN DURIYANGA. Educator, musician. Chen was a prominent musician and music teacher. During the period 1936-1954, he chaired a group of Thai musicians who wrote in musical score numerous traditional songs and melodies. These had previously existed only as oral traditions. Prior to this, Chen was active in aiding the development of Western classical music in Thailand. In the reign of King Vajiravudh (q.v.), he established the royal orchestra, the first of its kind in Siam. In 1934 his orchestra was transferred to and became the nucleus of the new Fine Arts Department of the Ministry of Education. Chen was awarded an honorific title by the king.

CHIANG MAI. One of the largest provinces in north Thailand, pop. 1,530,800 (est.). The nation's highest mountains are found here some of which are more than 1,700 meters (5,600 feet) high. The growing economy has prospered through tourism (q.v.), diversified agriculture, industry and cottage industries. In the uplands are found distinctive hill tribes (q.v.). The logging industry collapsed in 1989. However, logs continue to arrive from forests in Burma (q.v.). A national park in Chiang Mai Province has the greatest diversity of tree species found in any world temperate climate. Crude oil is pumped in the province and is processed at the Fang Oil Refinery. Mining operations are producing fluorite, tin and scheelite.

The provincial capital, Chiang Mai City, has a population of 200,000 (est.). It is a trade, tourist and educational center with a permanent colony of Western and Asian expatriates. The city has convenient rail and airline services, both international and domestic. Many Bangkok (q.v.) residents have second homes here to take advantage of the cooler climate. Chiang Mai is famous for its crafts such as silverware, umbrellas, cotton and silk cloth. Several companies provide a wide range of traditional celadons and modern porcelains.

CHIANG MAI FLOWER FESTIVAL. This popular and widely attended fair in February features a beauty pageant, a huge floral float parade and a variety of entertainments.

CHIANG SAEN. An early principality of Thai peoples in what today is northern Thailand with Chiang Saen as its capital. Relatively independent during the 10th to 12th centuries, it was later absorbed into a stronger principality. The ruins of the old city walls and moat can be observed along with several ancient Buddhist monuments. A small museum displays artifacts of the Chiang Saen art style which influenced the development of Sukhothai (q.v.) art. Chiang Saen is now a district (q.v.) and district capital in Chiang Rai Province.

CHINA, RELATIONS WITH. There is evidence of relations between China and the ancient Kingdom of Sukhothai (q.v.). For more than 500 years, Lan Na (q.v.), Sukhothai and subsequent kingdoms were nominally vassal states and periodically sent tributary missions to the Chinese emperor. This practice was ended in 1853 by King Mongkut (q.v.) with the support of the United States (q.v.) and other Western powers. When the People's Republic of China came to power in 1949, Thailand feared a possible southward expansion. In the 1960s, when China provided aid for insurgency (q.v.) to the Communist party of Thailand (q.v.), the threat appeared real. However, following Communist takeovers of the governments of Laos (q.v.) and Cambodia (q.v.) in 1975, Thailand sought accommodation with the victors. Diplomatic relations with China were established in July 1975 with the exchange of ambassadors.

Following the military defeat of the Khmer Rouge and the capture of Phnom Penh in early 1979, Vietnam set up a pro-Vietnam government in Cambodia. One result was the shared opposition to Vietnam by China and Thailand, which led to improved relations between them. For a time, Thailand was a conduit for Chinese arms sent to the Khmer Rouge and other forces resisting the Cambodian government. A Bangkok-Beijing hot line was created in 1985 to aid in coordinating efforts in the event of a Vietnamese attack on Thailand. Later, in May 1987, with a Vietnamese army division on its border, Thailand obtained an agreement for the purchase of Chinese arms and other military equipment for use when needed. Trade between Thailand and China has a long history. This has increased in recent decades as a result of the economic expansion in both countries. Thai businessmen are among those providing foreign investment in China.

CHINESE IN THAILAND. The role of the Chinese as merchants and government officials dates to early times in Siam (q.v.). King Taksin (q.v.), who reigned 1768-1782, had a Chinese father. During most of the 19th century and in the 20th to World War II, immigration from rural south China (q.v.) was very heavy. In Bangkok (q.v.) and the surrounding provinces, the immigration was encouraged by resident Chinese employers, who aided immigrants in order to meet their need for wage workers. These young single males took Siamese (q.v.) wives. The second generation in such marriages learned the Siamese language first which made assimilation easy. After the turn of the century, however, assimilation of the Chinese slowed. The new immigration brought in both men and women, mixed marriages became less common. The development of Chinese education and a Chinese language press soon followed.

The Chinese and their Sino-Siamese descendants built the modern sector of the economy centered in Bangkok. Canals, bridges, railways, government buildings, and small and large commercial buildings provide evidence of their industry. In the first half of the 20th century, they built the infrastructure essential to the rice-export economy. Because of their economic power, especially in Bangkok, and their alleged Communist Leanings, Prime Minister Phibunsongkhram (q.v.) secured laws and issued edicts that restricted Chinese schools and associations and placed controls on the press for most of a decade.

Today, the Chinese are largely assimilated or are regarded as Sino-Thai (q.v.). In the latest census, less than one percent of the population of Thailand were citizens of China. Success in the nation depends on a Thai education, Thai surnames, Thai language and even Sino-Thai intermarriage. However, many continue to retain some "Chineseness," through ancestor worship, use of the Chinese language, maintenance of Chinese customs and an orientation to commerce and business success. Businesses are often owned jointly by several inter-related families.

The Sino-Thai entrepreneurs have been a major component of the middle class in central Thailand and hold a major, if not dominant, role in the principal business organizations in Thailand. Political patronage has brought together the Sino-Thai business elite and many high officials in the government and military structure. The Sino-Thai are somewhat set apart by their occupations in banking, commerce, trade and the professions. A degree of Thai-Chinese integration has occurred in the last decade or two as numerous ethnic Thai are going into the occupations that for a long time have been dominated by the Chinese and Sino-Thai.

CHIT PHUMISAK (1930-1965). Thai author, intellectual and Marxist revolutionary. His brilliance as a scholar, as a critic and in political originality got him branded as a Marxist. He was suspended from his university studies. Later, after finishing his degree at Chulalongkorn University, his book *The Real Face of Thai Feudalism (1957)* was published. But since this was a scathing criticism of Thai society and government, he was jailed by the Sarit Thanarat (q.v.) regime. On his release from prison in 1964, he joined the insurgency (q.v.) in the northeast (q.v.) where he was killed in the fighting with government forces. His writings have provided inspiration for social and political change in Thailand.

CHITR BUABUSAYA. A well-known Thai painter, active in Thailand after World War II. His works reflect a Western orientation.

CHOEI. A Thai social value meaning to be still or cool, which are vital elements in the Thai reaction to situations of social stress. To have a cool heart is to be uninvolved, not annoyed and to remain in control of one's emotional self. The idea of *choei* marks the posture of a person being at ease and serene in spite of threats, anxiety or temptation.

CHON BURI AND PATTAYA. Chon Buri Province, pop. 925,000 (est.), just southeast of Bangkok (q.v.), is the locus of Pattaya, pop. 64,800 (est.), the famous resort and convention city. Pattaya is located on the Gulf of Thailand. However, its once popular beaches have been spoiled by pollution. Other resort areas in the province include Bang Saen, Bang Phra and Loi Island. The economy is strong, with important fisheries and prosperous agriculture (q.v.), especially pineapples, cassava (q.v.), coconuts (q.v.) and sugar cane. In addition, in the province there are extensive manufacturing (q.v.), the TORC petroleum refinery and the Royal Thai Naval base. Sichang Island, off the coast, has a port for large ocean-going vessels that are unable to dock in Bangkok.

CHRISTIANITY. In 1993, Christians in Thailand were estimated to number almost 300,000. The small number reflects the limited success of Christian Evangelism, which has been ongoing in Thailand for nearly 400 years. However, Christian missions have contributed to the transmission of Western ideas and technology to the Thai. The missions have founded hospitals, introduced Western medical knowledge, sponsored private elementary and secondary schools and established universities. (See EDUCATIONAL SYSTEM). Graduates of these schools played important roles as teachers in the new government schools.

Another asset of the Christian missions was the teaching of the English language. In time, the Thai officials recognized that English was a "window on the world." A number of officials in government, higher education and business are Christians. The children of the Thai elite are often enrolled in Christian schools. Christianity was first introduced to Thailand by the Portuguese Roman Catholic priests in 1606. Catholics in Thailand represent about 75 percent of all Christians. Protestant missionaries first arrived in Thailand in 1838. One of the early ones, Dan B. Bradley, a physician, was an advisor and teacher for Mongkut (q.v.) prior to his becoming King Mongkut. (See CATHOLICISM; PROTESTANTISM.)

CHUAN LEEKPAI. Prime minister of Thailand beginning in 1992 and an elected member of the House of Representatives (q.v.). Chuan was educated in the primary and secondary schools of Trang Province. He graduated from Thammasat University in 1962 and became a barrister-at-law in 1964. He practiced law in Trang Province and in Bangkok (q.v.). Chuan was elected a representative from Trang Province in 1975 under the Democrat party banner and was returned to the House of Representatives in each election since then.

He was elected deputy leader of his party in 1976. Chuan held cabinet posts under three previous prime ministers. In 1992, he became leader of the Democrat party. In the September 1992 general election, Chuan's Democrat party won more seats in the national assembly than any other political party. Following the election, a five-party coalition of pro-democracy parties named Chuan prime minister. In early 1994, efforts by the Chuan coalition to reduce by half the number of members of the upper house (senators) and enact several other democratic reforms were defeated by the conservative opposition. (See GOVERNMENTAL SYSTEM.)

CHULABHORN, PRINCESS (1957-). Princess Chulabhorn is the second daughter of King Bhumibol Adulyadej (q.v.) and Queen Sirikit (q.v.). She is a gifted scientist, having received her Bachelor of Science degree from Kasetsart University and a doctorate in organic chemistry from Mahidol University. She received the Einstein Gold Medal award in 1986. In 1987, she set up the Chulabhorn Research Institute to promote scientific research in Thailand. She is married to Flight Lieutenant Virayuth Didyasarin, a fighter pilot; they have two children.

CHULALONGKORN (1853-1910). King of Siam (reigned 1868-1910). Chulalongkorn was the first son of King Mongkut (q.v.) and became king at age 15. He initially served under the regent, Suriyawong (q.v.). During this period he continued his education and traveled in South Asia where he observed governmental systems. Chulalongkorn ascended the throne of Siam in 1868. His early attempts at reforms were resisted and delayed by older officials and older princes. In the meanwhile, Chulalongkorn aided in the education of his brothers and labored with them in many aspects of administrative affairs. In this way, he assessed their abilities and could assign them to government posts when older ministers and other officials died or retired.

Chulalongkorn, assisted by Devawongse (q.v.), introduced a new administrative system in 1892. This consisted of 12 ministries, functionally defined, in which each head was directly responsible to the king. This replaced an earlier system, the Mahatthai (q.v.) and the Kalahom (q.v.), in which the ministers had not been accountable to the king. A principal new Ministry of the Interior was assigned to Prince Damrong (q.v.), who was effective in getting it established. Similarly, Prince Rabi, the king's son, modernized the country's justice system.

Starting in 1873, Chulalongkorn initiated gradual measures to free slaves, and in 1905 slavery was abolished. The long-standing system of *sakdi na* (q.v.) was also ended. Early in his reign, he initiated changes from tradition such as wearing European-style clothes, abolition of prostration before the king and using chairs instead of pillows on the floor for seating. Chulalongkorn facilitated the development of schools for the children of officials, and a secondary school was opened for the children of non-officials. Sirirat Hospital was founded in 1887, which two years later started a School of Medicine for the training of doctors.

Chulalongkorn saw the need for modernization. Eventually, Siamese (q.v.) civil and criminal laws were revised to bring them into conformity with Western standards. These law revisions set the stage for new treaties between Siam (q.v.) and France (1904) and between Siam and Britain (1909). While Siam was able to retain its national independence, this came at the price of yielding border territories to these two rapacious colonial powers. The American advisor to King Chulalongkorn, Edward Strobel (q.v.), played a key role in the treaty negotiations.

In the diplomatic arena, Chulalongkorn made personal visits to Europe in 1897 and in 1907. He visited Denmark, Germany, Russia and other countries. He was accepted as an equal by heads of state and fellow kings. In the traditional polygynous pattern of Siamese kings, Chulalongkorn had many wives and fathered 77 children. About two-thirds of his offspring survived to maturity. Chulalongkorn did not enjoy being king, but liked to wander about Bangkok (q.v.) incognito, dressed as a peasant. His writings were impressive. These include *The Royal Ceremonies of the Twelve Months, Far from Home* and 25 volumes of his personal diary. When he died in 1910, Chulalongkorn had been king for 42 years.

CHULALONGKORN MEMORIAL DAY. This national holiday falls on October 23 in honor of King Chulalongkorn (q.v.) who occupied the throne from 1868 to 1910 and is the most famous of the Chakri (q.v.) kings. Near an equestrian statue of Chulalongkorn in an open plaza in Bangkok (q.v.), large floral and other wreaths are assembled and displayed. These are presented in a spirit of friendly competition by school organizations and other groups. The king also places a wreath in an official ceremony at the statue and pays homage to Chulalongkorn at the site where his ashes are buried. The occasion is marked in district (q.v.) and provincial capitals throughout Thailand.

CHULARAJAMONTRI. The official head of the Islamic religion in Thailand. He is appointed by the Thai government and is considered a government official. (See ISLAM.)

CIVIL AVIATION. Thailand is a crossroad for international air cargoes and travel. About 40 international airlines use the facilities of Don Muang (q.v.) International Airport in Bangkok (q.v.). Thai Airways International Corporation (TAC), a state owned airline, provides international flights to a wide range of cities abroad. In 1992, the management of TAC was transferred from military to civilian control. Bangkok is to a large extent a regional center for international air service especially to Asia and Europe. There is domestic air service to more than 25 cities and towns across the nation. In addition there is air service to Kunming, Rangoon, Penang, Vientiane, Ho Chi Minh City and Hanoi. Some of the latter flights originate in Chiang Mai (q.v.) and/or in Phuket.

CIVIL SERVICE. Employment in the Thai civil service or military service has traditionally been a major outlet for most ambitious and educated citizens. Since they are considered to be in a prestigious occupation, civil servants are accorded deference. However, since World War II, private commercial and industrial careers have become attractive, some of which are more prestigious than government careers because of higher incomes and better fringe benefits. The civil service employee is known in Thai as *karachakan* (q.v.).

Since 1975, public officials in the civil service system are divided into 11 position classifications (PCs), as follows:

PC 11   permanent secretary of a ministry;
PC 10   provincial governor (q.v.), deputy secretary of a ministry, department head;
PC 9   deputy department head;
PC 8   division head;
PC 6-7   section head;
PC 3-5   administrative clerk;
PC 1-2   clerk.

CLIMATE. Thailand has a tropical climate. Westerners from a temperate zone find the country hot and humid. On a simplified basis, four seasons may be recognized: (1) the dry season--which is the result of a northeast monsoon from December through February; (2) transitional hot weather and variable winds during March, April, and May; (3) the rainy season produced by the southwest monsoons from May to October; (4) a retreating monsoon, in October and November.

The amount of rainfall varies in different parts of Thailand, about 90 percent of which falls in the rainy season. It averages 100 to 150 centimeters (40 to 60 inches) in most of the northern mountains, the central Plain (q.v.), and in the Khorat Plateau. Precipitation is 230 to 250 centimeters (90 to 100 inches) in the western mountains and most of the peninsula (q.v.) region. Thunderstorms in the afternoon and early evening are common between May and October in the northern areas, and between March and November in the southern areas. Toward the end of the dry season, and again at the end of the rainy season, cyclonic storms often come into Thailand from the South China Sea, with associated flooding. The mean maximum temperature in Bangkok (q.v.) is approximately 32° C (90° F) and the mean minimum temperature there is 26° C (74° F). The hottest season is from March to September, the period of the wet monsoons, and the coolest period is in November and December.

CLOTHING. Western-style clothing has largely replaced the traditional clothing previously worn by the Thai people. Whether employees of the provincial governments, who have civil service (q.v.) rank, wear a standard uniform or Western-type clothing is decided by the provincial governor (q.v.). Traditional clothing is seldom seen except in remote areas or possibly in ceremonies or on special occasions. For men the garment is the *phakhawma*, a woven cloth long enough to be a wrap-around and extending from the waist to the knees. For women, the dress is the *pasin*, a tubular, long skirt wrapped around similar to a sarong. It is generally worn with a blouse.

COCKFIGHTING. A favorite pastime and effective method of redistributing rural wealth via the practice of betting. A good fighting cock costs up to 6,250 baht (q.v.) ($250) and elicits much pride and affection. The birds are especially bred and trained and are pitted against each other in the arena. Steel spurs are attached to their legs and they frequently fight to the death. Occasionally a bird will try to escape from the arena, in which case the remaining bird is adjudged the winner. Cockfighting is frowned upon by a majority of people, because it conflicts with Buddhist beliefs on the subject of cruelty to animals.

COCONUTS. The large nut fruits of the coconut palm tree. Coconuts are widely produced for domestic use and for export (q.v.). To some extent, production is concentrated on plantations in the south. Coconuts supply food, sugar and wine. The meat yields a fatty oil used for cooking, lighting and soap making. The husk provides a fiber that can be made into mats and rope.

COLOMBO PLAN. The Colombo Plan for Cooperative Economic Development in South and Southeast Asia was an international cooperative effort to assist countries of the area to raise their living standards. In 1970, member nations of the plan included Afghanistan, Bhutan, Burma, Cambodia (q.v.), Ceylon (now Sri Lanka), India, Indonesia, Iran, the Republic of Korea, Laos (q.v.), Malaysia (q.v.), the Maldive Islands, Nepal, Pakistan, the Philippines, Singapore, Thailand, the Republic of South Vietnam, Australia, Canada, Japan (q.v.), New Zealand, the United Kingdom, and the United States (q.v.).

COMMUNE. See LOCAL GOVERNMENT.

COMMUNICATIONS. Availability of telephone communication has been very limited in Thailand, but steps for improvement have begun. Most telephones are in Bangkok (q.v.) and its vicinity. In other cities, phones are less available and are chiefly in offices of government agencies and in business offices. During the early 1990s, there were on average less than four phone lines per 100 population. New line construction had until 1993 been handled solely by the Telephone Organization of Thailand (TOT), a state enterprise (q.v.). Starting in 1993, two private companies have started constructing phone lines. It is expected that the number of lines per 100 population will be doubled in a few years.

Plans are underway to use fiber optic technology to facilitate transmissions of cable television, interactive television and video conferences. The first Thai communications satellite was launched in December 1993. When operational, it will provide services for radio distribution, linking telephone switching units, computer networks and television broadcasting. The latter will include both relay of signals for station rebroadcasts and direct-to-home broadcasts.

COMMUNIST PARTY OF THAILAND (CPT). In the late 1920s and for more than 50 years, the Communist movement in Thailand attempted to exploit the dissatisfactions of the minority ethnic peoples who felt they had not been accepted by the Thai. In 1942, the CPT became organized through a merger of several small, widely scattered ethnic groups, led chiefly by ethnic Chinese (q.v.). However, a Communist political party was considered illegal under Thai law. The principal areas of clandestine activity were among the Hmong in northern

Thailand, the Thai-Lao in the northeast (q.v.) and among the Thai-Malay (q.v.) in southern areas. The vast majority of the people of Thailand clearly did not support the CPT, however, and continued to cherish their national identity and to feel an attachment to their king and to Thai Buddhism (q.v.). Although CPT membership grew somewhat, it reached a peak after the 1976 coup, when an attack against university students in Bangkok (q.v.) forced thousands to flee into the jungles.

Already in the mid-1970s the Thai government had underway a number of programs to counter the CPT insurgency (q.v.). Beyond military action, which was costly and sometimes ineffective, the economic, political and social needs of disaffected minorities were addressed. An amnesty program in the early 1980s brought the surrender of many CPT members. In addition, selective military attacks against guerilla bases were effective, and armed CPT forces had decreased from 12,000 in 1979 to less than 4,000 by 1983. At present, after defections, only a small core of dedicated persons remain in the CPT. Refugees (q.v.) from Cambodia, Laos and Vietnam, and their stories of repression and hardships caused by communism, have also contributed to a rapid decline of the movement. That the CPT had a significance out of proportion to its numbers was largely associated with Thailand's having socialist Burma (q.v.) on its western border and three Communist states on its eastern and northern borders: Cambodia (q.v.), Laos (q.v.) and China (q.v.). (See INSURGENCY.)

CONSTITUTION. The constitution promulgated in 1992 is the 13th such document since 1932 when Thailand (then Siam [q.v.]) changed in principle from an absolute monarchy (q.v.) to a constitutional one. Some basic concepts have been maintained in each successive constitution. The first concept is that the monarch is sacred and inviolable in his person. As head of state, he is empowered with the right to be consulted, the right to encourage and the right to warn. The latter can occur when the king considers that the government (the prime minister, his cabinet and the legislative assembly) have failed to administer the affairs of state in the best interests of the Thai people.

The second concept provided for a bicameral National Assembly (q.v.), consisting of a Senate, whose members are appointed, and a House of Representatives (q.v.), whose members are elected by popular vote. The third concept is the provision for an executive branch. In addition to serving as chief executive, the Thai prime minister is often seen as a protective figure, which reflects an extension of the patriarchal family into government. He is assisted by the persons appointed to be in charge of specific ministries, who with him constitute the Cabinet or Council of Ministers (q.v.).

COSMOLOGY. Traditional Thai beliefs concerning the nature of the cosmos were derived from ancient Indian and Babylonian sources. They give man his place within the universe and dictate his actions throughout life. In this legendary belief there are innumerable world systems, each with its own sun, moon, earth, continents and oceans. Central to it all is the legendary Mount Meru, up from which extend the heavens and the hells. Man inhabits a group of islands in the Great Ocean which is an outer circle of the cosmic system. The six forms of existence--man, animal, god, demon, ghost and souls in hell--are only of temporary duration and through which all human beings may at one time or another pass. A change in condition depends on one's *karma* (q.v.). Man in his human condition is the fundamental acting agent. (See BRAHMANISM.)

COTTAGE INDUSTRIES. Except for the busy periods of planting and harvesting, probably most farm families engage in the production of knives, thatches, cloth, musical instruments (q.v.), woven baskets for the storage and transport of agricultural products, and other items. These goods are produced in their own homes by family members and sometimes by hired labor. Surpluses beyond the needs of each farm family are sold or bartered.

COTTON WEAVING. This industry is very widespread in Thailand and great quantities of woven goods are exported. The traditional hand-woven materials compete with those made by machine. While soft cotton materials are most common, there is also a unique cloth of a linen-like texture, which is made in northern Thailand. Another interesting fabric is made from a mixture of Thai silk (q.v.) and cotton. It is washable and extremely long wearing.

COUNCIL OF MINISTERS (CABINET). The executive branch of the Thai government which is specified by the constitution (q.v.). The cabinet consists of the heads (ministers) of each government ministry, such as defense, interior, foreign affairs, finance and others. It also includes all deputy or assistant ministers and deputy prime ministers. The prime minister is the chief government official. He is typically the leader of the political party (q.v.) that has the most elected members of the House of Representatives (q.v.).

The prime minister has in the past been the real power in the Thai government. In fact, the executive branch and government power have usually been dominated by a military oligarchy since 1932. The past 60 years have seen some 20 coups d'etat by military leaders. Attempts to establish civilian control of the government have only rarely been successful. However, a 1992 election saw an elected prime minister take office amid hopes that a basic change has occurred.

A recent constitutional change requires that the prime minister also be an elected member. Ministers cannot be military officers (q.v.) on active duty or civil servants. Members of the cabinet are chosen from those political parties which have joined to provide a working majority in the House of Representatives. The cabinet not only dominates the legislative process, it handles all senior appointments and by law has control over all public agencies. These include control over most fiscal expenditures, foreign loans and policies that relate to citizen welfare and national stability. (See MILITARY OFFICERS.)

CREMATION. See FUNERAL RITES.

CULTURE, NATION BUILDING. While residents of Thailand very largely consider themselves as belonging to the Tai-language peoples, there are a number of ethnic groups with other distinctive cultural patterns. The Thai government has generally seen cultural differences from the viewpoint of the need for unity and national security. The chief policy has been to bring all diverse peoples under the authority of the national government. Assertion of this authority has at times encountered difficulties. To this end, a set of national symbols is emphasized. At the center of this set is the Thai monarch who legitimizes the power of the state. Members of its administrative bureaucracies, civil and military, are known as "servants of the crown." The legitimacy of the monarch is based on his connection with Buddhism (q.v.), the national religion. The king demonstrates this relationship through public acts of piety, and he serves as a patron of the Buddhist clergy. These cultural themes are pervasive in the society, but are also reemphasized on national holidays (q.v) and in other ways. A strong challenge to the foregoing concept of the national culture has come from the Thai-Malay (q.v.), especially those in the four southernmost provinces. The Thai-Malay espouse an Islamic religion. Gradually, the Thai government, which is Buddhist, has accepted this cultural variation and has even provided economic and other support to the Thai-Malay.

CURRENCY SYSTEM. The Thai currency unit is the baht (q.v.), which is divided into 100 stang. Notes in circulation are 10, 20, 100 and 500 baht denominations. Twenty-five baht are approximately equal to one U.S. dollar.

- D -

DAMRONG RACHANUPHAP, PRINCE (1862-1943). A son of King Mongkut (q.v.) and brother of King Chulalongkorn (q.v.). Damrong received a traditional education in the royal court. He served in the Ministry of Education, where he prepared what eventually became the standard texts in elementary education throughout Siam (q.v.). In 1890, he was an envoy to the royal court of Russia and to other European governments. In 1892, he was named minister of the interior, a post he held for 23 years. In this position, he pioneered a reorganization of the territorial administration of Thailand into 71 provinces (q.v.) and their respective sub-units. As a historian, Prince Damrong collected and compiled the Thai archives of the Bangkok period. He was a leader in establishing the National Museum (q.v.) and the National Library (q.v.). Due to his many scholarly treatises on history and archaeology, Prince Damrong is considered the "father of Thai history."

DANCE DRAMA. There are two significant forms of Thai dance drama, *(khon)* (q.v.) and *lakhon. Khon* is the classical masked drama. It takes its story from the Ramakian (q.v.), which is the Thai version of the Indian epic Ramayana. Performers wear ornate masks and brilliant costumes. The acting is vigorous, formalized and inseparable from dancing. Each step has a meaning defined by the music. Narrative verses are usually recited or sung by a chorus accompanied by a woodwind, gong and drum ensemble. The major characters are identifiable from the color of their costumes. The *lakhon* dance drama is less formal. The actors do not wear masks, but the costumes of *lakhon* and *khon* are the same. Plots are taken mainly from the Ramakian and from folktales. However, *lakhon* dance movements are more graceful, sensual and fluid. The upper torso and hands express emotions in conventionalized movements. (See KHON; LAM; LIKAY; NAIL DANCE.)

DANGREK RANGE. A mountain range oriented chiefly east-west, marking a part of the border between Thailand and Cambodia.

DEMOCRAT PARTY (PRACHATHIPAT). Formed in 1946 under another name, it was initially a political organization of the aristocracy. It became influential following the 1975 and 1976 elections, when its leader, Seni Pramoj (q.v.), became prime minister both times and formed coalition governments jointly with other parties.

In the 1992 elections, the Democrat party won the largest number of seats, and its leader, Chuan Leekpai (q.v.), became prime minister in a government coalition with three other parties. The Democrat party is a national party in the sense that it has a broad network of organization across the nation. When the party is part of the opposition in the House of Representatives (q.v.), cabinet ministers are often drawn from its ranks since they are respected seniors who serve the government in power.

DEVAWONGSE VAROPAKAR (1858-1923). Prince and foreign minister of Siam (q.v.) under two kings. Devawongse was a son of King Mongkut (q.v) and a half-brother of King Chulalongkorn (q.v.). He was educated in the royal court which included a British tutor. Early on, Devawongse gained administrative experience in the royal court as a secretary, body guard and auditor. At the age of 20, he became the personal secretary of the king and had some responsibility for foreign affairs. In 1885, he succeeded to the top post in foreign affairs. In this position, he modernized the ministry and had it organized to some extent along Western lines.

Devawongse made a careful observation of the organization of selected European governments in 1887 at the request of the king. In consequence, and with his help, King Chulalongkorn reorganized the government into 12 ministries. Devawongse was a strong force to bring Siam to the world scene as a modern and civilized nation and to gain Siam's rulers a status equal to that of other world monarchs. With diplomacy and skill, the independence of Siam was maintained at a time when both Great Britain and France were colonizing in Southeast Asia. Due to the expansionist policy of France, Siam was forced to give up territories in the Mekong (q.v.) valley. Devawongse was able to weather this action and led negotiations which ended major security threats to the kingdom.

DHANI NIVAT BIDYALABH BRIDHYAKORN (1885-1974). Popularly known as Prince Dhani, he graduated from Oxford University with honors and served under five kings. Entering the government, Dhani served in the Ministry of the Interior, was a private secretary to King Vajiravudh (q.v.) and the minister of education under King Prajadhipok (q.v.). In 1904, he had founded the Siam Society (q.v.) in which he served as president. He held many other high offices and in 1946 became regent of Thailand, a post he held until 1950. Later he served as president of the Privy Council (q.v.). He is the author of numerous scholarly publications chiefly on history.

DHARMA. An expression which conveys the sense of the duties of man. In the context of Thai Buddhism (q.v.), *dharma* generally means religion, especially the teachings of Buddha (q.v.). In a wider context, *dharma* also represents much of Brahmanism (q.v.) from which Buddhism evolved. The expression *dharma,* which is of Sanskrit (q.v.) origin, has the same meaning as *dhamma,* which is traced to the Pali (q.v.) language. *Dhamma* is typically the Thai spoken expression, while *dharma* is used for written communication. (See NEO-BUDDHISM.)

DISTRICT (AMPHOE). The name for any one of the six to 12 sub-units of a province *(changwat)* (q.v.), having its own governmental structure. The chief administrative officer is the district officer *(nai amphoe)* (q.v.). The number of such districts in Thai local government (q.v.) is in excess of 500. A sub-district of a large *amphoe* is headed by an assistant officer.

DISTRICT OFFICER (NAI AMPHOE). The chief administrative officer of a district *(amphoe)* (q.v.) which is a subdivision of a province. He is appointed by the minister of interior and is responsible to the governor (q.v.) of the province. The district officer operates at the lowest level of the central government and is a crucial link between the government and the people. Assisted by from three to ten officials, the district officer supervises the collection of taxes; issues certificates of birth, marriage, divorce and death; registers school children, young men for military service, aliens and buffaloes; arbitrates land disputes; and administers local elections. The district officer also meets regularly with the head men of the communes and villages to inform them of government policy and to guide them in their implementation of these policies.

DOKMAI SOT. See BUPPHA NIMMANHEIMIN.

DON MUANG. The airport serving Bangkok (q.v.) and its surrounding area. Its traffic is very largely international with numerous airline companies conducting passenger and freight operations. Don Muang is also the hub of domestic flights to some 30 nearby and remote cities of "up country" Thailand. The airport is Thailand's principal point of departure and arrival for international travel. (See CIVIL AVIATION.)

DONTRI PUEN MUANG. A native ensemble of instrumental musicians in northern Thailand, consisting of one to four lutes *(sueng)*, one or two spike fiddles *(salaw)*, a bamboo (q.v.) flute *(klui)*, a drum *(pon-pong)*, and one or two pairs of small cymbals *(chap)* or *(ching)*. Such a group would provide music for ceremonies in private homes. The lutes and flute are also used for solo work. (See also GONG AEW; MUSICAL INSTRUMENTS; PIPHAT ORCHESTRA.)

DRUMS. These instruments play an essential role in Thai instrumental ensembles. The *tapone* is a kind of hand timpanum, with drum heads at both ends; the *songna*, a drum similar in design to the *tapone*, is slightly longer but thinner. When the *song na* is used to accompany songs, it is called *poeng mang*. The *klong thad* is a thick large drum, both faces of which are used. It resembles somewhat the Western timpanum and thick sticks are used as beaters. (See MUSICAL INSTRUMENTS; PIPHAT ORCHESTRA.)

DURIAN. A popular fruit of the tree *Durio zibethinus*, which has a hard, prickly rind, pulpy, custard-like flesh and offensive odor. Nontha Buri Province is famous for this fruit.

DVARAVATI. The name of an early civilization of Mon (q.v.) peoples located chiefly in what today is the lower Chao Phraya River (q.v.) valley of Thailand. The best known sites include Nakhon Pathom, Suphan Buri, Lop Buri (q.v.), and U Thong. In addition, there is archaeological evidence of many other sites at long distances from these centers, most likely along trade routes to the north, the northeast and the east. The Mon inhabitants practiced rice (q.v.) agriculture (q.v.) and were adherents of Buddhism (q.v.). Mon remains include religious buildings, statues of Buddha (q.v.), other sculptures (q.v.) and numerous votive tablets. In the 10th century, the area occupied by the Mon people was incorporated into the Khmer Kingdom, which had its capital at Angkor (q.v.).

- E -

ECONOMIC AND SOCIAL COMMISSION FOR ASIA AND THE PACIFIC (ESCAP). (Formerly, ECAFE: Economic Commission for Asia and the Far East). One of four world regional commissions established by the United Nations in 1947; it has its headquarters in Bangkok (q.v.). ESCAP sponsors research and holds international conferences on economic development, trade promotion, inland transport, flood control, agriculture (q.v.), etc. Two of ESCAP's main projects have been of much help to Thailand. These are the Asian Highway and the Mekong River (q.v.) development projects. ESCAP has located its Asian Institute of Economic Planning in Bangkok. There are 48 member nations.

ECONOMIC DEVELOPMENT. For most of the past 30 years, Thailand has been one of the faster growing developing countries. There has been growth in personal income, a strengthening of the expanding middle class and a reduction in poverty as well as growth in other areas. A large part of this development has been due to the successive five-year economic development plans instituted by the national government. Goals of these plans included balanced economic growth, reduction of the income gap and improvement in the distribution of social services. The encouragement of private investment, both Thai and foreign, has resulted in an annual growth rate of the Gross Domestic Product (GDP) of seven to eight percent. In view of the excess of imports, especially machinery, transport equipment and many basic manufactured products, over exports (q.v.), a continued inflow to Thailand of foreign capital has been essential for economic stability. (See AGRICULTURE; BALANCE OF PAYMENTS; EXPORTS; FORESTRY; INDUSTRY; INVESTMENT PROMOTION; MANUFACTURING; ORGANIZATIONS THAT REPRESENT BUSINESS AS A WHOLE.)

EDUCATION, ADULT. Non-formal adult education has been conducted in Thailand since 1940. Programs aim to (1) promote and maintain literacy (q.v.) and (2) enhance vocational skills.

Instruction is offered throughout the country. Local education units reach out to remote areas offering lectures, mobile libraries, films and videotapes. Special programs are directed to new entrants into the labor market, the unemployed, those previously incarcerated, the homeless and persons sexually exploited.

EDUCATION, HIGHER. The late 1800s and early 1900s saw the beginnings of higher education in Thailand. A medical school was opened in 1889, a law school in 1897, civil servants school in 1902 and an engineering school in 1913. Chulalongkorn University, founded in 1916, took over the medical and engineering schools and other disciplines as well. Today, Chulalongkorn has the largest enrollment among the conventional universities. There are a total of 20 Thai public universities and institutes. In addition, there are 26 private colleges and universities, the first of which was Payap University in Chiang Mai (q.v.). Over time, 36 teacher training colleges were established to meet the growing demand for teachers in the elementary schools. Thammasat University, founded in 1933, took over the Civil Servants School and, like Chulalongkorn, has a broad curriculum. Three additional universities were added in 1943, Kasetsart, Silpakorn and Mahidol. The emphasis was on agriculture (q.v.), fine arts and medical sciences, respectively. Higher education is offered in the Police Cadet Academy and the Chulachomklao Military Academy.

Three regional universities were established during 1964-1967 to expand educational opportunity beyond Bangkok (q.v.), where higher education is concentrated. The schools were intended to facilitate economic and social development programs as well. One regional university was created in each Chiang Mai, Khon Kaen (q.v.) and Songkhla (q.v.). In 1966, the former Institute of Public Administration at Thammasat became the National Institute of Development Administration. It offers instruction at the postgraduate level only. Also, the Asian Institute of Technology was authorized to locate in Thailand (1967). It operates on subsidies, grants and donations secured worldwide and is staffed by a faculty from at least eight different nations. Master's degree programs are offered in at least ten state universities and at several of the private ones. Six universities offer doctoral degree programs, about one-half of which are at Chulalongkorn.

Two Buddhist universities, Mahamakut and Mahachulalongkorn, offer degree programs for Buddhist monks (q.v.). Five of the larger state universities have from one to seven research institutes which seek funding from their own institutions and from outside sources to carry on research projects. A significant recent development in Thai higher education was the founding in 1971 of Ramkhamhaeng University and in 1979 of Sukhothai Thammathirat University. These are "open" universities without admission standards that serve tens of thousands of students and have expanded educational opportunity especially for adults and for those who fail to gain admission to the conventional universities. Classes are provided at Ramkhamhaeng supplemented with television (q.v.) and radio programs. Sukhothai Thammathirat offers training by correspondence, radio, television and tutorial service.

EDUCATION, SECONDARY. See EDUCATIONAL SYSTEM.

EDUCATIONAL SYSTEM. Education as a responsibility of government dates from the latter part of the reign of King Chulalongkorn (q.v.). Much educational development has occurred and continues since then due in part to Western influence. Currently, the school system in Thailand follows a 6-3-3 pattern in which six years of primary education is compulsory. This is followed by three years of lower secondary schooling and three years of higher secondary schooling. Students in the upper secondary program can choose either a vocational or an academic curriculum. The secondary school in this way accommodates those who plan to enter college and also those who expect to seek employment after completion. Education in Thailand is also seen as a continuing lifelong process enabling persons to lead a useful life in society. Recent reports show that about 99 percent of Thai youth aged seven to 12 have attended primary school. Adult literacy (q.v.) among Thai citizens had advanced by 1990 to at least 90 percent compared to about 50 percent in the 1950s. Considerable public investment as well as foreign assistance were involved in achieving these gains.

Municipal primary schools have been administered by the Ministry of the Interior. Most primary education and all secondary education, teacher training colleges and vocational-technical education have been the domain of the Ministry of Education. There are a number of primary schools operated as a part of the Christian missionary programs in Thailand. Competition for admission to the best primary schools has led to the founding of a number of private kindergartens in the larger cities. In addition, there is a public demonstration kindergarten in the capital of each province. (See PRIVATE SECONDARY SCHOOLS.)

Public universities and institutes and private universities and colleges are administered by the Ministry of University Affairs. In addition, colleges of nursing are overseen by the Ministry of Public Health. Military training is supervised by the Ministry of Defense. (See EDUCATION, ADULT; EDUCATION, HIGHER; TECHNICAL COLLEGES.)

EKATOTSAROT. King of Ayutthaya (reigned 1605-1610). He previously ruled with his famous older brother, King Naresuan (q.v.). Ekatotsarot was concerned more with reorganizing Siamese (q.v.) finances than with military pursuits. During his reign, after contacts were made with the Dutch and Japanese, the first emissaries from Europe arrived in Ayutthaya (q.v.). The first Thai foreign mission was sent to a European country, the Netherlands, in 1608.

ELECTRIC POWER. Electricity was first produced by Thai government-owned companies in 1957 and 1958. A large hydroelectric power plant, which supplemented the privately owned power sources in Bangkok (q.v.) and adjacent provinces, began operating in 1964. From the beginning, state-owned enterprises have used lignite, which is available in Thailand, as well as oil to fuel the power plants and gas turbines which produce electricity. At least 20 plants have been in operation. A recent report indicated that about 70 percent of the electric power in Thailand is thermally produced and 30 percent is hydropower. Slowly, electricity has become available to about 90 percent of the more than 48,000 agricultural villages in the countryside. The remainder are expected to get electricity within a decade.

ELEPHANT GRASS. The grass *Imperata cyclindrica*, which grows to a height of 80 centimeters (32 inches), has flat, razor-sharp leaves, is impervious to fire, unsuitable for grazing, and impossible to plow without heavy, modern equipment. This secondary growth takes over when swidden (q.v.) fields are abandoned.

ELEPHANTS. Both a symbol of royalty and an important beast of burden, especially in the past. The elephant is indigenous to the tropical rain forests of Thailand. Their present numbers are greatly reduced, for they are unable to breed and survive in open forests and marginal slopes. In the past, Thai kings owned thousands of elephants, using them in the fields and the military. Elephants can work well only in the wet season. The white elephant has been prized by the kings of Thailand as a symbol of kingship (q.v.) and divine protection. Economic modernization has decreased the value of working elephants in logging. Mechanical vehicles and roads have lessened the use of elephants for transport as well. Although previously elephants had an important role to play in displaying the riches and grandeur of the Siamese (q.v.) Court, they no longer do. In 1900, there were 100,000 domestic elephants in Siam. In 1952, the number had dropped to 13,397; and by 1982, there were only 4,739, according to the Ministry of the Interior.

EMERALD BUDDHA. A historic Buddha (q.v.) image of green jasper or malachite, which is approximately 60 centimeters in height, is enshrined in the royal temple compound *(wat)* in Bangkok (q.v.) where it is supervised by the king. The Emerald Buddha was discovered in 1436 in Chiang Rai City and was regarded as a sacred object in two former kingdoms in what is now northern Thailand and Laos. The image was obtained by General Chakri at the time of a successful military campaign which he commanded and brought to the national capital in 1779. Later General Chakri, when he had become Siamese (q.v.)

King Rama I (q.v.), placed the Emerald Buddha in its present location.

EMPLOYERS ASSOCIATIONS. More recent than trade associations (q.v.), employers associations have been organized in response to a 1975 labor relations law. By the early 1990s, there were approximately 15 employers associations whose functions were to handle wage disputes and advise government officials on labor policy. To date they have had little influence on public policy. This is due in large part to the weakness of labor organizations (q.v.).

END OF LENT CEREMONY (OK PHANSA). The end of lent ceremony occurs on the 15th day of the waxing moon in October. The end of the three months period of Buddhist Lent (q.v.) is widely celebrated with morning worship services at the Buddhist temple and special illumination of homes and temples.

EPIGRAPHY. Ancient inscriptions relative to the history of Thailand are scarce. However, a stone inscription attributed to King Ramkamhaeng (q.v.) found in 1833 is perhaps the most famous. It is considered the first writing system devised (in 1283) as a language for Tai language speakers. Ramkamhaeng's orthographic system has influenced both modern Thai and modern Lao scripts. Other inscriptions record gifts to Buddhist temples or the dedication of Buddha images (q.v.). One inscription records a border agreement between the King of Lan Xang and the King of Ayutthaya (q.v.). The agreement was commemorated in 1560 by a *stupa* (q.v.) erected on the common border of the two kingdoms.

ETHICS OF THAI BUDDHISM. Guides for social relations, based chiefly on the principle that the fates of human beings are ruled by the moral law that good behavior causes good results. There are four types of ethically good behavior which bring merit (q.v.) to a person and improve his status in the world. These are *metta*, *karuna*, *mutthita* and *ubekkha*. *Metta* means benevolence or charity. It involves also the love of mankind for the sake of its humanity, and a generalized willingness to be kind and helpful.

Metta is the highest virtue which, in a sense, underlies the other three. *Karuna* is a passion to help a subordinate in difficulty. It is also sympathy or pity for those who have had misfortune and the willingness to sacrifice one's own advantage or happiness for others. *Mutthita* means sympathy for the joys and sorrows of others. *Ubekkha* signifies the Thai value of non-involvement, that is, an attitude of detachment in situations of social stress. When faced with an embarrassing experience, the Thai is very likely to react by not reacting. These ethics are generally manifested in the social behavior of the Thai.

EXPORTS, AGRICULTURAL AND AGRO-BUSINESS. In the early 1990s, exports of farm products and processed foods remained stable compared to previous years, although a year of drought caused some reductions. In order of monetary value, the leading exports were: canned and frozen foods, rubber products, rice (q.v.), tapioca (cassava [q.v.]) and sugar.

EXPORTS, GENERAL. In the early 1990s, exports of most products increased by 5 to 15 percent annually. A similar pattern of increases is expected to continue. Main markets for Thai export products are: the United States (q.v.), the European Community, Japan (q.v.) and the Middle East. Taken together, these markets account for about 70 percent of the total. Exports in general continue to be a major contributor to Thailand's approximate 7.5 percent annual economic growth rate.

EXPORTS, INDUSTRIAL. Industrial exports grew from 5 to 15 percent annually in the early 1990s and this rate of increase is expected to continue. In order of monetary value, the leading exports were: electronics and components, garments and textiles, gems and jewelry (q.v.), shoes and parts, and plastic products. To a large extent, industrial products are dependent on imports of capital goods. Such imports of course have a negative impact on the nation's trade balance.

- F -

FAMILY PLANNING. A family planning program initiated in Thailand in the 1960s has been in operation for three decades. The Thai population fertility rate has dropped from nearly seven percent to approximately two percent in 35 years. The annual population growth rate in the early 1990s has been about 1.4 percent.

FARANG. The term used by the Thai to refer to all Westerners. It is thought that the term originated in India by the Indians who used the word *feringhi* to refer to the French. The use of the term *farang* dates from the time the Portuguese arrived in Thailand in the early 16th century.

FAUNA. Wild elephants (q.v.), long a symbol of Thailand, still roam the limestone hills of the northern areas and the woodlands of the peninsula (q.v.). However, these huge animals have been wiped out in most other parts of the country. The single-horned rhinoceros can be found occasionally but apparently is disappearing. The tapir is sometimes seen in the forests along the Malaysian border, and the wild hog and several types of deer are common in the wooded areas.

Other forest dwellers are tigers, leopards, panthers and many small predators. The large Himalayan black bear and the smaller Malayan bear are found in the mountains. Gibbons and several varieties of monkeys are widely distributed. Of the numerous kinds of snakes in Thailand, many are poisonous including cobras, coral snakes, kraits and vipers. Sea snakes and lizards abound; crocodiles and several species of turtles are also present.

FINANCIAL ADVISOR. The foreign monetary expert, almost always British, employed by the Thai government in its Ministry of Finance during the 19th and 20th centuries. The persons employed as financial advisors had considerable power and their presence in Thailand continued from the latter 1800s to 1950.

FINANCIAL SYSTEM. Thailand has a substantial number of financial institutions, namely commercial banks, finance companies, agricultural cooperatives, savings cooperatives, life insurance companies, pawnshops and credit unions. In addition, specialized financial institutions include the Government Saving Bank, Bank of Agriculture and Agricultural Cooperatives (BAAC), Industrial Finance Corporation of Thailand (IFCT) and Government Housing Bank. Situated in Bangkok (q.v.), the Bank of Thailand, established in 1942, acts as the country's central bank. Its function is to issue currency, act as banker to the government and other banks, deal with international monetary organizations, manage public debt, maintain exchange controls and supervise commercial banks. Its three branches are located at Hat Yai, Khon Kaen (q.v.) and Lampang. As of the early 1990s, there were 15 local commercial banks with 2,127 branches, including head offices: 614 in Bangkok (q.v.) and 1,513 in the provinces. In addition, there were 25 overseas branches of Thai banks and 14 foreign banks operating in Thailand. In September 1992, the Thai government authorized the establishment of offshore banking units by local and foreign banks. In March 1993, 47 licenses were granted to banks to begin offshore operations.

FLAG, THAI. The national flag of Thailand consists of five horizontal red, white and blue stripes. The red stripes at both the top and the bottom represent unity of the nation, the white stripes next to the red stands for the purity of religion and the blue stripe in the center represents the king.

FON LEP. See NAIL DANCE.

FOOD. For the principal Thai meal in the evening, white rice (q.v.) is served accompanied by two to four vegetables mixed with diced meat (curries). A soup is common. Thai food varies in taste from bland to very spicy. A lunch may involve only a noodle soup or a dish of rice with one or two side dishes. Spicy soup *(gaeng)* with vegetables and/or diced meat is a common lunch. Desserts *(khanom)* range from cakes to cold or warm dishes of jelly or beans to which coconut (q.v.) milk or a sweet sauce is added.

FOREIGN ADVISORS. A tradition of foreign advisors and officials has been one of long standing in Thailand. Already in the 16th century Indian experts in law were called upon to assist in the revision of Thai laws. In the 17th century, a Greek advisor and later a Japanese advisor were employed by King Narai (q.v.). Later kings followed the same practice. For administrative and other reforms of the Siamese (q.v.) Kingdom, the services of foreigners were secured on a contract basis. They were chosen by King Chulalongkorn (q.v.) and his successors from nations judged to take a neutral role in any possible disputes with either France (q.v.) or Britain. Their contributions consisted essentially of "technical" advice and expertise, especially in negotiations with Western powers and other foreign governments. In 1892, Chulalongkorn engaged a Belgian general advisor named Gustave Rolin-Jaequemyns (q.v.) who retired in 1899. Robert J. Kirkpatrick (q.v.) was employed from 1894 to 1899 as a legal advisor. The second general advisor, Dr. E. H. Strobel (q.v.), took office in 1903. From that time to 1949, this post was reserved for an American, employed as an advisor in foreign affairs. Most advisors were Harvard-trained legal experts who had no affiliation with their government. Strobel was followed in this position by Jens I. Westengard (q.v.), W. H. Pitkin, Dr. Eldon James, Dr. Francis B. Sayre (q.v.), Courtney Crocker, Raymond Stevens, R. Dolbeare and Kenneth S. Patton. Traditionally, in finance, the advisor was British, beginning with E. Rivett-Carnac (1896-1903). Others were W. J. F. Williamson, Sir Edward Cook and W. M. A. Doll. The British advisors urged the Thai government to follow a cautious policy and build up reserves in the Treasury. R. L. Morant (1887-1893), W. G. Johnson and E. S. Smith helped to develop Thai education, police, surveying and railways. Danes were employed in the navy and gendarmerie, the French in law and public works, the Italians in architecture (q.v.) and construction work, and the Germans in the construction of the northern railway line. Chulalongkorn sent sons of princes and noblemen as well as commoners' sons for further studies in Europe. On their return, they gradually replaced the foreigners and participated actively in the improvement of the public services.

FOREIGN CHAMBERS OF COMMERCE. In the early 1990s, ten foreign chambers of commerce were active. Of these, the American, the Chinese and the Japanese were the most significant. Integration of foreign chambers into Thai business operations is secured through membership in the Board of Trade or in the Thai Chamber of Commerce (q.v.). Each of these is also a conduit for contact with Thai government agencies and officials concerned with public policy.

FORESTRY. The wide variety of hard and softwood forests, especially teak, has created a burgeoning timber industry in Thailand. The bulk of production is in the highlands of the north. Tree varieties include teak, tropical evergreens, deciduous and mixed deciduous types. Forest depletion in Thailand has become a serious problem. Between 1973 and 1989, forests as a percentage of total land area decreased from 43 percent to 28 percent. Major causes of this rapid loss of forests has been commercial logging, charcoal production and clearing land for cultivation. In coastal areas of the south, loss of mangroves has occurred from expansion of prawn farms.

In 1989, logging on public lands was banned and timber exports were prohibited by the government. Except for a few small privately owned areas, all forest land is the property of the Thai state. With these restrictions in place, loggers either poach or set up operations in a neighboring country. Since 1980, the Department of Forestry has been actively engaged in reforestation projects.

FOUR NOBLE TRUTHS. A central belief and teaching of Buddhism (q.v.). The truths are: (1) life is suffering, (2) life is the result of desire, (3) cessation of desire ends life and suffering, and (4) cessation of desire is attained by following the Noble Eightfold Path (q.v.). (See BUDDHISM; NOBLE EIGHTFOLD PATH.)

FRANCE, RELATIONS WITH. In the 1680s for a short time period, France and the Kingdom of Ayutthaya (q.v.) began diplomatic and commercial relations. This included the stationing of French troops in the kingdom and the exchange of ambassadors. This smooth relationship ended abruptly under King Phetracha (q.v.).

Two hundred years later in the closing decades of the 19th and first part of the 20th centuries, Siam (q.v.) experienced extremely difficult relations with France. This was the period of French colonization in Southeast Asia starting with Vietnam. Unfortunately for Siam, France had in its employ a capable and astute diplomat, Auguste Pavie (q.v.), who was instrumental in getting Laos (q.v.) and a portion of Cambodia (q.v.) detached from Siam. These areas, previously in a tributary relationship with Siam, became incorporated into French Indochina.

Initially there was the Franco-Siamese Crisis and Treaty of 1893 (q.v.), in which Siam gave up all its territories in Laos east of the Mekong (q.v.) to France. In a second treaty in 1904, Siam ceded to France another two Lao provinces west of the Mekong. In return, the French evacuated Chantaboun and eliminated the 25 kilometer protective zone west of the Mekong required previously. In a third treaty in 1907, Siam ceded three Cambodian provinces to France, and Siam obtained in return some minor territorial concessions plus an end to extraterritorial privileges for all Asian-French subjects.

With military and naval action and Japanese concurrence, Thailand in 1940-1941 secured the return of certain Lao and Cambodian territories lost to France previously. However, in a 1946 treaty, these short-lived gains were returned to French jurisdiction. In return, France supported Thailand's application to join the United Nations. Later in the 1940s, all French extraterritorial privileges in Thailand were eliminated.

A number of Thai students matriculated in the 1920s and subsequently at French universities. Today, bilateral diplomatic relations are friendly and cooperative. The French have for many years operated a French language and cultural center in Bangkok (q.v.). For Thailand, France is one of its European trading partners.

FRANCO-SIAMESE CRISIS AND TREATY OF 1893. Hostilities between resisting forces of Siam (q.v.) and French army units occurred when the latter were sent to take control of Laos (q.v.) early in 1893. There were hostilities also between Siamese and

French forces in the Paknam Incident (q.v.). These crisis producing events, together with others, led to an ultimatum delivered by Auguste Pavie (q.v.) which the king of Siam was unable to reject.

In the treaty signed in October 1893, Siam ceded all Lao territories east of the Mekong River (q.v.) to France (q.v.), which was expanding its Indochina colonies. The treaty also created a 25 kilometer demilitarized zone on the west side of the Mekong River and permitted France to occupy the port city of Chantaburi to ensure treaty compliance. The Siamese were also required to pay an indemnity to France for the losses it suffered.

FREE THAI (SERI THAI MOVEMENT). In 1942, in the United States and in Britain, an anti-Japanese underground movement was initiated. It was supported by Thai students who became stranded by the Indochina war. The movement was guided by Seni Pramoj (q.v.), the Thai ambassador to the United States, and by Pridi Phanomyong (q.v.) in Thailand, who was regent for the kingdom. Some 36 Thai students were trained by the British Army. Another 31 were trained by the Office of Strategic Services (OSS) in the United States. These young men were secretly returned to Thailand where they joined the local Free Thai group. The Allied war effort was aided by the Free Thai, and their existence reduced the demands that Thailand be treated as an enemy at the end of the war. Contacts by the Free Thai with resistance groups in neighboring countries had a considerable impact on Thailand's postwar foreign policy.

FRENCH TRADE, AYUTTHAYA PERIOD. Trade was officially begun with France (q.v.) in 1680 with the arrival of the French envoy Deslandes-Bourreau, and an exchange of embassies took place in 1684-1685, with Chevalier de Chaumont as the first French ambassador. Treaties were signed in 1685 and 1687 giving the French freedom of religious instruction, access to free trade, a monopoly on tin from the island of Phuket, the control of Songkhla (q.v.), and extraterritorial jurisdiction over doctors, teachers and other French citizens.

French influence ended abruptly with the death of King Narai (q.v.) in 1688. The throne was seized by Phetracha (q.v.), a distinguished general and leader of a strong anti-foreign movement. French troops were forced to withdraw, and all special privileges previously accorded to foreign missionaries and traders were rescinded.

FRUIT PRODUCTION. Thailand has become a leading exporter of tropical fruits and vegetables to Europe, the United States (q.v.), Hong Kong, Singapore, Malaysia, China (q.v.) and Japan (q.v.). The mainstay of these exports are dried beans to Japan and India, and canned pineapple and bamboo (q.v.) shoots to the United States, Europe and Japan. At present, baby corn and asparagus fetch a high price, while lychee, rambutan, mangosteen and longan are seen to have great future potential. On a smaller scale, papaya, mango, long beans, chili, capsicums and lemon grass are exported for the Asian and Southeast Asian communities in the West. Besides the country's commercial fruits, there are many other indigenous fruits and nuts raised for domestic consumption.

FUNERAL RITES. Such rites are the most elaborate of all life cycle ceremonies and may involve the following: Buddhist monks (q.v.) offering chants from Buddhist scriptures (q.v.) to benefit the deceased; expectation that the individual will experience rebirth; bathing ceremony in which friends and relatives pour lustral water over one hand of the departed; cremation within three days ordinarily using a pyre of wood (however, in urban areas the body may be burned in a permanent crematorium after which ashes may be collected and kept in an urn). Cremation of the bodies of prominent or wealthy persons may be deferred for periods of up to a year. This permits a longer period in which to show affection, respect and performance of religious rites which will benefit the deceased. Books or pamphlets are sometimes specially prepared for the funeral rites and distributed by wealthy persons.

- G -

GARUDA. The national and royal emblem of Thailand. The Garuda is a mythical bird with features of a man. As a symbol, it is incorporated into the labels or emblems of government departments and ministries. It is also displayed by banks when approved by the king in recognition of their public service.

GEMS AND JEWELRY. During the past two decades, the Thai gem and jewelry industry has grown rapidly. Gems and jewelry combined were the third largest earner of foreign exchange in 1992. After Italy, Thailand was the second leading exporter of gems and jewelry. Because Thailand has rich sources of sapphires, rubies, garnets, zircon beryle, quartz and jadeite, it has become one of the world's leading centers for the cutting and trading of gemstones. Each year an estimated 70 percent of the world's rubies and sapphires come from Thailand.

GOLDEN TRIANGLE. The famous opium-producing region of Southeast Asia, which includes the hills of eastern Burma, the highlands of northern Laos and the ridges of extreme northern Thailand. The civilization of the Golden Triangle dates back to the 13th century. It was a part of the ancient Kingdom of Lan Na (q.v.). Communities there were able to preserve their culture and traditions for years. The areas include Mae Sai, Chiang Khong, Chiang Saen, Doi Mae Salong and Chiang Rai. A few towns are famous for opium smuggling. They are largely controlled by descendants of former army officers and soldiers of the Chinese leader Chiang Kai-shek.

The inhabitants, who produce the opium poppies, belong to the hill tribes (q.v.) which live and survive in these higher elevation sites. While opium poppy production has decreased somewhat in Thailand, the country remains the principal trade route for marketing this crop. Interdiction efforts by Thai officials have been attempted and continue with United States' (q.v.) involvement. Major difficulties in interdiction are the remoteness of the production sites, deals with local officials and the lack of alternative economic opportunities for the producers.

GONG AEW. The name for a musical group in northern Thailand known as the long-drum ensemble and consisting of a long cannon drum *(gong aew)*, a short thin drum, two oboes and a pair of cymbals. The *gong aew* is used at festivals held in the temple compounds *(wat)* (q.v.) of northern Thailand when the traditional dance, the nail dance (q.v.), is a part of the ceremony. (See DONTRI PUEN MUANG; MUSICAL INSTRUMENTS; PIPHAT ORCHESTRA.)

GONG WONG YAI. A Thai musical instrument (q.v.) consisting of 16 metal resonance pieces, or gongs, arranged on a circular rattan frame. The gongs are graduated in size and are struck with beaters, one hard and one soft. The *gong wong yai* frequently carries the principal melody and is an essential part of a piphat orchestra (q.v.). It resembles the Western instrument called a glockenspiel. The *gong wong lek*, another Thai musical instrument, is built similarly to the *gong wong yai*, only smaller, and is played the same way. It resembles the Western musical instrument called a celesta.

GONGS. Gongs are essential instruments in most orchestras in central Thailand. Three such gongs are the *charb lek* or small cymbals, the *charb yai* or large cymbals, and the *mong*, a gong which is suspended on a tripod and beat with a stick. A fourth, the *ching*, is a small pair of thick cymbals which produce either short crisp notes or long ringing sounds. The *ching* sets the pace for the instrumental or singing group. (See MUSICAL INSTRUMENTS; PIPHAT ORCHESTRA.)

GOVERNMENTAL SYSTEM. The absolute monarchy (q.v.) which had governed Siam (q.v.) for more than six centuries was changed to a constitutional monarchy by the Revolution of 1932 (q.v.). The more or less authoritarian governments since then could be characterized as relatively stable, though controlled by a military elite. Changes in government administrations since 1932 have been, more often than not, the result of bloodless coups d'etat, which have been backed by military force. The coups ushered in new administrations headed by a military officer (q.v.). Sometimes, administrations were headed by a civilian who governed under more or less the control of the military. After a few years, an attempt at a democratic government in the 1970s was ended by a military coup. Another attempt at democratic government was initiated after the September 1992 election, when the Chuan Leekpai (q.v.) nonmilitary administration took office.

The elements of Thai governmental systems continue to be (1) the king (q.v.) as head of state, (2) the National Assembly (q.v.), which consists of two chambers, the House of Representatives and the Senate, (3) the Council of Ministers (q.v.) or Cabinet, (4) the Judiciary (q.v.), and (5) political parties (q.v.). An administration of the Thai national government operates in the House of Representatives as a coalition. This is a cooperating group of elected representatives from enough parties to achieve a working majority for legislative purposes.

GOVERNOR (PHUWARACHAKAN). The chief administrative officer of a province *(changwat)*. He is appointed by the minister of the interior, to whom he is responsible. In his province, the governor is the chief representative of the central government, the chief coordinator of governmental services from the various central government ministries and the chief administrator of provincial affairs. He is also the spokesman for local citizens to the central government.

GRAND PALACE. A grouping of royal palaces and associated buildings and courtyards inside an enclosure at the corner of Sanam Chai and Na Phralan roads in Bangkok (q.v.). Of general interest is the Chakri Throne Hall. Also found here are the Dusit Palace, Amarain Winichai Hall and Borophinman Palace. The palaces were built over a period of time by the kings of the Chakri dynasty (q.v.).

GREAT BRITAIN, RELATIONS WITH. An island nation, with a population of 57 million people (1991), at the extreme western part of Europe. It consists of England, Scotland, Wales, Northern Ireland and several adjacent small islands. Thailand and Great Britain have excellent international relations today. However, Thai-British relationships faced crises in the late-19th century and again during the World War II period. (See WESTERNERS.)

GREETING. The traditional form used by the Thai in greeting is called the *wai*. In this pattern, palms and fingers of the hands are placed together, fingers slightly bent toward each other and inward, in front of the chest or higher while the head is bowed. The basic posture has many variations according to the social position of the participants. The inferior (from position or age) offers the salute first and makes certain that his hands are raised high, and his bow lower than the salute of the superior. The superior grades his salute subtly to the position of the inferior, to the point where the persons of highest respect, the Buddhist monks (q.v.), refrain from responding to a *wai* at all.

The casual visitor is wise to be hesitant about using the *wai*, as there are subtleties involved. When introduced to Westerners, Thai men usually shake hands, as a concession to their customs.

- H -

HAMPE, RUDOLF W. E. An artist, born in Berlin in 1906, who arrived in Thailand in 1933. He has specialized in landscape painting, but also painted Thai temple scenes and the everyday life of the Thai people. Hampe was also a master of the graphic arts. He is famous for his copies, called "temple rubbings," of the bas-relief figures and carvings at Thai Buddhist temples. These copies are made on paper or on cloth using paint or crayon.

HANDICRAFTS. While not a major item in the national economy, traditional handicrafts are important to the villagers of many areas as a sideline to farming and other occupations. The "cottage or home industries" system implies part-time work. Many villages specialize in a single craft, often with each household of the village devoting attention to only one detail of that craft, e.g., the parasol village near Chiang Mai (q.v.) (see UMBRELLAS). (See BAMBOO; CERAMICS; COTTON WEAVING; LACQUERWARE; NIELLOWARE; RATTAN

FURNITURE MAKING; SUPPORT; THAI SILK; WOOD CARVING.)

HARIPUNCHAYA. Buddhist Mon (q.v.) kingdom located near Lamphun from about the early 9th to the 13th centuries. According to a 15th century Pali (q.v.) chronicle, Haripunchaya was founded by the Mon Princess Chamadevi (q.v.), who came from Lop Buri (q.v.) which was then a part of the Mon State of Dvaravati (q.v.). Haripunchaya maintained its independence though the Dvaravati State was largely conquered and absorbed by the Khmer Kingdom which was centered at Angkor (q.v.). However, Haripunchaya was overthrown in the 14th century by King Mengrai (q.v.) and incorporated into the Lan Na Kingdom (q.v.).

HEALTH AND SANITATION DISTRICT (SUKAPIBAN). A local sanitation or health district which has a population center and a tax base, but is not yet large enough to be a municipality. The capital towns of districts (q.v.), which are not municipalities, are generally sanitation districts. Governing each *sukapiban* is a committee chaired by the district officer (q.v.). Funds available are used for such functions as garbage collection, street paving, providing electricity, slaughterhouse regulation, water, sewage facilities and health care.

HIGHWAYS. The Department of Highways was organized in 1912. Most roads in Thailand run generally in a north-south direction in keeping with the configuration of the mountains and rivers of the country. From 1981 to 1991, total motor vehicle registrations quadrupled (2 million to 8.5 million), while truck, van and passenger car registrations doubled. Massive traffic jams and air pollution have become a serious problem in Bangkok (q.v.). The need for roads has increased extensively in the last decade. The road transportation network of the country totals 169,794 kilometers (106,121 miles), consisting of 15,899 kilometers (9,936 miles) of national highways and expressways, 25,895 kilometers (16,184 miles) of provincial roads and about 128,000 kilometers (80,000 miles) of rural roads. Throughout the country the government has established 175 bus stations for passengers.

These support the expansion of industrial zones. There are also several cargo stations.

HILL TRIBE DEVELOPMENT. The way of life of hill people was severely affected in the middle of the 1960s when both opium growing and swidden (q.v.) were declared illegal. A new development program of the Thai government encourages hill tribe farmers to grow agricultural crops other than opium and to use permanent agricultural sites. Since the mid-1960s members of the royal family have become patrons of hill tribes (q.v.). Members of the royal family have made well-publicized visits to tribal communities to open schools, sponsor rice (q.v.) banks and assist those who have suffered some calamity. Queen Sirikit (q.v.) also encourages them to expand their traditional handicrafts (q.v.), and sponsors the sale of tribal crafts nationwide and in many markets abroad. (See SUPPORT.)

HILL TRIBES. The term designates ethnic minorities most of whom live in the remote highland areas of the northern and southwestern parts of Thailand. They have their own traditions and customs which are different from the people in the lowlands. The type of shifting cultivation practiced by most of the hill tribes causes the deforestation and deterioration of highland watersheds. The principal ethnic groups are Karen (q.v.), Meo (Hmong) (q.v.), Lahu, Lisu, Yao, Akha, Htin, Lua (Lawa) and Khamu. The present hill tribes population is scattered over 21 provinces and 76 districts (q.v.). In 1988, it was estimated to total 550,000. Among these, the Karen were the largest group with 52 percent and Khamu was the smallest group with about 1 percent. The household is the basic socioeconomic unit charged with the responsibility of providing food (q.v.), shelter, welfare, health and education, including religious training and socialization of behavior. On July 6, 1976, the stated policy of the Thai government was to integrate these people into the Thai state and give them full rights to practice their religions and maintain their culture. According to the 1986 survey, 79 percent of the hill tribe population had no education (q.v.), and about 19 percent had education ranging from primary to university level.

HINAYANA BUDDHISM. See BUDDHISM.

HMONG. See MEO.

HOLIDAYS, NATIONAL. Five national holidays, celebrated annually, are dated by the Western calendar. Chakri Memorial Day (q.v.) is the 6th of April, Coronation Day is celebrated on the 5th of May, the Queen's Birthday (q.v.) occurs on the 12th of August, Chulalongkorn Memorial Day (q.v.) is on the 23rd of October and the King's Birthday (q.v.) is celebrated on the 5th of December.

HOUSE OF REPRESENTATIVES. See NATIONAL ASSEMBLY.

HOUSEHOLD RITES. Ceremonies at the home of Buddhist laity and in which Buddhist monks (q.v.) are included. The monks sing chants and offer blessings, lustral water and counsel. They are invited on occasions that mark births, housewarmings, marriages, severe illnesses and deaths. Gifts of food (q.v.) and other offerings to the monks, which make merit (q.v.) for the givers, are an essential part of these ceremonies.

HSINBYUSHIN. King of Burma (reigned 1763-1776), who led invasions of Siam (q.v). During his reign, Burmese military power was at its zenith. This occurred in spite of the king's difficulties with ministers and other high administrative officials. Hsinbyushin continued the plan of his father, Alaunghpaya, to conquer and dominate the Tai-speaking peoples east of the Salween River. Initially, during 1773-1775, the army of Burma forces subjugated Lan Na (q.v.) and Lan Xang along with adjacent regions. Then, using a large-scale pincer movement, the Burmese overcame the Thai state of Ayutthaya (q.v.) in early 1767, which was then ruled by the weak King Ekatat (or Suriyamarin). The capital city, Ayutthaya, was captured, plundered and left desolate, while thousands were taken captive to Burma. During the period 1765-1769, the Burmese under Hsinbyushin and his successor were also at war with China (q.v.).

- I -

IMAM. Islamic priest and leader of the religious congregation. (See ISLAM; THAI-MALAY.)

IN KHONG. A famous painter of the mid-19th century whose wall paintings at the Temple of the Emerald Buddha (q.v.) in Bangkok (q.v.) represent episodes from the history of the former capital of Ayutthaya (q.v.).

INDIANS IN THAILAND. One of the smaller minorities, Indians are immigrants or descendants of immigrants, chiefly from Ceylon (now Sri Lanka) or the west coast of India. They can be either Hindus, Sikhs or Muslims and are located mainly in urban centers, especially the Bangkok metropolis (q.v.). They are found in a variety of occupations but mainly in textiles, jewelry, metal products and food stores.

INDUSTRY. The growth rate of industrial production in Thailand has recently been relatively high at 7 to 10 percent annually. The largest component is manufacturing (q.v.). Agriculture (q.v.) and agri-business, transport and communications, construction, mining (q.v.) and quarrying, and public utilities are among the larger sectors of industry.

INSURGENCY. Since the 1950s, there have been segments of Thai society that have become aware of the income gap between the urban and rural workers. Dissatisfied segments of the population have been most noticeable among the Thai-Lao in the northeast (q.v.), certain minority hill tribes (q.v.) in northern provinces that are adjacent to the northeast, and the Thai-Malay (q.v.) in the extreme south of Thailand. There are separatists among the Thai-Malay who seek greater autonomy from the national government with regard to religion, education and local government (q.v.). Beginning in the 1950s, the Communist party of Thailand (CPT) (q.v.) has attempted to exploit the potential of these villagers to revolt. The CPT was also a conduit for financial aid and weapons from China (q.v.) and Vietnam.

When isolated armed clashes began to occur, counter insurgency measures were taken by the Thai Army and border police. From 1951 to 1976, they were assisted in their effort by the United States (q.v.), but the military actions undertaken brought only limited success. In 1980, a new approach was developed. Amnesty was offered, to which large numbers of insurgents responded, and accelerated rural development was begun. Military operations were conducted against a limited number of selected targets. As a result of this new approach, in addition to favorable political changes in Southeast Asia, insurgency threats have greatly diminished.

INTERNATIONAL COOPERATION. Cooperation through the United Nations has been an important part of Thai foreign relations since Thailand joined that body in 1946. Thailand holds membership in 14 of the United Nations special agencies as follows: Food and Agriculture Organization (FAO), International Atomic Energy Agency (IAEA), International Bank for Reconstruction and Development (IBRD), International Civil Aviation Organization (ICAO), International Development Association (IDA), International Finance Corporation of Thailand (IFC), International Labour Organisation (ILO), International Monetary Fund (IMF), International Telecommunications Union (ITU), United Nations Educational, Scientific, and Cultural Organization (UNESCO) (q.v.), Universal Postal Union (UPU), World Health Organization (WHO), World Meteorological Organization (WMO), Economic and Social Commission for Asia and the Pacific (ESCAP) (q.v.). Thailand also participates in a number of cooperative associations which consist of nations in the Pacific and Asian regions. (See ASEAN; ASPAC; COLOMBO PLAN; ESCAP; SEAMES; SEATO; UNESCO.)

INTERNATIONAL RESERVES. In the early 1990s, total international financial reserves of Thailand were significantly in excess of US$20 billion. This represents a continued growth pattern. The large excess of imports over exports, or negative trade balance, is more than offset by foreign investment in

Thailand and the huge foreign exchange earnings from tourism (q.v.).

INVESTMENT PROMOTION. Through its Board of Investment (BOI) the Thai government has an active program to encourage domestic and foreign investment. The major emphasis of the BOI is on labor-intensive industry exports (q.v.) and regional decentralization of industry. Certain categories of investment are eligible for promotional privileges and incentives. Foreign investors in promoted companies can own land, avoid certain taxes, enter and employ foreign nationals and remit foreign currency abroad. In addition, investors have available a wide range of business services. One of these is a center to aid the promoted companies to obtain required permits, licenses and visas. Agencies other than the BOI provide other help to new investors, including industrial estates and environmental management.

IRRIGATION. Rice (q.v.) producers in Southeast Asia have traditionally relied on rain and flood water, which characterizes the central Plain (q.v.). Records of rainfall and water for this area, over a long period, have indicated that one year in three there was insufficient water available for successful wet rice production. Controlled irrigation began in the central Plain in 1922. Since then the irrigated area in Thailand has been expanded to more than 3.7 million hectares (1.5 million acres). World Bank loans assisted in the construction of some dams and distribution systems. Two of these dams, completed in 1964 and 1973, have hydroelectric power generating potential. Responsibility for the development and maintenance of irrigation systems falls principally within the purview of the Royal Irrigation Department, founded in 1904.

Small irrigation projects have been completed in wet rice growing areas of all the regions. Besides bringing new lands into crop production, dams and irrigation systems contribute needed flood control. However, dams usually inundate previously farmed areas with water. This has led to the necessary resettlement of farm families with the resultant problems, including compensation for land lost, organizing new settlements and adapting to new soils and new crops. (See IRRIGATION SYSTEMS, TRADITIONAL.)

IRRIGATION SYSTEMS, TRADITIONAL. The land area available for wet rice (q.v.) cultivation has historically been extended by effectively managing water resources using irrigation (q.v.). For hundreds of years, agricultural villagers in northern Thailand have cooperatively operated their own irrigation systems. Using stakes of wood, stones and sand, dams have been constructed in rivers and repaired annually. The tasks involved are divided so that each village has a share in building and maintaining the dams and distribution canals. The communal ownership and maintenance of such water facilities under an elected dam chief was labeled by M. Bruneau "une petite démocratie rurale."

ISAN. See NORTHEAST.

ISLAM. Muslims constitute about four percent of the Thai population and are concentrated largely in the four southernmost provinces: Pattani (q.v.), Yala, Narathiwat and Satun. In these provinces, Thai-Muslim constitute about 75 percent of the population. The Islamic faith, like Buddhism (q.v.) in Thailand, has incorporated beliefs and practices which are not originally a part of the religion. The animistic practices, which seek to control evil spirits and are used in local Islamic ceremonies, are very similar to the animistic practices of Malays in Malaysia. In Thailand 38 provinces have more than 2,000 mosques, the great majority of which are of the Sunni branch of Islam. Each mosque has an *imam* (q.v.), its chief figure, the *katib* or preacher, and the *muezzin* or *bilal*, the crier. Islam demands a system of religious instruction and the Hajj or pilgrimage to Mecca.

- J -

JAPAN, RELATIONS WITH. Economic ties between Japan and the Kingdom of Ayutthaya (q.v.) existed already in the 17th century and have increased since then. At the turn of the 20th century when each nation had an embassy in the capital of the other, Japan sent legal advisors to Siam and assisted in improving the silk industry there. A blight on the bilateral relations of the two nations was the Japanese Occupation of Thailand 1941-1944 (q.v.). However, the frustrations, shortages and conflicts involved have been more or less forgotten by the Thai.

Longer lasting strains between Thailand and Japan have been the result of a marked trade imbalance. Large numbers of Japanese owned industries in Thailand import goods and services that far exceed in value the exports of Thailand to Japan. In response, Thailand has increased its export promotion activities. It also cooperates with the Association of Southeast Asian Nations (q.v.) in collective trade bargaining with Japan. While the bilateral relations are strictly economic, the wide range of Japanese consumer goods sold in Thailand has a cultural influence.

JAPANESE OCCUPATION (1941-1944). Japan in the 1930s sought to expand its trade and influence in Southeast Asia, with Thailand as one target. Phibunsongkhram (q.v.), the Thai prime minister from 1938 to 1944, supported the Japanese as a counterweight to the power of the British. Following an ultimatum and a military encounter at several coastal sites, the Thai acquiesced to military occupation by the Japanese in December 1941. Thailand served as a military and supply base for the Japanese, who attempted to construct a railroad link to Burma, part of which bridged the River Kwai. (See BRIDGE ON THE RIVER KWAI). It is remembered as the "famous railway of death," as the Kanchana Buri War Cemetery (q.v.) attests. As the war turned against Japan, Thai relations with the Japanese occupation worsened. Direct requisition of goods and labor by the Japanese was largely prevented. While the Thai prime minister issued a declaration of war against the Allies, there was also an effective Free Thai Movement (q.v.) working underground against the Japanese. The latter was of much help in restoring Thailand's good relations with the Allies after World War II. (See FREE THAI.)

JOINT PUBLIC AND PRIVATE SECTOR CONSULTATIVE COMMITTEES (JPPCCs). The central JPPCC was created by the government in 1981 as an organization to deal with important business and economic problems, and has provided a channel for business interests to present their complaints to the government. Problems presented are chiefly (1) reducing red tape and delays for needed approvals, (2) eliminating obstructive laws and rules and (3) relieving excessive taxation. The positive results achieved by the central JPPCC has led to the organization of a JPPCC in every province (q.v.) in Thailand. The JPPCCs have tackled both serious economic problems and promoted the development of business associations (q.v.).

JUDICIAL SYSTEM. Constitutional and legislative law provides for three levels of courts and for the independence of judges. There are numerous city and provincial Courts of Original Jurisdiction, the Intermediate Court of Appeals, and the Supreme Court. The latter two courts are located in the capital city, Bangkok (q.v.). Supervision of the courts is handled primarily by the Ministry of Justice which appoints and supervises the personnel of the courts and is responsible for reform in judicial practice and procedures. An additional minor supervisory body is the Judicial Service Commission which is composed of 11 members. In the courts of southern Thailand where cases involving Muslims are heard, there are Muslim judges who interpret the Islamic laws and usages. (See ISLAM.)

Most Thai jurists maintain that Thailand now has the civil law system as the basis for its jurisprudence. Yet, from outward appearance, it seems a common law system prevails fundamentally. The provisions of the Thai laws relating to commercial matters follow generally those of the British legal system. However, tort rules generally follow the German patterns. The laws of inheritance and domestic relations are generally based on ancient Thai customs, with some provisions taken from the civil law. The only death penalties in Thai law are for murder and high treason. In criminal cases, two or three judges sit when the penalty can be greater than one year of imprisonment. Cases can be initiated either by the public prosecutor or by the injured person. There is no provision for trial by jury. The judiciary (q.v.) as a whole enjoys a reputation for honesty and competence.

JUDICIARY. Both traditional and modern elements make up the Thai legal system (q.v.). Civil, criminal and commercial codes, adapted from Western legal systems, are an important feature of Thai laws. There are loans also from India, China and Japan. The levels of courts are those of first instance, the Court of Appeal and the Supreme Court. Administrative personnel of these courts and judicial reforms are handled by the Ministry of Justice. The appointment, promotion and removal of judges is handled by the Judicial Service Commission. The Central Labor Court was established in 1980 to adjudicate labor disputes. Juvenile offenses are handled by Juvenile Courts in several regional centers and by the Central Juvenile Court. (See JUDICIAL SYSTEM.)

JUTE PRODUCTION. A fiber plant, jute is cultivated mainly in the plateau area of northeast Thailand wherever there is sufficient water and loose soil.

- K -

KAEN (KHANE). In northeast Thailand and Laos, a mouth organ musical instrument (q.v.) that is widely used is the *kaen*. This instrument consists of 16 bamboo (q.v.) pipes and a hardwood wind chest inside of which is a small metal reed.

KALAHOM. Military organ of the government in the Kingdom of Ayutthaya (q.v.). Created by King Borommatrailokanat (q.v.) in the mid-15th century, the Kalahom handled military affairs. Its companion agency, the Mahatthai (q.v.), handled civil affairs. The administrative system was changed in the mid-17th century so that the Kalahom had charge of both military and civil affairs in the southern provinces of the kingdom. Similarly, the Mahatthai handled the affairs of the central and northern provinces. This system of government administration was retained until the end of the 19th century when it was modified to the system in operation today.

KAMMA. See KARMA.

KAMMAKAN WAT. A committee consisting of the head Buddhist monk (q.v.), several laymen and one or more junior monks who organize the practical affairs of a Buddhist temple compound *(wat)* (q.v.), such as communication between the monks and the laity, management of properties, arrangements for ceremonies and coordination of alms giving.

KAMNAN. The leader or headman of a commune *(tambon)*. He is normally chosen by the headmen of the villages that make up the commune, from among their own members. He is the principal link between the district (q.v.), which is the lowest branch of the national government, and the people of the commune he represents. In addition to participation in ceremonial duties, the recording of vital statistics and tax collection, the *kamnan* supervises law and order and agricultural extension projects in the commune.

KANCHANA BURI WAR CEMETERY AND MUSEUM. Near Kanchana Buri City, some 125 kilometers (78 miles) west of Bangkok (q.v.), is found the infamous "Bridge on the River Kwai" (q.v.). The bridge was built in 1944, during World War II, by the Japanese using exploited Allied prisoners of war (POWs) and slave-laborers from countries then occupied by the Japanese Army. In the cemetery are the remains of approximately 16,000 Allied POWs and 50,000 Southeast Asians who died there from lack of medical care, starvation and torture during bridge construction. The War Museum displays war memorabilia, photographs, personal recollections and descriptions of tortures perpetrated by the Japanese. The cemetery is maintained by a private British foundation.

KARACHAKAN. Any civil servant employed in the Thai government, whether at national, provincial, district (q.v.), or municipal level. Literally the name can be translated "a servant in the king's service." (See CIVIL SERVICE.)

KAREN (KARIANG, YANG). Of the highland or hill peoples, the Karen are probably the largest group and speak a non-Tai language (q.v.). They are located along the entire western border of Thailand with Burma. They share a culture with the Karen population along Burma's southeastern border with Thailand. The Karen were already present in earlier centuries, when the Mon (q.v.), Burmese, the ancestors of the Thai peoples and other ethnic groups were migrating into the area. Currently, the Karen in Thailand number at least 100,000. Different dialects are spoken by different subgroups, but village leaders also communicate in the Thai language.

The Karen subsist on upland agriculture (q.v.), which is in large part swidden (q.v.). They grow a variety of vegetables and crops as well as poultry, pigs and livestock. In addition, plants and animals are hunted in the jungle. In religion, the Karen are predominantly animists, although both Buddhism (q.v.) and Christianity (q.v.) are expanding into their communities. Elementary schools are gradually being established by the Thai government. In many ways the Karen are largely autonomous since they live in somewhat inaccessible areas.

KARMA. The Thai notion from Hinduism and Buddhism (q.v.) that every act, work or thought of a person has some ultimate and associate reward or punishment in this life or the next because of the existence of the law of causation. Hence, all of one's deeds, verbal, physical or mental, create one's *karma*. It follows that a person is born according to his past *karma* which together with his present *karma* will determine his future existence. This assumes, of course, belief in the transmigration of souls. The word *karma*, derived from the Sanskrit (q.v) language, has the same meaning as *kamma*, an expression of the Pali (q.v.) language. In Thailand, *kamma* is typically the spoken form and *karma* the written.

KATHIN. Colorful and varied ceremonies which occur within one or two weeks following the end of the Buddhist Lent (q.v.) holy days, normally in October. At this time, robes and other essentials are presented to the men who continue permanently in the temple as Buddhist monks (q.v.). There is usually a parade to mark the occasion in which participants carry their gifts to the presentation ceremony at the temple compound *(wat)* (q.v.). In some cities there are also boat races or other attractions. In the Bangkok metropolis (q.v.), the king leads a procession of large and beautifully decorated royal barges on the Chao Phraya River (q.v.) laden with gifts for presentation to the monks at the Temple of Dawn (Wat Arun [q.v.]).

KAVILA. Ruler of Chiang Mai (reigned 1775-1813). Kavila was a former local chieftain subservient to the King of Burma. However, he and his army went over to the side of Siam (q.v.) in a 1774 war in which the armies of Burma were defeated. As a result of his continued support of the Siamese (q.v.), he became the new head of the successor to the former Lan Na Kingdom (q.v.), but as a vassal to the Siamese king. Kavila was a capable military leader and held off Burmese attacks until Siamese aid arrived. He moved his capital from Lampang to Chiang Mai (q.v.) in 1781. Kavila was confirmed as ruler of all the northern region by Rama I (q.v.) in 1782. In his efforts to increase the population, Kavila brought in captured peoples through raids into territories in the domain of the Burmese. His descendants continued to rule in Chiang Mai, the capital city, until 1939.

KHAM BUNNAG. See THIPHAKORAWONG.

KHANE. See KAEN.

KHAO. See RICE.

KHAO PHANSA. See BUDDHIST LENT.

KHAO YAI. Thailand's most popular national park on a site about 200 kilometers (125 miles) northeast of Bangkok (q.v.). The cooler air of the high elevation, the natural vegetation and wildlife--including numerous species of orchids, elephants (q.v.)

and other protected wildlife--combine to make Khao Yai an attractive resort. The park was opened in 1962.

KHMER. A Khmer-speaking ethnic grouping found in southeastern Thailand and along the entire border region with Cambodia (q.v.). The Khmers in Thailand have been estimated to number between 185,000 and 400,000 and share the language of the Cambodian people. They occupy areas which, in the 18th century and earlier, were part of a Khmer Kingdom (q.v.) later conquered by the Thai. In their economy, religion, customs, and other cultural features, the Khmer are very similar to the Thai. They are gradually becoming assimilated into Thai society and use of the Thai language is increasing. The Khmer tongue, of an Austro-Asiatic language stock, is widely spoken. (See ANGKOR.)

KHMER KINGDOM. See ANGKOR.

KHON. The masked play in the classical form of Thai dance drama (q.v.) in which the performers in general are male. They wear masks having a wide variety of design each indicating the personality of its wearer. The dance drama is built on episodes from the Ramakian, a Thai version of the well-known Indian epic, the Ramayana (q.v.) of the poet Valmiki. Music forms an important part of the dance drama which is greatly bound by tradition and includes both singing tunes and action tunes. Each action tune is connected with certain dances and actions. The actors respond to each, a walk tune, a marching tune, a weeping tune, a love-making tune, and so on.

KHON KAEN. A large province of the northeast (q.v.), pop. 1,700,000 (est.). The provincial capital, Khon Kaen, pop. 131,000 (est.), has experienced impressive growth in the past two decades. To a large extent, this has resulted from government action. Khon Kaen has become a center for government programs of development for the western and central parts of the northeast. Khon Kaen University, opened in 1964, provides higher education (q.v.) in 15 schools or colleges. Four of these offer graduate programs. Recent enrollment has been about 7,000.

Other development efforts have focused on construction of dams to provide water for irrigation (q.v.) as well as for electric power. Agriculture (q.v.) is characterized chiefly as subsistence, although commercial farming is increasing. A television (q.v.) center and transmitting station are also located here. Khon Kaen City is an important center for air and surface transportation. In Gross Domestic Product per capita, Khon Kaen ranks first among the provinces of the northeast.

KHORAT. See NAKHON RATCHASIMA.

KHORAT PLATEAU. See THE NORTHEAST.

KHRU. Those who teach are addressed with the title *khru*. It is not limited to a particular profession. *Khru* is used to show respect to qualified persons in the arts, including those who offer private lessons.

KHRUBA SIWICHAI (1878-1939). Famous Buddhist monk. Khruba Siwichai was ordained a Buddhist novice *(nen)* (q.v.) in his home village temple *(wat)* at age 18. Three years later he was ordained a Buddhist monk *(bhikkhu)* (q.v.). During his life-long vocation as a monk, Khruba demonstrated his ability to organize villagers and others in the construction or repair of important religious buildings. These include two famous temples that house important relics and another major temple which is in Chiang Mai City (q.v.). His success in these endeavors reflects a capacity he had to persuade his followers to donate their labor and wealth for building projects. His efforts occasionally resulted in conflict with secular and religious authorities. However, such events and their outcomes seemed to enhance his reputation among his followers.

Khruba is remembered also for the high degree of asceticism that characterized his life-style, and for assisting the laity to attain merit (q.v.). His concern for fellow Buddhists has been noted by those who knew him. One writer stated: "Khruba saw as useful only actions for the collectivity while doing nothing useful for himself." Khruba has been acclaimed a saint by his followers. Following his death and cremation, his remains were preserved and distributed. These relics have been accorded divine status by his devoted followers and are believed to have intrinsic power that can be utilized.

KHUANG APHAIWONG (1902-1974). Descended from hereditary rulers of Siam's former Cambodian dominions, Khuang studied engineering in France. He entered government service in the Telegraph Department of which he later became director-general. He was a cabinet (q.v.) minister under Prime Ministers Phahon and Phibun (q.v.). Khuang was elected a number of times to the Thai National Assembly (q.v.), where he was a leader, becoming vice-president in both 1943 and 1944. He was prime minister for three short terms. In his first term, he released all political prisoners and restored to the nobility the ranks and titles which had been abolished by the previous prime minister. He became leader of the Democrat party (q.v.) Prachatiphat in 1955, a post he held until his death. He was known for his good humor and incorruptible character.

KHUN. A polite term used before the name of a person who is addressed or spoken of. *Khun* is the equivalent of Mr., Miss or Mrs. The same term is used to address both men and women.

KHUNYING. The title *khunying* is given to married women whose contributions to society are recognized by the royal family.

KHWAN. See VITAL ESSENCE.

KING, AS HEAD OF STATE. In a formal and ceremonial role, the king is head of state in Thailand. While he approves the selection of the prime minister and the acts of the legislature, he does not have veto power. He is not directly involved, according to the constitution (q.v.), in decisions about government policy. To the extent that the king has influence, it is indirect; it flows from the respect he enjoys as the embodiment of religion and history.

KING'S BIRTHDAY. On December 5th, the celebrations of the birthday of King Bhumibol Adulyadej (q.v.) and National Day are combined. The latter commemorates the anniversary of the 1932 coup d'etat which introduced a constitution (q.v.) and a limited monarchy (q.v.) form of government. The king's birthday is marked by brilliant illuminations of urban buildings at night, decorations of flags, portraits of the king, parades and parties. Religious aspects include the presentation of food (q.v.) to the Buddhist monks (q.v.) and special services at the Buddhist temple compounds *(wat)* (q.v.).

KINGSHIP. His Majesty Bhumibol Adulyadej (q.v.), king of Thailand since 1946, is the ninth reigning monarch of the house of Chakri (q.v.). He reigns from a Thai throne that consciously asserts a historical tradition of more than 700 years. The Thai people see their king as the living symbol of the hierarchy of respect that operates throughout Thai society. The king's court and the national capital represent to the people the highest realization of their cultural values. A previous concept of the king as absolute was changed in the Revolution of 1932 (q.v.) which ushered in a constitutional monarchy (q.v.) in Thailand. However, the traditional royal prestige continues, and the king is respected more than any other national leader or national symbol.

The Thai kingship as an ideal conception appears to have incorporated through accretion the following four ideas: *phaw khun, chakraphat, deva raja* and *phra chao phaen din. Phaw khun* is the notion of the king as the father of the people, the leader in war, the wise counsellor and judge in peace. *Chakraphat* is the idea of the wheel-rolling king or emperor, which is a Hindu-Buddhist concept which came to the Thai from the Mon (q.v.). The concept of the wheel-rolling monarch maintains that by virtue of his adherence to the principles of the law, the norm and the right, he gains universal power.

According to the concept of *deva raja* from Brahmanism (q.v.), the king is an earthly incarnation of a Hindu god. As a god, the king is the proper object of a cult to be conducted by officials in the king's retinue. Such a cult includes a structure of cosmological symbols which transforms the kingdom into the universe and the king into the lord of the universe. The king as *phra chao phaen din* is lord of the land. This designation is meant to distinguish the appearance and behavior of the monarch from the point of view of his subjects. In this sense the Thai throne displays qualities of splendor and majesty.

There are certain theoretical limitations inherent in the concept of Thai kingship. From the Hindu-Buddhist code of law called the Dharmasattham, the king is bound to uphold the principles of justice, to abide by the kingly virtues and to uphold the moral precepts.

KIRKPATRICK, ROBERT J. The first and most important Belgian legal advisor was R. J. Kirkpatrick who served King Chulalongkorn (q.v.) from 1894 to 1899. He held several government positions and was known for his indefatigable work and for his achievements as a judicial commissioner in Bangkok (q.v.), Ayutthaya (q.v.), Sara Buri and Ban Plasoi. Kirkpatrick also served part-time as the general advisor.

KIT SANGKHOM. See SOCIAL ACTION PARTY.

KITE-FLYING. A favorite game in Thailand, played by persons of all ages. Kites are flown chiefly from February to April, the period during which the southwest monsoon blows strong and steady. Kites are made of bamboo (q.v.) and rice (q.v.) paper in sizes ranging from 13 centimeters to 8 meters and in the shapes of butterflies, fish, hawks, serpents, etc., in many colors. Kite-fighting between the huge, star-shaped male kite *(chul)* and the tiny, diamond-shaped female kite *(pakpao)* is a big-league sport in which there are established teams, umpires, official rules and a national championship.

KLONG. The name for canals which are everywhere in the lowland areas of the central Plain (q.v.). The heart of Thailand is an alluvial plain and much of it is less than three meters above sea level. In the agricultural areas of the lowlands, there is an enormous latticework of canals which is tied into the rivers.

Klong are essential both as a source of water and as a means of travel.

KRAISRI NIMMANAHAEMINDA (1912-1992). Famous scholar, businessman, Thai government official for finance and banker. Kraisri, one of the best-known Chiang Mai (q.v.) residents at the time of his death, was born in Chiang Mai City. He was educated there, also in Bangkok (q.v.) and at Harvard University (M.B.A., 1938). At the latter he became interested in Lan Na (q.v.) culture, which he pursued on his return home. With his brothers and sisters he had a key role in the business activities of the Waroret Market in central Chiang Mai City. In addition, he managed the state enterprise the Industrial Finance Corporation. He was also a regional director of the Luang Thai Bank, 1946-1955, and of the Bangkok Bank Ltd., 1956-1964. His scholarly work and writings included research on ancient pottery kilns, old Lan Na inscriptions and many other aspects of early northern Thai culture. Kraisri helped in revitalizing interest in northern Thai wood carving, celadon, textiles and lacquerware (q.v.) as well. In recognition of his scholarly contributions, he was recognized in 1981 as an "Outstanding Person in the Field of Culture Preservation" by the National Council of the Office of the Prime Minister. Then, in 1982 he was awarded an honorary doctorate by Chiang Mai University. He was known to his friends and others as Acharn (q.v.) Kraisri.

KRIANGSAK CHOMANAN (1917-). Prime minister, politician, army commander. Kriangsak was educated in Thailand. He graduated from the Chulachomklao Thai Military Academy in 1939 and attended the U.S. Army Command and General Staff College in 1954. He was awarded the honorary degree of Doctor of Law by the University of Bridgeport, Connecticut, U.S., 1979. In the Thai Army, he rose from the rank of lieutenant to that of general in 1973. He commanded troops that fought in the Shan States and in Korea.

Following the political instability and the infamous riot against university students on October 6, 1976, Kriangsak, as Armed Forces supreme commander, and in concert with other army officers, asserted military control of the national government.

The junta that he led named Thanin Kraivichien (q.v.) as prime minister. Sensing that Thanin was in a weak position because of his overly repressive regime, on October 20, 1977, Kriangsak took over the government, making himself prime minister. In 1978 he sponsored a new national constitution (q.v.). This was part of a broader effort to promote democracy and reconciliation with those who had rebelled against the regime. A 1979 election established a new National Assembly (q.v.) which, in 1980, rejected Kriangsak in favor of Prem Tinsulanonda (q.v.) for the post of prime minister. Later, Kriangsak was elected to the House of Representatives (q.v.) from Roi Et Province in 1981 and became leader of the Democrat party (q.v.).

KRUNG THEP. See BANGKOK.

KUKRIT PRAMOJ (1911-   ).   Politician, writer and social critic. Kukrit studied abroad at Trent College and Queen's College in the United Kingdom. He was prime minister of Thailand, 1975-1976, after serving as deputy finance minister and leader of the Social Action party which he helped to organize. During World War II, his relationships with the United States (q.v.) and European countries were friendly. However, after the war, he sought the removal of all foreign troops from Thailand. In 1975 and 1976, the U.S. military forces were withdrawn under Kukrit's supervision.

　　He was the primary author of the 1974 constitution (q.v.), the product of a convention that he served as chair. He is well known among other activities as owner and columnist of the newspaper *Syam Rat*. His work in diverse fields as educator, artist, actor, banker and dancer met with unusual success. All of this brought him fame as one of Thailand's most colorful personalities. It is debated whether he will be remembered best as a political figure or as a scholar, writer and social critic. His work *Sii Phaeaendin* (1954, *Four Reigns*) was acclaimed as a great literary creation. It is a two-volume novel depicting a panorama of court life.

KULAP SAIPRADIT (pseudonym, SI BURAPHA). Prominent novelist of the pre-World War II period.   Kulap's *Songkhram*

Chuvit (War of Life), which appeared in 1932, is probably the best of his seven novels. They all reflect the opportunities for personal achievement of young people that arise through education and the expansion of government bureaucracy in Siamese (q.v) society. However, a main theme of his first novel, *Luk Phuchai (A Gentleman)*, is the belief that virtue leads to success and vice to failure.

- L -

LABOR ORGANIZATION. Labor unions sprang up in Thailand in the 1950s. However, the 1956 Labor Law with its protection was abolished after the 1958 coup d'etat of Sarit Thanarat (q.v.). For the next 14 years formal labor organization did not exist. Then, in a 1972 announcement of the government executive council, labor unions were legalized. The strength of organized labor has increased gradually with the growth of the Thai economy. Union membership today is in excess of 300,000, but this represents less than five percent of the industrial labor force.

A large number of strikes in the mid-1970s led to a five-year ban on such action in 1976. In 1981, the bans were lifted in the interest of efficient industrial production. Unions are now recognized as giving stability to labor market conditions. In addition, unionists as working class leaders voice the interests of that class which has begun to share the fruits of the recent economic boom in Thailand.

In a recent study in three cities, the degree of unionization was the highest among textile and clothing workers, the next highest for chemical/industrial labor and the lowest for workers in industries that produce building materials or food. Skilled workers had a higher degree of unionization than unskilled workers. Those preferred as labor leaders were persons who could resolve conflict and deal in a practical way to help the workers.

LACQUERWARE. The handicraft (q.v.) of making lacquerware originated in China. Widespread production in Thailand began during the Ayutthaya (q.v.) period (1350-1767). The craft declined but in recent years has been revived with improved techniques from Japan. The best lacquerware comes from Ban Khoen village near Chiang Mai (q.v.). A natural varnish, derived from the sap of the sumac tree, is used to coat furniture, decorative panels, book cases and small or large boxes to contain manuscripts or personal items, bowls, dishes, vases, water jars and cigarette boxes. The base material can be woven split-bamboo (q.v.), carved teak, papier-mâché or earthenware. In the early Bangkok period, the lacquerware makers began to copy narrative scenes from temple murals. Designs are engraved or painted, inlaid with mother-of-pearl or gilded. Usually black and red are used as basic tints. Thai patterns are the most popular.

LAKHON. See DANCE DRAMA.

LAKMUANG. The name of the foundation stone of Bangkok (q.v.). It is located in the center of the city. When distances from Bangkok to other places are measured, it is done from this stone. The Lakmuang, which is in the form of a lingam, is held in great respect by the city inhabitants.

LAM (LUM). In both northeast Thailand and Laos, the Lam is a musical performance in town and village festivals. The Lam is a singing repartee, which is a staged or pretend courtship. It is performed typically by a man and a woman who trade singing insults and jibes. The songs are accompanied by music of the *kaen* (q.v.) and possibly other instruments.

LAN NA. An early historical kingdom in what today is northern Thailand. Speakers of the Tai-language dialects have long been present there and possibly had migrated into the region in the 5th to 10th centuries. Gradually, the Tai-language speakers gained ascendancy in the region. This followed mainly from their success as producers of wet rice (q.v.) agriculture (q.v.). They based their settlements in the river valleys where there were fertile soils and abundant water. Local chronicles indicate that there were one or more small kingdoms there in the 8th century as vassals to either Mongolian or Burmese kings. In the 13th century, Mangrai (q.v.) was able by diplomacy and military strength to unite a number of principalities where Tai-language speakers predominated. By 1296 an independent city-state had emerged with Mangrai as king. He then established a capital at Chiang Mai (q.v.). The diverse population also included Mon (q.v.), Lawa and several tribal peoples. Since then the regional kingdom has sometimes been called Chiang Mai after the name of its capital. While the mountainous terrain made governing difficult, there was a long line of kings who succeeded Mangrai, including Tilokaracha (1441-1487) (q.v.). In the reign of the latter, Lan Na reached a high point in power and prosperity, when Theravada Buddhism (q.v.) of the Sinhalese form prevailed.

Later, the region succumbed to the armies of Burma (q.v.) and became a vassal kingdom (1558-1774). During the period of Burmese control, the area served the rulers as a base for launching attacks against the Siamese (q.v.) of Ayutthaya (q.v.). When Burmese control over the population of Lan Na had become oppressive, the people there joined the forces of Siam (q.v.) in defeating their masters of two centuries. However, the Burmese contributed to the region's distinctive architecture (q.v.), handicrafts (q.v.), cuisine, language and religion.

The Siamese, whose capital was Bangkok (q.v.), gained control of the Lan Na Kingdom in 1774. Kavila (q.v.), who had been a chieftain under the Burmese, and his successors ruled Lan Na first in Lamphun and later in Chiang Mai City under the suzerainty of Siam. The several principalities of the region enjoyed considerable autonomy until the reign of King Chulalongkorn (q.v.). During this time they were able to strengthen Lan Na's agricultural economy as well as its religious and cultural traditions. Administrative control was gradually increased by Siamese rulers until Lan Na was transformed into a number of provinces with appointed governors (q.v.).

LAND TENURE AND TENANCY. At the turn of the 20th century, land for farming was readily available. However, four hectares (ten acres) was the maximum that one cultivator could obtain. At this time, a national pattern of small independent farms characterized Thai agriculture (q.v.). An important exception was the previous large land grants to nobles and government officials primarily in the area near Bangkok (q.v.). Another widespread pattern by mid-century was that of part owner-part tenant. These were cultivators who owned part of their operation and rented additional land. At this time, full tenancy was less than 10 percent. However, in some districts (q.v.) near Bangkok, about 80 percent of cultivators were full tenants by 1973-1974, as indicated in a survey. This was the area of the large estates owned by Bangkok landlords.

Due to their heavy debts and the lack of low-cost farm credit, a large proportion of Thai farmers have lost their lands in recent decades. During this period there has been a rapid increase in the number of landless farmers, who support themselves by wage labor. Their numbers are estimated to be in excess of 500,000. A 1975 Land Reform program was to make additional small farms available through purchases from private owners and then sales to cultivators. Other sources of land are crown properties and forest lands. Unfortunately, implementation of this government land reform has been limited, and it has been strongly opposed by large landowners.

Another way that landless farmers have secured small plots of land is to squat in suitable parts of the national forest. This has been an outlet for thousands of land seekers, but has led to an enormous reduction in the total forest lands of the nation. In several cases, new village groups have been forced to evacuate their new lands, which were previously forest, by government agencies seeking to preserve the forests. A study by the Thailand Development Research Institute (1986) found that the cultivated area in Thailand totals about 152 million rai or 48 percent of the country's area, suggesting that about half of the country is now permanently owned or occupied by private individuals.

LANGUAGE AND THAI PEOPLES. More than 80 percent of the population of Thailand speak languages that are part of the Tai-language family. Others who speak a language of this family are residents of the Shan state of Burma (q.v), Laos (q.v.), northwestern Vietnam and southern China (q.v.). Standard Thai, the language taught in schools, is used in printed materials and is the official language. It originally was the mother tongue or dialect of the Siamese (q.v.) inhabitants of the central Plain (q.v.), who constitute about 30 percent of the present Thai population. In the early 20th century, the national government established this central Tai version, also known as "Thai," as the official language of the nation.

For the most part, inhabitants elsewhere in the nation speak Tai-languages other than standard Thai. In northeastern Thailand (q.v.), several interrelated Tai dialects are used. These are generally referred to as Lao or Isan by the residents who use them and are more or less the same as the languages in Laos. In northern Thailand (q.v.), inhabitants speak a language they call *kham muang*, meaning the language of our principality. In written form it is called *Yuan*. The Kham Muang and Lao dialects are closely related to each other. In south Thailand, the dialects spoken, called *pak tai* (q.v.), are considered by their users as distinctive. Scattered throughout Thailand there are pockets of inhabitants who speak still other dialects of Tai. Among certain minority groups in Thailand, there are other languages in use also. Chief among these are Teochiu used by the Chinese (q.v.), Malay used by the Thai-Malay (q.v.), and Khmer (q.v.). Standard Thai provides an effective means of communication in schools, in printed materials, in government and elsewhere, throughout the nation.

The origin of the Thai script is not clear, but it dates from the reign of King Ramkhamhaeng (reigned 1219-1317 [q.v.]), who adapted the Mon (q.v.) and Khmer scripts of that time into what is now Thai. There have been modifications and loan words incorporated since then. The Thai language is tonal, uninflected and predominantly monosyllabic. Each syllable has an inherent tone that, no less than the consonants and vowels, determines the meaning of the syllable or word. In standard Thai, there are five tones. Grammatical functions are shown by word order. The alphabet consists of 44 consonants and 32 vowels and diphthong forms. Tones are indicated by special tone marks or diacritics in some but not all cases.

LANGUAGE, ENGLISH. Since the 1950s, the English language has been taught in the schools and universities of Thailand. As a result, there is a large population of people in business and the professions who are able to write and converse in English, especially in the large urban centers, and particularly Bangkok (q.v.). Knowledge of a foreign language, especially English, has been seen as facilitating contacts with the West. Many government documents are published in both the Thai and English languages. Among their books and pamphlets, publishers include some that are in English. University instruction in a limited number of graduate and undergraduate courses is in the English language exclusively. These include specific programs in engineering, economics and business administration. In Bangkok, an English TV program known as *Good Morning* is available, and programming on several radio stations is conducted in English by Thais.

LANGUAGE, MALAY. In general, the Thai-Malay (q.v.) of the extreme southern provinces of Pattani (q.v.), Yala, Narathiwat and a small portion of Satun are ethnically Malay. Predominantly, their speech is a Malay dialect similar to that of Kelantan in Malaysia. Only a small proportion are able to use the Tai-language (q.v.). For the Thai-Malay, language enables them to perceive their past and interpret the future and embodies the social history of a people. For this ethnic group, the Malay language is also the language of Islam (q.v.) and the medium used in each local Muslim religious school *(pondok)*. Current government policy allows the Thai-Malay to use either Malay or Tai-language to communicate with government officials.

LAOS, RELATIONS WITH. The small nation of Tai-language speaking peoples located on Thailand's eastern border. The total population of Laos is less than four million. Its lowland inhabitants are Buddhist wet-rice (q.v.) farmers. They share the Lao language with the much larger population of Thai-Lao speakers in northeastern Thailand (q.v.). In the upland areas, especially in northern Laos, other languages prevail.

Three parts of Laos, loosely integrated, include an area in the north centered around Luang Prabang (q.v.), a middle part based on Vientiane, the nation's capital, and the area around Champassak in the south. There the Mekong River (q.v.) is the principal common border. The nation of Laos is the remaining portion of the Kingdom of Lan Xang. That earlier kingdom was divided into two kingdoms, Luang Prabang and Champassak, which were invaded and disrupted by the armies of Burma. Late in the 18th century, both principalities became vassals to kings of Siam (q.v.). Lack of adequate protection by the Siamese led to the Lao obtaining French support in 1887. This occurred during the period of colonization by both Britain and France (q.v.) in Southeast Asia.

Eventually, Lao territories were divided between Siam and France following the Franco-Siamese Crisis and Treaty of 1893 (q.v.). Auguste Pavie (q.v.) was the key figure who almost single-handedly negotiated this transfer of territories. Attempts by Thailand to regain the Laotian territories it lost in connection with World War II were not successful.

Up to 5,000 Thai Army troops fought in Laos on the side of the king during the protracted civil wars there in 1965 to 1974 after which they were withdrawn. Many of the Lao people fled to Thailand during this time resulting in large refugee (q.v.) camps. Thai-Lao relations were strained after the Lao People's Democratic Republic took power in 1975, but were improved by agreements in 1979. Thai-Lao border conflicts occurred in 1984 and again in 1987-1988. Border agreements were made in 1991. Thai-Lao relations in the 1990s have been friendly and trade has increased.

LEGISLATIVE PROCESS. While legislation is introduced in the House of Representatives (q.v.), it is typically brought there by the prime minister. The making of new government policy is dominated by the prime minister and his cabinet (q.v.). Citizen participation in policy-making decisions scarcely exists. The legislative initiatives of the prime minister and his coalition of party representatives in the national legislature (q.v.) typically face opposition from the members of parties that are not in the coalition.

One power the House has is its prerogative to pass a no confidence motion. When this occurs, the prime minister and the entire cabinet are dismissed. The House, with prior approval of the prime minister, can initiate an appropriations bill. A bill passed by the House is sent on to the Senate for its action. If there are disagreements between the two houses, a committee is appointed to resolve the dispute. Legislative acts that pass both houses are presented to the king for approval, who responds to the prime minister's wishes.

LIKAY (LI KE). In contrast to the classical art of *khon* (q.v.) and *lakhon*, *likay* is a burlesque with pantomime, comic folk opera and social satire. As a form of people's theater, performers interact with the audience, who respond to local references and anecdotes. The *likay* dialog is spontaneous, witty and risqué, with emphasis on word play.

LITERACY. Reports by UNESCO show literacy rates of better than 90 percent for Thai adults. In 1990, illiteracy was seven percent for men and between eight and nine percent for women. The government sponsored adult education (q.v.) programs help to maintain literacy.

LO THAI. King of the Sukhothai Kingdom (q.v.) (reigned 1298-1346). While he was the son and heir of the great King Ramkhamhaeng (q.v.), he was not a military leader. He could not retain the vast territories ruled by his father and reigned only over the area near the capital. The classic Sukhothai bronze sculptures (q.v.) were cast during his reign. He is known also for the promotion of Sinhalese Buddhism (q.v.).

LOCAL GOVERNMENT. In Thailand local government consists of three separate inter-related patterns of authority. The first of these is territorial or provincial administration, which consists of hierarchical units staffed by officials of the central government. At the top of the hierarchy are 73 provinces *(changwat)* (q.v.), each of which is administered by a governor *(phuwarachakan)* (q.v.). Provinces are subdivided into districts *(amphoe)* (q.v.) and sub-districts which are headed by district officers *(nai amphoe)* (q.v.).

In a second pattern of authority are the traditional village leaders who have local responsibility and who have largely been incorporated into the territorial administrative framework. Each of the more than 50,000 villages *(muban)* (q.v.) has an elected village headman *(phu yai ban)* (q.v.). For purposes of administration, villages are grouped into communes *(tambon)*, which consist of a cluster of about ten villages. Typically, village headmen of the commune choose one of their members to be the leader of the commune *(kamnan)* (q.v.). The third pattern of authority in local government includes four types of units which as yet have been implemented in only a part of Thailand. These include: the provincial council, an appointed or elected group of representatives who are intended to act as a legislative organ; municipalities *(thesaban)*, committees at the district level; and commune councils at the commune level.

LOP BURI, HISTORY OF. An old and historic city, which today is both a Thai province and provincial capital. Initially, a site of prehistoric settlers, Lop Buri became in the 6th to 10th centuries a major center of the Dvaravati Kingdom (q.v.) called Lavo. In the 10th to 13th centuries, Lop Buri was a military outpost of the Angkor Kingdom (q.v.). During this three-decade period, the Lop Buri style of art and architecture (q.v.) emerged. Traditional Mon (q.v.) styles were integrated with those of Angkor to produce a distinctive art movement. Later, in the 17th century, King Narai (q.v.) of the Kingdom of Ayutthaya (q.v.) used Lop Buri as an alternative capital.

LOTUS SYMBOL. The popular lotus flower grows in ponds, swamps, canals and roadside ditches. It is treasured by the Thai for its beauty, its many uses and its symbolism. The numerous synonyms of the lotus are revealed when the flower is used in poetry, e.g., *prathum* and *ubon*. These synonyms are often used to name people, temple compounds *(wat)* (q.v.), provinces (q.v.), districts (q.v.) and villages.

The lotus is also the traditional flower of Buddhism (q.v.). Many Buddha (q.v.) images (q.v.) are traditionally placed in a stylized lotus in full bloom. The lotus has also been used widely as an artistic form to express Buddhist thought. The lotus represents purity uncontaminated by the mud from which it grows. Buddhism as truth is comparable to the lotus as having inherently the power to rise above ignorance in a chaotic world.

LOY KRATONG. A famous and charming festival of lights which honors both Buddha (q.v.) and ancient water spirits on the night of the full moon in November. Participants make or purchase a small tray or leaf float bearing a lighted candle. Large floats may be constructed by school groups or business firms. At dusk, they gather at the bank of a river or canal and set their *kratong* afloat amid cheers and fun making. The vista of an innumerable array of tiny lights on the water is a breathtaking sight. In Chiang Mai (q.v.) and other cities some residents also decorate their houses for *loy kratong.*

LUANG PRABANG. A city in northern Laos (q.v.) formerly the royal capital and official residence of the Laotian king. The name Luang Prabang in previous centuries also designated a kingdom whose capital had the same name. Its location on the Mekong River (q.v.) and its proximity to Thailand has led to vassalage to the Thai Kingdom from 1778 until 1893 when the French colonized Laos.

LUE. A Thai ethnic group of possibly 50,000 residing chiefly in the eastern part of northern Thailand. The Lue, who live in the plains, have a tradition of trade with various hill tribes (q.v.) in the region and serve as intermediaries between the hill peoples and the dominant Thai society in the plains. The Lue are wet-rice (q.v.) agriculturalists, and glutinous rice is the main crop. Besides rice, the products of domestic animals are important in their diet.

LUK SIT WAT. See. TEMPLE BOYS.

- M -

MAAG. See BETEL.

MAE CHI. See NUNS.

MAHA. The term *maha* is a title of a person or place that has the connotation "great." It is also a title used with the name by a Buddhist monk (q.v.) after he passes a certain high-level examination.

MAHATHAMMARACHA. King of Ayutthaya (reigned 1569-1590). As a member of the court under the previous king, Mahathammaracha was leader of a plot that put Chakraphat (q.v.) on the Siamese (q.v.) throne in 1548. He was rewarded with the title *maha* (q.v.) and marriage to the king's daughter. In Siam's (q.v.) struggle with Burma (q.v.), Mahathammaracha provided aid to the enemy when the Ayutthaya (q.v.) capital was captured in 1569. For this he was made king of Siam (q.v.) under the suzerainty of the Burmese king. He began to restore Siam's independence, but military action was left to his sons Naresuan (q.v.) and Ekathotsarot (q.v.) who succeeded him.

MAHATHAMMARACHA I. King of Sukhothai (reigned 1347-1368 or 1374). A great scholar and patron of Buddhism (q.v.). Mahathammaracha wrote a treatise on Buddhist cosmology (q.v.), which is considered to be one of the oldest specimens of Thai literature. He also wrote *Phra Ruang's Proverbs* and the *Nophamas Story.* He built monasteries, Buddha images (q.v.), roads, canals and a brick palace, and founded a school for Buddhist monks (q.v.) on the palace grounds. Mahathammaracha I set the precedent of becoming a Buddhist monk, an example followed by kings of Thailand to the present day. An able statesman and military leader, King Mahathammaracha I expanded the territory of Sukhothai (q.v.). He recognized that the Kingdom of Ayutthaya (q.v.) was too powerful to oppose. Instead he cultivated diplomatic relations with it.

MAHATTHAI. Military organ and agency of civil government in the Kingdom of Ayutthaya (q.v.). Created in the mid-15th century by King Borommatrailokanat (q.v.), the Mahatthai organ initially had charge of all civil government in the kingdom. At this time, military matters were handled by the Kalahom (q.v.). However, this was changed in the mid-17th century when the Mahatthai was placed in charge of both military and civil affairs in the northern and central provinces of the kingdom. Similarly, the

Kalahom organ was placed in charge of military and civil affairs in the southern provinces. This pattern of administration was modified to its present system in the late-19th century.

MAHORI. A traditional orchestra of central Thailand consisting of four instruments: a castanet, a three-stringed violin, a drum and a lute. (See MUSIC.)

MAHOUT. An elephant driver and handler. There is usually a lifetime partnership between the man and the elephant (q.v.).

MAKHA BUCHA. See BUDDHIST ALL SAINTS DAY.

MALAYSIA, RELATIONS WITH. Western Malaysia is a neighboring state whose northern border coincides with Thailand's border on the Peninsula (q.v.). Always trading partners, Malaysia along with Thailand and several others nations formed the Association of Southeast Asian Nations (ASEAN [q.v.]). This has led to continued cooperation between Thai and Malaysian officials in order to deal with economic and political affairs of the region. Communist insurgency (q.v.) in both countries from the 1950s to the 1970s was a threat to both countries. Cooperative efforts to control insurgency and terrorism has also characterized relations between Thailand and Malaysia.

Before achieving independence in the late 1950s, Malaysia was a British colony. In the Anglo-Siamese Treaty of 1909, Thailand gave up to the British the tributary relationship it then had with the four Malay states Perlis, Kedah, Terengganu and Kelantan. These are now the four northern states of the Federation of Malaysia.

MAN PHURITHATTA (1871-1949). Famous Buddhist monk. Man was ordained a Buddhist novice *(nen)* (q.v.) at age 15 in his home village in Ubon Province. Later at age 21 he was ordained a Buddhist monk (q.v.) and began almost immediately a life of renunciation, asceticism and meditation. Rejecting a permanent residence, he became a wandering monk dwelling mostly in forests. A traveling monk is typically noticeable for the saffron colored tents he uses and carries. Man ate only one meal each day and possessed only essential robes. Man's example had much appeal not only to other monks. He also had a following among the laity in both rural and urban areas.

Man was widely regarded as a teacher *(acharn)* (q.v.) though his instruction was more by example than verbal presentation of the Buddhist *dharma* (q.v.). He was known for most of his life as Acharn Man Phurithatta. The accounts of one biographer reflect visions and mystical encounters that Man had during meditation. One of these accounts reveals Man's capacity for mind-reading, healing and other supernatural powers. Thus, to this biographer, Man's life was a supreme example that others can imitate. Evidently, many of his monk-followers did try to practice an ascetic life-style of meditation. Man was considered by many of his followers as one of the holiest of men.

Man's heritage for his followers was his powerful example of the development of the human mind and spirit as taught by Buddha (q.v.). He is considered to have achieved enlightenment *(nirvana)* (q.v.). After his death and cremation, Man's remains were distributed as relics to which unusual qualities were subsequently attributed.

MANGRAI. King of Lan Na (reigned 1259-1317). Born a prince, he succeeded his father as ruler of a small principality, which was a vassal of the Mongolian king. He extended his kingdom, then a city-state in what today is northern Thailand, through both conquests and strategic alliances. Mangrai's expanded kingdom eventually included the former principalities of Chiang Rai, Luang Prabang (q.v.), Nan, Haripunchaya (q.v.) and Pagan. Subsequent to each military conquest, Mangrai moved the capital of his kingdom southward as far as Lamphun. These were protective moves in a situation of threats from hostile powers.

Later, in 1296, when he had become independent and had friendly neighboring rulers, he built a new capital which he named Chiang Mai (q.v.). While the elite around Mangrai were chiefly Tai-language speakers, the kingdom also embraced large populations of Mon (q.v.), Lawa, and other tribal and indigenous peoples. The northern Thai of today are descendants of this mixed population, and they trace their unique identity, in large part, to the kingdom-building of Mangrai and his successors, especially Tilokaracha (q.v.).

MANOPAKORNNITITHADA (1884-1948).   The first prime minister of Thailand following the Revolution of 1932 (q.v.) that ended the absolute monarchy (q.v.).   A lawyer educated in Britain, he had been a chief justice of the Supreme Court of Appeals under King Prajadhipok (q.v.). The promoters of the Revolution saw Manopakorn as the capable person that they needed as a front man during the period when they were consolidating their power. In 1933, after a disagreement with the revolutionary group, he dissolved the National Assembly (q.v.), lost power and fled to Penang, where he lived in exile until his death.

MANUFACTURING. More than a quarter of the Gross Domestic Product (GDP) of Thailand comes from manufacturing, which is the leading sector of the economy. The principal products in the early 1990s were garments and textiles, computers and computer parts, gems and jewelry (q.v.), and food (q.v.) and beverages. This industrial production represents a significant change from 25 years earlier when industries were in their infancy and agriculture (q.v.) alone was first in economic importance. Today, manufacturing accounts for approximately 70 percent of the country's exports (q.v.) and has had an annual growth rate of 12 to 15 percent compared to a 7.5 percent annual growth rate in the economy as a whole in recent years.

MASS MEDIA. Mass media can be classified in order of greatest influence as follows: radio (q.v.), television (q.v.), newspapers, videotapes, journals and magazines and films. There are educational broadcasting stations throughout Thailand. The media have a strong impact on Thai society and culture. Noteworthy are videotapes showing aspects of foreign cultures, especially Japanese cartoons, Hong Kong movies and Chinese films. (See MOTION PICTURES; PUBLISHING; RADIO; TELEVISION.)

MEKLONG. The name of a river in the southwestern part of the central Plain (q.v.) associated with mountains on the Thai-Burmese border. It empties into the Gulf of Thailand at the city of Samut Songkhram.

MEKONG. A river, about 2,000 kilometers (1,250 miles) in length, and the longest in Southeast Asia. It originates in the western Yunan Province of China and flows generally in a southerly direction. It flows through or marks the national boundaries (q.v.) of Burma, Laos, Thailand and Cambodia. Finally, the Mekong flows through the southern part of Vietnam, where it has formed an enormous delta as it empties into the south China Sea. That portion of the Mekong River which borders on northeastern Thailand is navigable and is an important means of transportation. The Mekong is also, together with its tributaries, an important source of water for irrigation (q.v.) and hydroelectric power.

MEO (HMONG or MONG). A Sino-Tibetan ethno-linguistic group, approximately 77,000 or 14 percent of the total hill tribe (q.v.) population. The Meo are one of the most widespread minority groups. They are scattered throughout the south China provinces, in communities in northern Vietnam and Laos, as well as Thailand, and a few in Burma. Meo settlements are concentrated in 13 northern provinces of Thailand. They are separated into Blue Meo (Mong Njua), White Meo (Hmong Daw) and Gua Mba Meo (Hmong Gua Mba). The religion of the Meo is a combination of pantheism and shamanism with the emphasis on ancestor-worship. The Chinese influence is obvious in their beliefs and practices. Meo establish their villages at high altitudes usually above 1,500 meters (5,000 feet). Rice (q.v.) and corn are the main subsistence crops; opium is the principal cash crop. (See HILL TRIBES.)

MERIT-DEMERIT. An idea central to Buddhism (q.v.) that the good deeds or morally positive actions of a person will accumulate and lead in the future to some valued state of being. Individuals attempt to "make merit" *(tham bun)* by performing such acts as giving support to members of the Buddhist monkhood (q.v.), e.g., food (q.v.), clothing and other needed items, and by helping parents, relatives and the needy. Conversely, one's evil deeds or behavior that contradicts the moral rules of Buddhism can also accumulate and lead to pain or suffering at some future time. Such acts will bring about "demerit" *(bap)*. These religious patterns are an expression of the law of *karma* (q.v.), which is incorporated in Thai Buddhism.

MILITARY ASSISTANCE, UNITED STATES. For 26 years, from 1950-1975, Thailand received major military assistance grants from the United States (q.v.) government. The goal was to strengthen Thailand's military capability in the face of supposed Communist threats in the region. In the 1960s aid was increased over that of the 1950s to assist the Thai government's counter-insurgency efforts. (See INSURGENCY.)

American military specialists and advisors, beginning in the 1950s, came to Thailand under the Joint U.S. Military Assistance Group. They sought to help Thailand qualify for military aid and to supervise U.S. field operations in its war with Vietnam. The opportunity to operate from bases in Thailand was an enormous advantage for the American conduct of the war. U.S. forces were permitted to use naval facilities at Sattahip and seven air bases from which American aircraft flew combat missions. However, facilities at the bases had initially required construction and modernization, which was done at U.S. expense amounting to millions of dollars. At its peak, about 45,000 United States air force and army personnel were serving in Thailand with a considerable impact on the Thai economy. Withdrawal of the American forces began in 1969 and was completed by July 1976. Facilities at the seven bases were then turned over to the Thai government.

Direct grants for military assistance to Thailand declined after 1975 and were discontinued in 1979. However, in the same year, $4 million worth of arms and military material were sent to Thailand in view of Vietnam's invasion of Cambodia (q.v.). Additional grants followed periodically. Thai and American military forces staged joint exercises in the 1980s and, in 1986, the two countries agreed to establish a reserve weapons pool.

MILITARY OFFICERS, THEIR ROLE IN NATIONAL LIFE. Early in the 20th century, efforts were made by Siamese (q.v) kings to build a professional military establishment. By 1920, the country had a sizable army trained on the European model. The Siamese officers, as well as civilians studying in France and Britain, acquired a new social and political awareness. The Revolution of 1932 (q.v.), which ushered in a constitutional monarchy (q.v.), was led by those who had studied abroad. This marked the beginning of the military as a significant force in national life. Financial and other support of the United States (q.v.) for Thailand, from 1950 to 1976, brought modernization, training, equipment and base construction. (See MILITARY ASSISTANCE.)

The military establishment's support for the king (q.v.), country and Buddhism (q.v.) resulted in widespread acceptance. Coups d'etat led by military officers were often justified as maintaining peace, order and security. In the 1960s and 1970s, the Thai military was credited with conducting successful operations against Communist insurgents. (See INSURGENCY). They were also seen as providing security from Indochina threats. However, in recent decades, senior military officers were found to be doing more than pursuing military careers. They used their power to take on business activities and to amass wealth. This has led to civilian allegations of repression, greed and corruption.

The dominance of the military in Thai government affairs has undergone change in the 1980s among its members. One aspect is the sharp factionalism within the military. Another aspect is a growing awareness that military coups are not only undemocratic but actually harmful. To emphasize this change, a number of military officers in retirement entered politics by joining the Thai Nation party (q.v.).

MINING. Tin (q.v.) is one of the dominant minerals in the mining industry of Thailand and is a big export (q.v.) earner. Other minerals which produce export earnings include gems (q.v.), tungsten, fluoride, antimony, zinc, gypsum, lead, barite, columbite-tantalite, oil and gas, lignite and iron. Large quantities of lignite which is used for fuel, limestone which the cement industry uses, and gypsum are mined and processed for use in

Thailand. Altogether, more than 40 minerals are produced. The Minerals Act, 1967, as amended, governs onshore and offshore mining activities. (See TIN.)

MISIEM YIPINTSOI (1906-1988). Famous for her paintings and sculpture. Misiem was born in Thailand to elite Indonesian-Chinese merchant parents and started her art in mid-life after an extended trip to Europe. First as a painter and then as a sculptor, her work is considered some of Thailand's most innovative among productive artists. Silpakorn University honored her posthumously by establishing a sculpture garden of her work. Misiem was a three-time gold medalist at the kingdom's National Art Exhibition.

MON. The Mon, also known as Ramaan or Taleen, are to be found in scattered communities in Thailand, in and around the central valley, and in Lower Burma. The Mon are a respected minority with an ancient past. They were exposed to Brahmanism (q.v.) and Theravada Buddhism (q.v.) more than a thousand years before the arrival of the Thai and the Burmese in the area.

The Mon language has been very influential on other languages of the mainland, including Karen (q.v.), Burmese, and Thai. The Mon speak a language related to Cambodian (Khmer [q.v.]) and to the languages of a large number of hill tribes (q.v.) throughout Southeast Asia. Mon script has been adopted first by Burmans at Pagan in the 12th century, then later by northern Thai at Lamphun/Chiang Mai (q.v.) in the 14th century and subsequently by Lao-speaking groups in northeastern Thailand.

The younger generation is educated in Thai and illiterate in Mon, but a number of older people, mostly men educated in Mon temples, can still read the language. There are several temples where Mon manuscripts are read and sermons preached in Mon. Near Bangkok (q.v.) there are Mon villages where Mon customs and language still survive. Most strikingly, Mon houses are completely different from standard rural Thai houses. Physically too, the Mon appear different from the Thai. Their food (q.v.) is similar to Thai food, however. Traditionally, the Mon are rice (q.v.) farmers.

MONARCHY. Since the Revolution of 1932 (q.v.), Thailand has had a constitutional monarchy. The former pattern of kings to have absolute power was ended at that time. The role of the king in relation to the society and to the government has been gradually emerging. The present Thai king, Bhumibol Aduladej (q.v.), has won the Thai monarchy a high level of prestige and respect.

From the earliest times and up to 1932, the people of what today is Thailand had been ruled by kings having absolute power. For centuries the kings of Sukhothai (q.v.), Lan Na (q.v.), Ayutthaya (q.v.) and Bangkok (q.v.) attained the right to rule through their military successes. In addition, they projected an image of royal paternalism and divine right. Patronage of the Buddhist religion underscored the legitimacy of the king's status. The power of these kings, as elsewhere in Southeast Asia, reached over as much territory as they could control either militarily or through the loyalty of local chieftains who received protection. In addition, subservient kings of other principalities became vassals and paid tribute. Fluidity characterized the kingdom's territorial boundaries until the late-19th century. The several dynasties of kings in the history of Thailand indicates that at times a usurper gained the throne from the hereditary heir.

In the mid-15th century, a new pattern of royal control began to be effected. Government officials were appointed by the king to administer specific areas in the vicinity of the capital of the kingdom. However, control in outer regions continued as before. Use by the king of governors (q.v.) and a bureaucratic system for control became more general throughout the kingdom in the latter part of the 19th century. At this time, Thailand saw threats of becoming a colony of Britain or of France (q.v.). The kings of Thailand, especially Mongkut (q.v.) and Chulalongkorn (q.v.), were successful in reorganizing government control along the lines of administration in the West and colonization was avoided. (See CHAKRI DYNASTY; KINGSHIP; TAKSIN.)

MONDOP. A square, planned cubicle structure in the Buddhist temple compound *(wat)* (q.v.) which may be plain or have a range of pillars around it. Its superstructure is a curved pyramidal mass formed by many low dome-shaped roofs superimposing each other and having a slender pinnacle as its apex. Buildings of the *mondop* design are used either for libraries or to house relics. There is a famous *mondop* at Wat Phra Buddhabhat (q.v.) near the city of Sarap Buri. (See WAT PHRA BUDDHABHAT.)

MONGKUT (1804-1868). King of Siam (reigned 1851-1868). By birth, Mongkut was a crown prince and ascended the throne of Siam (q.v.) at age 47. He joined the Buddhist monkhood (q.v.) at age 20 and remained there until he became king. While he was a Buddhist monk (q.v.), he acquired fluency in English and most Southeast Asian languages. His studies also included Sanskrit (q.v.), Pali (q.v.) and several of the sciences, especially astronomy. As a devout Buddhist, he aided the movement toward a more strict observance of the discipline and teachings of the Buddha (q.v.). In this way, a more rational response to modern science would be possible. Mongkut's own reform teachings were found in his sermons and were published also as tracts.

As king, Mongkut did much to improve the international standing of Siam. He had extensive correspondence with foreign heads of state, including those of Great Britain, France (q.v.), the United States (q.v.) and the Pope. Mongkut and his advisors recognized the colonization threat presented by the British and French and gradually met their demands. These included extraterritoriality for the benefit of European subjects in Siam and the removal of trade barriers. A pattern of accommodation was seen as essential in order to maintain the independence of Siam. Aware of the merits of modernization, Mongkut set in motion a number of changes. These included dropping certain ancient customs, establishing new rights for citizens and publishing an official gazette. The necessity for reform and maintaining national independence were emphasized in the education of his sons. Chulalongkorn (q.v.), the son who succeeded Mongkut as king, actually put into practice these ideas.

MONK. See BUDDHIST MONK.

MOTION PICTURES. At least half of the urban population of Thailand is estimated to attend weekly motion pictures, now widely available. However, except for occasional visiting governmental teams with education exhibits, motion pictures are generally not available to the vast rural population of Thailand. Most films are imported, and the majority come from the United States (q.v.). Several cinemas in Bangkok (q.v.) regularly show Chinese language movies made in Hong Kong and Singapore. Most of these films are dubbed in Teochiu, the dialect spoken by most Chinese (q.v.) in Bangkok. Other foreign films are seldom dubbed. However, a commentary may be provided after the film is completed or during intermission. The film showing frequently includes one or two professional performers who accompany the film and provide translation of selected scenes. However, the great majority of Thai films are made for entertainment purposes. Historic Thai films are preserved by the National Film Archives. In 1991, Thailand had 575 cinemas, with a total capacity of 390,000.

MUANG. A term with several meanings: as *amphoe muang*, it designates a district *(amphoe)* (q.v.) of a province in which a provincial capital is located; as *muang thai*, it refers to the Thai nation; as *muang*, it refers to a class of municipalities in which the population of each is at least 10,000.

MUBAN. Any population center (village) in rural Thailand with at least five households. Typically, the *muban* consists of 50 or more households in which the able-bodied workers are engaged predominately in farming. To a small extent, there may be craftsmen and merchants in the village as well. The *muban* is also a unit of governmental administration and for this purpose has a headman *(phu yai ban)* (q.v.). There are more than 50,000 *muban* in Thailand. (See LOCAL GOVERNMENT.)

MUN. The name of the river in the Khorat Plateau which flows in a southeastern direction and empties into the Mekong River (q.v.) near Ubon Ratchathani.

MUNICIPALITY (THESABAN). Cities with a population of 50,000 or more have been established by law as municipalities. They provide citizens with experience (though limited) in self-government. Urban centers of 10,000 or more can be municipalities also, as are most provincial capitals. Some municipal mayors have been elected while others have been appointed by the provincial governor (q.v.). The municipal executive committee consists of the mayor and two to four others members who are also appointed. Local taxation does not produce sufficient revenue to meet expenses of municipalities. Reliance on the national government for budget support is accompanied by considerable control over municipal affairs by the national government. The Bangkok Metropolis (q.v.) is a special case and is governed by a special unit created by law in 1971. (See LOCAL GOVERNMENT; URBANIZATION.)

MUSICAL INSTRUMENTS. There are many different Thai musical instruments. The most common are flutes and oboes of various types, stringed instruments, drums, percussion-melody pieces and gongs. (See DRUMS; GONG WONG YAI; GONGS; PINAI; RANAD EK; RANAD THUM.)

MYANMAR. After the mass protests in 1988, the ruling Council dropped the term "Socialist Republic" and renamed the country "The Union of Burma." On June 18, 1989, the Council again changed the name in English to "The Union of Myanmar." The nation is referred to as Burma in this dictionary. (See BAYINNAUNG; BURMA, RELATIONS WITH.)

- N -

NAI. The term *nai* means literally master. In one use, it refers to the lowest rank in the traditional nobility. *Nai* is also used as a mark of respect for employers or any person of superior status.

NAI AMPHOE. See DISTRICT OFFICER.

NAIL DANCE (FON LEP). A dance which is popular in northern Thailand. It is performed frequently in Chiang Mai (q.v.), and other cities and towns, during festivals and ceremonies (q.v.). (See GONG AEW.)

NAK THAM. The name given to a person who, as a novice (q.v.) or Buddhist monk (q.v.), completed an elementary *dharma* (q.v.) course. Such a course is offered in a *dharma* school and conducted in certain Buddhist temple compounds *(wat)* (q.v.) in Thailand. The course is taught by a qualified Buddhist monk. (See BUDDHISM.)

NAKHON PATHOM SHRINE. The oldest Buddhist shrine and also the largest in Thailand. In design it is a *chedi* (q.v.) 127 meters (420 feet) in height located in the city of Nakhon Pathom. It was completed in 1860 and encases a previous *chedi* that was built about 500 AD and that was later remodeled by the Mon (q.v.). The shrine is also known as Phra Pathom Chedi which means "The First Chedi." It is widely believed that Buddhism (q.v.) first came to be established in Thailand at this place. The golden-tiled inverted bowl of the *chedi* can be seen against the skyline from afar.

NAKHON RATCHASIMA (KHORAT). The largest province of the northeast (q.v.), both in area and in population, 2,405,000 (est.). The provincial capital, Khorat, pop. 203,000 (est.), is the largest city outside of the Bangkok (q.v.) area and serves as a point of entry to the northeast. It has well-developed communications as well as good air and surface transportation facilities. In sum, it is a major military and commercial center. The province has sufficient water resources to sustain its general agriculture (q.v.) and is a silk-producing area. Khorat was the leading Thai province in both crop and livestock production in 1989. It also was the leader in wholesale and retail trade for 1989, outside of Bangkok and vicinity. The province has extensive resources of rock salt. The ancient Pimai Stone Palace is found here.

NAKHON SI THAMMARAT. City in southern Thailand and an ancient principality there. Today it is the capital, pop. 74,250 (est.), of a province of the same name. It has a favorable coastal location on the peninsula (q.v.) with an excellent harbor, is the terminus of overland trade routes and is the rice (q.v.) market for a large fertile agricultural area. For about ten centuries up to the 13th, Nakhon Si Thammarat was a prominent principality with its own chieftain. As a vassal, it gave tribute at different times to kingdoms based in Indonesia, Pagan in Burma or Angkor (q.v.). One of these was the Dvaravati Kingdom (q.v.). In the latter half of this period, Buddhism (q.v.) had a growing influence.

Late in the 13th century, Nakhon Si Thammarat, along with neighboring principalities, became allied with the Thai Kingdom of Sukhothai (q.v.). Besides the Thai peoples, the Nakhon population at that time included Khmer (q.v.), Mon (q.v.) and Malay. A century later, the alliance was with the Siamese (q.v.) Kingdom of Ayutthaya (q.v.), albeit with some autonomy. In the mid-16th century, as trade prospects improved, the Siamese took full control of Nakhon Si Thammarat, and in later years controlled the other principalities of the peninsula as well.

In Nakhon Si Thammarat City, there is today a museum that displays many prehistoric artifacts and art works. The traditional shadow plays (q.v.), more common to Indonesia, are performed during festivals.

NANG TALUNG. See SHADOW PLAY.

NARAI. King of Ayutthaya (reigned 1656-1688). A major king of Ayutthaya (q.v.), he had considerable success in expanding contacts with the West and in building commerce. By 1680, Ayutthaya had become a center for foreign trade, which was aided by resident foreigners, especially Japanese, Malay and Persian, and the Dutch and British East India Companies. In order to promote relations with France (q.v.), Narai named Constantine Phaulkon (q.v.) to the powerful position of minister of finance and foreign affairs in 1685. Two Siamese (q.v.) missions were sent to Paris and three French missions came to Siam (q.v.). The third one included 500 French troops.

However, opposition to Phaulkon developed among traders and government officials when he attempted to convert King

Narai and his son to Christianity (q.v.). In addition, there were anti-foreign attitudes toward the stationing of French troops in the kingdom. When King Narai died in 1688, Phetracha (q.v.), who was reared as a foster brother of the king, led a coup that usurped the throne, and he became the next king of Ayutthaya. Phaulkon was executed and the French troops were removed. King Narai's reign saw a revival of Thai literature, with the court becoming a focal point for writers and poets to gather under the king's patronage.

NARESUAN. King of Ayutthaya (reigned 1590-1605). Born in 1555, he succeeded his father King Mahathammaracha (q.v.). He is considered one of the few great kings because he restored Siamese (q.v.) sovereignty after its defeat by the Burmese in 1569. Naresuan became a hostage in the Burmese court when his father assumed the throne of Siam (q.v.). While there, he observed Burmese military strengths and strategy. On his return, he joined his father in rebuilding the army and the fortifications of Siam. Naresuan's armies inflicted defeats on the Cambodians and reestablished security on the eastern borders of the nation. In 1584, following a successful battle against the Burmese, Naresuan declared Siam's independence from Burma (q.v.). The Siamese still commemorate a crucial engagement in 1553, in which King Naresuan single-handedly turned back the army of Burma when he killed their crown prince in a duel on an elephant's back.

By 1600, Naresuan's campaigns against the Burmese contributed to the breakup of Burma into many warring factions and eliminated it as a threat to Ayutthaya (q.v.) for 175 years. Armies under Naresuan, who was noted for many acts of personal bravery in battle, conquered Cambodia in 1594. During his reign, contacts with the West were continued in the form of a treaty with Spain, signed in 1598, and in the beginning of trade with the Dutch.

NATIONAL ASSEMBLY. The present constitution (q.v.), as well as previous ones, provide for Thailand to have a bicameral legislature as part of the government, with the king (q.v.) as titular head of state. The members of the upper chamber, the

Senate, are nominated by the prime minister for a proforma appointment by the king. The body typically is made up of Thai military and bureaucratic elite. Senator's terms are for six years, but they can be reappointed. The other chamber of the National Assembly is the House of Representatives, whose members are elected for a term of four years. To run for election, candidates must be members of a political party (q.v.). The number of representatives, approximately 360, is based on a ratio of one member for each 150,000 inhabitants in a province (q.v.). However, a province has at least one seat regardless of population. Business in the chambers is conducted separately and each has a "speaker" or president. The office of president of the National Assembly is taken by the person selected as president of the House of Representatives.

NATIONAL EDUCATION COUNCIL (NEC). Supervision of education in Thailand is highly centralized, since responsibility for education is largely in the national government. Direction comes chiefly from the Ministry of Education and from the National Educational Council, which is located in the Office of the Prime Minister. The Council coordinates the general plan for education (q.v.) and participates in the allocation of resources.

NATIONAL LIBRARY. When the first printing press was brought to Siam (q.v.) in 1835, libraries had already existed in the kingdom for centuries. Buddhist temple libraries were repositories of sacred manuscripts. Ancient Thai books were written on strips of hand-made paper or palm leaf, as were recorded laws, art, medical formulas and religious teachings. In 1881, King Chulalongkorn (q.v.) established a library for collecting Siamese (q.v.) and foreign literature. Since 1990, Wat Benchamaborpitr (q.v.) has had a library that houses all the books pertaining to the Buddhist (q.v.) faith, not only in Pali (q.v.) and Siamese, but also in Lao, Burmese, Chinese, Japanese, Singhalese and Sanskrit (q.v.). In 1905, the Wachirayan (q.v.) library was established as a National Library within the precincts of the Grand Palace. In 1966, a new National Library, with a capacity of more than 1,000,000 volumes, was opened at Thavasukri on Samsen Road. A depository library, it now holds

900,000 volumes and 200,000 manuscripts. According to the printing act, two copies of each publication printed in Thailand are kept in the National Library. Branches of the National Library are now functioning in several provinces. Through the years, the Library has expanded to include records or tapes of lectures, Thai folktales, music and parliamentary debates. The library also offers many rare materials on microfilm; photocopying facilities are available.

NATIONAL MUSEUM. The National Museum is located on Na Pra Tat Road in west-central Bangkok (q.v.) and housed in an old palace and two new buildings which were added in 1966. This outstanding collection of Thailand's treasures includes historic artifacts, ancient weapons, royal regalia, funeral chariots, illustrated books, marionettes, textiles, clothing, jewelry, furniture, ceramics (q.v.), bronze and stone sculptures (q.v.), ceremonial equipment and musical instruments (q.v.). The historian can find in the library important records and ancient manuscripts, as well as stone inscriptions. Indian and Chinese sculptures and pottery, together with archaeological artifacts which show ancient Khmer (q.v.) and Thai workmanship are included in the collection.

NEN. See NOVICE.

NEO-BUDDHISM. The path taken by educated Thais in response to the influence of scientific and philosophical thought from the West. As a result, the Thai urban intelligentsia have developed an orientation based more upon the actions and examples of the Buddha (q.v.) and less upon his teachings. They stress his cooperative and sympathetic nature and his respect and love for people. Neo-Buddhism is strongly social and altruistic. Desire is acceptable when directed toward other social ends. The ancient cosmological theories, animistic beliefs in the supernatural and ghosts, or dependence upon astrology (q.v.), while not eliminated, are seen as elements of the popular Buddhism (q.v.) of the uneducated Thais. Such beliefs are no longer a sufficient basis for governmental patterns nor adequate legitimation of ceremonies (q.v.) and festivals. (See COSMOLOGY; KARMA.)

NIELLOWARE. Niello is the art of decorating metal with engraved designs which are filled with an alloy consisting of sulfur combined with silver, copper or lead. The resultant pattern is coal black. This metalware has been hand-crafted for several centuries at Nakhon Si Thammarat (q.v.) on the peninsula (q.v.). Vases of pure silver take many shapes: bowls, betel nut boxes, jewelry, picture frames, and trays. Less expensive mass-produced pieces, often composed of silver and brass, are made in Bangkok (q.v.). (See HANDICRAFTS.)

NILAWAN PINTONG, KHUN (1915-   ). The daughter of Rong Ammat Dho Waet and Jang Pintong, she was born in Thonburi. She received her B.A. degree from Chulalongkorn University in 1937, and began her career as a teacher. In 1949, she become an editor of a well-known women's magazine, *Satri Sarn*, and has remained in that position to the present. In 1961, Khun Nilawan was the first Thai woman to be honored for public service by the Magsaysay Foundation. She held several voluntary positions in non-governmental organizations. She has received several decorations from the king and honorary Ph.D. degrees from Chulalongkorn and Ramkamhaeng Universities.

NIRVANA. The ultimate end of religious persons according to the teachings of Buddha (q.v.), attained by release from desire, defilement and ignorance. Nirvana is the cessation of processes which involve the above characteristics.   It is attained by following faithfully the Noble Eightfold Path (q.v.). He who has attained nirvana is said to be an *arahat.* (See BUDDHISM; FOUR NOBLE TRUTHS; KARMA.)

NOBLE EIGHTFOLD PATH. A central belief and teaching of Thai Buddhism (q.v.). It is called the "middle way" between the austere ascetic and the sensuous worldling. It consists of: (1) right belief, (2) right aspiration or feeling, (3) right speech, (4) right actions, (5) right livelihood, (6) right effort, (7) right mindfulness and memory, and (8) right contemplation and meditation. (See FOUR NOBLE TRUTHS.)

NONG HAN LAKE. The lake of the northeast (q.v.), the largest lake in Thailand. It is located in and provides water for the entire province of Sakon Nakhon.

NONTHA BURI. Though relatively small in geographic area, Nontha Buri Province, pop. 710,000 (est.), in the past was an area of abundant agricultural production. Today the province is experiencing rapid urbanization. The location of Nontha Buri City, pop. 265,000 (est.), 12 kilometers (8 miles) north of Bangkok (q.v.) makes it a fast growing suburb of the nation's capital. Commuters have easy access to employment in Bangkok by both land and water transportation. In agriculture, rice, commercial vegetables and fruits predominate. Nontha Buri City is the location of national occupational training centers, hospitals and the largest prison in Thailand.

THE NORTHEAST. A very large part of the rural population of Thailand resides in the northeast. Historically, much of the region was formerly a part of Laotian kingdoms. In the late-18th and 19th centuries, the Siamese kingdom of Bangkok (q.v.) established control over the northeast by military conquest. Integration into the Thai nation since then has been limited. A sense of regional identity has developed among the people of the northeast since the start of the 20th century. This was heightened in the 1930s and 1940s when the National Assembly (q.v.) was an important forum in the Thai national government. Political leaders with ties to the region rose to positions of influence. The mysterious assassination of three northeast political leaders in 1948 and a fourth in 1952 was seen as a government response to their dissent. In the late 1950s and early 1960s, many so called "leftist" politicians from the northeast were arrested and imprisoned.

While the Thai-Lao of the northeast have gradually become more identified with the Thai nation, there have been obstacles. Cultural differences between the central Thai and the Thai-Lao is one of these. In the late-19th century, a national Thai government reform established control through provinces (q.v.) and districts (q.v.). In the northeast, this replaced the local chieftains or lords. However, the national government officials' failure to understand Thai-Lao patterns and traditions led to errors and inadequate reform measures. Thai-Lao resistance and demonstrations were met with heavy-handed measures by the national government.

NORTHEAST ECONOMIC DEVELOPMENT. The economy of northeast Thailand (q.v.) is based primarily on agriculture (q.v.). Due mainly to soils of limited productivity and a lack of other opportunities, per capita income is only about two-thirds as much as elsewhere in Thailand. A principal export from the northeast is labor. Unskilled workers go to the Bangkok (q.v.) metropolitan area where they have largely replaced Chinese immigrants. Activities that contribute to economic improvement of the northeast include irrigation (q.v.) and energy projects. The three largest cities of the region are Nakhon Ratchasima (q.v.) pop. 203,000 (est.), Khon Kaen (q.v.) pop. 131,000 (est.), and Ubon Ratchathani pop. 99,500 (est.).

In the 1960s, the Thai government with United States (q.v.) financial and technical support began to improve welfare and security. The people of this large area were perceived as having low income and as facing a threat of insurgency (q.v.). One program involved training the local police. Another emphasized self-help community improvement projects. These programs and others that sought to strengthen channels available and provide facilities were (1) religious and educational training in the Buddhist temple compounds (q.v.), (2) civil service employment open to all with training and (3) an improved educational system (q.v.). In addition to the several teacher training colleges in the northeast, a new regional university was established at Khon Kaen in 1964.

During the Vietnam War, the United States (q.v.) military forces operated from several bases in the region, giving the northeast one of the better transportation systems in Asia. Rapid population growth ensued. As the villagers needed farm lands, they cleared forested areas. The loss of forests (see FORESTRY) has been strongly opposed by the national government, but without success.

2001
1964
37

NORTHERN AND WESTERN MOUNTAIN REGION. An area of broken and dissected ranges running parallel north and south, separated by narrow alluvial valleys. The average height of the ranges in the region is about 1,600 meters (5,300 feet) above mean sea level. Several peaks are considerably higher. The heavy rains of the summer monsoons give rise to rivers that support rice (q.v.) cultivation in the valleys. Some of these flow northward or to the northwest. The major drainage is southward, consisting chiefly of the Ping, Wang, Yom and Nan Rivers. Vegetables, tobacco and various fruits are produced in addition to rice.

NOVICE (NEN). A Thai male under 20 years of age who takes the vows of commitment to a role of self-denial, discipline and study of the scriptures of Buddhism (q.v.). Following an ordination (q.v.) ceremony, the novice takes up residence in a Buddhist temple compound *(wat)* (q.v.). There the novice will be supervised in his activities by the abbot (q.v.) or by a senior Buddhist monk (q.v.). In northern Thailand most males begin their Buddhist temple compound experiences as novices. After the novice has reached 20 years of age, he can be ordained as a monk. Novices observe the ten precepts (q.v.) in their daily lives. Becoming a novice is similar to becoming a Buddhist monk in that it is a highly meritorious act of self-denial and commitment. Merit (q.v.) is accumulated not only by the novice, but also by his parents, his sponsor and others who assist in his ordination.

NUNS (MAE CHI). Women, called nuns, often seek training in Buddhism (q.v.) while residing in the temple compound *(wat)* (q.v.). Because their integration into the monkhood is minimal, they are regarded as part of the lay section of society. They shave their heads and wear white robes similar in style to the monks' habit. Most nuns attach themselves to a particular abbot (q.v.) or particular meditation teacher. They may learn the plaintive, minor-keyed chants of Buddhism (q.v.), but there are no vows of silence, poverty or obedience, nor is there in Thailand a Buddhist cloistered order. There are no obstacles in the way of a nun who wishes to return to a householder's life. Nuns have eight precepts (q.v.) to uphold and may have two meals a day before noon. Traditionally, they have devoted themselves to cleaning, food (q.v.) preparation, gardening and other activities which are prohibited to monks. Today, nuns are trained to go into the rural areas of Thailand to teach home economics, nursing skills, meditation, and most important, the *dharma* (q.v.).

- O -

OK PHANSA. See END OF LENT CEREMONY.

ORDINATION. The ceremony which takes place when a male makes the vows of commitment to be a Buddhist monk (q.v.) or a Buddhist novice (q.v.). The ordination ceremony is performed in the *bot* (q.v.) of the Buddhist temple compound *(wat)* (q.v.). At least five Buddhist monks are needed to carry out the rites for the person being ordained. The active cooperation of a sponsor, family members and friends is also essential. Persons ordained as a monk must be at least 20 years of age. Young men and youth who are not yet 20 can be ordained as novices.

ORGANIZATIONS THAT REPRESENT BUSINESS AS A WHOLE. Several business organizations are able to speak for all or a large part of the business sector of Bangkok (q.v.) where the predominant part of the Thai economy is located. Five of these groups are the following: The Board of Trade works with the Ministry of Commerce to set both export quotas and minimum prices. The Board also represents Thai business in international forums. The Thai Chamber of Commerce (TCC), founded in 1993, began to be very active in the 1980s. As the TCC membership of provincial chambers of commerce rose to 72, the TCC became equal to the Board of Trade in overall influence as a spokesperson for Thai business. The Federation of Thai Industries (FTI) is widely accepted as speaking for industry as a whole. In the early 1990s, the FTI had a staff of 84 and is widely represented on government commissions and committees. The Mining Industry Council, created in 1983 by national legislation, is regarded as the official representative of all mining-related industries. Its membership consists of individuals or firms. The

Joint Standing Committee on Commerce, Industry and Banking was founded in 1977. It helps member associations reach common positions on key issues and represents them in national and international forums.

- P -

PAI THIAW. A custom in which young Thai men individually or in small groups leave their home villages, often going to urban areas or elsewhere to obtain wage labor, engage in a trade and to "have fun." They usually return after an absence of a few months to a year or so.

PAKNAM INCIDENT. An incident in July 1893 at Paknam, the mouth of the Chao Phraya River (q.v.), when approaching French warships were fired upon by Siamese guards acting in self-defense. The French government seized this as an opportunity and pressured the Siamese to grant France (q.v.) jurisdiction over former territories of Siam east of the Mekong River (q.v.). Payment of an indemnity by Siam was also compelled. Anticipated British support for the Siamese failed to arrive. (See FRANCE, RELATIONS WITH.)

PALI. An ancient language used for the writings of the Buddhist scriptures (q.v.). Spoken Pali is used in all Thai Buddhist religious ceremonies.

PANYANANDA BHIKKHU (1911-   ). A Buddhist lecture-monk, abbot, and educator. Panyananda was born and educated in Phatthalung Province. He was ordained as a novice *(nen)* (q.v.) about 1930 and as a Buddhist monk (q.v.) two years later. In 1938 he began a long association with Buddhadasa Bhikkhu (q.v.). This led to his study of the Pali (q.v.) language at a temple in Bangkok (q.v.). He traveled considerably in Thailand and to other countries, including Burma, India and Malaysia, during and after World War II. In 1954 he visited Europe and North America in support of the "moral rearmament" movement.

His goal in all of his travels was to spread Buddhism (q.v.) and raise the morale of Buddhist monks that he contacted.

Panyananda is best known in Thailand as a lecture-monk *(nak thet)*. He has lectured in many temple compounds *(wat)* (q.v.) on the Buddhist scriptures and probably more than any other Buddhist monk. To his credit he has provided, in his lectures, meaning and understanding of the traditional rituals. He has served as abbot (q.v.) of several temple compounds. At one of these, Wat Cholprathan in Nontha Buri (q.v.), he was invited to serve as abbot in 1960. Later, he opened there a Pali language school and a meditation center. Besides his lectures on Saturdays and Sundays there, he conducted a long period of Sunday morning lectures on television.

PARAMANUCHIT CHINOROT (1790-1853). Poet, Buddhist philosopher and writer, and supreme patriarch (q.v.). Paramanuchit was a son of King Rama I (q.v.) and was educated in the royal court. At age 12, he entered the Buddhist monkhood (q.v.) which became central to his life career. His writings were both religious and literary. Many of Paramanuchit's poems are considered to be masterpieces. He developed a command of the arts and disciplines of the Ayutthaya (q.v.) period. Paramanuchit communicated this knowledge to his contemporaries and this made him a kind of bridge between two periods of Siamese (q.v.) history. He also contributed to the style and refinement of the Siamese language. Paramanuchit also had a complete knowledge of Pali (q.v.). In this language he wrote three famous works. For his literary contributions, Paramanuchit was honored by UNESCO (q.v.) in 1990.

PARLIAMENT. See NATIONAL ASSEMBLY.

PASTEUR INSTITUTE (SATAN SAOWAPA). The Pasteur Institute in Bangkok (q.v.) is operated by the Thai Red Cross Society (q.v.). A main attraction to the public is the snake farm where, on certain days, specialized workers extract venom from snakes. This venom is used to prepare anti-snakebite vaccine which is then distributed all over Thailand. Venom is extracted from such snakes as cobras, king cobras, kraits, Russell vipers and other snakes. Thai villagers are sometimes bitten by poisonous snakes when they are working in the fields, so the vaccine of the Pasteur Institute serves a useful function.

PATIMOKKHA. That section of the Buddhist scriptures *(tipitaka)* (q.v.) comprising 227 highly specific rules of conduct which Buddhist monks (q.v.) are expected to follow.

PATTANI. An important coastal city, located at the eastern end of east-west trade route that crossed the peninsula (q.v.) on the gulf of south Thailand. It was also an ancient principality. As a port city near a rice (q.v.) plain, Pattani made history as a trade center in the 6th and 7th centuries. In the 13th century, the Pattani principality was overcome and absorbed into the Thai-Buddhist principality of Nakhon Si Thammarat (q.v.), which was adjacent on the north.

The population was converted to Islam (q.v.) about the 15th century. Later, on becoming a powerful trade center, Pattani enjoyed a large degree of independence in the 16th to 18th centuries. However, it was conquered by the Siamese (q.v.) from Ayutthaya (q.v.) in 1785 and subsequently was divided into several provinces. The Pattani people waged unsuccessful rebellions against the Siamese government in 1901-1902 and again in 1946-1948.

Today, Pattani is a center of Islamic religious scholarship and propagation. Strong opposition to the control of the Thai authorities continues. A part of Prince of Songkhla University was located at Pattani in 1967. Programs of study are offered in science and technology, humanities and social sciences, and education. Both undergraduate and graduate programs are available. The other part of this university is located near Hat Yai in Songkhla Province (q.v.).

PATTAYA. See CHON BURI.

PAVIE, AUGUSTE (1848-1925). Colonial civil servant of France (q.v.) who became a vice-consul and served in Laos (q.v.). Previously he led a 17-year exploration and scientific group in Cambodia. As a diplomat in 1887, he became the leading exponent of French expansion in Laos and Cambodia (q.v.). He sought to protect these peoples from alleged imperialism of Siam (q.v.). In perspective, there was a system conflict between an Asian kingdom using a vassalage system and the European pattern of diplomacy backed by military force.

Pavie lobbied his government to put Laos under French control when he was in Bangkok (q.v.) as French consul-general. Some hostile incidents between the French and the Siamese occurred in 1893. This led to a French ultimatum delivered to the Siamese king by Pavie and resulted in huge territorial losses to France. (See FRANCE, RELATIONS WITH; FRANCO-SIAMESE CRISIS OF 1893.)

THE PENINSULA. The topography of the peninsula region is mostly rolling to mountainous. There is a small amount of flat land and numerous small streams. The northern part of the peninsula is shared with Burma, and the border is the Bilauktaung Range (q.v.). Just south of this range is the narrow part of the peninsula, which is called the Isthmus of Kra. Here there is an overland crossing of only 25 kilometers (16 miles). South of the Isthmus, Thailand widens to occupy the full width of the peninsula down to the border with Malaysia (q.v.). The Gulf of Thailand borders on the east and the Andaman Sea borders on the west. Numerous islands are scattered along the western coast; the largest one is the tin-rich Island of Phuket (q.v.). The east coastal plain is from 5 to 35 kilometers (3 to 22 miles) wide, and there are several river plains and basins which extend far inland. Well to the south is the large inland sea, Thalesap.

Soils in the northern part of the peninsula are sandy and generally unproductive; in the southern part, however, soils consist of sand and clay loams, in which rubber (q.v.) trees thrive. The peninsula is also rich in tin (q.v.) deposits. The Malay population, to a lesser extent than the Thai and Chinese, engage in tin mining (q.v.), the production of rubber, and the cultivation of other tropical crops.

PETROLEUM AND NATURAL GAS. During the past decade, Thailand has covered from one-half to two-thirds of its needs for petroleum from local reserves and has expanded its oil refining capacity. Dependence on foreign oil sources and the possibility of price fluctuations represent a serious potential problem for Thailand's balance of payments (q.v.). Oil reserves have been discovered in several places in Thailand. This includes large quantities of oil shale, the use of which is limited due to high production costs. Development and management of oil production and refining has been partly by private companies and partly by state-owned enterprises.

PHAHONYOTHIN (1889-1958). Prime minister (1933-1938), army officer. Phahon was educated in Thailand, Germany and Denmark. His career in the army was a distinguished one. He was a member of the group that promoted the Revolution of 1932 (q.v.) and the second prime minister (1933-1938) of Thailand. Phahon came to power following a bloodless coup which he led, assisted by Phibunsongkhram (q.v.). Important events during his term of office included the unsuccessful Bowaradet rebellion (q.v.), the first national election of representatives to the House of Representatives (q.v.) in 1933 and the abdication of King Prajadhipok (q.v.) in 1935. Phahon was noted for his modesty, personal integrity and pleasing personality.

PHAULKON, CONSTANTINE (1647-1688). Leading official in the government of King Narai (q.v.). Phaulkon, who was born in Greece, was an adventurer who arrived in the Kingdom of Ayutthaya (q.v.) by way of employment in the East India Company. He readily mastered English, Portuguese, Malay and the Tai-language. As an interpreter, he entered the service of King Narai in 1679. Phaulkon rose in status and responsibility when his remarkable talents became known. King Narai used him as an advisor and an unofficial "prime minister." However, Phaulkon's actions antagonized the British, but facilitated the French goals of Christian missions and establishment of military posts in the kingdom. Opposition to Phaulkon resulted in his execution for treason in 1688 after the death of King Narai. At that time, Phetracha (q.v.) led a bloody coup that usurped the throne.

PHETCHABUN RANGE. A mountain range in central Thailand at the extreme eastern edge of the central Plain (q.v.) and the western limit of the Khorat Plateau.

PHETRACHA. King of Ayutthaya (reigned 1688-1703). Phetracha had been a general under the previous king, Narai (q.v.), and a commoner. He usurped the throne, which included arranging the murders of royalty who were next in line after the death of King Narai whose foreign policies he opposed. French soldiers who were stationed in Bangkok (q.v.) and Mergui were expelled by Phetracha and also some French priests who had come as missionaries. However, he showed favor to the Dutch, who supported him. Constantine Phaulkon (q.v.), who had served King Narai, was seen by his enemies as too influential. The king had him arrested, charged with treason and executed. Phetracha was confronted with a series of rebellions during his reign, all of which he successfully put down.

PHI CULT. The Thai peoples, who were animists before they became Buddhists (q.v.), acknowledged the existence of spirits of all kinds. Spirits were associated with natural objects, but also included restless souls of the dead. Such spirits *(phi)*, can have a material existence which may interfere in human affairs. Hence, these spirits are to be propitiated, cajoled, outwitted and dealt with as persons. Propitiation typically includes the presentation of food and other offerings. Certain spirits are enjoined as moral agents enforcing public norms, the violation of which would result in illness, difficulties or misfortune. In some hill tribes (q.v.), religious life centers entirely on such beliefs and forces. The *phi* cult has a central place in the Thai world. When the Thai peoples became Buddhists, animistic beliefs and the *phi* cult became more or less incorporated into the Buddhist cosmology (q.v.).

An example of a spirit is the *chao thi* (q.v.), the spirit of the place, such as a home or a village settlement. Individual spirit houses in appropriate locations are constructed and used as a place to contact and make offerings to a guardian spirit on ritual occasions. Another spirit central to Thai culture is the Rice Goddess. Offerings and appropriate ceremonies are performed for this spirit on selected occasions related to the production of rice (q.v.).

PHIBUNSONGKHRAM (1897-1964). Prime minister (1938-1944) and (1948-1957). Phibun's tenure in that office was the longest of any Thai prime minister. Born into a village farm family and a student in temple schools, he graduated from the Royal Military Academy in 1915. Upon his graduation as valedictorian from the Army General Staff College in 1924, he was awarded a prestigious scholarship to study artillery science in France. There he became friends with other Siamese (q.v.) students who became involved with him in the Revolution of 1932 (q.v.). Phibun advanced rapidly in the Siamese Army, largely due to the respect that he attained as an outstanding student, as a teacher and writer in military science.

In Phibun's first tenure as prime minister, prominent policies of his regime were: militarism, a nationalism that penalized the Chinese (q.v.), and the recovery of lost territories. Changing the name of the country to Thailand in 1939 reflected a Phibun policy of uniting all Tai-language (q.v.) peoples, including those in adjacent countries.

Under great pressure in 1941, Phibun permitted the Japanese military forces to use Thailand as a staging area and a source of supplies for attacks elsewhere. With aid from the Japanese, Thailand got back, temporarily, formerly held territories in Burma (q.v.), Laos (q.v.), Cambodia (q.v.) and Malaya. However, the Phibun regime was greatly weakened by war expenditures, inflation and scarcity of essential commodities. These problems and Japan's (q.v.) war losses increased the political opposition to Phibun and forced him to resign his post in 1944.

Phibun returned as prime minister as a result of a 1947 coup that reasserted military government and displaced the civilian regimes of the previous three years. This time, Phibun's policies included taking actions against Communists and giving Thailand a central role in SEATO (q.v.). He also instituted an anti-Chinese campaign and measures suppressing the Thai-Malay (q.v.) in southern Thailand. His pro-Americanism was rewarded in 1950 and thereafter by large annual dollar grants by the United States (q.v.) to Thailand. Phibun now assumed great personal power. For a time he held four ministerial posts in his cabinet while being the commander of three armies. There were unsuccessful coups against Phibun in 1948, 1949 and 1951. He also lost face and reputation for several actions perceived to be against the monarchy (q.v.). When Phibun was replaced as prime minister in a 1957 coup d'etat, he went into exile in Japan where he died in 1964.

PHOT SARASIN (1906-   ). Thai diplomat and political leader. Phot was educated in Thailand, the United States (q.v.) and Britain after which he joined a law firm in Bangkok (q.v.). He developed a friendship with Prime Minister Phibunsongkhram (q.v.) and was appointed senator in 1947. In 1952, he became ambassador to the United States and to the United Nations. Phot returned to Thailand in 1954 to serve as secretary general of the newly formed Southeast Asia Treaty Organization (SEATO [q.v.]) . He became interim prime minister for three months in 1957 following the coup against Phibun which brought Sarit Thanarat (q.v.) to power. Later, Phot was minister of development in the Thanom Kittikachorn (q.v.) administration.

PHRA. The title *phra* or *phraya* is (1) a traditional princely title designating that its bearer is a relative of the king, or (2) a functional title given to holders of the highest ranks in the civil administration, or (3) an honorific for monks or persons and certain objects having religious significance. Uses (1) and (2) are no longer practiced.

PHRA PHUM. See CHAO THI.

PHRAYA. See PHRA.

PHU YAI. The Thai name for a superior or person of high status.

PHU YAI BAN. The Thai village headman, who is normally elected to this post. Formally, the term of office is five years, but headmen tend to remain in office until death or retirement. In a sense he is a middle-man in that he represents the village to the government authorities at the district (q.v.) level, while he must also represent the district government to his village constituency. The village headman is supposed to keep records on everything from animal slaughtering to births. He plans festivals and acts as patron in weddings. He is responsible for reporting calamities such as flooding and for obtaining help in emergencies. The headman has the authority to make arrests in cases of theft and other violations. He receives a nominal pay of 75 to 100 baht (q.v.) per month. (See LOCAL GOVERNMENT; MUBAN.)

PHUKET. A small island province in extreme south Thailand, pop. 188,500 (est.), with an area of 550 square kilometers (250 square miles). Phuket is one of the more prosperous and developed of Thailand's provinces due chiefly to tourism (q.v.) and the production of tin (q.v.) and coconuts (q.v.). Its resorts are the most popular of any beaches in the nation. Tin mining, begun in the 14th century, flourishes though surface deposits are waning and water dredging for tin is increasing. Phuket city, the provincial capital, pop. 48,500 (est.), is 900 kilometers (550 miles) south of Bangkok (q.v.). There is an excellent international airport, good highways and the island can be reached by sea.

PHUTHAI. A Tai-speaking ethnic group with a distinctive dialect located in the eastern part of northeast Thailand. The Phuthai, numbering more than 100,000, are agriculturalists. Their cultural traits resemble those of people of northern Laos and Vietnam, from where they presumably immigrated in the 19th century.

PHUWARACHAKAN. See GOVERNOR.

PI NAI. An oboe-like musical instrument (q.v.) with a reed and a conical bore with six holes. In the simple music of a *piphat* ensemble, the *pi nai* carries the melody. (See PIPHAT ORCHESTRA.)

PING. A major river in the northern region of Thailand. It flows southward and is a tributary of the Chao Phraya River (q.v.).

PIPHAT ORCHESTRA (WONG PIPHAT or GONG TENG TING).
The Thai percussion orchestra which consists of three groups of instruments: the *pi nai* (q.v.), a woodwind; a melodic percussion section, with xylophones and glockenspiel or celesta; and finally the rhythmic percussion section, consisting of drums, cymbals and the *ching*. The latter instrument resembles the Western triangle, but in the *wong piphat* its ringing notes control the rhythm of the music. While the number of instruments used may vary, the *piphat* orchestra is used widely in restaurants, especially those that feature Thai classical dancing. It is also heard frequently at large temple festivals and at village spirit ceremonies. (See also DONTRI PUEN MUANG; GONG AEW; MUSIC; MUSICAL INSTRUMENTS.)

POH TEK ASSOCIATION. A Chinese charity organization based in Bangkok (q.v.) with an annual budget, which conducts or supervises most of the benevolent and charitable work of the Chinese (q.v.) community. It was founded in 1910. It provides hospitalization for the sick, aid to the indigent and immediate food (q.v.) and shelter for the victims of fires, floods and other disasters.

POLITICAL PARTIES (PHAK KANMUANG). Political parties, while active following World War II, became more significant after legislation in 1983 required minimal membership in each of the nations's four geographical regions. In addition, a party must have at least 50 members in each of five provinces per region. Political parties typically become active as an election approaches and tend to be organized around charismatic persons of wealth. However, a party occasionally is known for its ideology or programmatic objectives.

During the 1980s, more than 30 parties presented candidates for election to the House of Representatives (q.v.). More than half of these eventually disbanded. Problems faced by political parties include lack of organization, factionalism, vote buying and emphasis on personality over issues.

In the September 1992 election, 11 parties succeeded in getting one or more candidates elected to the house. Four parties had 47 or more successful candidates. Two of these were new parties in 1992. Prominent political parties of long-standing include the Democrat party (q.v.), the Thai Nation party (q.v.), and the Social Action party (q.v.). Political parties also field candidates for election to the city council of the Bangkok Metropolis (q.v.).

PONG TEUK. An archaeological site in Kanchana Buri Province about 15 kilometers (9 miles) west of Ban Pong village where the railway from Bangkok (q.v.) to Singapore turns south. It is one of the oldest sites in Thailand; diggings in 1926 unearthed a temple and several monuments. A bronze Roman lamp in the Pompeian style decorated with the mask of Silenus indicates that Greek or Roman merchants were establishing contacts between China and the West. A small bronze Buddha (q.v.) statue in the Dvaravati (q.v.) style, probably made in India, was also found here. Both pieces are in the National Museum (q.v.) in Bangkok.

POPULATION. One of the 20 most populous nations in the world, Thailand had a population of approximately 60 million people in 1994, with an average growth rate of 1.4 percent a year. This total was divided about equally between males and females. The regional breakdown was approximately 17 million in the central region (including the Bangkok [q.v.] metropolitan area), 11 million in the north, 7 million in the south, 21 million in the northeast and 4 million in the east. Approximately, 30 percent of the population was between the ages of 15 and 29.

PRACHATHIPAT. See DEMOCRAT PARTY.

PRAJADHIPOK (1893-1941). King of Siam (reigned 1925-1935). Prajadhipok, the youngest son of former King Chulalongkorn (q.v.), was educated in Bangkok (q.v.), Britain and France. He ascended the throne on the death of King Vajiravudh (q.v.). As he lacked preparedness, he called as advisors senior princes whom his predecessor had ignored. However, the conservatism of these princes was questioned by the liberal Siamese (q.v.) elite. The financial difficulties then facing Siam (q.v.) were to some extent overcome, but the low public esteem of the monarchy (q.v.) remained. A conspiracy of civil and military officials acted to force King Prajadhipok to end the absolute monarchy and agree to a constitutional one. This event has since been referred to as the Revolution of 1932 (q.v.). Previously, ideas of increased public participation in political decisions, favored by Prajadhipok, were rejected by his senior advisors. After several unsuccessful attempts to negotiate such ideas with the new ruling junta, he became disillusioned. In March 1935 Prajadhipok abdicated the throne to be followed by Ananda Mahidol as the next king.

PRAMARN ADIREKSARN (1913-   ). Politician and party leader, former army general and businessman. Pramarn was educated in Thailand, graduated from the Royal Thai Military Academy in 1935 and studied in the United States (q.v.). In the army, Pramarn advanced to major general. With his organizational skills, in his army command, he was in charge of state-run transportation services, state-run communications systems and both state-owned and private industry. Pramarn resigned from the army in 1951 and was elected to the House of Representatives (q.v.) in 1956 from Sara Buri Province. He held ministerial posts in the cabinets of four prime ministers. With Chatchai Choonhavan (q.v.) and Siri Siriyothin, Pramarn founded the Thai National party *chat thai* in 1974 and served as its leader for 12 years. He was, for a time, leader of the "opposition" in the House. (See POLITICAL PARTIES.)

PRANG. A tower-like masonry structure ending in a blunt pinnacle. The upper portion of a *prang* resembles a heavy cylinder compared to the tapering spire of the *chedi* (q.v.) and the former is usually taller. It may contain a relic chamber in which art objects or ashes of royalty are kept. The design of the *prang* is said to have originated with the ancient Khmer (q.v.) of mainland Southeast Asia.

PRAPHAS CHARUSATHIAN (1912-   ). Army officer and government official. He gained prominence for his part in the army's quelling of a 1949 rebellion, and he served in the cabinet of Prime Minister Sarit Thanarat (q.v.). After Sarit's death, Praphas shared top power with Prime Minister Thanom

Kittikachorn (q.v.), 1963-1973, as deputy prime minister, minister of the interior and commander-in-chief of the army. Following the student-led uprising of 14 October 1973 (q.v.), which resulted in a new government, both Praphas and Thanom were forced into a brief exile.

PRAYUDH PAYUTTO (1939-   ). Famous Buddhist monk, author and scholar. Prayudh's early education was chiefly in Buddhist temple schools in his home province *(changwat)* of Suphan Buri and in Bangkok (q.v.). After becoming a novice *(nen)* (q.v.), Prayudh completed all nine levels of Pali (q.v.) language study. This was an outstanding accomplishment. He graduated from Mahachulalongkorn Buddhist University in 1962. He taught at his alma mater from 1962 to 1974. As part of his teaching role, he aided in curriculum improvement and served as an administrator. His publications include a *Dictionary of Buddhism* and *Buddha-Dhamma*. The latter is his masterpiece on Buddhist doctrine and theology.

Over a period of 35 years of his teaching, study and writing he has earned five Buddhist honorary titles, each award being higher than the previous one. Since 1982, Prayudh has been awarded honorary doctorates from five major Thai universities in Bangkok. He has been a superior example of a monk-scholar and a major figure in Thai Buddhism (q.v.).

PRECEPTS. Certain moral injunctions to which Buddhists (q.v.) are expected to conform as closely as possible. The Buddhist layman should refrain from (1) taking life, (2) stealing, (3) speaking falsely, (4) being unchaste and (5) drinking intoxicating liquors. The first three of the precepts are taught to young children and others are emphasized later in life. When Holy Day services are held, the devout Buddhist laymen and Buddhist nuns (q.v.) observe the above five precepts and also three additional ones: (6) refrain from eating after midday, (7) refrain from cosmetics and bodily ornaments and (8) refrain from sitting or lying on a high or wide mattress filled with cotton. Novices (q.v.) observe the above eight precepts and also two additional ones, viz., (9) refrain from dancing, singing, music and entertainment and (10) refrain from receiving gold or silver. In addition to these ten precepts the Buddhist monks (q.v.) observe 227 specific rules of conduct.

PREM TINSULANONDA (1920-   ). Prime minister, army commander and minister of defense. Prem was educated in Thailand and graduated from the Royal Military Academy in 1941. He attended the U.S. Army Cavalry School and U.S. Army War College. In the Thai Army, Prem rose from the rank of lieutenant to general. He served as a cabinet officer under prime minister Kriangsak Chomanan (q.v.). A number of influential assemblymen and senators who were high army officers joined to bring about Prem's selection as prime minister in 1980. Prem began his tenure as an army general and was not an elected representative to the National Assembly. Later, during his long term as prime minister, he resigned from the army and thereafter served as a civilian.

The widespread support for Prem and his administration included that of the Thai king, Bhumibol Adulyadej (q.v.), the person with the highest prestige in the nation. Prem's standing was indicated when he remained in power in spite of coup attempts against him in 1981 and 1985. He also weathered elections that were somewhat disorderly and a crisis of the national currency. Prem's term of eight-and-a-half years as prime minister was one of the longest in Thai history. It was also a time in which the political system began to move toward a bit more democracy. He was able, as a strong leader, to checkmate the military when needed and to maintain a balance between competing elements of the elite. On his 68th birthday, the king awarded Prem a rare and noble honor, the "Ancient Auspicious Order of the Nine Gems," *(Nopparat Rajavaraporn)*.

PRIDI PHANOMYONG (1900-1983). Political leader, senior statesman. Pridi, the precocious son of a farmer, completed secondary education and then law studies by the age of 19. He studied in France, where he interacted with other Siamese (q.v.) students who later became his political colleagues. He had a prominent role in the group of reformers that overthrew the Siamese absolute monarchy (q.v.) in the Revolution of 1932 (q.v.). Pridi was active in politics from 1932 to 1949. He was a strong leader and held positions in several administrations. These included the cabinet posts of finance, interior, justice and prime minister. He served as regent for a youthful king of Thailand.

Pridi was recognized for outstanding public service and was awarded several of the highest Thai orders and decorations. Four foreign nations, France (q.v.), Great Britain, Sweden and the United States (q.v.), also awarded Pridi high honors. Pridi's wife, Poonsuk, was honored with the Thai title Than Phuying. Pridi contributed to the national constitution (q.v.) and to the structure of local government (q.v.). As finance minister, he placed the Thai finance and monetary system on a sound basis. He led in the founding of Thammasat University where he was rector for 18 years. During World War II, when Thailand was aiding Japan (q.v.), Pridi and Seni Pramoj (q.v.) led a Free Thai (q.v.) underground movement which helped in obtaining lenient peace terms with the Allies after the war. Pridi was discredited by opponents when the young King Ananda Mahidol died mysteriously. Banishment from Siam (q.v.) was the way his enemies used to block his potential power. He was forced into permanent exile in 1949 and died in Paris in 1983. Some of his admirers have established the Pridi Phanomyong Institute in Bangkok (q.v.).

PRIVATE SECONDARY SCHOOLS. Private schools are prominent in the conduct of secondary education in Thailand. These include those owned and operated by private individuals or by religious organizations. Since 1970, as a result of expansion, the public or government-supported schools account for more than half of all secondary school enrollment. Supervision of both private and public schools is provided through the Thai Ministry of Education. (See EDUCATION, ADULT; EDUCATION, HIGHER; EDUCATIONAL SYSTEM.)

PRIVY COUNCIL. The Privy Council is a royally appointed group that assists the king in discharging his formal duties. The members cannot hold any other public office, show partisan loyalty or belong to a political party (q.v.). When the throne becomes vacant, the Council acts to appoint a new king. Until the heir ascends the throne, the president of the Privy Council serves as regent and substitutes temporarily for the king.

PRO-DEMOCRACY DEMONSTRATION AND MILITARY CRACKDOWN. Widespread protests occurred in Bangkok (q.v.) on May 7th and 8th of 1992 demanding Suchinda Kraprayoon to resign since he was not an elected prime minister. Up to 100,000 demonstrators marched in Bangkok streets from May 17th to May 20th. These were initiated by educated middle-class persons and joined by others. Chamlong Srimuang (q.v.) was the principal leader of the movement.

Soldiers of the Thai Army were ordered to put down the disturbance after fires had been set. In army clashes with unarmed demonstrators, 52 persons were killed and hundreds were injured. King Bhumibol Adulyadej (q.v.) intervened on May 20th and asked Chamlong and Suchinda to settle the dispute peacefully.

Prime Minister Suchinda resigned on May 24th. The interim prime minister, Anand Panyarachun (q.v.), demoted a number of military officers for their part in the death of demonstrators. The new coalition government and general assembly that took office after the September 1992 elections passed a law requiring prime ministers to be elected. (See CHUAN LEEKPAI.)

PROTESTANTISM. Introduced in Thailand by American Presbyterian missionaries in 1828. Today, nine denominations operate a cooperative mission--The Church of Christ in Thailand--with more than 40,000 Thai members in approximately 135 congregations. They are served by ministers, more than half of whom are Thai. Thirteen other Protestant churches individually conduct missionary work in Thailand, having a total of approximately 180 congregations. They are served by some 160 ministers of whom about three-fourths are Thai. The Protestant groups combined operate some ten hospitals and nearly 50 schools providing elementary and/or secondary education for Thai students. (See CHRISTIANITY.)

PROVINCE (CHANGWAT). The name for any of the 73 territorial units of Thailand, each serving as a major unit of local government (q.v.). The chief administrative officer of the province is the governor (q.v.), who is appointed and supervised by the Ministry of the Interior. Provinces are subdivided for administrative purposes into two to 20 districts (q.v.), each having a district officer *(nai amphoe)* (q.v.). The city in which the provincial headquarters is located is the provincial capital and has the same name as the province, e.g., Ayutthaya is the capital of Phra Nakhon Si Ayutthaya Province; Chiang Mai (q.v.) is the capital of Chiang Mai Province, etc.

PUBLISHING. The press is the oldest of the mass media (q.v.) in Thailand. In 1835, Christian missionaries introduced the first printing press in Thailand. Publishing was confined mostly to the royal court, the foreign missionaries and businessmen. *The Royal Gazette*, founded in 1858 by King Mongkut (q.v.), exists to the present day as the official medium. Other newspapers and periodicals were published in the mid-19th century. Although prior to World War II few publications lasted for any length of time, the number of publications and the size of readership grew steadily.

The mass media are under the supervision of the Public Relations Department in the Office of the Prime Minister. All major daily newspapers are privately owned, but radio (q.v.) and television (q.v.) stations are controlled by the government and operated as commercial enterprises. By 1988, there were 40 daily newspapers in Thailand and 245 non-daily newspapers; 11 were in Chinese and 4 in English. There were 58 weekly magazines and 20 fortnightly ones. For journals there were 140 monthlies, 37 quarterlies and 8 biannuals. There were 55 other publications in the Tai-langauge, 13 in Chinese and 11 in English. By 1990, the number of daily newspapers appearing in Thailand jumped to 51, and magazines to 380.

Newspapers and other periodicals in Thailand today enjoy a freedom that is unequaled in the rest of Southeast Asia, though the private press in Thailand has been subject to censorship from time to time. It was especially strict during World War II, during the period of Sarit's (q.v.) rule and in the immediate aftermath of the October 6, 1976 coup. Even during these periods, however, the press was allowed to publish many nonpolitical stories. However, in the May 1992 coup, much of the news was censored in newspapers as well as on television. Thai newspapers exercise self-censorship and have been careful to present a positive coverage of the monarchy (q.v.), government affairs, internal security matters and Thailand's international image. Soon after their appearance abroad, many foreign best-sellers were translated into Thai. Standards of production have improved dramatically and high-quality color printing is common.

PUEY UNGPHAKORN (1916-   ). Puey was educated in Thailand and Britain. He was a student at the London School of Economics when the circumstances of the Indochina War caused him to join the Pioneer Corps of the British army in 1942. This enabled him to secretly return to Thailand where he served as an interpreter and supporter of the Free Thai Movement (q.v.). In 1949, he completed his doctorate in economics at the London School. Puey was governor of the Bank of Thailand, 1959-1971. He was appointed rector of Thammasat University in 1975. In October of the following year, when rightist groups used force against demonstrating students at Thammasat, Puey was forced into exile because he had championed human rights.

- Q -

QUEEN'S BIRTHDAY. Queen Sirikit's (q.v.) birthday is a national holiday and is celebrated on August 12th. She is married to King Bhumibol Adulyadej (q.v.) of Thailand and is widely admired and respected for her beauty and talent.

- R -

RACHASAP. See ROYAL LANGUAGE.

RADIO. The Public Relations Department is responsible for Radio Thailand, the official government broadcasting station, which transmits the local and international news. Thailand's 480 radio stations are under the aegis of the Department. Except for the

Ministry of Education and the Radio Thailand broadcasts, the rest of the stations are commercial and rely heavily on advertising revenue.

RAEK NA. See ROYAL PLOWING CEREMONY.

RAILWAYS. The State Railways of Thailand have operated since 1890. They provide passenger and freight services. The construction of the first line was begun in Bangkok (q.v.) in 1892 and reached Nakhon Ratchasima (q.v.) in 1900, with a distance of 264 kilometers (165 miles). In 1990, the total network of meter gauge lines was 4,478 kilometers (2,800 miles). The main line, running 3,825 kilometers (2,390 miles), connects 42 provinces and consists of four routes. Railways extend from Bangkok north to Chiang Mai (q.v.), northeast to Nong Khai and Ubon Ratchatani, east to Prachin Buri/Aranyaprathet, and south to Songkhla (q.v.) and Padang-Besar with links to the Malaysian Railway.

RAIN-MAKING CEREMONIES. Rites aimed at producing rain are frequently conducted in areas which have experienced drought. This can consist of public prayers, a procession carrying an animal or a holy image, or daily worship services. The nature of such ceremonies varies from one locality to another and reveals Brahmanic (q.v.), Buddhist (q.v.) or animistic (q.v.) origins.

RAINY SEASON RETREAT. See BUDDHIST LENT.

RAMA I (YOT FA) (1737-1809). King of Siam (reigned 1782-1809), founder of the Chakri dynasty (q.v.). Born to a noble family as Thong Duang, he and his younger brother led the Siamese (q.v.) in a series of military successes against the armies of Burma and against the forces of Siam's eastern neighbors. For his achievements, Thong Duang was named chief minister of Chakri and general over all Siamese forces by King Taksin (q.v.). Due to his capable leadership and suitable kin ties, he was chosen king. This occurred when King Taksin was removed from the throne because he was found unfit to reign. The name Rama was given to him and later kings by a great grandson, King Vajiravudh (q.v.).

As king, Rama I engaged in a campaign to rebuild and restore the country after its catastrophic defeat in 1767 by the armies of Burma (q.v.). The Law Code of 1805-1807 was a revision of earlier laws. The Grand Palace (q.v.) and other Ayutthaya-type buildings were constructed in Bangkok (q.v.), the new Siamese capital. Rama I gave support to and strengthened the Buddhist monastic order. Important Buddhist texts were reconstructed. Trade with China and other countries was revived. During his reign, five major Burmese attacks were successfully repelled. Rama I eventually ruled a united Siam (q.v.), the Laotian principalities, most of the Malay states and what today is southwest Burma.

RAMAKIAN. A Thai version of the Ramayana (q.v.) epic.

RAMATHIBODI I. Founder of the Kingdom of Ayutthaya (reigned 1351-1369). As a ruler of the independent principality of U Thong, he moved his people and his capital to the trading center of Ayutthaya (q.v.). The site for the new capital was at a strategic junction of two rivers. Meanwhile, he held outposts at Lop Buri (q.v.) and Suphan Buri. This move enhanced communications and trade with interior areas as well as increasing international contacts.

Ramathibodi is known for his early attempts to centralize governmental administration through the appointment of four officers of state, who can be considered forerunners of cabinet ministers. In addition, he developed a system of laws in which he codified earlier Thai patterns. In this system, he put together bureaucratic skills from the former Khmer Kingdom of Angkor (q.v.) that he knew and local manpower resources. These laws, with some modification, served as the basis of the Siamese (q.v.) legal system until the mid-19th century.

RAMAYANA. A great epic of Indian literature generally credited to the writer Valmiki. It is the story of Rama, who with his half brother was the incarnation of the god Vishnu. Though heir to the throne, he and his wife Sita were by guile driven into exile.

There Sita was abducted by a demon. He recovered her with the help of the wise monkey King Hanuman and the monkeys. He regained the throne, but gossip caused Sita to be put away. However, she proved her virtue and bore Rama twin sons. Portions of the epic are frequent drama presentations in Southeast Asia. Scenes from this epic, called Ramakian in Thailand, are presented in dance drama (q.v.), shadow plays (q.v.) and in puppet shows.

RAMBHAI BARNI, QUEEN (1911-1984). Wife of King Prajadhipok (q.v.) of Thailand. After the Revolution of 1932 (q.v.), both the king and queen were self-exiled and lived in Britain. After World War II, Rambhai came back to Thailand and settled in Chanthaburi. She was active in promoting Thai handicrafts (q.v.).

RAMKHAMHAENG. King of Sukhothai (reigned 1279-1298). Ramkhamhaeng achieved a large and powerful kingdom by the end of his reign. He was an outstanding warrior, statesman, scholar and diplomat. His armies conquered much of what is present-day Thailand, at the expense of the then Khmer Kingdom of Angkor (q.v.). He also gained hegemony over what today is the northern part of Laos (q.v.), the peninsula (q.v.) and a part of Burma (q.v.). His control was consolidated through diplomatic relations with neighboring kingdoms and principalities. He visited China (q.v.), then ruled by the Mongols, and accepted vassalage.

Ramkhamhaeng's reign was a period of development for the Thai peoples within his domains. From the Mon (q.v.), whose civilization preceded the Thai in Southeast Asia, he became a believer in Theravada Buddhism (q.v.). He invited Buddhist monks (q.v.) to come from Ceylon and later made Buddhism the state religion. He initiated the notion of the king as a paternalistic ruler. He placed a bell outside the palace so that any citizen could ring and gain an audience in order to present the king with a grievance. Ramkhamhaeng's reign is credited with creating the alphabet which, with minor changes, is in use today in Thailand. It was adapted from the then existing Mon and Khmer (q.v.) scripts.

RANAD EK. A Thai treble xylophone, consisting of 21 seasoned wooden bars, which are graduated and mounted on a boat-shaped sound box. The bars are tapped with both soft and hard beaters. The *ranad thong ek* or *ranad lek*, another treble xylophone, has steel bars and is played the same way as the *ranad ek.* Both instruments are used in the *piphat* orchestra (q.v.).

RANAD THUM (THUM YAI). An alto xylophone with 17 wooden resonance bars. It resembles, and is played the same way as, the *ranad ek* (q.v.), but is larger and has deeper tones. The *ranad thong thum* (also *thum lek*), another alto xylophone, has 18 steel resonance bars. It resembles, and is played the same way as, the *ranad thong ek*, but is larger and has deeper tones. (See PIPHAT ORCHESTRA.)

RATTAN FURNITURE MAKING. A craft which uses the stems of plants of the *genera calamus*, a climbing palm. *Rattan* cane is slender, flexible, tough and of uniform diameter. It is used both whole and split for wicker work and for wrappings. Products include chairs, stools, couches and other furniture pieces, all of which are not expensive. (See HANDICRAFTS.)

REFUGEES. Throughout its long history, Thailand has given shelter to refugees of various nationalities. Major groups in Thailand include the Vietnamese nationals who, in 1945, fled the Dien Bien Phu War into the northeastern part of the country, and the soldiers of the 93rd Chinese Army Division and their families who, in 1949, fled Mainland China (q.v.). Hundreds of thousands of Indochinese have continued their endless influx unto the eastern part of the country after the upheavals in Cambodia (q.v.), Vietnam and Laos (q.v.) in 1975. The government has provided the refugees with immediate assistance. After 1975, due to the biggest and endless influxes of refugees, the government had called for international assistance and adopted a policy of giving only temporary asylum, pending either resettlement in third countries or repatriation. (See CAMBODIA, RELATIONS WITH.)

RELIGIOUS FESTIVALS. There are four principal Buddhist religious days. (1) Buddhist All Saints Day *(makha bucha)* (q.v.) commemorates the miracles which occurred just prior to the death of the Buddha (q.v.). (2) Triple Anniversary Day *(visakha bucha)* (q.v.) is the most sacred of Buddhist religious days and commemorates the birth, death and enlightenment of the Buddha. (3) Buddhist Monkhood Day *(asalha bucha)* (q.v.) commemorates the Buddha's sermon to his first five disciples. (4) End of Lent Ceremony *(ok phansa)* (q.v.) occurs on the 15th day of the waxing moon in October. The end of the three months' period of Buddhist Lent is widely celebrated. After the End of Lent ceremony, on a day during the next month, a *kathin* (q.v.) ceremony is performed.

REVOLUTION OF 1932. The events of June 1932 marked the end of the absolute monarchy (q.v.) in Thailand and the beginning of the constitutional era. Since that historic event, the government system invests power in a "Council of Ministers" which generally has had military backing, a National Assembly (q.v.), and a king (q.v.) with limited prerogatives but who is head of state. The overthrow of the power of the Thai king in 1932 was precipitated by a bloodless coup d'etat led by a group of civilian and military officers (q.v.) who had the support of a Thai Army unit.

Key persons in the coup group, often called the "promoters," included men educated in European universities such as Pridi Phanomyong (q.v.), a brilliant intellectual, Phahonyothin (q.v.), a disaffected old-line military officer, and Phibunsongkhram (q.v.), a young ambitious army officer. At the time of the coup, Thailand was in the grip of the worldwide depression and had just reduced by one-fourth its civil service employees. The then Thai monarch, Prajadhipok (q.v.), had taken some steps toward a constitution, but did not pursue such a drastic move effectively.

RICE (KHAO). Rice is the main food (q.v.) in the Thai diet. For centuries, rice has been the dominant crop in the nation's agriculture (q.v.). Both glutinous and nonglutinous rice in numerous varieties is grown. The former is preferred for home consumption in northern Thailand and the northeast (q.v.). Nonglutinous rice predominates in the rest of Thailand and is produced for domestic use and for export (q.v.). In general, farmers grow rice in the valleys near streams which provide the water for wet-rice agriculture. Fields are laid out in a manner which guides the water into them during annual floods. The water flow is also controlled by dams and canals. In recent decades, large-scale irrigation (q.v.) works have been constructed by government agencies, which have done much to enhance rice production.

In the upland areas on the margins of the valleys, dry-rice farming occurs. Sometimes the fields are cleared by the "slash and burn" or swidden (q.v.) method in which land is cleared for growing crops. Upland rice is totally dependent on rainfall for successful growth. In the lowlands, water buffaloes (q.v.) are a power source for preparation of rice fields except in the central Plain (q.v.) and in parts of northern Thailand. In these two areas, mechanization and new agricultural technology (q.v.) are used widely. In addition, motor vehicles have largely replaced animals for the transport of farm products and other commodities. Rice production by farm families, who reside in small villages, continues today, as in the past, as a basic feature in the structure of Thai society. (See AGRICULTURAL TECHNOLOGY.)

RICE MILLS. Large commercial mills separate rice (q.v.) into five or six grades and mill from 15 to 100 tons per day. Small mills have a three or four ton capacity and simply separate the rice from the husk and bran. The rice bran is the thin layer that surrounds the rice kernel and is sold as animal feed. The rice husk is the thick layer that surrounds the bran layer and rice kernal. It is used as fuel to run the large capacity mills and normally has no other commercial value. Labor in this industry has a guaranteed annual wage. The government imposes a rice milling tax.

RIVERINE COMMERCE. The agricultural and commercial activities of Thailand--especially of the central area--utilize a vast network of inland canals and rivers that exceed 5,000 kilometers (3,125 miles) in length. A variety of river craft, including storeboats, barges and tour boats, all predominantly motorized, are utilized in this commerce by the entrepreneurs who represent several different ethnic groups. The less heavily capitalized and more common forms of trade, such as movement of agricultural produce, minerals and construction aggregates are handled by the Thai. The Sino-Thai (q.v.) are prominent in the highly specialized and capital-intensive activities such as rice (q.v.) trade, wholesale and retail trading of consumer goods, luxury items and marketing of fresh produce.

Riverine commerce is greater during April to November, which is also the period of greatest agricultural activity. Competition from trucks operating on a growing network of roads in Thailand has caused a decline in the amount of riverine commerce during the past decade. While transportation by train and truck is faster, it is also costlier than water transportation. (See STOREBOAT MERCHANT.)

ROCKET FESTIVAL (BUNGBANGFAI). This is a widely celebrated festival in northeast Thailand (q.v.) in the agricultural areas. It is primarily a rain-making ritual addressed to guardian spirits but has overtones regarding the health and general well-being of the villagers. This festival, which occurs on a date between mid-May and mid-June, is climaxed with firing of locally made rockets and may include a procession and a fair at the Buddhist temple compound *(wat)* (q.v.). There is much gaiety with uninhibited songs, dances, sexual innuendoes and crude pantomimes.

ROLIN-JAEQUEMYNS, GUSTAVE (1835-1901). Belgian general advisor to King Chulalongkorn (q.v.) from 1892 to 1899. He was a son of a cabinet minister and was trained as a lawyer. He assisted in Thai judicial reform and supported the founding of the law school. During the hostilities of 1893 with France (q.v.), he energetically advocated reliance on Great Britain. In 1896, he was awarded a high noble rank by the king.

ROSE GARDEN. A privately owned picturesque country resort near Nakhon Pathom City, 32 kilometers (20 miles) west of Bangkok (q.v.). It consists of landscaped flower gardens, tree-lined roads, orchards and park lands, bordered by the Nakhon

Chaisri River. There are tourist attractions including a typical Thai village, a Thai wedding ceremony, village handicrafts (q.v.), Thai sports and games, folk dancing, sword fighting and elephants (q.v.) at work. The Rose Garden also boasts an 18-hole golf course.

ROYAL LANGUAGE (RACHASAP). A special language used especially in conversations with or about Thai royalty and, in different degrees, with lesser persons. The Thai recognize five categories or ranks of spoken *rachasap*. The highest form is that used in speaking with the king and queen; the second category is used for the crown prince and all those of royal blood down to and including the rank of *mom chao*; the third, is used for all other nobility; the fourth, for the priesthood; the fifth consists of all the polite forms of language used among ordinary people.

The words of *rachasap* used indicate the degree of respect or reverence shown, which in turn depends on the rank of those addressed. This special language has a history of use in Thailand since the Sukhothai (q.v.) period 700 years ago. (See ROYAL RANKS AND TITLES.)

ROYAL PLOWING CEREMONY (RAEK NA). The plowing ceremony, an event in Bangkok (q.v.) near the Grand Palace (q.v.), occurs in early May. It is intended to commence the rice-growing season for the nation's farmers. It supposedly foretells rainfall amounts and ensures good crops. Brahman (q.v.) priests have charge of the rites which are presided over by the king. The director-general of the Rice Departments, who is Lord of the Ceremony, guides a plow drawn by oxen. He is followed by four women who scatter rice (q.v.) on the ground. The rice seed used was blessed in religious rites the previous evening in a ceremony also conducted by the king. Farmers who attend pick up the scattered grains and mix them with their own rice to enhance its productivity. Farmers take comfort that the omens were consulted, the seed blessed and the season inaugurated with religious rites.

ROYAL RANKS AND TITLES. To address the king or persons of royal birth in Thai requires the use of a complicated set of pronouns whereby each term reveals the relevant distinctions of the status of the speaker and the person spoken to. A foreigner, fortunately, may resort to simpler European usage and terminology. The king or queen are addressed as "your majesty." The child of a king and queen has the rank *chao fa* and is addressed "your royal highness." The grandson of a king and queen has the rank *mom chao* and is addressed "your highness." Prior to Rama VI, when polygamy was practiced, the child of a king and minor wife had the rank *phra ong chao* and was addressed "your royal highness." Since 1910, the Thai royal family has been monogamous. *Mom chao* is the lowest princely rank, but the offspring of *mom chao* have a noble rank of *mom rajawongse*, and their grandchildren have the noble rank *mom luang*. After this fifth generation, there are no further ranks of titles and royal descendants become commoners.

RUBBER. Rubber trees were introduced into southern Thailand by the British in 1901. As a result of government regulations, the industry was developed by local landowners whose holdings averaged 12 to 15 rai (five to six acres). Rubber trees are tapped regularly and the liquid is processed into sheets by the owner. After the sheets are cured by smoking, they are sold. Thai rubber has long had a reputation for low quality, due to the continued use of old trees. With government assistance, rubber farmers have nearly completed an extensive replanting program. The new trees have increased the potential for a better quality product. Rubber continues to be an important export (q.v.) crop.

RUSK-THANAT AGREEMENT OF 1962. A foreign affairs protocol in which the United States (q.v.) was committed to the defense of Thailand if the need arose, without prior agreement by other SEATO (q.v.) members. This agreement was broadened and used as a basis for American support of the Thai government's action against Communist insurgency (q.v.) in the 1960s and 1970s.

- S -

SAFFRON ROBE. The distinctive orange-colored garb worn by Buddhist monks (q.v.) in Thailand.

SAISUREE JUTIKUL (1934-   ).   Educator, social worker, politician. Saisuree was educated in Thailand and in the United States (q.v.). She served as minister of education in the cabinet of Prime Minister Anand Panyarachun (q.v.). The daughter of Pornsil and Sudsawat Jutikul, she was born in Bangkok (q.v.). She received her Ph.D. degree in educational psychology and guidance from Indiana University in 1962. Saisuree held several important positions: dean of the Education Faculty, Khonkaen University, 1969-1975; director, Long-Term Planning Board for Children's Development, 1979-1981.   She has also received several decorations from the king and honorary doctorates from Khonkaen University and Whitworth College, Washington, D.C. She is married and has two children.

SAIYASAT. The practice of magic, of Hindu origin, used by certain ritual specialists to ward off evil, tell horoscopes and confer happiness.   While most of those who practice *saiyasat* are Buddhist monks (q.v.), only a tiny proportion of all monks engage in this magic.   However, more acceptance is given to a magical practitioner who is also a Buddhist monk.

SAKDI NA. A system of land tenure that historically provided income for the king and all civil and military officials. *Sakdi na* was instituted by King Borommatrailokanat (q.v.) in 1454. Its use continued until late in the 19th century when King Chulalongkorn (q.v.) had public officials paid in cash. The amount of productive land assigned to officials reflected their rank in a system of statuses. As all land was owned by the king, *sakdi na* was the system for temporary use of it by his subjects. A portion of agricultural produce was the property of the king who alone could levy taxes and require unpaid labor from his subjects.

SALWIDHAN NIDHES, LT. GEN. PHRAYA (1892-). Salwidhan has served the kings of Siam (q.v.), five in all, for more than 75 years, beginning with King Chulalongkorn (q.v.) and continuing today with King Bhumibol Adulyadej (q.v.). In 1909, he was the first of the king's scholars to study in the United States (q.v.) and the first Siamese (q.v.) to graduate from Harvard University. In 1913, he earned a degree of Bachelor of Science in engineering and in 1914 a Master's degree in mathematics. Upon his return, he began his work with the Royal Survey Department under the Ministry of Defense. Along with all his other work, he spent more than six decades lecturing at Chulalongkorn University, at both the Faculty of Sciences and the Faculty of Engineering. He was given the title of Phraya in (q.v.) 1929, and became the director of the Royal Survey Department in 1930. In the same year, he was the last person to obtain the rank of major general before the Revolution of 1932 (q.v.). In 1950, he was appointed lieutenant general and special aide-de-camp to King Bhumibol.

SANAM LUANG. The main square or center of Bangkok (q.v.) and a traditional meeting place of the Bangkok residents. It is also called the Pramane Ground. This is a broad open space near the Grand Palace (q.v.). The Sanam Luang is transformed each weekend into a large open-air market which is one of the attractions of Bangkok. The merchants bring their wares and set up shop on Friday evening and Saturday morning, and for two days this is an enormous hub of activity. There are innumerable stalls where one can buy almost anything imaginable. By Sunday evening everything is cleared out and there is just the open space of the Pramane Ground.

SANEH CHAMARIK. Educator and writer. Saneh was educated in Thailand at Thammasat University and in Britain at Manchester University. Since 1960, he has been a member of the Political Science Faculty of Thammasat University. In Bangkok (q.v.), Saneh is a prominent worker in the group known as The Development of Human Rights in Thailand. He also leads the Social Science Textbook Project, which produces texts for higher education (q.v.). Saneh's many books and articles deal with such subjects as peace, politics, development, human rights and education.

SANGHA. See BUDDHIST MONKHOOD.

SANSKRIT. Classical standard language of India. Valuable religious and literary chronicles have been preserved in the Sanskrit language. These works include religious texts of Hinduism and Mahayana Buddhism (q.v.). The Tai-language (q.v.) contains many words borrowed or adapted from Sanskrit.

SANUK. Activities that are fun-loving or pleasure seeking such as games, dancing, music, shows and travel; also enjoying food (q.v.) and drink with companions or talking, teasing and joking among friends. The Thai like and respect those who can make them laugh and feel happy. Even in work, the *sanuk* value operates to give the more interesting occupations higher prestige than jobs that are boring or routine. In Thai culture, the *sanuk* value is integrated with the emphasis on suffering in Buddhist dogma. The Thai accept this idea only in the sense that suffering is unavoidable in life and death and will occur eventually. But, they assert that to reduce suffering, we should enjoy ourselves as much as we can. Some writers hold that the *sanuk* value has led to the development of two other values among the Thai: the avoidance of hard work and the emphasis on present-time consumption.

SANYA DHARMASAKTI (1907-). Jurist, educator, prime minister and privy councillor. Sanya was educated in Thailand and Britain. He studied law in both countries and was admitted to the English bar. In Bangkok (q.v.), he served as a judge and later as chief judge of the Court of Appeals. Later he was appointed to the Supreme Court of which he was president during 1963-1967. Sanya became dean of the Faculty of Law, Thammasat University, where he served as university rector, 1972-1974.

Sanya was named prime minister in 1973 by King Bhumibol Adulyadej (q.v.), when the previous prime minister was forced into exile in the aftermath of the 1973 student-led uprising (q.v.). Sanya was named to the Privy Council in 1968. He became president of that organization in 1975, and continues in that post. Sanya's attempt, in 1974, while prime minister, to install a national constitution (q.v.) that reflected democracy was not successful.

SAOWABHA PONGSRI, QUEEN (1863-1919). Saowabha was a daughter of King Mongkut (q.v.) and the mother of Kings Vajiravudh (q.v.) and Prajadhipok (q.v.). During her years as queen to King Chulalongkorn (q.v.), she exerted an influence that encouraged countless Thai women (q.v.) from all walks of life to do social welfare work, to continue their education and to study abroad under her sponsorship. She was a pioneer in bringing modern methods of childbirth to the kingdom. In 1897, she established, with her own funds, a midwifery school in Thailand and also founded the Thai Red Cross Society (q.v.), of which she was an active president for 26 years.

SARIT THANARAT (1908-1963). Prime minister (1959-1963) and military leader. Sarit was born in Bangkok (q.v.), the son of a Siamese (q.v.) army linguist and a graduate of the Royal Military Academy. He gained distinction with the Thai Army in World War II and as an able military administrator. In 1945, he commanded a regiment located in the nation's capital, and his troops played a central role in a 1947 coup that ushered in Phibunsongkhram (q.v.) as prime minister for a second time. Sarit's troops also suppressed two other rebellions. His career advanced and he became supreme commander of the Armed Forces and minister of defense.

In 1957, Sarit led a coup against Prime Minister Phibun who stepped down and went into exile. After Sarit obtained medical treatment abroad, he assumed full power serving as prime minister until his death in 1963. He abolished the National Assembly (q.v.) and established what he called a "revolutionary government" that was authoritarian. Neither religious, intellectual nor political dissension was permitted. Dissenters were treated harshly. In dealing with the Communist threat, Sarit had the cooperation of the United States (q.v.). One of his accomplishments was a restoration and redefinition of the monarchy (q.v.), which he felt was essential for the benefit of society. As a result, the king, Bhumibol Adulyadej (q.v.), became more active with the revival of neglected public ceremonies and tours of the provinces.

Sarit's support of the monarchy bolstered his government's authority. Social and economic development (q.v.) included highway construction, irrigation (q.v.), rural electrification, new farming techniques and an increase in the Gross Domestic Product. Sarit paid particular attention to improvement of primary education (q.v.) in the villages. He was a take-charge person and was known as one who got things accomplished.

SATTAHIP. A modern military port and district (q.v.) center in Chon Buri Province (q.v.), located southeast of Bangkok (q.v.). It is the main naval base in Thailand. Much of it is a restricted military zone.

SAW. A traditional singing form in northern Thailand which consists of an impromptu repartee style of song between a man and a woman on any subject, religious, romantic, etc. The singing may be accompanied by several persons, each playing a reed wind instrument *(pi)*.

SAYRE, FRANCIS B. (1885-1972). Advisor to and representative of Thai kings, 1923-1932. Sayre was an American professor of law, 1914-1923, United States (q.v.) government official, 1931-1942, and United Nations advisor, 1944-1952. King Vajiravudh (q.v.) engaged Sayre to serve first as treaty negotiator and foreign affairs advisor and later as Siam's official representative to the Permanent Court of Arbitration at The Hague. As Siam's representative from 1924-1925, Sayre concluded in Europe treaty negotiations with ten nations, the disadvantageous extraterritoriality that had been imposed on Siam during the mid-19th century. The new treaties also ended trade restrictions on Siam and reestablished tariff autonomy.

SCULPTURE, RELIGIOUS. Buddhism (q.v.) has been the dominant influence in sculpture, and the Thai gained wide recognition for their representations of Buddha (q.v.). Images of the Buddha produced in the period from the 13th to the 15th centuries are considered to be the finest examples of pure Thai sculpture. The most common Buddha images (q.v.) were of stucco; stone, popular in neighboring countries, was not commonly used. Poses were fairly standard: seated, with legs folded and in a mood of contemplation, reclining, or walking. Because Buddha was sacred, he was usually represented in idealized form.

SECOND KING. A title, first used in King Borommatrailokanat's (q.v.) reign (1448-1488), granted by the reigning monarch; the holder was second in status only to the king. The title was seldom used. It involved more substantive duties than did the *uparaja* (q.v.) appointment but did not necessarily imply that the holder was the heir apparent. King Mongkut (q.v.) in 1851 was the only king of the Chakri dynasty (q.v.) to appoint a second king.

SENATE. See NATIONAL ASSEMBLY.

SENI PRAMOJ (1905-   ). A distinguished government official, elected to the House of Representatives (q.v.) several times. In 1975, he was the leader of the Democrat party *(prachatiphat)* (q.v.), which has a conservative orientation. Long a lawyer by occupation, he has also served in Thailand's Diplomatic Service. As prime minister, he headed the Thai government for nearly six months in 1945-1946, when Thailand was recovering from World War II. During that war, Seni was ambassador to the United States (q.v.). At this same time, he was active in a Free Thai Movement (q.v.), which sought to drive out the Japanese military occupation (q.v.) of Thailand. When the Japanese pressured Thailand to declare war on the United States, Seni refused to notify the United States government.

SERI THAI MOVEMENT. See FREE THAI.

SHADOW PLAY (NANG TALUNG). A traditional dance drama. The shadow play or Nang Talung is a form of dance drama (q.v.) performed by casting shadows of cowhide figures or puppets on a screen. The figures dance the roles and the story is provided by a narrator, with an accompanying orchestra and sometimes a chorus. The shadows are cast by manipulating the hide figures between a bright light and the back of a screen of white cloth. Presentations of the shadow-play drama are decreasing. It is occasionally seen in southern Thailand during festivals at the Buddhist temple compound *(wat)* (q.v.). A similar drama, popular in Java and Bali, is called the Wayang Kulit.

SI BURAPHA. See KULAP SAIPRADIT.

SI SATCHANALAI. An archaeological site of the ruins of pottery kilns 65 kilometers (41 miles) north of the city of Sukhothai. It is located some 11 kilometers (7 miles) south of the town of Si Satchanalai on the Yom River. Ceramics (q.v.) of the Sukhothai type were produced here in the 14th to 15th centuries.

SI THEP. An archaeological site (also called Si Deva) 110 kilometers (70 miles) south of Phetchabun City in the district (q.v.) of Wichian Buri, Phetchabun Province. It was excavated in 1935-1936 by Dr. Quaritch Wales. The ruins are of an Indian settlement of the 5th century. During the 9th century, it was an outpost of the Khmer Kingdom, which had its capital at Angkor (q.v.).

SIAM. The nation known today as Thailand was, prior to 1939, called Siam in European languages and Syam in the Tai-language. The name Siam was first used by James Lancaster in 1592. In the 17th century, Siam was generally used as the country's name among Europeans. However, the Thai called the nation by the official name of its capital city. Thus, there was the Kingdom of Sukhothai (q.v.) (1238-1378), the Kingdom of Ayutthaya (q.v.) (1350-1767) and the Kingdom of Bangkok (since 1967). Siam became the official name of the nation in 1856, at the time of the Bowring Treaty (q.v.) between Siam (Thailand) and Great Britain. In 1939, the name Prades Thai was adopted in place of Prades Sayam and its equivalent in English was the name Thailand. The latter name change occurred during the government of Prime Minister Phibunsongkhram (q.v.). Historically, the Thai people have referred to themselves as *muang thai. Muang* (q.v.) corresponds to "land" and *thai* signifies "free." Hence, Thailand means "land of the free."

SIAM SOCIETY. A learned society, dealing with all aspects of the arts and sciences in Thailand and neighboring countries. Founded in 1904, the Society publishes the *Journal of the Siam Society* and other scholarly works on Southeast Asian culture, arts, science and literature. Since 1910, the king has been the royal patron of the Society, whose membership includes many distinguished Southeast Asian scholars. The new and present home and library of the Society was opened in 1922. The Natural History Society was founded as a section of the Society in 1925. The *Natural History Bulletin* is published as a separate but companion piece to the *Journal of the Siam Society*.

SIAMESE. Until 1939 the name by which the Thai people of the Chao Phraya (q.v.) Valley were known. This distinguished them from the Tai-language people of Laos, northern Thailand, northern Vietnam, southwestern China, and northern Burma. The word Siamese is a variant of the word Syam appearing in ancient Southeast Asian inscriptions. Between 1939 and 1946 and since 1949 preferred usage has been to employ "Thai" and not "Siamese" to describe the dominant ethnic group of Thailand and "central Thai" to denote the Thai of the Chao Phraya Valley or central Plain (q.v.).

SILPA BHIRASRI (1892-1962). Sculptor and art educator. Born in Italy, Professor Silpa Bhirasri (originally Corrado Feroci) secured an education in Italy and gained recognition there for his work in art, especially in sculpture (q.v.). He came to Thailand in 1923 at the request of King Vajiravudh (q.v.). While in the Fine Arts Department he sculpted many significant monuments, including some of famous Thais. In 1932, Professor Silpa Bhirasri organized a school of fine arts which later was expanded into Silpakorn University. He was highly regarded as a teacher as well as for his books and articles. Some consider him the father of Thai modern art.

SINGH. A mythical lion, a stone statue of which guards pagodas and temples, usually located in pairs at their entrances.

SINO-THAI. Those persons in Thailand who have a Chinese background. The Sino-Thai have adopted Thai surnames, secured a Thai education and have obtained Thai citizenship. All this indicates that the so-called "ethnic Chinese" have been culturally assimilated. A high proportion of the business enterprises in Thailand are owned and operated by the Sino-Thai. (See CHINESE IN THAILAND.)

SIPHATCHARINTHRA (1830-1920). Queen and philanthropist. Siphatcharinthra was a daughter of King Mongkut (q.v.). She married and became queen of King Chulalongkorn (q.v.). She bore him nine children. Queen Siphatcharinthra promoted education for girls and social welfare. She assisted financially in the founding of Sirarat Nursing School. The health center, Sapha Unahondoing, that she opened in 1920, later became the headquarters for the Thai Red Cross Society (q.v.). She was given the title *somdet phra* by King Chulalongkorn.

SIPSONG CHAU TAI. An area of what today is the border region of both northern Vietnam and southeastern China that is supposedly the place of origin of the Tai speaking peoples. There in the mountainous region west of the Black River was a federation of 12 Tai principalities called Sipsong Chau Tai. This was preceded by an earlier political grouping of Tai speakers before they became consolidated into a kingdom. The chief town in this region, Dien-Bien-Phu, was built on an earlier site of a Tai town named Muang Theng which means "city of gods." The foregoing represents the "South Asian Coastal Regions" theory of the origin of the Tai speaking peoples. (See LANGUAGE AND THAI PEOPLES.)

SIRIDHORN, HER ROYAL HIGHNESS PRINCESS MAHA CHAKRI (1955-   ). Daughter of King Bhumibol (q.v.) and Queen Sirikit (q.v.) of Thailand. In 1979, she obtained a Master of Arts in Oriental epigraphy from Silpakorn University, a Master of Arts in Pali (q.v.) and Sanskrit (q.v.) studies from

Chulalongkorn University in 1981 and a Doctoral Degree in educational development from Sri Nakharinwirot University in 1986. Princess Siridhorn assists King Bhumibol in his court functions and serves as his private secretary. She introduces the king at official and religious ceremonies and at charitable events, promotes friendly relations with other countries by receiving foreign dignitaries visiting Thailand, as well as paying visits to foreign countries upon invitation. She accompanies the king and the queen on rural development missions to inspect the various royal projects sponsored in remote villages throughout the country. She founded the Sai Jai Thai Foundation of which she serves as chairman of the board. The Foundation's objective is to assist and care for the soldiers, policemen and civilians wounded and disabled in the line of duty.

In December 1977, after the passage of a constitutional amendment permitting a royal daughter to succeed to the throne, King Bhumibol (q.v.) granted Princess Siridhorn the title of Crown Princess Somdej Phra. Her contribution to Thai culture has led to the national proclamation of her birthday, April 2, as the Thai Cultural Heritage Day, which is celebrated nationwide. Apart from her duties in service to the throne, she participates in academic functions and carries on her duties as President of the Thai Red Cross (q.v.). Princess Siridhorn loves music and plays a number of classical Thai instruments and also encourages musical training at all educational levels. She supervises the conservation of classical Thai music.

SIRIKIT, HER MAJESTY QUEEN (1932-   ). Born as Mom Rajawongse Sirikit Kitiyakara, she began her education in the tradition of children of the royal court. Sirikit's parents then broke with precedent by sending their daughter to the St. Francis Xavier Convent School in Bangkok (q.v.). She continued her advanced education in Britain. She was engaged to Crown Prince Bhumibol on July 19, 1949 and was married on April 28, 1950. On May 5, 1950, King Bhumibol Adulyadej (q.v.) was crowned ninth monarch of the Chakri dynasty (q.v.), and Sirikit became Queen Sirikit of Thailand.

The queen has devoted her time to family life. The offspring are: Princess Ubolratana, born in 1951; Crown Prince

Vajiralongkorn, 1952; Crown Princess Maha Chakri Siridhorn (q.v.), 1955; and Princess Chulabhorn (q.v.), 1957. On November 1, 1991, Queen Sirikit was awarded the First International Humanitarian Award by the Friends of the Capitol Children's Museum in Washington, D.C., in recognition of her outstanding contribution to humanitarian activities in Thailand, particularly the activities of SUPPORT (q.v.) established in 1976. In 1976, on the birthday of the queen, August 12, Thailand's Mother's Day was established. Early in 1992, Queen Sirikit received the first UNESCO Borobodur Medal in honor of her 60th birthday. This was followed on August 2, 1992 by awards from UNICEF in recognition of her dedication and profound commitment to improving the lives of mothers and children in Thailand and from UNIFEM in recognition of her earnest commitment to and support of the Thai women's contribution to their country. In 1993, the queen received an honorary doctorate from Georgetown University in Washington, D.C., and the Women of the Year award from Stanford University, in California. In 1995, the queen received the 1995 Charles Lindbergh Award, for her educational and humanitarian efforts on behalf of the people in Thailand and other countries. As queen of Thailand, she has acted with dedication, courage and character which has endeared her to the Thai people. She is devoted to her husband, her family and the welfare of her nation.

SOAI (KUI). An ethnolinguistic group numbering more than 100,000 located on both sides of Thailand's border with northern Cambodia (q.v.). The majority of the Soai are in Thailand, and they may speak Tai-Lao (q.v.) or Khmer in addition to their own language. The Soai were probably in the area prior to the coming of the Thai and the Khmer (q.v.). Their agriculture (q.v.) is very similar to that of the Thai. Some have become skilled in elephant (q.v.) hunting or in iron forging. The Buddhist (q.v.) religion has been widely adopted although animism (q.v.) is also practiced.

SOCIAL ACTION PARTY (KIT SANGKHOM). Formed in 1974 the Social Action party was then led by Kukrit Pramoj (q.v.) who resigned in 1986. The current leader is Montri Pongpanich. The

Kukrit style of leadership was authoritarian and that along with recent intra-party squabbles helps to explain the party's decline since it won 101 house seats in 1983. However, in spite of winning only six percent of the house memberships in the September 1992 election, the Social Action party became a part of the new coalition government. This was headed by Chuan Leekpai (q.v.) leader of the Democrat party (q.v.).

In 1976 and subsequently, the Social Action party promoted reforms. Its agenda focused on medical assistance to the poor, improvement of wage scales for labor and needed public housing. Another program of Kukrit and his party was the building of infrastructure. This was done by distribution of funds to council representatives of villages for schools, health centers, roads, irrigation works, etc. The program was halted in a few years because of opposition by army leaders and other conservatives.

SOCIAL MOBILITY. Thai society is generally regarded as "open" for those who seek to advance in prestige and status. The main channels used for upward social mobility are (1) the Buddhist monkhood *(sangha)* (q.v.), (2) the civil service (q.v.), (3) advanced secular education (q.v.), and (4) *pai thiaw* (q.v.).

SOMPONG SUCHARITKUL (1931-   ). Diplomat, specialist in international law. Sompong completed law and other studies in Thailand, Britain, France and the United States. He taught briefly in two law schools in Thailand after which he served his country in several high-level capacities. Entering the Foreign Ministry in 1959, he held, over time, positions as secretary to the minister, director-general of economics, and director-general of treaty and legal affairs. In a series of ambassadorial appointments, he served in The Netherlands and Belgium, Japan, France and Portugal, Italy and Greece. Sompong represented Thailand in international conferences and other matters including trade law, UNESCO (q.v.), international law and the International Court of Arbitration. His publications include books and articles on international law.

SONGKHLA. A large province on southern Thailand's east coast, pop. 1,097,200 (est.). Urban centers in Songkhla include

Songkhla City, the capital, pop. 82,170 (est.), and Hat Yai, pop. 142,400 (est.). Hat Yai is the fourth largest city located outside of the Bangkok (q.v.) area. It is the commercial center and transportation hub for southern Thailand. Its shops and bazaars attract many people from the neighboring country of Malaysia as well as those from Thailand.

Nearby Hat Yai is the principal campus of the Prince of Songkhla University, which is a regional center of higher education (q.v.). It offers programs of study in eight different schools or departments. In five of these, programs of postgraduate study are offered as well. Songkhla Province is a leader in commercial fisheries. It also ranks near the top among all provinces in commercial agricultural products. Tin (q.v.), wolfram concentrates and rubber (q.v.) are other products.

SONGKHLA LAKE. A large lake located on the peninsula (q.v.) in Songkhla Province (q.v.). Songkhla City is located at the point where the lake waters flow into the Gulf of Thailand.

SONGKRAN. A major festival in mid-April celebrating the beginning of the New Year according to the Thai lunar calendar. The old Songkran celebration is in part religious. In villages, almost everyone visits the local temple to sprinkle or bathe the Buddha images (q.v.). Also, senior Buddhist monks (q.v.) and important Buddha images are paraded through the streets in a solemn procession. Often small sand pagodas are constructed in the temple grounds to earn merit (q.v.), and elaborate offerings of flowers and incense are made. Homes are given a thorough cleaning, and younger members of the family show respect for their elders by pouring water over their hands. Water throwing came first to Chiang Mai (q.v.) from Burma and then spread throughout the country. Silver bowls, sizable buckets, and even water pistols are freely used to ensure that every passerby gets a thorough soaking. Everything is done in a spirit of good fun.

SOUTHEAST ASIA TREATY ORGANIZATION (SEATO). A collective security arrangement initiated by the United States (q.v.) and formed in September 1954. Other member nations were Britain, France (q.v.), Australia, New Zealand, Pakistan, the

Philippines and Thailand. If necessary to defend against Communist aggression in Southeast Asia, member nations would act jointly in defense. SEATO headquarters was in Bangkok (q.v.). The role of secretary general was handled by a prominent Thai official. Prior to the disbanding of SEATO in 1977, it helped to create the Asian Institute of Technology located in Bangkok.

SOUTHEAST ASIAN MINISTERS OF EDUCATION ORGANIZATION (SEAMEO). It was set up in 1965. This regional group of nations is engaged in cooperative research in agriculture (q.v.), tropical biology, tropical medicine and public health, education in science and mathematics and language study. Other studies include vocational and technical education, archaeology and fine arts, educational innovation and technology. Thailand is a member of this group along with nine other Southeast Asian countries: Brunei, Cambodia (q.v.), Indonesia, Laos (q.v.), Malaysia (q.v.), Myanmar (q.v.), Philippines, Singapore and Vietnam.

SPIRIT HOUSE. See CHAO THI.

SRI INDRADITYA. A founder and first king (reigned 1240-1270) of Sukhothai (q.v.). This new kingdom was located in what today is the northern part of central Thailand (q.v.). Sri Indraditya together with another local chieftain joined forces and overthrew the ruler of Syam. The latter was an administrative center and outpost of the Angkor Kingdom (q.v.). For his bravery and heroism in this victory, Sri Indraditya was called *Pra Ruang* which means "Glorious Prince."

SRI NAGARINDRA, SOMDEJ PHRA (1900-   ). Known as the princess mother, the mother of rural medicine in Thailand, wife of Prince Mahidol, mother of King Ananda Mahidol and King Bhumibol (q.v.). Her given name was Sangwal. Trained as a nurse in the United States, she created one of the largest voluntary medical services, the Voluntary Flying Doctor Foundation, in 1969. It is a network of efficient and dedicated medical and dental care personnel, radio medical clinics and radio district (q.v.) hospitals operating almost all over the country, where such care is inaccessible. She also inspired the Foundation for Phra Sri Nagarindra Park project, which was initiated in 1981. Its committee is composed of representatives from both the government and private sectors to provide recreational grounds for children, youths and the general public. At present ten out of 12 planned parks have been completed and opened to the public.

STATE ENTERPRISES. State-owned enterprises and their intrusion into the national economy began in 1933 when the Department of Defense set up the Fuel Division to import petroleum. Today there are almost 60 state enterprises, at least half of which are in three government branches. These are the Ministries of Agricultural and Cooperatives, Interior, and Transport and Communication.

Three motivational factors in the Thai government's entry into the private economy can be identified. Two interrelated elements were nationalism and modernization. The third was to benefit the public. Relative to nationalism, the Thai wished to acquire for themselves the fruits of economic activity already exploited by the Chinese (q.v.) and foreigners. Early on, state enterprises entered into rice milling, commercial banking, shipping, imports and manufacturing in all of which the Chinese were felt to have a monopoly.

The entry of the government into economic affairs had a symbolic effect of stimulating Thai entrepreneurs to engage in business. The state enterprises were useful in strengthening the national infrastructure also. Other public ownership resulted from the government rescuing troubled finance companies. The Ministry of Finance also held shares in a large number of private firms.

STOREBOAT MERCHANT. A small scale entrepreneur engaged in riverine commerce (q.v.). The boat used is usually small (20 to 40 tons gross) made of hardwood and powered by an outboard motor. The bins, racks and shelves in the cargo hold of the boat are arranged for the maximum display of the merchandise. Other goods are tied, hung or piled on the decks and superstructure. The boat also serves as the home of the merchant.

The storeboat businessman does both wholesaling and retailing, chiefly in consumer staples and various luxury items. In addition, he may act as money-lender, rice (q.v.) broker, middleman and transport broker. He plies a regular trade circuit or route. Customers along the route predict fairly accurately the time of arrival of the storeboat trader.

STROBEL, EDWARD HENRY. The first American to be appointed general advisor to the king of Thailand. He held that office from 1902 to 1908. Strobel was instrumental in negotiating Thai-French Treaties in 1904 and in 1907. The latter treaty ended French extraterritoriality in Thailand which resulted in a significant advance in the national status of Thailand. However, in exchange, Thailand ceded to France (q.v.) territories over which it previously claimed suzerainty. Strobel also initiated the negotiations leading to a similar Thai-British treaty. Strobel was highly regarded by King Chulalongkorn (q.v.) and others for his achievements in Thai foreign affairs.

STUDENT UPRISING OF 1973. An event in October 1973 of ten days' duration that involved huge demonstrations in the city of Bangkok (q.v.) against the government headed by Prime Minister Thanom Khittikachorn (q.v.) and Deputy Prime Minister Praphas Charusathian (q.v.). Both leaders were toppled from power in the turmoil and violence which occurred. King Bhumibol Adulyadej (q.v.), the reigning monarch of Thailand, who normally remains aloof from politics, provided leadership in the crisis. The principal demands of the students, who were organized largely through the National Student Center of Thailand, were for a new national constitution (q.v.) and parliamentary elections. These demands were eventually met. A new constitution was promulgated in October 1974 and members of the House of Representatives (q.v.) and other officials were elected in January 1975.

STUPA. A conical monument or tower named after the Sanskrit (q.v.) word for mound. The *stupa* was likely a pre-Buddhist burial mound which in time developed into the pagoda and other structures of religious significance in India and Southeast Asia. It often served as a burial site for the relics of royalty or great religious leaders. (See also CHEDI.)

SUCHINDA KRAPRAYOON. Army officer and prime minister. Suchinda graduated from the Military Academy where he was president of class number five. By the 1980s, he and other members of his class had attained high positions in the Thai Army and were influential in public affairs. In February 1991, Suchinda led a coup against the then Prime Minister Chatchai Choonhavan (q.v.) and his administration. Following a March 1992 election, Suchinda was named prime minister by a coalition of five conservative political parties. Since Suchinda was not an elected representative to the National Assembly (q.v.), he immediately became the center of a storm of controversy. Mass demonstrations in the streets of Bangkok (q.v.) occurred during May 17-19, 1992. These were led in large part by Chamlong Srimuang (q.v.) who demanded the resignation of Suchinda. Attempts to suppress the group actions by the army resulted in hundreds killed or injured. Suchinda resigned his post when King Bhumibol (q.v.) acted to restore law and order.

SUKAPIBAN. See HEALTH AND SANITATION DISTRICT.

SUKHOTHAI, KINGDOM OF. Sukhothai was the first major kingdom ruled by Tai-language speakers within the territory of modern Thailand and was founded in the 13th century. Contemporaneous with it was the Lan Na (q.v.) Kingdom in what today is northern Thailand. There were also other enclaves of Tai-language speakers in a variety of areas of Southeast Asia. These included the Shan of Burma (q.v.) and the Lao (q.v.). At the time Sukhothai was founded, approximately 1240 AD, Sri Intraditya (q.v.) and another local chieftain joined their forces to capture the Angkor Kingdom (q.v.) outpost at Syam. Sri Intraditya became the first king and established a dynasty of eight kings who collectively ruled for almost 100 years. The Sukhothai Kingdom was identified in Chinese sources as *siem* in the late-13th century.

The kingdom initially was small, but under its third king, Ramkhamhaeng (q.v.), its territory was greatly expanded and its influence has been important. The Buddhist (q.v.) religion was adopted and supported by Sukhothai kings. Buddhist monks (q.v.) used the royal throne as a place to preach the *dhamma* (q.v.). The art and sculpture that flourished in the Sukhothai Kingdom had a style that is prominent today. The population included, in addition to Tai speakers, Mon (q.v.) and Khmer (q.v.) peoples. The Tai-language was used in administration. To facilitate this, a written Tai script was invented or adapted from the Mon and Khmer scripts. This Tai-language, with changes, is in use today in Thailand. The Kingdom of Sukhothai weakened after the death of Ramkhamhaeng. Subsequently, it was absorbed into the Kingdom of Ayutthaya (q.v.) in 1438.

SUPARB YOSSUNDARA, KHUNYING (1920-1974).   Suparb graduated from Birmingham University, Britain, in 1942. During the war, Khunying Suparb, as a member of the Free Thai Movement (q.v.), worked as a translator/announcer on the Thai Program at All India Radio, India. In 1947, she joined the Bank of Thailand and, in May 1966, became a director. She also served as an assistant to the Bank's governor, covering the fields of international relations and economic policy. In the 1970s, she acted as chairman of the Advisory Committee of the Asian Development Bank study of Southeast Asia. In 1971-1972, she played an important role in the formation of an informal grouping of various central banks in Southeast Asia known as the Southeast Asian Central Bank Group (SEACEN). In 1971, she became an executive director of the World Bank.

SUPATRA MASDIT, KHUNYING (1950-). The daughter of Surin and Suda Masdit, she was born in Nakhon Si Thammarat (q.v.). She received her M.A. degree in communications from the University of Hawaii. She also received several decorations from the king. She is very progressive and has been a member of the Democrat party (q.v.) from 1984 to the present as well as of several important committees.

SUPATRA SINGHOLKA, KHUNYING (1910-). The daughter of Praya Rajmontri and Khunying Boonpa Rajamontri, she was born in Bangkok (q.v.). She received her Bachelor of Law degree from Thammasat University in 1939. Khunying Supatra holds many important positions both in her own business enterprise and in the social services. She has fought for the advancement of the status and rights of Thai women. Her success supports efforts to give Thai women equal legal rights with men. She is married and has two daughters.

SUPPORT. The handicraft (q.v.) training school, Supplementary Occupations and Related Techniques Foundation (SUPPORT), was established by Queen Sirikit (q.v.) in 1976. The major training center was established in Chitralada Villa in 1979. In 1993, there were about 500 students learning 21 different crafts including a few which are nearly extinct, such as *kram*, the art of gold or silver wires inlaid in steel. Today, SUPPORT has expanded to four regional craft training centers involving more than 200 villages nationwide with at least 9,000 artisans employed in various projects. Many villagers work full-time on handicraft production while others are involved only part-time. The Foundation buys and pays high prices for all the craft items that meet its quality standards, and sells them at Chitralada stores in Bangkok (q.v.), Chiang Mai (q.v.), other tourist destinations and abroad.

SUPREME PATRIARCH. The head of the Buddhist monkhood *(sangha)* (q.v.) in Thailand. The supreme patriarch is appointed by the king in consultation with leaders of the monkhood. He presides over the Sangha Supreme Council, which has both legislative and judicial functions. The current supreme patriarch is Somdet Nyanasamvara.

SURIN ELEPHANT ROUNDUP. This tourist attraction is held on the third Saturday in November outside the city of Surin in northeast Thailand (q.v.).

SURIYAWONG (CHUANG BUNNAG) (1808-1883). King's advisor and government official. Suriyawong was a prominent and influential member of the Bunnag family (q.v.) and served as regent for the boy-king Chulalongkorn (q.v.). A very able and powerful government official, he served both King Mongkut (q.v.) and King Chulalongkorn as minister governing the southern Siamese (q.v.) provinces. In concert with his father, Dit Bunnag, and his uncle, That Bunnag, Suriyawong brought about Mongkut's elevation to the throne of Siam (q.v.) in 1851. He had a central role in treaty negotiations with Britain and other Western nations. These arrangements were designed to maintain Siam's independence while promoting trade. Many needed reforms sought by King Chulalongkorn were opposed and delayed, owing to the power of Suriyawong, until the latter's death in 1883. Suriyawong was given the semi-royal title *somdet* by King Mongkut.

SURYOTHAI. Queen and wife of King Chakraphat (q.v.). During an attack by the army of Burma in 1549, she went into battle with her husband, two sons and a daughter. Seeing that her husband was in danger, she drove her elephant (q.v.) between him and the enemy, and was killed in his place. She is considered a major heroine of Thai history.

SWIDDENS. An abbreviation for swidden farming. It refers to discontinuous cropping of particular fields which are slash-cleared and burned for one or more years' crops. After this they are allowed to return to natural vegetation for several years before being used again. This widespread practice of upland farmers has caused serious soil erosion and loss of forests.

- T -

TAI. See LANGUAGE AND THAI PEOPLES.

TAKRAW. A game in which a light, woven rattan ball about the size of a softball is kicked, kneed, butted and shouldered. It takes skill to keep the ball moving without letting it touch the hand or fall to the ground.

TAKSIN. King of Siam (reigned 1768-1782). Sin (later named Taksin) was born of a Chinese (q.v.) father and a Siamese (q.v.) mother. He was adopted and reared by an aristocratic family which saw to his education. Entering government service, he advanced to governor (q.v.) of the province of Tak. When, in 1767, a disastrous victory by armies of Burma over the Siamese (q.v.) at Ayutthaya (q.v.) seemed imminent, Taksin escaped to eastern Siam (q.v.) with his loyal troops. In early steps to rebuild the country, he chose Thonburi as a national capital. From that base and with support of the Chinese community and others, he obtained food (q.v.) for the needy and supplies for his successful military campaigns.

Within a few years, Taksin had overcome his four chief rivals and reestablished Siam as a state to be reckoned with. In subsequent wars with Burma (q.v.) and other opponents, Taksin's Army General Chakri (later King Rama I [q.v.]) and his brother General Surasi proved to be successful military commanders in the king's service. During Taksin's reign the Kingdom of Lan Na (q.v.) was wrested from control by Burma and made a vassal state of Siam. Toward the end of his reign, Taksin saw himself as a living Buddha (q.v.). This resulted in controversy and the loss of elite support. He was judged insane and put to death in 1782.

TEACHER SUPPLY. There has long been a shortage of qualified teachers in many rural elementary schools of Thailand. This is related to both the large annual increases in student enrollment and to a high rate of population growth. Difficulties faced include low salaries and the preference of teachers to locate in urban areas. Many elementary teachers do not have certificates or diplomas. (See EDUCATIONAL SYSTEM.)

TECHNICAL COLLEGES. Practical training centers in several of the larger cities which offer more advanced instruction than the vocational schools. A certificate of ten years' prior education is required for admission. Training is offered in such fields as building trades, auto mechanics, electronics, printing, photography, tailoring, nutrition, accountancy and secretarial. Completion of the three-year course leads to a diploma.

TELEVISION. In 1955, Thailand acquired television services. Today, there are five channels, two operated by the government, two by the army and one private. There are variety shows, such as sports, boxing, soccer and soap operas which are imported from United States (q.v.) television series. The most popular TV shows are locally produced sports programs and serial dramas. Educational programs are a part of the open-university teaching project.

TEMPLE BOYS (LUK SIT WAT). Typically, several boys are affiliated with the Buddhist monks (q.v.) in the Buddhist temple compound *(wat)* (q.v.), and perform services such as cleaning, running errands and collecting gifts. In return, they may receive food (q.v.), lodging, instruction and other advantages. Often such temple boys and novices (q.v.) form a kind of pool from which any monk may secure assistance. In Bangkok (q.v.), students from distant provinces may assume the role of temple boy in order to have a place to live while pursuing higher education (q.v.).

THAI. See LANGUAGE AND THAI PEOPLES.

THAI BOXING. Two male boxers, flyweight to lightweight, confront each other in a ceremonial combat which originated in the medieval Siamese (q.v.) art of fighting with the feet. A three-piece ensemble provides a rhythmic musical accompaniment to the three stages of action: pre-fight prayer ritual, ceremonial dance, and fight. Kicking with bare feet, hitting below the belt, and unrestricted use of elbows and knees are allowed. The boxer's costume consists of boxing gloves and trunks, a charm cord worn around the biceps, and a sacred headband worn during the preliminaries but removed for the main fight.

THAI-LAO. See THE NORTHEAST.

THAI-MALAY (THAI-ISLAM). A Malayo-Polynesian ethnolinguistic group comprising more than two million Muslims who are the second largest minority within Thai society. They reside for the most part in four provinces on the southern border of Thailand: Pattani (q.v.), Yala, Narathiwat and Satun. It has been the policy of the Thai government to refer to all Muslims in Thailand as "Thai-Islam" and to stress the unity of all citizens regardless of race, religion or ethnic identity. However, the religion and related characteristics of those in Thai-Islamic communities have been firm obstacles to efforts of the Thai government at assimilating minorities. Two distinct groupings of Muslims should be recognized. These are the Thai-Malay and the Thai-Islam.

The Thai-Malay constitute 75 percent of the population of the four Thai provinces adjacent to the northern part of West Malaysia. In religion, language (see LANGUAGE, MALAY) and general culture, they are as Malay as their counterparts on the other side of the border excepting, of course, for their provincial and national government. The Malay provinces were made part of Thailand in the 18th century when they were held as vassals of the Thai king. Previous to this in the 15th century, the Malay people were converted to Islam (q.v.). Only in the 20th century has governmental administration at the province (q.v.) and district (q.v.) levels been established by the Thai. Thai-Malay culture differs sharply in some respects from its Thai counterpart, particularly in the role of religion in social life. In these Malay provinces, religious studies in both primary and secondary Islamic schools are valued above secular education in the government schools, attendance in which is resisted by the Muslim clergy. Ability to recite the Koran by rote is expected of all adult males. For these and other reasons, the Thai-Malay are resistant to assimilation into the national culture of Thailand.

In Thai-Malay areas, agricultural villagers predominate as elsewhere in Southeast Asia. Their dwellings in clusters are placed on stilts among rice fields, rubber trees and kitchen gardens. Somewhat unique is the village mosque and its associated buildings. Rice (q.v.) is the principal food (q.v.) crop but mostly grown in small lots of a size that one family can handle. Other cash crops include coconuts (q.v.), cassava (q.v.), and varied fruits.

The religion of the Thai-Malay is Islam which is combined with Brahmanism (q.v.) and animism (q.v.). It includes the organization of a congregation around a mosque with the imam (q.v.) as clerical leader. There are rites of circumcision, marriage, burial, and others, in keeping with Islamic law. A variety of spirits are propitiated to avoid illness and misfortune, with assistance from practitioner specialists.

The term Thai-Islam refers to the remainder (about one-fifth) of the Muslim population who live in scattered clusters in some 24 of Thailand's other provinces. In contrast to the Thai-Malay, the Thai-Islam are regarded, and consider themselves, as Thai. They differ very little from the Thai except in religion; some no longer speak Malay. Where there are differences in dress, behavior, and patterns of living, these may be ascribed to origin in southern Thailand rather than specifically to Malay ancestry. For the most part, the Thai-Islam have become interspersed with Thai and occasionally may predominate in some villages. In places with a large proportion of Thai-Islam families, the village headman may be Thai-Islam.

THAI-MALAY SEPARATISM. Political difficulties arising from separatist activity among Thai-Malay (q.v.) in southern Thailand is a serious threat to the territorial integrity of the nation. The Malay ruling aristocracy in Pattani (q.v.), Yala, Narathiwat and Satun provinces was replaced in the early 20th century by Thai administrators who applied new policies. The change in administration was part of a national reorganization of all provinces (q.v.). This resulted in a gulf between the Thai-Malay and the new state bureaucracy. The former saw this as a threat to their religion and way of life. Violence, which has resulted in arson, numerous deaths, banditry and guerilla insurgency (q.v.), has erupted from time to time. Several organized Thai-Malay separatist movements have sprung up in the past 40 years. Their objectives have been to obtain autonomy for the region they occupy, to improve their standard of living and to revive Malay culture. Separatist movements have been due not only to perceived Thai oppression, but to outside influences as well. The latter include support from the neighboring country, Malaysia (q.v.), sympathy and financing from other Islamic countries, and success in obtaining international forums for airing their grievances.

In response to separatist movements, the Thai government has abandoned its previous restrictive policies. Religious pluralism is stressed, the building of mosques has been sponsored and Muslim pilgrimages to Mecca have been facilitated. However, these and other similar policies face the criticism that the government cannot be a patron of Islam (q.v.). Rather, the purity of Islamic religion is achieved when the state is an instrument of the Divine Will. Some success has occurred in Thai efforts to broaden the local Islamic schools to include secular subjects and the Thai language (q.v.). Through secular education, a body of Muslims, who will be acceptable as administrators to the Thai government, will be created.

THAI MUSLIMS. See THAI-MALAY.

THAI NATION PARTY (CHART THAI). Organized in 1974, the Thai Nation party was led initially by Police General Pramarn Adireksan (q.v.). It was one of the political parties (q.v.) backed by the Thai Army, and it supports conservative candidates for election to the House of Representatives (q.v.). The Thai Nation party has been one of the most successful ones in the past ten years in having a large number of members in the House of Representatives. In 1983, 1988 and again in 1992, its leader became prime minister (q.v.). In the 1992 election, its leader was Somboon Rahong. The party illustrates how power is shared among a number of key individuals. Faction leaders of the party wield influence over a number of representatives under their patronage. This enables the party to act in unison on important issues.

THAI PEOPLES. See LANGUAGE AND THAI PEOPLES; INTRODUCTION.

THAI RED CROSS SOCIETY. The Society was established in 1893, when fighting broke out between the French and Thai forces on the eastern border of Siam (q.v.). Queen Saowabha (q.v.), the ladies of the palace, and the wives of officials set up a volunteer aid society. It was named *Sabha Unalom Daeng* (Red Unalom Society). The Siamese (q.v.) Red Cross Society gained full recognition from the International Red Cross Committee in Geneva in 1920 and joined the League of Red

Cross Societies in 1921. The activities of the Red Cross Society are divided into five basic sections: Hospital Section, Relief Section, Health Section, Scientific Section, and Junior Red Cross Section. Throughout the past century, the Society has served the people and the country in various ways: by establishing a hospital, blood bank, eye-bank for corneal transplants, nurses' training school, program for training volunteers, etc. The Society's laboratories produce vaccines to control smallpox, rabies and cholera, make serum for snake bites and conduct medical research.

THAI SILK. Mudmee silk, a genuine and exquisite traditional fabric that has been produced in the northeast (q.v.) for centuries. Whether spun and woven by hand or machine, the silk is available in several weights, suitable for men's and women's clothing and house furnishings. Thai silk comes in solid colors, plaids, stripes, checks, brocades and prints. In 1972, a mudmee silk weaving project, encouraged and supported by Queen Sirikit (q.v.), was started in the northeastern province of Nakhon Phanom. The weavers have introduced a few modern modifications in the weaving process but have carefully preserved the traditional methods of weaving and dyeing. The industry has expanded to employ hundreds of small home weaving units, producing high-quality, multicolored shimmering mudmee silk. The northeast is still the main center of production; near the northeastern town of Pak Thong Chai, the company which James Thompson (q.v.) founded has built the largest hand-weaving facility in the world. Today Thai silk is the best known of all the country's handicrafts (q.v.), not only in Thailand but throughout the world as well.

THAMMAYUTIKA. A very small reform sect within Thai Buddhism (q.v.). A movement for religious reform initiated by King Mongkut (q.v.) led in 1894 to recognition by the Buddhist monkhood *(sangha)* (q.v.) of two sects. The Thammayutika sect adheres more strictly to the rules of conduct for Buddhist monks (q.v.) than the Mahanikai sect and places more emphasis on study than on pastoral services performed for the laity. (See BUDDHIST MONK; BUDDHIST MONKHOOD.)

THANG. A rice (q.v.) basket having a capacity of 20 liters and weighing approximately 16 kilograms. It is a traditional Thai unit of measurement. (See WEIGHTS AND MEASURES.)

THANIN KRAIVICHIEN (1927-   ). Jurist and politician. Thanin studied law and other subjects in Bangkok (q.v.) and London. He practiced law and soon began a career as a judge in Thailand. Eventually he was appointed to senior judge positions. These were consecutively at the Civil Court, Court of Appeals and Supreme Court. He was also a senator in the National Assembly (q.v.) in October 1976 when he was chosen to be prime minister. This came about following a coup against the previous Prime Minister Seni Pramoj (q.v.), which was led by a military junta. Thanin was deposed in October 1977 in a coup led by Kriangsak Chomanan (q.v.). The coup group contended that there was social unrest due to Thanin's repressive administration. Thanin wrote numerous publications on history, politics and legal systems.

THANOM KITTIKACHORN (1911-   ). Prime minister, army officer, politician. Thanom graduated from the Royal Military Academy in 1929. A capable and effective career military officer, Thanom advanced to commander of strategic units in Bangkok (q.v.). In 1955, an appointment to the cabinet of Prime Minister Phibunsongkhram (q.v.) gave him an increased role in politics. In the 1957 coup d'etat led by Sarit Thanarat (q.v.), Thanom became a "right-hand man" and stand-in prime minister for one year. When Sarit returned from abroad and took over the prime minister position, Thanom became deputy prime minister and minister of defense.

Thanom again became prime minister in 1963 after the death of Sarit. In his administration, Thanom was allied with General Praphas Charusathian (q.v.), the deputy prime minister. During their ten year rule, they were much involved with the United States (q.v.) and the Vietnam War. They emphasized the promotion of trade, investment and modernization. Meanwhile, there was an inescapable trend toward democratic political development and public discussion of the nation's problems. The authoritarianism of the Thanom regime was opposed by students and Bangkok residents who also pressed for a new constitution (q.v.).

Large student-led demonstrations occurred and these culminated in a bloody confrontation on October 14, 1973. Thanom and Praphas were forced into exile. The king, Bhumibol Adulyadej (q.v.), intervened to prevent chaos. A new civilian prime minister was appointed. When, in 1976, Thanom returned from exile and joined the Buddhist monkhood, student demonstrations led to the 1976 military coup. (See STUDENT UPRISING OF 1973.)

THESABAN. See MUNICIPALITY.

THEWADA. The Thai name for gods of various grades who inhabit the heavens above Mount Meru. The Thewada are beings who have risen to their exalted state through accumulated merit (q.v.). Belief in the *thewada* is associated with belief in other gods of the Hindu pantheon such as Siva, Brahma and Vishnu. (See COSMOLOGY.)

THIPHAKORAWONG (KHAM BUNNAG) (1813-1870). Government official and scholar. Kham was the son of Dit Bunnag and had aided in Mongkut's (q.v.) accession to the throne in 1851. He was appointed by King Mongkut in 1855 to the Phrakhlang, where he served as treasurer and was in charge of trading monopolies and foreign relations. The term Phrakhlang was both the name of an administrative post and the title of the person in charge. Kham earned fame for his use of historiography in writing a two-volume history of the first four Chakri (q.v.) kings. He also wrote a survey of modern science. (See BUNNAG FAMILY.)

THOMPSON, JAMES H. W. (1906-1967). Thompson was an American-born entrepreneur who helped develop the modern Thai silk (q.v.) industry. In 1946, he became interested in the production of Thai silk and founded the Thai Silk Company Ltd. To the ancient manufacturing process, he introduced modern dyes and new designs and set standards of production. In 1962, in recognition of his contribution to Thailand, the Thai government awarded him the Order of the White Elephant. Increasingly interested in Thai architecture (q.v.) and Southeast Asian art, he built a house in Bangkok (q.v.) along the Klong (q.v.) that eventually became a leading tourist attraction. While on a holiday with friends in Malaysia, on an Easter weekend in 1967, he disappeared under mysterious circumstances.

THREE FUNDAMENTAL PRINCIPLES. Basic to the essential teachings of Buddha (q.v.) are the Three Signs or Fundamental Principles: (1) the impermanence of every individual, (2) the non-reality of a separate self or soul, and (3) sorrow and suffering as inherent in individuality. In light of Buddha's other teachings, this means that all existence is illusion or continual change and there is no "being" but only eternal becoming. The second principle asserts that there is no connection between the individual who exists one moment and the same individual who exists the next moment. The only link between them is *karma* (q.v.), the result of all of an individual's acts both good and evil. Thirdly, there is no relief from sorrow and suffering except through understanding Buddha's teaching and the extinction of desire by following the monastic role which Buddha exemplified. (See BUDDHISM; BUDDHIST MONK; BUDDHIST SCRIPTURES; PRECEPTS.)

THREE GEMS. Three elements for which reverence and devotion are expressed at the opening of religious observance: the Buddha (q.v.), *dharma* (q.v.) and *sangha* (q.v.). Buddhists believe that with these they can overcome suffering and danger. (See BUDDHISM.)

THREE REFUGES. See THREE GEMS.

THUDONG BHIKKHU. The Buddhist monk (q.v.) who, during the approved season, goes on foot to visit various Buddhist shrines that are scattered throughout the country. (See BUDDHIST MONK.)

THUM YAI. See RANAD THUM.

TILOKARACHA (TILOK). King of Lan Na (reigned 1441-1487). Tilok was the son of and successor to King Sam Fang Kaen who ruled Lan Na (q.v.). History has recorded the frequent military actions involving Tilok due to his precarious status as king and leader of the Lan Na Kingdom. There were challenges from the king of Ayutthaya (q.v.), from rivals for the throne, and from the ruler of the state of Nan. However, Tilok was victorious over his adversaries. With a sense of security in 1450, Tilok began to expand the kingdom with limited success. For at least two decades, there were continued but inconclusive wars against the forces of King Borommatrailokanat (q.v.) of Ayutthaya. However, Lan Na was enlarged and strengthened by Tilok. His reign was a high point in Lan Na's so-called Golden Age (1355-1558). Tilok is also remembered for his construction of the famous Buddhist temple Maha Chedi Luang.

TIMLAND. The name of an amusement park in rural surroundings where typical aspects of country life and Thai handicrafts (q.v.) have been assembled. The park caters to tourists who have little time to explore Thailand as a whole. Here one can see teams of elephants (q.v.) at work, spinners and weavers of cloths, wood carvers, several Thai-style houses, typical canals and so on. Timland also organizes cock fights (q.v.), Thai boxing (q.v.) shows, kite-flying (q.v.) competitions, and classical music and dance performances.

TIN. Tin is the leading mineral in Thailand's mining (q.v.) industry and is a high export (q.v.) earner. As early as the 13th century, tin was available in the country and was used with copper in making bronze images of the Buddha (q.v.). In the past two decades, the chief tin operation has been in the coastal areas of the peninsula (q.v.). Phuket (q.v.) has become the main center of tin activities. However, the large number of firms, many of them unregistered, has brought about political controversy and social problems. Attempts by the government to establish order and regulation have been only partly successful. The Minerals Act of 1967, as amended in 1973 and 1979, is the chief legal instrument which governs both onshore and offshore mining activities.

TIPITAKA. See BUDDHIST SCRIPTURES.

TOURISM. The major source of foreign exchange in the present-day Thai economy. Thailand's official promotion of tourism began during the reign of King Chulalongkorn (q.v.) when publicity materials were sent to the United States (q.v.). Since 1924, tourism has been promoted by a succession of governmental bodies: the Ministry of Commerce and Transport, Publicity Department and finally Tourist Organization of Thailand (TOT). Tourism, Thailand's largest source of foreign exchange from 1981 to 1986, increased by almost 25 percent in 1987 when "Visit Thailand Year" was promoted as part of the 60th birthday celebrations of King Bhumibol Adulyadej (q.v.). Tourists have continued to flock to Thailand during the 1990s. Although generally valued as a means of strengthening the Thai economy, tourism has come under strong criticism because it has been closely linked to the growth of prostitution and acquired immune deficiency syndrome (AIDS).

TRADE ASSOCIATIONS. Organizations focused on trade are very largely dominated by the Sino-Thai (q.v.), descendants of Chinese immigrants who are legally and culturally Thai. Of the more than 175 trade associations in the early 1990s, only about one-fourth are active in influencing public policy. The others serve chiefly as social clubs or are concerned with the welfare of members. The trade associations are of seven principal types: (1) Agricultural export associations deal with exports such as rice (q.v.), tapioca and maize. (2) Industry associations, the most active of which seek to improve the technology and managerial capability of members. Others focus on public policy formation. (3) Tourist industry associations have successfully lobbied the national government because tourism (q.v.) is the number one foreign exchange earner of Thailand. (4) Financial associations, the most prominent being the Thai Bankers Association (TBA) which has as members all of the 16 government-owned banks. It has been both active and influential in public policy-making. (5) Insurance associations have worked closely with the Ministry of Commerce in regulating the insurance industry. (6) Domestic trade associations are quite numerous. They have capable leaders and focus on public policy and legislative concerns. (7) Service associations have a long history in charitable works and in promoting the welfare of members. The Chinese Construction Association and the Lottery Dealers Association are examples.

TRIPLE ANNIVERSARY (VISAKHA BUCHA). Triple Anniversary Day is the most sacred of Buddhist (q.v.) religious festivals. It commemorates the birth, death and enlightenment of the Buddha (q.v.). The event occurs at the full moon of the sixth lunar month. Worshippers walk in procession around the chapel *(bot)* (q.v.) in the temple compound *(wat)* (q.v.) after which they listen to sermons given by Buddhist monks (q.v.). Merit (q.v.) making is done in a manner similar to All Saints Day.

TUNG SALENG LUANG NATIONAL PARK. This park is in the Phetchabun Mountain Range (q.v.) midway between Phitsanulok City and the town of Lom Sak in Phetchabun Province. The highway between these two towns runs through the park, which covers 1,280 square kilometers (500 square miles) of wooded mountains. Types of animals found here include deer, wild buffaloes, boars, tigers, panthers and elephants (q.v.). The flora and fauna (q.v.) are protected insofar as the authorities are able to patrol such a large area.

- U -

UBOLRATANA, PRINCESS (1951-). The eldest daughter of King Bhumibol (q.v.) and Queen Sirikit (q.v.).

UBOSOT. See BOT.

UMBRELLAS. Making umbrellas is a handicraft (q.v.) derived either from Burma or from Yunan, a province in southern China, over two centuries ago. Bo Sang village near Chiang Mai (q.v.) specializes in the craft of parasol-making. Each household in the village concentrates on a single detail of manufacture. One household may split and shape bamboo (q.v.), while another assembles the bamboo strips into parasol skeletons, and others fasten the paper coverings, or waterproof them with resin oil, or paint on the floral designs. Nowadays, the umbrella coverings are fashioned out of cotton, silk, or sa-paper, which is made from the mulberry tree. (See HANDICRAFTS.)

UNITED NATIONS. See ESCAP; INTERNATIONAL COOPERATION; UNESCO.

UNITED NATIONS EDUCATIONAL, SCIENTIFIC AND CULTURAL ORGANIZATION (UNESCO). The Principal Regional Office for Asia and the Pacific (PROP) is located in Bangkok (q.v.). PROP was set up as the Regional Office of Education in 1961, but expanded to include culture in 1976, and social and human sciences in 1977. In 1987, the office was further expanded to provide information programs and social services. There are 33 member states of UNESCO in Asia and the Pacific. PROP encourages the development and reform of education at all levels from early childhood to the university, promotes the study of social and human sciences, particularly as they relate to women, fosters human rights and peace, and works toward the preservation of the cultural heritage, traditions and cultural identity among the youth.

UNITED STATES, RELATIONS WITH. Prior to 1945, Thai-American relations can be described as "cordial but distant." In this period there were useful missionary activities and Americans advising government officials. The early teaching of English, the creation of schools and the publishing of newspapers have had a significant impact on development of the nation. Another long-lasting early contribution was in the area of medicine and public health.

Beginning in 1945, Thai-American relations became close and were based largely on security ties. The United States aided Thailand in reestablishing friendly relations with Great Britain and in getting Thailand admitted to the United Nations. After 1950, the U.S. provided much military and financial assistance to Thailand to support anti-Communist activities. In the context of the Cold War, it seemed important to prevent any further Communist takeovers. In the 1960s, Thailand facilitated the construction of bases in its country for the U.S. war with Vietnam. In addition, the Thais permitted their country to be a vast staging area for the air war and the search and rescue operations conducted by the U.S. During this time there was very close cooperation between the two nations. Several cities in Thailand also served as "rest and recuperation" spots for American troops. In a sense, Thailand was, for a time, a bastion of U.S. power in Southeast Asia.

In the mid-1970s, Thai-American relations became more cautious. By 1975, a considerable degree of anti-American sentiment had developed in Thailand. As a result, in 1975, all U.S. troops and equipment were withdrawn from Thailand at the latter's request. More recently, Thai-American relations have broadened to include not only security, but also trade, investment, science and technology. It appears that the Thais see relations with the United States as important because Thailand has at many times felt threatened by other nations. However, it has never been colonized. Since the 1960s, the United States has continued to contribute to the educational development of many Thai colleges and universities. The USAID (q.v.) has been a principal conduit for this financial aid. There are also many non-governmental cooperative relationships between Thai and U.S. universities. Cooperation more recently also involves emphasis on two sectors, the creation of jobs in rural areas and assistance in science and technology transfer. (See also MILITARY ASSISTANCE.)

UNITED STATES AGENCY FOR INTERNATIONAL DEVELOPMENT (USAID). The agency responsible for channeling American economic development assistance to Thailand after 1962. It superseded the International Cooperation Administration which has operated as part of the United States Operations Mission (q.v.). Technical and financial assistance were directed chiefly at village development in the northeast (q.v.). In addition, aid to Thai education occurred including buildings, equipment and books. Thai educators and officials were provided training in the United States (q.v.) and American consultants were brought from United States universities.

UNITED STATES OPERATIONS MISSION (USOM). The United States (q.v.) agency responsible for channeling financial, military and technical assistance to Thailand from the mid-1950s to the mid-1970s. During the war with Vietnam, roads, airfields and other infrastructure were constructed in Thailand with the Mission's assistance.

UPARAJA. Heir apparent or deputy king. This title was created by King Borommatrailokanat (q.v.) in the 15th century in an attempt to make the operation of royal succession smoother. Appointed by the reigning monarch, he was usually (1) the eldest son of the king's senior queen or (2) the king's full brother. The title became defunct after the royal succession act of 1924. The office of *uparaja* is often confused in Western historical accounts with the much less common title second king (q.v.).

URBANIZATION. The urban population of Thailand is concentrated in one city, Bangkok (q.v.). Its six million people dwarfs all other cities of the nation. When the population of other cities in the vicinity are added to that of Bangkok, there is a metropolitan area of approximately nine million. Four cities that are larger than 150,000 are Nonthaburi (q.v.), Chiang Mai (q.v.), Nakhon Ratchasima (q.v.) and Hat Yai in Songkhla Province (q.v.). Approximately 15 other cities have a population in excess of 50,000. Taken as a whole, Thailand continues to be largely rural, as two-thirds of the nation's population are agricultural villagers and other rural residents.

- V -

VAJIRALONGKORN, CROWN PRINCE (1952-   ). Prince Vajiralongkorn is the son of King Bhumibol Adulyadej (q.v.) and Queen Sirikit (q.v.). He completed his primary education in Thailand and continued his secondary education in England. He was also trained in the Royal Military College, Duntroon, Australia. Upon his return, he took up his duties in the Royal Thai Army. He makes provincial tours and represents King Bhumibol at official functions and ceremonies. As His Majesty's representative, the crown prince makes state visits to foreign countries. He is married to Princess Somsawali; they have one daughter.

VAJIRAVUDH. King of Siam (reigned 1910-1925). The son of King Chulalongkorn (q.v.), Vajiravudh was educated in Bangkok (q.v.) and in Britain at Oxford University and Sandhurst Military Academy. Early in his reign he organized the Wild Tiger Corps, a nationwide paramilitary movement, to build a following. Vajiravudh decreed that all persons have surnames. He started compulsory education (q.v.) and promoted Western hairstyles and dress among Siamese (q.v.) women. Vajiravudh enjoyed literary pursuits and wrote plays and essays. He popularized his ideas about patriotism, the virtue of hard work and willingness to die for king and country. However, his personal life was felt by many to be undignified, and his expenditure of national funds was extravagant. Thanks to the skill of his foreign minister, Devawongse (q.v.), treaties with European governments, Japan (q.v.) and the United States (q.v.) were renegotiated between 1920 and 1926. These treaties restored Siamese judicial and fiscal autonomy and abolished extraterritoriality previously granted to those foreign powers.

VILLAGES, AGRICULTURAL. About two-thirds of the Thai people are farmers who predominantly grow rice (q.v.). A variety of other crops is also grown. Small farms average no more than 15 rai (6 acres) of land, a part of which is owned and the remainder rented. In the southern part of the Central Plain (q.v.), farmers are predominantly landless and work as wage laborers. The agricultural village consists typically of a cluster of 50 or more households set among fruit trees, palms and rice fields or in linear fashion along a waterway or road. In the alluvial plains, clusters may contain only a few farmsteads.

Members of farm families also engage in seasonal wage labor if available. They also carry on various crafts such as carpentry, home weaving, mat fabrication for house walls or floors and basket making. Some village craftsmen specialize in pottery, metal work, lacquer gilding, inlays, gold or silversmithing and jewelry making carried on as full-time occupations.

There are daily markets in the towns and larger villages where handicrafts (q.v.), farm produce and imported items are bought and sold. After the harvest, rice is milled for family use or sold to an itinerant buyer who may also handle the farmers' other cash crops. Better transportation in Thailand in recent years has improved marketing opportunities for farmers.

VISAKHA BUCHA. See TRIPLE ANNIVERSARY.

VITAL ESSENCE (KHWAN). Originally an animistic belief that each person is animated by a vital essence *(khwan)*. Eventually this belief was incorporated into the Buddhist cosmology (q.v.). The vital essence is transmitted to the mother's womb along with the male sperm. It is nourished by the mother and by rice (q.v.). Vital essence is also interpreted as morale, and something that can be aided or promoted. For example, efforts are made to give military personnel feelings of security. This promotes their vital essence (morale). Company employees have good morale when they receive high pay and excellent fringe benefits. In rural areas, as part of a welcome for visitors, ceremonies which promote vital essence are held.

- W -

WACHIRAYAN WAROROT (VAJIRANANA VARORASA) (1860-1921). Prince Wachirayan was the son of King Mongkut (q.v.) and a younger half-brother of King Chulalongkorn (q.v.). Inspired by each of these two people he greatly admired, Wachirayan was ordained a Buddhist monk (q.v.) in 1879. As a result of the exemplary work he did in his Pali (q.v.) studies, King Chulalongkorn conferred on him the rank of prince. As deputy patriarch of the Thammayutika (q.v.) order of Buddhism (q.v.), Wachirayan improved Buddhist education and ecclesiastical organization in significant ways. His strengthening of the intellectual content of Siamese (q.v.) Buddhism is a lasting tribute to his remarkable ability. For the 11 years prior to his death, he was the supreme patriarch (q.v.) of Buddhism in Siam.

WAI KHRU. Each year a day is set aside when students at all levels of education pay respect to their teachers. A ceremony is normally held for each school, either in a temple compound *(wat)* (q.v.) or in a school auditorium, where a Buddha image (q.v.) is positioned on an altar. Buddhist monks (q.v.), on a raised dais at the front, participate in the ceremony. This may include a chanted prayer, flower arrangements and the sprinkling of lustral water on those assembled. A student leader from each grade level makes the gift presentation and a speech on respect for teachers. (See EDUCATIONAL SYSTEM.)

WANG. A major river in the northern region of Thailand. It flows southward and is a tributary of the Chao Phraya River (q.v.).

WAT. See BUDDHIST TEMPLE COMPOUND.

WAT ARUN. Widely known as the Temple of Dawn, this temple is located on the Chao Phraya River (q.v.) in Thon Buri. It was constructed in the early-19th century and includes one large central tower and four smaller towers forming a quadrangle. Its porcelain ware decorations sparkle in the sun. The towers rest on a series of terraces, seemingly supported by rows of statues of demons and angels. Crowning each of the towers is the trident of the god Siva. Wat Arun is a popular tourist attraction.

WAT BENCHAMABORPITR. Commonly known in English as the Marble Temple, this religious center was built in the early 1900s and is located on Si Ayutthaya Street, in Bangkok (q.v.). It is unique in blending 19th-century architecture (q.v.) with adaptations from earlier periods of Thai architectural history. Except for the roof, it was constructed of marble from Carrara, Italy. Wat Benchamaborpitr is also famous for the marble lions at the entrance, Chinarat Buddha image (q.v.) in its *bot* (q.v.), and the more than 50 life-size Buddha images in its gallery. A sacred bo (pipal) tree, a monk's quarters *(kuti)* and other buildings are part of the temple complex.

WAT HARIPUNCHAYA. One of the best-kept Buddhist temple complexes in Thailand, located near Chiang Mai (q.v.) in the city of Lamphun. This city is on the site of the capital of the old Mon (q.v.) principality of Haripunchaya and the *wat* dates from that early period, before political control was in Thai hands. It is also famous for its large golden *chedi* (q.v.), 51 meters (170 feet) high. Other buildings include a *bot* (q.v.), several *wihan* (q.v.), a library, and a museum which has no equal in northern Thailand.

WAT MAHATHAT. A temple in the city of Nakhon Si Thammarat (q.v.) and the second oldest Buddhist shrine in Thailand, after the Nakhon Pathom Shrine (q.v.). It is impressive for its large central *chedi* (q.v.) surrounded by a score of other *chedi* of considerable height. Wat Mahathat is famous as the site where, at the time of his reign, King Rama I (q.v.) was able to obtain copies of the Buddhist scriptures (q.v.) following the destruction in 1767 of Ayutthaya (q.v.), a former Thai capital.

WAT PHRA BUDDHABHAT. One of the most famous Buddhist temple compounds in Thailand, located at the city of Sarapburi, 115 kilometers (72 miles) north of Bangkok (q.v.). A large footprint believed to be that of the Buddha (q.v.) is enshrined in a magnificently constructed *mondop* (q.v.). This Buddha symbol is highly venerated and attracts throngs of worshippers from Thailand and other countries. There are many temple bells of various sizes in the courtyard. (See BUDDHA.)

WAT PHRA KEO. A Buddhist temple complex, on Sanam Chai Road in Bangkok (q.v.), which is known as the Thai Royal *wat*. It has been used for ceremonial purposes only by the Thai kings of the Chakri dynasty (q.v.) for many decades. Wat Phra Keo was founded in 1782 and is a very interesting and famous Bangkok religious center. The most revered Buddha image (q.v.) in Thailand, the Emerald Buddha (q.v.), is housed in the *bot* (q.v.) (royal chapel) of this *wat*. The doors of the *bot* are decorated with mother of pearl inlays. Black and gold lacquer work is seen both inside and outside, and murals on the walls of the *bot* depict scenes from the life of the Buddha (q.v.). Also in this *wat* is a royal pantheon which contains life-size statues of the past monarchs of the Chakri dynasty. Also in Wat Phra Keo is a religious library, numerous other buildings, *stupa* (q.v.) and bronze images. The covered gallery, which runs around the *bot* courtyard, contains wall paintings which represent episodes from the Ramakian (q.v.).

WAT PHRA SINGH LUANG. An important Buddhist religious center founded in 1345 in the city of Chiang Mai (q.v.). The chapel *(bot)* (q.v.) contains one of only three famous Phra Singh Buddha images (q.v.). The others are at the Thai National Museum (q.v.) in Bangkok (q.v.) and at Wat Mahathat in Nakhon Si Thammarat (q.v.). The word *singh* here means a perfect gold alloy for use in casting Buddha images. Wat Phra Singh Luang is the place for regular meetings of the Buddhist monk (q.v.) of the fifth circle of *sangha* (q.v.). The abbot (q.v.) here is a *sangha* administrator, which explains the addition of the word *luang* to the name of the *wat*.

WAT PHRATHAT. One of the leading Buddhist religious centers of Thailand, located on Mount Suthep, near the city of Chiang Mai (q.v.). Built in the 14th century, the *wat* has long been famous for the Phrathat Buddha image (q.v.) found here and for a large *chedi* (q.v.), 12 meters (40 feet) high, in which a relic of the Buddha (q.v.) is enshrined. The *chedi* is covered with copper or brass plates overlaid with gold. Murals in the adjoining cloisters depict incidents in the life of the Buddha. The mountain location of the *wat* affords an excellent view of Chiang Mai valley.

WAT PO. This Buddhist religious center, located on Maharaj Road in Bangkok (q.v.), is the most extensive temple complex of its kind in Bangkok (also called Wat Phrachetuphon). It is best known for its colossal reclining Buddha image (q.v.), 45 meters (150 feet) long and 15 meters (50 feet) high. This posture of the Buddha represents his entrance into nirvana (q.v.). Other features in this *wat* are a chapel *(bot)* (q.v.) with adjoining galleries where nearly 400 Buddha images are displayed. The galleries are also used by out-of-town visitors for overnight accommodations. There are four small *wihan* (q.v.) and a large display of anatomical drawings, which have value in medical instruction. In addition, there are four great *chedi* (q.v.) and a school for the instruction of both the laity and Buddhist monkhood *(sangha)* (q.v.) members.

WAT POMAN KUNARAM. A temple complex, the largest in Thailand, that serves the ethnic Chinese (q.v.) minority, located on the Satha Pradit Road in Bangkok (q.v.). It was constructed in the 1960s under the leadership of Pra Po Cheng, currently the top leader at this center of Mahayana Buddhism (q.v.). Mainly Chinese in style, Wat Poman Kunaram reflects a blend of Tibetan and Thai architecture (q.v.). (See CHINESE IN THAILAND.)

WAT SRAKET. A temple compound in downtown Bangkok (q.v.) which is famous for having ashes believed to be remains of the Buddha (q.v.) and for being located on a man-made hill or "mount." It is therefore also called the Wat of the Golden Mount. The Buddha relics were enshrined there in 1899. Wat Sraket also has the Phra Buddha Chinoros, a very large Buddha image (q.v.) in bronze nine meters in height. A festival connected with the worship of the Buddha relics is held at Wat Sraket each November; along with its religious events, it includes a bazaar and entertainment.

WAT SUTAT. One of the largest of Bangkok's (q.v.) temple complexes, it is located at Sikak Sao Ching Cha (the Great Swing Square). It was constructed in the early 1800s. The large *wihan* (q.v.) of Wat Sutat is surrounded by galleries which display 160 gilt Buddha images (q.v.). The distinctive brass Buddha image in the *wihan* is a copy of a Sukhothai period (1250-1450) sculpture (q.v.). The large *bot* (q.v.) at Wat Sutat contains a huge Phra (q.v.) Trilokachet Buddha image. From an altar it looks down on 80 life-size images of disciples of the Buddha (q.v.). Murals and panelling depict the life of the Buddha and also Hindu imagery.

WATER BUFFALO. A domestic animal that historically has been and continues to be a principal source of farm power in Thailand and elsewhere in South and Southeast Asia. The water buffalo has been essential in plowing and preparing the soil for wet-rice (q.v.) production and has been used for transportation. It is not certain why the word buffalo is preceded by the word water, but one can assume that association plays a role. The animal works best in hot weather when it can be allowed to submerge periodically in a pond or river. In recent decades, the buffalo has gradually been replaced by tractors where their use is feasible. The demand for water buffaloes in the central Plain (q.v.) and in parts of northern Thailand has sharply declined. This change has had a significant effect in the northeast (q.v.), where the farmers have been the chief producers of water buffaloes.

WAY OF THE ELDERS. Another name for Hinayana or Theravada Buddhism (q.v.). This form of Buddhism is considered to be the closest to the original teachings of the Buddha (q.v.) in contrast to the other chief form--Mahayana Buddhism.

WEIGHTS AND MEASURES. The metric system became the basic standard when the Law of Weights and Measures was promulgated in Thailand on December 17, 1923. Local terms in common usage were standardized in a definite round-number relationship to basic metric terms. For example: 1 *pikul* (or *hap*) = 60 kilograms (132.3 pounds); 1 *kwian* = 2000 liters (440 gallons); 1 *thang* = 20 liters (4.4 gallons); 1 hectare = 2.47 acres; 1 *rai* = 0.16 hectare (0.4 acre).

WESTENGARD, JENS IVERSEN. The second American to be appointed general advisor to the king of Thailand. He served first as assistant advisor and then as advisor from 1908 to 1915. He was instrumental in negotiating the Anglo-Thai Treaty of 1909. In exchange for four states in the Malay peninsula, Britain relinquished its extraterritorial rights over its subjects, both European and Asian, in Thailand. He also led the negotiations between Thailand and Denmark resulting in a similar treaty in 1913. Westengard enjoyed the full confidence of the Thai government, which conferred on him the Order of the White Elephant and other honors.

WESTERNERS. A tiny part of the population in Thailand, estimated at between 5,000 and 10,000, are Westerners who have much importance because of their diplomatic, missionary, business and other activities. Most Westerners are concentrated in Bangkok (q.v.), with smaller numbers in Chiang Mai (q.v.) and other cities. While the size of the Western community is relatively stable, individuals within it are constantly being replaced. Few gain more than a superficial knowledge of Thai culture and most retain the perspective of their country of origin.

WHEEL OF THE LAW. A symbol of Buddhism (q.v.) used by writers and teachers in their expositions on the doctrine of Buddha (q.v.). The Wheel was especially important between 300 and 100 BC before the use of Buddha images (q.v.) became acceptable. Turning the Wheel is to preach or set in motion the Law.

WICHIT WATHAKAN (1898-1962). Political leader, dramatist, intellectual. After he studied law in Thailand and France, Wichit was employed in the Thai Foreign Service in 1915. Later he served in several cabinet posts and became ambassador to Japan under Prime Minister Phibunsongkhram (q.v.) until the end of World War II. Later he became ambassador to Switzerland. His skills as a literary figure led to his writing several dramas commissioned by Phibun in 1936-1940. While some persons see these dramas as propaganda, they were also genuinely popular. Wichit also produced historical works and radio scripts. All of his writings aided the growing popularity of Thai novels and short stories.

At least one historian credits Wichit with assigning the proper meaning to the Revolution of 1932 (q.v.), which resulted in the Thai monarchy (q.v.) becoming a constitutional one. In his histories, Wichit depicted the 1932 event as reflecting Thai nationalism and as paralleling a similar change in the aging dynasties of Europe. This interpretation and his other writings may make Wichit a competitor with Prince Damrong Rachanuphap (q.v.) for the title "father of Thai history." Wichit was awarded the title of Luang, signifying his distinct loyal service.

WIHAN. The worship or preaching hall in the temple compound *(wat)* (q.v.). The building is without chairs but may have mats on the floor and a raised dais near the altar for the Buddhist monks (q.v.) who chant the services.

WOMEN. Historically, Thai society has been male-dominated and to some extent remains so today. Nevertheless, Thai women have always wielded considerable power, both in the home and outside. Throughout the long history of the Thai people, women were rather fortunate in comparison with their counterparts in other parts of Southeast Asia, where tradition often gave fathers and husbands authority over female family members. During the reign of King Mongkut (q.v.), the common practice of husbands selling their wives was abolished. At that time, a woman was permitted to marry without parental approval, but she remained subordinate to her husband in property ownership, divorce and other legal matters.

The relative position of women continued to improve, and during the reign of King Vajiravudh (q.v.), Thai women began to receive formal education, the first in Asia to do so. Women gained the right to vote in 1932 when a coup d'etat established a constitutional monarchy (q.v.). However, women did not take an active part in Thai politics until 1949. Since that date, there have always been women candidates and members of the National Assembly (q.v.). In 1974, the Thai constitution (q.v.) stated for the first time that men and women have equal rights. In Thailand, as elsewhere, however, the removal of legal barriers has not ended all forms of discrimination.

Today, women constitute half of Thailand's population and are an integral part of the labor force. Because Thailand is an agrarian society, most of the female labor force is engaged in work related to agriculture (q.v.). However, recent rapid industrial development has increasingly brought women into the industrial work force. The number of successful career women has grown rapidly, too, in modern Thai society. Women can be found in almost every profession and career, from engineering to politics. The government and several nongovernmental organizations attempt to improve and expand the role and status of women. Greater momentum in these activities was gained during the United Nation's Decade of Women (1975-1985), particularly as it followed the restoration of constitutional government between 1973 and 1976. In 1992, the first Muslim woman was elected to the House of Representatives (q.v.) and the first woman governor (q.v.) was appointed.

WOOD CARVING. An ancient Thai craft that has experienced a considerable upsurge since the mid-1960s. Details of the temples and palaces of Thailand have for centuries reflected the great skill of Thai woodcarvers. In recent years, carved bowls, animal figures, and wall plaques as well as designs on lamp bases, have been in great demand. Teak is the most popular wood. (See HANDICRAFTS.)

- Y -

YAK. Sculptured art objects representing mythological giants which as large statues stand at the gate of the Buddhist temple compound *(wat)* (q.v.). Supposedly, they provide protection from evil spirits.

YOM. A major river in the northern region of Thailand. It flows southward and is a tributary of the Chao Phraya River (q.v.).

YOUNG BUDDHIST ASSOCIATION. An organization of young Buddhist laymen, founded in 1949, having more than 25 affiliated chapters. Its aims include the propagation of the *dharma* (q.v.), the inculcation of moral behavior in young people and social service activities, especially the guidance of their leisure time pursuits and other assistance for young people. While the Buddhist and Young Buddhist associations are similar in orientation, the latter places more emphasis on social service. It has promoted a number of work camps in which university students assisted farmers in construction of roads, bridges and reservoirs. (See BUDDHISM.)

- Z -

ZOOS. There are several zoos in Thailand. The biggest, Khao Din Zoo, also known as Dusit Zoo, is situated between the Grand Palace (q.v.) and the National Assembly (q.v.). This is one of the most popular places in Bangkok (q.v.) for family outings. By tradition, every white elephant (q.v.) found in Thailand belongs to the king and is kept in the zoo. It also houses a fine collection of birds, giraffes, kangaroos, crocodiles, monkeys, quaint little mouse-deer (native of Thailand) and bears. There is another zoo in Chiang Mai (q.v.), and it houses most of the region's wild animals. In 1983, the queen established a natural zoo, covering an area of 975,000 rai (156,000 hectare), on a large tract of virgin forest and jungle in Phu Khieo.

BIBLIOGRAPHY

Introduction

The field of Thai studies has expanded so rapidly in the past four decades that the amount of materials available for compilation now exceeds the ability of one compiler to organize, classify and rationally select them. The case then is all the stronger for beginning the immediate compilation of more specialized, critical and selective bibliographies. Source materials concerning Thailand are worldwide. Relevant monographs, articles and serials available in the United States alone are enormous.

This bibliography assumes no prior knowledge of the subjects it treats. Its presentation is not designed for specialists, students or scholars, but for general readers. All of the items in the bibliography are written in English and are available in the United States. Dissertations and unpublished papers are not included. The bibliography necessarily contains many entries which cover more than one subject.

There now exists a wide range of bibliographies on many Thai subjects that are strongest in areas of contemporary political, economic and social development. There are also numerous bibliographies on relatively concrete subject areas such as agriculture, demography, history, religion and rural development, but none on psychology and psychiatry. The best general bibliographies, vital to the beginner in Thai studies, are now largely available. The Social Research Institute at Chulalongkorn University, Thailand, publishes various annotated bibliographies.

Work dated as early as 1879 to 1974 cited in *Thailand: An Annotated Bibliography of Bibliographies*, by Donn V. Hart (1977), provides some general measurement of previous work for readers interested in Thai studies. The majority of entries are monographic titles. The arrangement of entries is in alphabetical order by author. The latest annotated bibliography, *Thailand,* by Michael Watts (1986), is classified with 32 subject headings. The annotations also refer to many works not included as main entries, but the names of the authors have been included in the index. *Statistical Yearbook: Thailand*, by the National Statistical Office, is a good source of statistics on Thailand.

Students and general readers will find an overview of Thai history in Prince Chula Chakrabongse's *Lords of Life* (1960). *Siam Becomes Thailand: A Story of Intrigue*, by Judith A. Stowe (1991), includes a detailed analysis of the Revolution of 1932-33, the gradual evolution of military regimes, and the war between Thailand and French Indochina in 1940-1941. It is essential reading for all who seek to understand Thailand. While rich in anecdotal material, Bass Terwiel's *History of Modern Thailand* (1983) tells only part of the story, limiting its narrative to the years 1767-1942; all the same, the book is informative.

In *Thailand: A Short History*, by David K. Wyatt (1984), the emphasis is on politics, policies and changes at the highest levels. The author has examined Thai history from its beginning to the 1980s. *The End of the Absolute Monarchy in Siam*, by Benjamin A. Batson (1984), offers the crucial phase of modern Thai history based on a real grasp of a wide range of sources. The book covers the controversy over the seventh reign of the Chakri dynasty, and its royal family, and a full account of the impact of the Great Depression on Siam. *Thailand: Buddhist Kingdom as Modern Nation-State*, by Charles F. Keyes (1987), is a readable, comprehensive and accurate study of Thai history, economics, politics, ethnic and cultural diversity, the media, religion, Buddhism as both a religion and a way of life, and modern literature. *Thailand: A Country Study*, edited by Barbara Leitch LePoer, 6th ed. (1989), describes and analyzes its political, economic, social and national security systems and institutions, and examines the interrelationships between those systems and the way they are shaped by cultural factors. *Thailand in the 90s*, published by the National Identity Office of the Office of the Prime Minister of Thailand (1991), presents a comprehensive overview of the economic and social conditions of Thailand.

The best study on the culture of politics in Thailand, with particular reference to the period from 1963-1977, is presented in *Thailand: Society and Politics*, by John L. S. Girling (1981). It is concerned primarily with the structure and patterns of Thai political relationships and their roots in changing Thai society. *Institutionalization of Democratic Political Processes in Thailand: A Three-Pronged Democratic Polity*, by Pisan Suriyamongkol (1988), is informative and well worth reading. The author sets out different concepts and models used in the interpretation of recent Thai history and analyzes clearly the growth of social and economic development and the way it has changed the distribution of power.

The Military in Thai Politics, 1981-1986, by Suchit Bunbongkarn (1987), includes more recent developments and an updated analysis of Thai politics. For understanding the role of the Thai military in politics since 1973, *The Thai Young Turks*, by Chai-Anan Samudavanija (1982), is highly useful, with particular reference to the "Young Turks" who staged the abortive coup of 1981. Being experienced as a member of the Communist party, Gawin Chutima (1990) wrote an inside story of *The Rise and Fall of the Communist Party of Thailand (1973-1987)*. *History of the Malay Kingdom of Patani*, by Ibrahim Syukri, translated by Conner Bailey and John N. Miksic (1985), presents an original Malay work in Jawi, written by a Patani Malay, about a mid-20th century perspective of the history of the former Malay state of Patani, a Malay community of south Thailand.

An account of a U.S. foreign assistant on modern Thai development and a history of the United States Agency for International Development (USAID) in Thailand is provided in *Thailand and the United States: Development, Security, and Foreign Aid*, by Robert J. Muscat (1990). *U.S.-Thailand Relations in a New International Era*, edited by Clark D. Neher and Wiwat Mungkandi (1990), is a valuable source book on a broad range of issues including bilateral economic conflicts, trade in services, security cooperation, conflict in Cambodia, obstacles to the economic integration of the ASEAN nations and Japan's changing role in the world economy.

American, British, Thai and other scholars have carried out research on rural communities since the late 1940s. Until the 1970s, Americans were the leaders in Thai studies but this dominance no longer exists. Since the improvement of education in Thailand, Thai scholars have become involved in studying their institutions. Australia and Japan have also taken an interest in Thailand and its history. The latest addition to the literature on Thai-Japanese relations during the World War II era is *"The Tragedy of Wanit"*: *A Japanese Account of Wartime Thai Politics*, by Benjamin A. Batson and Shimizu Hajime (1990). *Thai-Japanese Relations in Historical Perspective*, edited by Chaiwat Khamchoo and Bruce Reynolds (1988), gives solid reason to anticipate further valuable contributions to the study of Thai-Japanese relations. In providing vast quantities of data from Japanese, Thai and Western sources, the account demonstrates how economic relations between the two countries moved from relative insignificance to considerable importance.

Several studies are available on the Thai economy. A lucid historical narrative of economic change and the importance of trade in the first half of the 19th century is stressed in *Thailand in the Nineteenth Century: Evolution of the Economy and Society,* by Hong Lysa (1984). It also provides an interesting attempt to open new perspectives in the discussion on the politics of Thai development and economics. *Capital Accumulation in Thailand, 1855-1985,* by Suehiro Akira (1989), analyzes the recent Thai business scene and role of the Overseas Chinese community in the country. Lucid, well-written and an insightful work, *Business Associations and the New Political Economy of Thailand: From Bureaucratic Polity to Liberal Corporatism,* by Anek Laothamatas (1992), centers on the influence of business on the economics and politics of Thailand. *The Political Economy of Productivity: Thai Agricultural Development, 1880-1975,* by David Feeny (1982), is a detailed economic history of the political economy of agriculture in Thailand, with primary emphasis on developments prior to World War II.

Buddhism, Legitimation, and Conflict: The Political Functions of Urban Thai Buddhism, by Peter A. Jackson (1989), provides an insight into the changing relationship between Buddhism and politics in contemporary Thailand. *The Buddhist Saints of the Forest and the Cult of Amulets,* by Stanley J. Tambiah (1984), considers the model of the Buddhist saint and how this model has been employed in shaping the roles of monks in Thailand today. It also examines the way in which the charismatic power of monks is believed to be made concrete in the form of Buddhist amulets. In *Gender, Power and the Construction of the Moral Order: Studies from the Thai Periphery,* edited by Nancy Eberhardt (1988), the authors have used symbolic interpretation and contextual analysis of normative behavior in their search for the subjective meanings attached to gender.

The Malay-Muslim minority of southern Thailand is one of the major minority problems within Southeast Asia. To understand the political process in south Thailand, *Islam and Malay Nationalism: A Case Study of the Malay-Muslims of Southern Thailand,* by Surin Pitsuwan (1985), is a unique source of insight and the first scholarly work by a Malay-Muslim about his own people, the Malay-Muslims in Thailand. Literature on the Muslims in both Thailand and the Philippines has been increasing. A comparative study of the problem of Moro separatism in the southern Philippines and Malay separatism in southern Thailand is *Muslim Separatism: The Moros of Southern Philippines and the Malays of Southern Thailand*, by W. K. Che Man (1990).

Sources on the Chinese in Thailand can be found in *Chinese in Thailand with Supplements on the Chinese Haws and the Kuomintang*, by G. William Skinner (1983), and *Perceptions and Boundaries: Problematics in the Assimilation of the Chinese in Thailand*, by Tong Chee Kiong (1988).

Sangha, State and Society: Thai Buddhism in History, by Yoneo Ishii (1986), demonstrates the structure and history of the Thai Sangha, especially in the 19th and 20th centuries. *Buddhism and Politics in Thailand: A Study of Socio-Political Change and Political Activism in the Thai Sangha*, by Somboon Suksamran (1982), evaluates the relationship of the Sangha with politics, particularly in the 1970s. The author presents a remarkable amount of new information including confidential documents, and a comprehensive Thai and Western source bibliography.

A Life Apart: View from the Hills, by Jon Boyes and S. Piraban (1989), presents interviews with members of the six major hill tribes of northern Thailand (Yao [Nien], Akha, Lau, Hmong, Lisu, and Karen). In an earlier work, a brief historical and ethnographic introduction of *Peoples of the Golden Triangle*, by Paul and Elaine Lewis (1984), provides descriptions of all the tribal peoples in Thailand as well as excellent photographs of them.

A book written in the 14th century by a Thai prince became the major source for popular Buddhist cosmological ideas not only among the Thai but also among other Southeast Asian Buddhists. This work was translated and appears under the title *Three Worlds According to King Ruang: A Thai Buddhist Cosmology*, by Frank E. and Mani B. Reynolds (1982). The worldview based on this Buddhist cosmology was dominant in Thailand until the end of the 19th century and remains significant for many sectors of the population in Thailand.

An Anthropology of Curing in Multi-Ethnic Thailand, by Louis Golomb (1985), provides an informative account of modern and traditional medical practices, and ethnographic and historical material shedding light on such diverse topics as healing practices, ethnic relations and interpersonal relations in southern and central Thailand. *Thai Temples and Temple Murals,* by Rita Ringis (1990), tells a great deal about both the structural, decorative and symbolic features of the principal architectural forms encountered in the monastic compounds as well as the formal properties, techniques and themes presented in the mural paintings which embellish the interior walls of buildings or galleries. *The Arts of Thailand,* by Steve Van Beek and Luca Invernizzi Tettoni, 2nd ed. (1991), a visual pleasure, is divided into classical arts and minor arts.

The first and foremost reference guide to a wide range of groups and bibliographic sources relevant to gender studies in Thailand is *By Women, For Women: A Study of Women's Organizations in Thailand,* by Darunee Tantiwiramanond and Shashi Ranjan Pandey (1991). It also provides background information on women's non-governmental organizations (NGOs) in Thailand. *Thai Women in Buddhism,* by Chatsumarn Kabilsingh (1991), is the first book on the history and the plight of Buddhist women in Thailand.

In addition, articles of historical interest, political events, issues, personalities, and good accounts of contemporary events and institutions involved in the political evolution of Thailand appear in *Journal of the Siam Society, Journal of Southeast Asian Studies (Singapore), Asian Survey, Crossroads: An Interdisciplinary Journal of Southeast Asian Studies, Pacific Affairs, Far Eastern Economic Review, The Economist,* and *Asian Wall Street Journal. Far Eastern Economic Review Asia Yearbook, Europa World Yearbook* and an annual publication of *Country Report: Thailand, Burma* by the Economist Intelligent Unit (U.K.) present overall events in the year and include statistics.

1. GENERAL

A. Bibliographies

Bibliography on Community Development in Northern Thailand. Chiang Mai, Thailand: Research and Community Development Center, Payap College, 1983.

Chaveelak Boonyakanchana. *Thai Reference Books and Their History*. Bangkok: Dept. of Library Science, Chulalongkorn University, 1981.

Compilation of Publications in English on the Chakri Dynasty. Bangkok: Office of His Majesty's Principal Private Secretary, 1983.

Corruption: An Annotated Bibliography. Bangkok: Chulalongkorn University, Social Research Institute, 1983.

Environmental Pollution: An Annotated Bibliography. Bangkok: Chulalongkorn University, Social Research Institute, 1982.

Gehan Wijeyewardene and Ann Buller. *Bibliography: The First 1,500 Hundred Entries*. Canberra, Australia: Research School of Pacific Studies, Australian National University, 1989.

Hart, Donn Vorhis. *Thailand: An Annotated Bibliography of Bibliographies*. DeKalb, IL: Center for Southeast Asian Studies, Northern Illinois University, 1977.

Housing: An Annotated Bibliography. Bangkok: Chulalongkorn University, Social Research Institute, 1982.

Hughes, Phlip J. *Thai Culture, Values, and Religion: An Annotated Bibliography of English Language Materials*. Rev. ed. Chiang Mai, Thailand: Payap College, 1982.

Investment: An Annotated Bibliography. Bangkok: Chulalongkorn University, Social Research Institute, 1982.

Ishii, Yoneo. *A Selected Thai Bibliography on the Reign of King Chulalongkorn*. Osaka, Japan: Thai Section, Osaka University of Foreign Studies, 1972.

Lan Na Literature: Catalogue of Secular Titles among the 3,700 Palm-Leaf Manuscripts Borrowed from Wats throughout Northern Thailand and Preserved on Microfilm at the Social Research

Institute of Chiang Mai University. Bangkok: Distributed by the Chulalongkorn University Bookstore, 1986.

Mabbett, Ian W. *Early Thai History: A Select Bibliography.* Melbourne, Australia: Monash University, 1978.

Migration: An Annotated Bibliography. Bangkok: Chulalongkorn University, Social Research Institute, 1983.

Padmadin, Sanan. *Mass Communication in Thailand: An Annotated Bibliography.* Singapore: Asian Mass Communication Research and Information Centre, 1983.

Religious Traditions among Tai Ethnic Groups: Selected Bibliography. Ayutthaya, Thailand: Ayutthaya Historical Study Centre, 1991.

Slum: An Annotated Bibliography. Bangkok: Chulalongkorn University, Social Research Institute, 1982.

Social Values: An Annotated Bibliography. Bangkok: Chulalongkorn University, Social Research Institute, 1982.

Srisunan Narintharangkura Na Ayudha. *Thai Fisheries Bibliography, 1981-1985.* Bangkok: Southeast Asian Fisheries Development Center in Cooperation with the International Development Research Center, 1986.

The Thai (Gedney) Collection of the University of Michigan Library: A Union Catalogue. Ann Arbor, MI: University of Michigan Library, 1987.

Thailand: An Annotated Bibliography on Local and Regional Development. Tokyo: United Nations Centre for Regional Development, 1982.

Thapa, Gopal B. *Land Settlement through the Kaleidoscope: Annotated Bibliography of Asian Experiences.* Bangkok: Asian Institute of Technology, 1986.

Union Catalog of Books in University Libraries in Thailand. Bangkok: The Library, 1982.

Union Catalog of the Chulalongkorn University Libraries, 1980. Bangkok: The Library, 1981.

Union List of Serials in Thailand. 3rd ed. Bangkok: Ministry of University Affairs, 1987.

Watts, Michael. *Thailand.* Denver, CO: Clio Press, 1986.

Working Bibliography on Gender and Development in Thailand. North York, Canada: Women in Development Consortium in Thailand and Thai Studies Project, 1988.

B. Statistics

1980 Population & Housing Census, Whole Kingdom. Bangkok: National Statistical Office, 1980.

1983 Intercensal Survey of Agriculture, Changwat Chai Nat. Bangkok: National Statistical Office, 1984.

1983 Intercensal Survey of Agriculture, Changwat Sing Buri. Bangkok: National Statistical Office, 1984.

1983 Intercensal Survey of Agriculture, Phra Nakhon Sit Ayutthaya. Bangkok: National Statistical Office, 1984.

1983 Intercensal Survey of Agriculture, Whole Kingdom. Bangkok: National Statistical Office, 1984.

1990 Population and Housing Census: Preliminary Report. Bangkok: National Statistical Office, 1990.

1990 Population and Housing Census. 73 v. Bangkok: National Statistical Office, 1992.

Census 1970. Bangkok: National Statistical Office, 1977.

The Children and Youth Survey, 1982. Bangkok: National Statistical Office, 1985.

Chintana Pejaranonda and Fred Arnold. *Census Subject Reports.* 2 v. Bangkok: National Statistical Office, 1981.

Chiswick, Carmel Ullman. *Statistical Data for Thailand: Surveys of Households and Individuals.* Chicago, IL: University of Illinois at Chicago, 1987.

Data Analysis on Population and Family Health. Bangkok: Sun Pramuan Khaosan Kananamai Khropkhrua, 1990.

Data Analysis on Women and Health. Bangkok: Sun Pramuan Khaosan Kananamai Khropkhrua, 1990.

Employment and Unemployment. Survey no. 2. Bangkok: Sathaban Sapphayakon Manut, Mahawitthayalai Thammasat, 1990.

A Glance at Educational Statistics during the Fifth Plan (1982-1986). Bangkok: Office of the National Education Commission, 1988.

Laing, John E. *Findings on Contraceptive Use Effectiveness from the 1989 Thailand Demographic and Health Survey.* Honolulu, HI: East-West Center, 1992.

Mineral Statistics of Thailand. Bangkok: Dept. of Mineral Resources, 1981.

The Morbidity and Mortality Differentials: ASEAN Population Programme Phase III, Thailand: A Report on the Secondary Data Analysis. Bangkok: Institute for Population and Social Research, Mahidol University, 1985.

Public Health Statistics, A.D. 1977-1981. Bangkok: Krasuang Satharanasuk, 1983.

Report: The Survey of Hill Tribe Population, 1987. Nan Province. Bangkok: National Statistical Office, 1988.

Bibliography of Thailand / 207

Report: The Survey of Population Change, 1989. Bangkok: National Statistical Office, 1990.

Report of the 1986 Household Socio-Economic Survey, Greater Bangkok Metropolitan Area. Bangkok: National Statistical Office, 1988.

Report of the Mass Media Survey (Radio and Television), 1984. Bangkok: National Statistical Office, 1987.

Report on Education Statistics 1984. Bangkok: National Statistical Office, 1987.

Report on Employment and Unemployment of Migrants to the Bangkok Metropolis, the Vicinity of Bangkok Metropolis and the Regional Urban Growth Centre. Bangkok: National Statistical Office, 1988.

Social Indicators in 10 Years and Social Indicators, 1987. Bangkok: National Statistical Office, 1989.

Statistical Handbook of Thailand. Bangkok: National Statistical Office, 1993.

Statistical Reports of Region (in Brief). Bangkok: National Statistical Office, 1990.

Statistical Yearbook: Thailand. Bangkok: National Statistical Office, 1994.

Statistics on Women and Health, Thailand. Bangkok: Kananamai Khropkhrua, Kong Anamai Khropkhrua, 1990.

Thailand Economic Information Kit. Bangkok: Thailand Development Research Institute Foundation, 1990.

Thailand in Figures 1990. Bangkok: Tera International, 1990.

Uraiwan Kanungsukkasem. *Comparative Population and Health Statistics for Thailand: Regional and Provincial Levels.* Bangkok:

Institute of Population and Social Research, Mahidol University, 1983.

C. Description and Travel

Bock, Carl Alfred. *Temples and Elephants: The Narrative of a Journey of Exploration through Upper Siam and Lao.* Bangkok: White Orchid Press, 1985.

Campbell, Reginald. *Teak-Wallah: The Adventures of a Young Englishman in Thailand in the 1920s.* Singapore: OUP, 1986.

Carroz, Jean. *The Fascination of Bangkok.* Bangkok: White Lotus, 1985.

Cummings, Joe. *Thailand: A Travel Survival Kit.* 2nd ed. South Yarra, Victoria, Australia: Lonely Planet Publications, 1984.

An Englishman's Siamese Journals, 1890-1893. Bangkok: Siam Media International Books, 1983.

Finlayson, George. *The Mission to Siam and Hue, 1821-1822.* Singapore: OUP, 1988.

Garrett, Stephen A. *Bangkok Journal: A Fulbright Year in Thailand.* Carbondale, IL: Southern Illinois University Press, 1986.

Hoskin, John. *Chiang Mai: The Tranquil Valley.* Bangkok: Artasia Press, 1989.

Krannich, Ronald L. *Shopping in Exotic Thailand.* Manassas, VA: Impact Publications, 1989.

Mortlock, Elizabeth. *At Home in Thailand: A Guide for Americans Living with Thai Families.* Bangkok: USIS, 1987.

Nicholl, Charles. *Borderlines: A Journey in Thailand and Burma.* London: Secker & Warburg, 1988.

Parkes, Carl. *Thailand Handbook.* Chico, CA: Moon Publications, 1992.

Raemakers, Jeremy. *The Singing Ape: A Journey to the Jungles of Thailand.* Bangkok: The Siam Society, 1990.

Reid, Daniel. *Bangkok.* Hong Kong: The Guidebook, 1990.

Siam: 16th and Early 17th Century Accounts Published in the Early 17th Century and in 1617. Bangkok: Chalermnit Press, 1968.

Smith, Malcolm Arthur. *A Physician at the Court of Siam.* Kuala Lumpur, Malaysia: OUP, 1982.

Smithies, Michael. *Old Bangkok.* Singapore: OUP, 1986.

Terwiel, B. J. *Through Travellers' Eyes: An Approach to Early Nineteenth-Century Thai History.* Bangkok: Editions Duang Kamol, 1989.

Thailand at Cost: A Traveller's Guide. Bedford, U.K.: Little Hills Press, 1989.

Thailand from the Air. Bangkok: Sparkle Media, 1984.

Van Beek, Steve. *Bangkok.* Singapore: APA Publications, 1988.

Warren, William. *Thailand: A View from Above.* Singapore: Times Editions, 1986.

Winterton, Bradley. *The Insider's Guide to Thailand.* Edison, NJ: Hunter, 1989.

D. Guidebooks and Directories

Brown, Robin. *A Guide to Buying Antiques, Arts & Crafts in Thailand: Including Hill Tribe, Burmese, Cambodian and Laotian Artefacts.* Singapore: Times Books International, 1989.

Business Visitors' Guide for Tourists, Exporters and Importers. Bangkok: Intertrade Publications, 1985.

Directory of Science and Technology Services in Thailand. Bangkok: Thailand Development Research Institute Foundation, 1990.

The Federation of Thai Industries Directory. Bangkok: Business Thailand, 1990.

Fodor's Thailand. New York, NY: Fodor's, 1991.

Frommer's Comprehensive Travel Guide. Thailand '92-93. New York, NY: Prentice-Hall Travel, 1992.

Khon Khaen Guide & Directory. Khon Khaen, Thailand: s.n., 1991.

Kornfield, Jack. *A Brief Guide to Meditation Temples of Thailand.* Bangkok: Thaikasem Press, 1972.

Nidda Hongvivat, ed. *Ayutthaya: The Former Thai Capital.* Bangkok: Muang Boran, 1980.

____. *Chiangmai: The Cultural Center of the North.* Bangkok: Muang Boran, 1980.

Official Listings, Thailand 1991. Bangkok: Tawana Holdings, 1991.

The Siam Directory 1990/92: The Books of Facts & Figures. Bangkok: Tawana Publishing, 1991.

A Survey of Thai Arts and Architectural Attractions: A Manual for Tourist Guides. Bangkok: Faculty of Arts, Chulalongkorn University, 1987.

Thailand Company Information. Bangkok: A. R. Business Consultant, 1990.

Thailand Export-Import Monitor, 1989-1990. Bangkok: Thera International, 1989.

Thailand, Guide to Business and Investment. Brookfield, VT: Gower, 1986.

Thailand Profiles, 1990/91. Bangkok: Tawana Publishing, 1990.

Trade Directory 1990/1991. Bangkok: Board of Trade of Thailand, 1990.

E. Biographies

Bunchana Atthakor's Memoirs: Life and Dreams, tr. by Jotika Savanananda. Bangkok: B.A. Foundation for Education and Research, 1987.

Davis, Reginald. *The Royal Family of Thailand.* London: Nicholas Publications, 1981.

His Majesty the King. Bangkok: Bangkok Post/World, 1981.

Hoskin, John. *Ten Contemporary Thai Artists.* Bangkok: Graphis, 1984.

Jackson, Peter A. *Buddhadasa: A Buddhist Thinker for the Modern World.* Bangkok: The Siam Society, 1988.

Kukrit Pramoj, M. R. *M. R. Kukrit Pramoj, His Wit and Wisdom: Writings, Speeches and Interviews,* compiled by Vilas Manival, ed. by Steve Van Beek. Bangkok: Editions Duang Kamol, 1983.

Somboon Suksamran. *Military Elite in Thai Politics: Brief Biographical Data on the Officers in the Thai Legislature.* Singapore: ISAS, 1984.

Thanin Kraiwichian. *His Majesty King Bhumibol Adulyadej, Compassionate Monarch of Thailand.* Bangkok: Katavethin Foundation, 1982.

Who's Who in Petroleum and Petrochemical Industries of Thailand. 2nd ed. Bangkok: Petroleum Institute of Thailand, 1990.

Who's Who in Thailand 1986. Bangkok: Advanced Pub., 1986.

2. HISTORY

A. General

Chula Chakrabonse, Prince. *Lords of Life: A History of the Kings of Thailand.* 3rd. rev. ed. Bangkok: D D Books, 1982.

Early Accounts of Phetchaburi. Bangkok: The Siam Society, 1987.

Gosling, Betty. *Sukhothai: Its History, Culture, and Art.* Singapore: OUP, 1991.

Hall, E. R. *The Burma-Thailand Railway of Death.* Armadale, Victoria, Australia: Graphic Books, 1981.

Haseman, John B. *The Thai Resistance Movement during the Second World War.* DeKalb, IL: Center for Southeast Asian Studies, Northern Illinois University, 1978.

How Thailand Lost Her Territories to France. Bangkok: Dept. of Publicity, 1940.

Jones, Robert B. *Thai Titles and Ranks, Including a Translation of Traditions of Royal Lineage in Siam by King Chulalongkorn.* Ithaca, NY: Cornell University Press, 1971.

Jumsai, M. L. Manich. *History of Thailand & Cambodia: From the Days of Angkor to the Present.* Bangkok: Chalermnit Press, 1970.

LePoer, Barbara Leitch, ed. *Thailand: A Country Study.* 6th ed. Washington, D.C.: Dept. of the Army, 1989.

Keyes, Charles F., W. J. Klausner and Sulak Sivaraksa. *Phya Anuman Rajadhon: A Reminiscence.* Bangkok: Satirakases-Nagapradita Foundation, 1973.

Laugesen, Mary. *Scandinavians in Siam*. Bangkok: Skaninavisk Samfund Siam, 1980.

Leeuw, A. and David K. Wyatt. *Hikayat Patani: The Story of Patani*. 2 v. The Hague, The Netherlands: Martinus Nijhoff, 1970.

Manas Chitakasem and Andrew Turton, eds. *Thai Constructions of Knowledge*. London: School of Oriental and African Studies, University of London, 1991.

Mulder, Niels. *Java-Thailand: A Comparative Perspective*. Yogyakarta, Indonesia: Gadjah Mada University Press, 1983.

Proceedings of the 4th International Conference on Thai Studies, 11-13 May, 1990. Kunming, China: ISAS, 1990.

Proceedings of the International Conference on Thai Studies, The Australian National University, Canberra, 3-6 July, 1987. Canberra, Australia: The University, 1987.

Rong Syamananda. *A History of Thailand*. 7th ed. Bangkok: Thai Watana Panich, 1990.

Syukri, Ibrahim. *History of the Malay Kingdom of Patani*, tr. by Conner Bailey and John N. Miksic. Athens, OH: Center for International Studies, Ohio University, 1985.

Thailand: Country File. 2 v. Kuala Lumpur, Malaysia: Asian and Pacific Development Center, 1993.

Thailand and the Islamic World. Krungthep, Thailand: War Veterans Organization of Thailand, 1987.

Traditional and Changing Thai World View. Bangkok: Chulalongkorn University Social Research Institute, 1985.

Vliet, Jeremias van. *The Short History of the Kings of Siam*. Bangkok: The Siam Society, 1975.

Wilson, Constance M. *Thailand: A Handbook of Historical Statistics*. Boston, MA: G. K. Hall, 1983.

Wilson, Constance M. and Lucien M. Hanks. *The Burma-Thailand Frontier over Sixteen Decades: Three Descriptive Documents*. Athens, OH: Ohio University, Center for International Studies, 1985.

Wyatt, David K. *Thailand: A Short History*. New Haven, CT: Yale University Press, 1984.

Yoshihara, Kunio, ed. *Japan in Thailand*. Kuala Lumpur, Malaysia: Falcon Press, 1990.

Yuting, Du and Chen Lufan. "Did Kublai Khan's Conquest of the Dali Kingdom Give Rise to the Mass Migration of the Thai People to the South?" *Journal of the Siam Society* 77, 1 (1989): 33-41.

B. TO 1782

Anderson, John. *English Intercourse with Siam in the 17th Century*. London: Kegan-Paul, 1890.

Beze, Claude de. *1688 Revolution in Siam: The Memoir of Father de Beze, s.j.*, tr. by E.W. Hutchinson. Bangkok: White Lotus, 1990.

Charnvit Kasetsiri. *The Rise of Ayudhya: A History of Siam in the Fourteenth and Fifteenth Centuries*. New York, NY: OUP, 1976.

Gervaise, Nicolas. *The Natural and Political History of the Kingdom of Siam*, tr. and ed. by John Villiers. Bangkok: White Lotus, 1989.

History of Siam in the Reign of H.M Somdetch Pra Narai and Other Kings, tr. from the French by Samuel J. Smith. Bangkok: S. J. Smith, 1880.

Loubere, Simon de la. *A New Historical Relation of the Kingdom of Siam*. 2 v. Kuala Lumpur, Malaysia: OUP, 1969

Luce, Gordon H. "The Early Syam in Burma's History." *Journal of the Siam Society* 46, 2 (Nov. 1958): 123-214 & 47, 1 (June 1959): 59-101.

The Ram Khamhaeng Controversy: Collected Papers. Bangkok: The Siam Society, 1991.

Smith, Ronald Bishop. *Siam or the History of the Thais from Earliest Times to 1569 A.D.* 2 v. Bethesda, MD: Decatur Press, 1966.

Sunait Chutintaranond. "Cakravartin: Ideology, Reason, and Manifestation of Siamese and Burmese Kings in Traditional Warfare (1538-1854)." *Crossroads* 4, 1 (Fall 1988): 46-56.

____. "'Mandala,' 'Segmentary State' and Politics of Centralization in Medieval Ayudhya." *Journal of the Siam Society* 78, 1 (1990): 88-100.

C. 1782-20th Century

Apha Phamonbut. *The Chakri Dynasty*. Bangkok: Abha Bhamorabutr, 1983.

Batson, Benjamin A. *The End of the Absolute Monarchy in Siam*. New York, NY: OUP, 1984.

Bhumibol Adulyadej, King of Thailand. *The Royal Speeches and Address of His Majesty King Bhumibol Adulyadej of Thailand*. Bangkok: Marketing Operation Office of The Royal Initiation Projects, 1984.

Catalyst for Change: Uprising in May. Bangkok: Post Publishing, 1992.

The Chakri Monarchs and the Thai People: A Special Relationship. Bangkok: National Identity Board, 1984.

Corfield, Justin, ed. *Rama III and the Siamese Expedition to Kedah in 1839, the Dispatches of Luang Udomsombat,* tr. by Cyril Skinner. Clayton, Victoria, Australia: Center of Southeast Asian Studies, Monash University, 1993.

Direck Jayanama. *Siam and World War II,* ed. by Jane Godfrey Keyes. Bangkok: Social Science Association of Thailand Press, 1978.

Evers, Hans Dieter. "Trade and State Formation: Siam in the Early Bangkok Period." *Modern Asian Studies* 21 (Oct. 1987): 751-771.

Hong, Lysa. *Thailand in the Nineteenth Century: Evolution of the Economy and Society.* Singapore: ISAS, 1984.

Jumsai, M.L. Manich. *Foreign Records of the Bangkok Period up to A.D. 1932.* Bangkok: Office of the Prime Minister, 1982.

Khoo Kay Kim. "Patani During the Turn of the 20th Century: A Malayan Perception." *Journal of The Malaysian Branch of Royal Asiatic Society* 61, 1 (1988): 87-116.

Likhit Dhiravegin. *The Meiji Restoration, 1868-1912, and the Chakkri Reformation, 1868-1910: A Comparative Perspective.* Bangkok: Research Center of the Faculty of Political Science, Thammasat University, 1984.

Mongkut, King of Siam. *A King of Siam Speaks.* Bangkok: Siam Society, 1987.

Prachoom Chomchai, ed. *Chulalongkorn the Great.* Tokyo: Centre for East Asian Cultural Studies, 1965.

Rabidhadana, Akin. *The Organization of Thai Society in the Early Bangkok Period, 1782-1863.* Ithaca, NY: SEAP, Cornell University, 1969.

Sivaram, M. *The New Siam in the Making: A Survey of the Political Transition in Siam, 1932-1936.* Bangkok: Stationers Printing Press, 1936.

Sorasak Ngamkhachonkunlakit. *The Free Thai Movement and Thailand's Internal Political Conflicts, 1938-1949.* Bangkok: Institute of Asian Studies, Chulalongkorn University, 1991.

Stowe, Judith A. *Siam Becomes Thailand: A Story of Intrigue.* London: Hurst, 1991.

Terwiel, B. J. *A History of Modern Thailand, 1767-1942.* St. Lucia, Australia: University of Queensland Press, 1983.

Thailand in the 90s. Rev. ed. Bangkok: National Identity Office, 1991.

Thipakorawong, Chao Phraya. *The Dynastic Chronicle, Bangkok Era, the Fourth Reign B.E. 2394-2411 (1851-1868)* 5 v., tr. by Chadin and E. Thadeus Flood. Tokyo: Centre for Asian Cultural Studies, 1965-74.

Tips, Walter E. J. *Gustave Rolin-Jaequemyns (Chao Phraya Aphai Raja) and the Belgian Advisers in Siam (1892-1902): An Overview of Little-Known Documents Concerning the Chakri Reformation Era.* Bangkok: Published by the Author, 1992.

Two Views of Siam on the Eve of the Chakri Reformation. Gartmore, Scotland: Kiscadale, 1989.

Vella, Walter Francis. *Siam under Rama III, 1824-1851.* Locust Valley, NY: J. J. Augustin, 1957.

Vella, Walter Francis and Dorothy B. *Chaiyo! King Vajiravudh and the Development of Thai Nationalism.* Honolulu, HI: University Press of Hawaii, 1978.

Vichitvong Na Pombhejara. *Pridi Banomyong and the Making of Thailand's Modern History*. Bangkok: Printed by Siriyod Printing, 1983.

Wenk, Klaus. *The Restoration of Thailand Under Rama I, 1782-1809*. Tucson, AZ: University of Arizona Press, 1968.

Wright, Joseph J. *The Balancing Act: A History of Modern Thailand*. Bangkok: Asia Books, 1991.

Wyatt, David K. "The Abridged Royal Chronicle of Ayudhya of Prince Paramanuchitchinorot." *Journal of the Siam Society* 61, 1 (Jan. 1973) 25-50.

____. "The Bangkok Monarchy and Thai History." *Crossroads* 2, 2 (1985): 131-139.

3. POLITICS AND GOVERNMENT

A. General

Bartak, Elinor. *The Student Movement in Thailand 1970-1976*. Clayton, Victoria, Australia: Monash University, 1993.

Chaichana Ingavata. "Community Development and Local-Level Democracy in Thailand: The Role of *Tambol* Councils." *Sojourn* 5, 1 (Feb. 1990): 113-143.

Chakrit Noranitipadungkarn. *Elites, Power Structures and Politics in Thai Communities*. Bangkok: National Institute of Development Administration, 1981.

Country Report: Thailand, Burma. London: The Economist Intelligence Unit, 1992.

Guyot, James. *Between Two Coups: The Continuing Institutionalization of Democracy in Thailand*. Madison, WI:

Center for Southeast Asian Studies, University of Wisconsin-Madison, 1989.

Hewison, Kevin. "Of Regimes, States and Pluralities: Thai Politics Enters the 1990s." In *Southeast Asia in the 1990s: Authoritarianism, Democracy and Capitalism*, ed. by Kevin Hewison, Richard Robinson and Garry Rodan. London: Allen & Unwin, 1993: 161-189.

Hirsch, Philip and Larry Lohmann. "Contemporary Politics of Environment in Thailand." *Asian Survey* 29, 4 (1989): 439-451.

Jackson, Peter A., ed. *The May 1992 Crisis in Thailand: Background and Aftermath*. Canberra, Australia: National Thai Studies Center, Australia National University, 1993.

Likhit Dhiravegin. *Nationalism and the State in Thailand*. Bangkok: Faculty of Political Science, Thammasat University, 1985.

____. *The Postwar Thai Politics*. Bangkok: Faculty of Political Science, Thammasat University, 1986.

Merely the Truth - Distress, Painful and the Challenging Future. Bangkok: Student Federation of Thailand (SFT) Movement for Democracy and Civil Society (MODEM), 1992.

Moller, Kay. *The Thailand Communist Movement and China-Vietnam Competition in Asia*. Cologne, Germany: Federal Institute for Asian and International Studies, 1982.

Morell, David L. and Chai-Anan Samudivanija. *Political Conflict in Thailand: Reform, Reaction, Revolution*. Cambridge, MA: Delgeschlager, Gunn & Hain, 1981.

Murashima, Eiji, Nakharin Mektrairat and Somkiat Wanthana. *The Making of Modern Thai Political Parties*. Tokyo: Institute of Developing Economies, 1991.

Murray, David. *The Coup d'Etat in Thailand, 23 February, 1991: Just Another Coup?* Nedlands, Australia: Indian Ocean Centre for Peace Studies, 1991.

Neher, Clark D. and Budsayamat Bunjaipet. "Political Interaction in Northern Thailand." *Crossroads* 4, 2 (1989): 35-52.

Reynolds, Craig J., ed. *National Identity and Its Defenders: Thailand, 1939-1989.* Clayton, Victoria, Australia: Center of Southeast Asian Studies, Monash University, 1991.

The September 9, 1985 Coup Memoirs. Bangkok: Royal Thai Army, 1986.

Somboon Suksamran. *Buddhism and Politics in Thailand: A Study of Socio-Political Change and Political Activism of the Thai Sangha.* Singapore: ISAS, 1982.

Somsakdi Xuto, ed. *Government and Politics of Thailand.* Singapore: OUP, 1987.

Tan Lian Choo. "Personality Politics in Thailand." In *Southeast Asian Affairs 1991.* Singapore: ISAS, 1991: 279-297.

Tapp, Nicholas. "Political Participation among the Hmong of Thailand." *Journal of the Siam Society* 76 (1988): 145-161.

Wedel, Yuangrat and Paul Wedel. *Radical Thought, Thai Mind: the Development of Revolutionary Ideas in Thailand.* Bangkok: Assumption Business Administration College, 1987.

B. Government and Administration

Bunnag, Tej. *The Provincial Administration of Siam, 1892-1915: The Ministry of the Interior under Prince Damrong Rajanubhab.* New York, NY: OUP, 1977.

Choo, Tan Lian. "Personality Politics in Thailand." In *Southeast Asian Affairs 1991.* Singapore: ISAS, 1991: 279-297.

Girling, John L. S. *Thailand: Society and Politics.* Ithaca, NY: Cornell University Press, 1981.

Jackson, Peter A. *Thai Government Cabinets: April, June and September 1992.* Canberra, Australia: National Thai Studies Center, Australian National University, 1993.

Likhit Dhiravegin. *Demi Democracy: The Evolution of the Thai Political System.* Singapore: Times Academic Press, 1992.

Murashima, Eiji. "The Origin of Modern Official State Ideology in Thailand." *Journal of Southeast Asian Studies* 19, 1 (1988): 80-96.

Neher, Clark D. "Political Development and Political Participation in Thailand." In *Asia, Case Studies in the Social Sciences: A Guide for Teaching,* ed. by Myron L. Cohen. Armonk, NY: M.E. Sharpe, 1992: 1415-1426.

Prizzia, Ross. *Thailand in Transition: The Role of Oppositional Forces.* Honolulu, HI: University of Hawaii Press, 1985.

Saneh Chamarik. *Problems of Development in Thai Political Setting.* Bangkok: Thai Khadi Research Institute, Thammasat University, 1983.

Suchitra Punyaratabandhu-Bhakdi. "Structural Problems in the Governance of Bangkok." *Crossroads* 2, 2 (1985): 113-127.

Surin Maisridrod. "Thailand 1992: Repression and Return of Democracy." In *Southeast Asian Affairs 1993.* Singapore: ISAS, 1993: 327-349.

____. *Thailand's Two General Elections in 1992: Democracy Sustained.* Singapore: ISAS, 1992.

Tanet Charoenmuang. "General Prem's Eight-Year Premiership and Its Implications for Thai Democracy." *Asian Profile* 16, 6 (1988): 501-514.

"Thailand." In *Military Powers Encyclopedia: The South-East-Asia.* Paris, France: Société IC (Compact, International Company), 1991.

Thailand on the Move: Stumbling Blocks and Breakthroughs. Bangkok: Thai University Research Association, 1990.

Tin Prachyapruit. *Thailand's Elite Civil Servants and Their Development-Orientedness: An Empirical Test of National Data.* Bangkok: Chulalongkorn University Social Research Institute, 1986.

Wales, Horace Geoffrey Quaritch. *Ancient Siamese Government and Administration.* New York, NY: Paragon, 1965.

Weatherbee, Donald E. "Thailand in 1989: Democracy Ascendant in the Golden Peninsula." In *Southeast Asian Affairs 1990.* Singapore: ISAS, 1990: 337-359.

C. Constitution and Law

Acts on the Administration of the Buddhist Order of Sangha. Bangkok: Mahamakuta Educational Council, The Buddhist University, 1963.

Archer, R. W. *Land Subdivision in Thailand: A Translation of the Land Subdivision Regulations and the Guidelines for Relaxing the Regulations.* Bangkok: Asian Institute of Technology, 1988.

Engel, David M. *Law and Kingship in Thailand during the Reign of King Chulalongkorn.* Ann Arbor, MI: Center for South and Southeast Asian Studies, University of Michigan, 1975.

____. "Litigation across Space and Time: Courts, Conflict, and Social Change (Chiang Mai, Thailand)." *Law & Society Review* 24, 2 (1990): 333-344.

Kachadpai Burusapatana. "Thai Government Policies on Minorities." *Southeast Asian Journal of Social Science* 16, 2 (1988): 47-60.

Mya Saw Shin. *The Constitutions of Thailand*. Washington, D.C.: Law Library, Library of Congress, 1981.

Surakiart Sathirathai. *Thailand and International Trade Law*. Bangkok: Graduate Institute of Business Administration of Chulalongkorn University, 1987.

Tanham, George Kilpatrick. *Trial in Thailand*. New York, NY: Crane, Russak, 1974.

Vickery, Michael. "Prolegomena to Methods for Using the Ayutthayan Laws as Historical Source Material." *Journal of the Siam Society* 72 (1984): 37-58.

D. Armed Forces

Ananya Bhuchongkul. "Thailand 1991: The Return of the Military." In *Southeast Asian Affairs 1992*. Singapore: ISAS, 1992: 313-333.

Chai-Anan Samudavanija and Suchit Bunbongkarn. "Thailand." In *Military-Civilian Relations in South-East Asia*, ed. by Zakaria Haji Ahmad and Harold Crouch. Singapore: OUP, 1985: 78-156.

Chai-Anan Samudavanija. *The Thai Young Turks*. Singapore: ISAS, 1982.

Gill, R. Bates. "China Looks to Thailand: Exporting Arms, Exporting Influence." *Asian Survey* 31 (June 1991): 526-539.

Hagelin, Bjorn. "Military Dependency: Thailand and the Philippines." *Journal of Peace Research* 25 (Dec. 1988): 431-448.

Neher, Clark D. "Political Succession in Thailand." *Asian Survey* 32 (July 1992): 585-605.

____. *Southeast Asia in the New International Era.* Boulder, CO: Westview Press, 1991.

Suchit Bunbongkarn. *The Military in Thai Politics, 1981-1986.* Singapore: ISAS, 1987.

____. "The Thai Military in the 1990s: A Declining Political Force?" In *The Military in Politics: Southeast Asian Experiences*, ed. by Wolfgang S. Heinz, Werner Pfennig and Victor T. King. Hull, U.K.: Center for South-East Asian Studies, University of Hull, 1990: 106-122.

____. "Thailand in 1991: Coping with Military Guardianship (Part of a Symposium on: Asia in 1991)." *Asian Survey* 32 (Feb. 1992): 131-139.

Thompson, James Plyler. *The Thai Military: An Analysis of Its Role in the Thai Nation.* Claremont, CA: Thompson, 1974.

E. International Relations

1. General

Aldrich, Richard. "A Question of Expediency: Britain, the United States and Thailand, 1941-42." *Journal of Southeast Asian Studies* 19, 2 (1988): 209-244.

The Burney Papers. 5 v. Bangkok: Printed by the Committee of the Vajiranana National Library, 1910-1914.

Charivat Santaputra. *Thai Foreign Policy, 1932-1946.* Bangkok: Thai Khadi Research Institute, Thammasat University, 1985.

The Kampuchean Problem in Thai Perspective: Positions and Viewpoints Held by Foreign Ministry Officials and Thai Academics. Bangkok: Institute of Asian Studies, Chulalongkorn University, 1985.

Mayoury and Pheuiphanh Ngaosyvathn. "World Super Power and Regional Conflicts: The Triangular Game of Great Britain with Bangkok and the Lao during the Embassies of John Crawfurd (1821-1822) and of Henry Burney (1825-1826)." *Journal of the Siam Society* 76 (1988): 121-133.

Phuangkasem, Corrine. *Determinants of Thailand's Foreign Policy Behavior.* Bangkok: Faculty of Political Science, Thammasat University, 1986.

____. *An Empirical Analysis of Thailand's Foreign Policy Behavior, 1964-1977.* Bangkok: Faculty of Political Science, Thammasat University, 1982.

____. *Thailand's Foreign Relations, 1964-80.* Singapore: ISAS, 1984.

Sayre, Francis B., ed. *Siam: Treaties with Foreign Powers, 1920-27.* Bangkok: Royal Thai Government, 1928.

Thailand's Policy toward the Vietnam-Kampuchea Conflict: Issues on Thai National Interest, Policy Objectives and Alternatives on the Kampuchean Problem as Seen by the Thai Foreign Ministry Officials and the Academics. Bangkok: Institute of Asian Studies, Chulalongkorn University, 1985.

Wilson, H. E. "The Best of Friends: Britain, America and Thailand." *Canadian Journal of History* 25 (Apr. 1990): 61-83.

2. With China

Anuson Chinvanno. *Thailand's Policies towards China, 1949-54.* Oxford, U.K.: St. Anthony College, 1992.

Bartle, G. P. *Sir John Bowring and the Chinese and Siamese Commercial Treaties.* Bulletin of the John Rylands Library 44, 2 (Mar. 1962): 286-308.

China and Thailand, 1949-1983. Atlantic Highlands, NJ: Humanities Press, 1984.

Sukhumbhand Paribatra, M. R. *From Enmity to Alignment: Thailand's Evolving Relations with China.* Bangkok: Institute for Security and International Studies, Chulalongkorn University, 1987.

Wilson, David A. *China, Thailand and the Spirit of Bandung.* Santa Monica, CA: Rand, 1962.

3. With Great Britain

Isorn Pocmontri. *Negotiations between Britain and Siam on the Agreement for the Termination of Their State of War, 1945: An Instance of Intervention by the United States in British Foreign Policy.* Bangkok: Chulalongkorn University, Social Research Institute, 1982.

Jumsai, M. L. Manich. *King Mongkut of Thailand and the British: The Model of a Great Friendship.* Bangkok: Chalermnit Press, 1991.

Tarling, Nicholas. *The Fall of Imperial Britain in South-East Asia.* Singapore: OUP, 1993.

Xie, Shunyu. *Siam and the British, 1874-75: Sir Andrew Clarke and the Front Palace Crisis.* Bangkok: Thammasat University Press, 1988.

4. With Japan

International Dimensions of Japanese Financial Development: Implications for Asean and Thailand: Proceedings of an International Conference on Thai-Japan Relations. Bangkok: Faculty of Economics, Chulalongkorn University, 1991.

The Lion and the Mouse?: Japan, Asia and Thailand: Proceedings of an International Conference on Thai-Japan Relations. Bangkok: Faculty of Economics, Chulalongkorn University, 1986.

Proceedings on the Joint Symposium on Thai-Japanese Relations: Development and Future Prospect: January 15-16, 1987, at Japanese Studies Center, Rangsit Campus, Thammasat University. Bangkok: Office of Foreign Relations, Thammasat University, 1988.

Reynolds, E. Bruce. "Aftermath of Alliance: The Wartime Legacy in Thai-Japanese Relations." *Journal of Southeast Asian Studies* 21 (Mar. 1990): 66-87.

____. *Thailand and Japan's Southern Advance: 1940-1945.* New York, NY: St. Martin's Press, 1994.

Sulak Sivaraksa. *Thai Thoughts on the One Hundredth Anniversary of Diplomatic Relations between Japan and Siam.* Bangkok: Pridi Banomyong Institute, 1987.

Swan, William L. "Thai-Japan Monetary Relations at the Start of the Pacific War." *Modern Asian Studies* 23 (May 1989): 313-347.

____. "Thai-Japanese Relations at the Start of the Pacific War: New Insight into a Controversial Period." *Journal of Southeast Asian Studies* 18 (Sep. 1987): 270-293.

"Thailand." In *ASEAN-Japan Relations.* Bandung, Indonesia: Padjadjaran University, 1990: 136-223.

5. With the United States

A Century and a Half of Thai-American Relations. Bangkok: Chulalongkorn University, 1982.

Indorf, Hans H., ed. *Thai-American Relations in Contemporary Affairs.* Singapore: Executive Publications for Chulalongkorn University, 1982.

Jackson, Karl D. and Wiwat Mungkandi, eds. *United States-Thailand Relations.* Berkeley, CA: Institute of East Asian Studies, University of California at Berkeley, 1986.

Neher, Clark D. and Wiwat Mungkandi, eds. *U.S.-Thailand Relations in a New International Era.* Berkeley, CA: Institute of East Asian Studies, University of California at Berkeley, 1990.

Ramsay, Ansil and Wiwat Mungkandi, eds. *Thailand-U.S. Relations Changing Political, Strategic, and Economic Factors.* Berkeley, CA: Institute of East Asian Studies, University of California at Berkeley, 1988.

Randolph, R. Sean. *The United States and Thailand: Alliance Dynamics 1950-1985.* Berkeley, CA: Institute of East Asian Studies, University of California at Berkeley, 1986.

Songsri Foran. *Thai-British-American Relations during World War II and the Immediate Postwar Period, 1940-1946.* Bangkok: Thai Khadi Research Institute, Thammasat University, 1981.

Surachat Bamrungsuk. *United States Foreign Policy and Thai Military Rule, 1947-1977.* Bangkok: Editions Duang Kamol, 1988.

6. With Others

Facts and Data on Lao-Thai Relations in the Past Ten Years (1975-85). Vientiane, Laos: K.P.L. News Agency, 1985.

Kobkua Suwannathat-Pia. "The 1839-41 Settlements of Kedah: The Siamese Compromise." *Journal of the Malaysian Branch of Royal Asiatic Society* 59, 1 (1986): 33-48.

____. "The 1902 Siamese-Kelantan Treaty: An End to the Traditional Relations." *Journal of the Siam Society* 72 (1984): 95-139.

____. *Thai-Malay Relations: Traditional Intra-Regional Relations from the Seventeenth to the Early Twentieth Centuries.* Singapore: OUP, 1988.

Kosa Pan. *The Siamese Embassy to the Sun King: The Personal Memorials of Kosa Pan.* Bangkok: Editions Duang Kamol, 1990.

Ling, Trevor Onsward. *Buddhism, Imperialism and War: Burma and Thailand in Modern History.* London: G. Allen & Unwin, 1979.

Pheuiphanh Ngaosyvathn. "Thai-Lao Relations; a Lao View." *Asian Survey* 25 (Dec. 1985): 1242-1259.

Relations between Burma and Thailand, papers collected by King Bagyidaw of Burma. 2 v. Bangkok: The Siam Society, 1959.

Smithies, Michael, ed. *The Discourses at Versailles of the First Siamese Ambassadors to France, 1686-7: Together with the List of Their Presents to the Court: In the Original French Together with a Translation into English.* Bangkok: The Siam Society, 1986.

Thailand and Portugal: 470 Years of Friendship. Lisbon, Portugal: Calouste Gulbenkian Foundation, 1982.

Viraphol Sarasin. "Reflections on Thai-Lao Relations." *Asian Survey* 25 (Dec. 1985): 1260-1276.

F. Insurgency

Gawin Chutima. *The Rise and Fall of the Communist Party of Thailand (1973-1987)*. Canterbury, Kent, U.K.: Center of Southeast Asian Studies, University of Kent at Canterbury, 1990.

Kanok Wongtrangan. "The Revolutionary Strategy of the Communist Party of Thailand: Change and Persistence." In *Armed Communist Movements in Southeast Asia*, ed. by Lim Joo-Jock with Vani S. Aldershot. Singapore: ISAS, 1984: 131-185.

Kusuma Snitwongse. "Thai Government Responses to Armed Communist and Separatist Movements." In *Governments and Rebellions in Southeast Asia*, ed. by Chandran Jeshurun. Singapore: ISAS, 1985: 247-275.

Randolph, R. Sean and W. Scott Thompson. *Thai Insurgency: Contemporary Developments*. London: Sage, for the Center of Strategic and International Studies, 1981.

Saiyud Kerdphol. *The Struggle for Thailand: Counter-Insurgency, 1965-1985*. Bangkok: S. Research Center, 1986.

Wedel, Yuangrat. *The Thai Radicals and the Communist Party: Interaction of Ideology and Nationalism in the Forest, 1975-1980*. Singapore: Maruzen Asia, 1983.

G. Refugees

Brown, William A. "Indochinese Refugees and Relations with Thailand (Statement, February 24, 1988)." *Department of State Bulletin* 88 (May 1988): 37-41.

The CCSDPT Handbook: Refugee Services in Thailand. Bangkok: DuMaurier Associates International for the Committee, 1982.

Cambodians in Thailand: People on the Edge. Washington, D.C.: U.S. Committee for Refugees, 1985.

Indochinese Refugees: Asylum and Resettlement. Bangkok: Institute of Asian Studies, 1988.

Khmer Rouge Abuses Along the Thai-Cambodian Border. Washington, D.C.: Asia Watch Committee, 1989.

Long, Lynellyn D. *Ban Vinai: The Refugee Camp.* New York, NY: Columbia University Press, 1993.

Marisa Benyasut. *The Ecology of Phanat Nikhom Camp.* Bangkok: Institute of Asian Studies, Chulalongkorn University, 1990.

Reynell, Josephine. *Political Pawns: Refugees on the Thai-Kampuchean Border.* Oxford, U.K.: Refugee Studies Programme, 1989.

Seeking Shelter, Cambodians in Thailand: A Report on Human Rights. New York, NY: Lawyer's Committee for Human Rights, 1987.

Shawcross, William. *The Quality of Mercy: Cambodia, Holocaust and Modern Conscience.* London: André Deutsch, 1984.

Thailand, a First Asylum Country for Indochinese Refugees. Bangkok: Institute of Asian Studies, Chulalongkorn University, 1988.

4. ECONOMY

A. General

Albritton, Robert B. and Thosaporn Sirisumphand. "Trade-Offs between Military Spending and Spending for Economic Development in Thailand, 1961-1982." *Southeast Asian Journal of Social Science* 16, 1 (1988): 63-80.

Anek Laothamatas. *Business Associations and the New Political Economy of Thailand: From Bureaucratic Polity to Liberal Corporatism.* Boulder, CO: Westview Press, 1992.

Basic Needs and Government Policies in Thailand. Singapore: Maruzen Asia, 1982.

Brown, Ian. *The Elite and the Economy in Siam, 1890-1920.* Singapore: OUP, 1988.

Colombant, Laurent and Peter Trager. *The Capital Markets of Thailand and Hongkong: A Study of the Present Structures and an Analysis of the Post-1997 Era.* Thailand: s.n., 1989.

Cooper, Robert. *Thais Mean Business: The Foreign Businessman's Guide to Doing Business in Thailand.* Singapore: Times Books International, 1991.

Drud, Arne. *Thailand: An Analysis of Structural and Non-Structural Adjustments.* Washington, D.C.: World Bank, 1982.

Hewison, Kevin. *Power and Politics in Thailand: Essays in Political Economy.* Manila, Philippines: Journal of Contemporary Asia Publishers, 1989.

Korff, Rudiger. *Bangkok and Modernity.* Bangkok: Chulalongkorn University, Social Research Institute, 1989.

Napaporn Havanon. *The Impact of Family Size on Wealth Accumulation in Rural Thailand.* Bangkok: Institute of Population Studies, Chulalongkorn University, 1990.

Narongchai Akkharaserani. *Thailand and ASEAN Economic Cooperation.* Singapore: ISAS, 1980.

Pisit Leeahtam. *Thailand's Economic Adjustment: From Crisis to Double Digit Growth.* Bangkok: Dokya Pub., 1991.

Takashi Tomosugi. *A Structural Analysis of Thai Economic History: Case Study of a Northern Chao Phraya Village.* Tokyo: Institute of Development Economics, 1980.

Thailand: Income Growth and Poverty Alleviation. Washington, D.C.: World Bank, 1980.

Thailand: Prospects and Policies. London: Economist Intelligence Unit, 1984.

Warr, Peter G. *Thailand's Economic Miracle.* Canberra, Australia: National Thai Studies Center, Australia National University, 1993.

B. Agriculture and Land Policy

Agricultural Development Planning in Thailand. Ames, IA: Iowa State University Press, 1982.

Archer, R.W. *Directory of Urban Land Organizations in Thailand, 1990.* Bangkok: Asian Institute of Technology, 1990.

CARE - Mae Chaem Highlands Resource Integration Project: Some Guidelines on Baseline Surveys and Project Monitoring. Chiang Mai, Thailand: Payap Research and Development Institute, Payap University, 1991.

Chiengkal Witayakorn. "The Transformation of the Agrarian Structure of Central Thailand, 1960-1980." *Journal of Contemporary Asia* 13, 3 (1983): 340-360.

Chintana Chantachaeng. *Land Settlement Policy, Agricultural Income and Farm Organization in Thailand: A Case Study of Khuan Phumiphol and Lamnamnan Land Settlement Projects.* Kiel, Germany: Wissenschaftsverlag Vauk, 1988.

Chote Suvatti. *Fishes of Thailand.* Bangkok: Ratchabandit Sathan, 1981.

Dohrs, Larry S. *Commercial Agriculture and Equitable Development in Thailand: Success or Failure?* Ann Arbor, MI: Center for South and Southeast Asian Studies, University of Michigan, 1988.

Dowling, J. Malcolm. *Agricultural Supply Response of Some Major Crops in Thailand*. Bangkok: Thammasat University, Faculty of Economics, 1983.

Durrenberger, E. Paul and Nicola Tannenbaum. *Analytical Perspectives on Shan Agriculture and Village Economics.* New Haven, CT: Yale University Southeast Asia Studies, 1990.

Economic and Social Conditions among Farmers in Changwad Khonkaen. Bangkok: Faculty of Economics and Cooperative Science, Kasetsart University, 1983.

Feeny, David. *The Political Economy of Productivity: Thai Agricultural Development, 1880-1975*. Vancouver, Canada: University of British Columbia Press, 1982.

How to Develop the Small Farming Sector: The Case of Thailand. Bangkok: Faculty of Social Administration, Thammasat University, 1986.

The Impact of Agricultural Irrigation Projects on Fertility in Northeastern Thailand. Bangkok: Vichit Hattakorn Press, 1981.

Jaroon Soopharb. *An Analytical Survey of Thailand Fundamental Economic Organization Development and Agricultural-Industrial Potentials and Democratic Secularization*. Tokyo: Institute of Developing Economies, 1981.

Judd, Laurence C. *Chao Rai Thai: 1987 Update*. Bangkok: Suriyaban Pub., 1987.

Land Policy Study. Bangkok: Thailand Development Research Institute Foundation, 1990.

Murray, David. *Current Forest Land Use Conflicts in Thailand: No Room to Move?* Nedlands, Australia: The Indian Ocean Centre for Peace Studies, University of Western Australia, 1992.

Nicol, Kennth J., Somnut Striplung and Earl O. Heady, eds. *Agricultural Development Planning in Thailand*. Ames, IA: Iowa State University Press, 1982.

O'Reilly, F. D. *Thailand's Agriculture.* Budapest, Hungary: Akademiai Kiado, 1983.

Rice from Our Field. Bangkok: Catholic Council of Thailand for Development, 1990.

Seri Phongphit and Robert Bennoun, eds. *Turning Point of Thai Farmers*. Bangkok: Thai Institute for Rural Development, 1988.

Somphong Shevasunt and Cheeraporn Wuthiprapai. *Introduction of Multiple Cropping System to Farmers in Northern Thailand: Constraints and Strategies: A Report of Survey Data, 1978-1979*. Chiang Mai, Thailand: Social Research Institute, Chiang Mai University, 1981.

Suthad Setboonsarng. *The Structure, Conduct and Performance of the Seed Industry in Thailand*. Bangkok: Thailand Development Research Institute Foundation, 1991.

Tambon and Village Agricultural Systems in Northeast Thailand: Report of a Workshop Held at Khon Kaen University, February 22-26, 1982. Khon Kaen, Thailand: Faculty of Agriculture, Khon Kaen University, 1982.

"Thailand." In *Southeast Asia Rainforests: A Resource Guide & Directory*. San Francisco, CA: Rainforest Action Network, 1993: 39-73.

Thavivongse Sriburi. "Forest Resources Crisis in Thailand." In *Proceedings of the "Conference on Forest Resources Crisis in the Third World" 6-8 September 1986*. Penang, Malaysia: Sahabat Alam Malaysia, 1987: 93-129.

Theodore Panayotou, ed. *Food Policy Analysis in Thailand*. Bangkok: Agricultural Development Council, 1985.

Torell, Magnus. *Fisheries in Thailand: Geographical Studies about the Utilization of Resources in Semi-Enclosed Seas.* Goteborg, Sweden: Kulturgeografiska Institutionen, Goteborgs Universitet, 1984.

Vanpen Surarerks. *Historical Development and Management of Irrigation System[s] in Northern Thailand.* Chiang Mai, Thailand: Faculty of Social Sciences, Chiang Mai University, 1986.

Verhagen, Kuenrad. *Co-operation for Survival: An Analysis of an Experiment in Participating Research and Planning with Small Farmers in Sri Lanka and Thailand.* Amsterdam, The Netherlands: Royal Tropical Institute, 1984.

Water Management Conflicts in Northern Thai Irrigation Systems. Chiang Mai, Thailand: Faculty of Social Sciences, Chiang Mai University, 1980.

Wilson, Constance M. "The Thai Rice Trade and Government Revenues, 1885-1890." *Crossroads* 4, 2 (1989): 19-33.

Wolz, Axel. *Rural Employment under Closing Land Frontier: The Case of Selected Villages in Phitsanulok Province, Thailand.* Fort Lauderdale, FL: Breitenbach, 1987.

C. Finance and Banking

Anan Panyarachun. *Coping with the Recession in ASEAN: The Case of Thailand.* Singapore: Heineman Asia, 1988.

Brown, Ian. *The Creation of the Modern Ministry of Finance in Siam, 1885-1910.* London: Macmillan, 1992.

Hewison, Kevin. *Bankers and Bureaucrats: Capital and the Role of the State in Thailand.* New Haven, CT: Yale University Southeast Asia Studies, 1989.

____. "The Structure of Banking Capital in Thailand." *Southeast Asian Journal of Social Science* 16, 1 (1988): 81-91.

Kanitta M. Meesook. *Income and Price Policy.* Bangkok: Dept. of Economic Research, Bank of Thailand, 1980.

Robinson, David et al. *Thailand: Adjusting to Success: Current Policy Issues.* Washington, D.C.: International Monetary Fund, 1991.

The Role of Private Enterprise in Intra-ASEAN Trade and Investment: Proceedings of Conference Held in Chiang Mai, Thailand, 16-19 January, 1986. Chiang Mai, Thailand: ASEAN and Private Enterprise Studies, Chiang Mai University, 1986.

Ruangthong Chaiprasop. "The Thai Economy in 1987: An Overview." In *Southeast Asian Affairs 1988.* Singapore: ISAS, 1988: 287-294.

Setting up in Thailand: A Guide for Investors. Bangkok: BLC Pub., 1988.

Somjai Phagaphasvivat. *Thai Capital Market: Background, Development and Issues.* Bangkok: S.S. Consultant & Research, 1988.

Suehiro, Akira. *Capital Accumulation in Thailand, 1855-1985.* Tokyo: Centre for East Asian Cultural Studies, 1989.

____. "Bangkok Bank: Management Reforms on Thai Commercial Banks." *East Asian Cultural Studies* 28 (Mar. 1989): 101-126.

Tax and Investment Profile: Thailand. Bangkok: Jaiyos, 1982.

Thailand's Budget in Brief: Fiscal Year 1993. Bangkok: Bureau of the Budget, 1993.

D. Industry and Trade

Ayal, Eliezer B. "The Interpretation of the Economic Development of Thailand." *Crossroads* 2, 2 (1985): 103-112.

Bell, Peter. "Gender and Economic Development in Thailand." In *Gender and Development in Southeast Asia*, ed. by Penny and John Van Esterik. Ottawa, Canada: Canadian Council for Southeast Asian Studies, 1991: 61-82.

Borawornsri Somboopanya. *Thailand's Interzonal Input-Output Tables in Reference to East Thailand.* 3 v. Bangkok: UN Asian and Pacific Development Institute, 1980.

Bowie, Katherine A. "Unraveling the Myth of the Subsistence Economy: Textile Production in Nineteenth-Century Northern Thailand." *Journal of Asian Studies* 51 (Nov. 1992): 797-823.

Briggs, M. *The Climate for Private Business, Thailand.* Manila, Philippines: Asian Development Bank, 1985.

Business and Investment Environment in Thailand. Kuala Lumpur, Malaysia: Asian and Pacific Development Center, 1987.

Chira Hongladarom and Medhi Krongkaew, eds. *Comparative Development, Japan and Thailand.* Bangkok: Thammasat University Press, 1981.

Cushman, Jennifer W. *Family and State: The Formation of a Sino-Thai Tin-Mining Dynasty, 1797-1932,* ed. by Craig J. Reynolds. New York, NY: OUP, 1991.

Ekacit Wongsupbhasatigul. *Regional Industrial Development in Thailand: Theory and Practice.* Bangkok: Wacharin Pub., 1986.

Forbes, Andrew D. W. "The 'Cin-Ho' (Yunnanese Chinese) Caravan Trade with North Thailand during the Late Nineteenth and Early Twentieth Centuries." *Journal of Asian History* 21, 1 (1987): 1-47.

Friel, Patrick C. "The International Competitiveness of Thailand's Petrochemical Industry." *Journal of Southeast Asia Business* 7, 1 (1991): 1-38.

Gordon, Alec. "Production and Distribution of Smallholder's Economic Surplus: Thailand's Rubber Sector." *Journal of Contemporary Asia* 19, 1 (1989): 3-25.

Hillman, John. "The Freerider and the Cartel: Siam and the International Tin Restriction Agreements, 1931-1941." *Modern Asian Studies* 24 (May 1990): 297-321.

Hong, Lysa. "The Tax Farming System in the Early Bangkok Period." *Journal of Southeast Asian Studies* 14 (Sep. 1983): 379-399.

Ichikawa, Nobuko. "Geographic Implications of Foreign Investment in Thailand's Industrialization." *Southeast Asian Journal of Social Science* 19, 1 & 2 (1991): 64-81.

Industrial Restructuring Study for the National Economic & Social Development Board Final Report. Bangkok: Industrial Management, 1985.

Juanjai Ajanant, Supote Chunanuntathum and Sorrayuth Meenaphant. *Trade and Industrialization of Thailand.* Bangkok: Social Science Association of Thailand, 1986.

Kroekkiat Phiphatseritham. *Business Groups in Thailand.* Singapore: ISAS, 1983.

Likhit Dhiravegin. "Demi-Democracy and the Market Economy: The Case of Thailand." *Southeast Asian Journal of Social Science* 16, 1 (1988): 1-25.

Lumholdt, Niels and William Warren. *The History of Aviation in Thailand.* Hong Kong: Travel Publishing Asia, 1987.

Ministry of Industry, Activities & Services. Bangkok: The Ministry, 1990.

Narongchai Akrasanee and Atchana Wattananukit. "Changing Structure and Rising Dynamism in the Thai Economy." In *Southeast Asian Affairs 1990.* Singapore: ISAS, 1990: 360-382.

Odhnoff, Jan. *Industrialization and the Labour Process in Thailand: The Bangkok Area.* Stockholm, Sweden: Arbetslivscentrum, 1983.

Phisit Pakkasem. *Leading Issues in Thailand's Development Transformation, 1960-1990.* Bangkok: National Economic and Social Development Board, 1988.

Praiphol Koomsup. *Energy Demand Management Policies in Thailand.* Bangkok: Asian Development Bank, 1986.

Proceedings of the Conference on Challenge to Thai Exports: 23-24 September 1986, Bangkok. Bangkok: Thammasat University, 1987.

Ramsay, Ansil. "The Political Economy of Sugar in Thailand." *Pacific Affairs* 60, 2 (1987): 248-270.

Ruland, Jurgen. *Another Asian Miracle Economy in the Making?: Thailand's Prospects for Becoming a NIC in the Nineties.* Freiburg/Breisgau, Germany: Arnold-Bergsträsser-Institut, 1989.

Sippanondha Ketudat. *The Middle Path for the Future of Thailand: Technology in Harmony with Culture and Environment.* Honolulu, HI: Institute of Culture and Communication, 1990.

Somphop Manarangsan. *Economic Development of Thailand, 1850-1950: Response to the Challenge of the World Economy.* Bangkok: Institute of Asian Studies, Chulalongkorn University, 1989.

Spontaneous and Planned Settlement in Southeast Asia: Forest Clearing and Recent Pioneer Colonization in the ASEAN Countries and Two Case-Studies on Thailand. Hamburg, Germany: Institute of Asian Affairs, 1984.

Suchart Prasith-Rathsint. *Thailand: A Socio-Economic Profile.* New York, NY: Apt Books, 1992.

Suntaree Komin. *Social Dimensions of Industrialization in Thailand.* Bangkok: National Institute of Development Administration, 1989.

Suphat Suphachalasai. *Export Growth of Thai Clothing and Textiles.* Canberra, Australia: National Centre for Development Studies, Australian National University, 1989.

____. *Thailand's Growth in Textile Exports.* Adelaide, Australia: Centre for International Economic Studies, University of Adelaide, 1989.

Thailand: Industrial Development Strategy in Thailand. Washington, D.C.: World Bank, 1980.

Thailand: Natural Resources Profile. Singapore: OUP, 1988.

Uphoff, Elisabeth. "Thailand." In *Intellectual Property and US Relations with Indonesia, Malaysia, Singapore and Thailand.* Ithaca, NY: SEAP, Cornell University, 1991: 37-53.

Voravidh Charoenloet. "The Crisis of State Enterprises in Thailand." *Journal of Contemporary Asia* 19, 2 (1989): 206-217.

Wira Wimoniti. *Historical Patterns of Tax Administration in Thailand.* Bangkok: Institute of Public Administration, Thammasat University, 1961.

E. Development

Angel, Shlomo. "Where Have All the People Gone? Urbanization and Counter-Urbanization in Thailand." *Journal of the Siam Society* 76 (1988): 245-259.

Archer, R. W. *The Possible Use of Urban Land Pooling/Readjustment for the Planned Development of Bangkok.* Bangkok: Asian Institute of Technology, 1985.

Belassa, Bela. *Industrial Development Strategy in Thailand.* Washington, D.C.: World Bank, 1980.

Douglass, Mike. *Regional Integration on the Capitalist Periphery: The Central Plains of Thailand.* The Hague, The Netherlands: Institute of Social Studies, 1984.

Everything Begins in the Countryside. Bangkok: Armed Forces Information Office, 1989.

Gohlert, Ernst W. *Power and Culture: The Struggle against Poverty in Thailand.* Bangkok: White Lotus, 1991.

Judd, Laurence C. *A Vision to Some: A Case Study of Rural Development Activities by a NGO in Thailand: The Rural Life Department of the Church of Christ in Thailand, 1961-1970.* Bangkok: Suriyaban Pub., 1987.

Kanok Rerkasem. *The Assessment of the UNDP Fourth Country Programme for Thailand: Production, Marketing, Research and Development of New Technologies.* Chiang Mai, Thailand: Cooperative Development Group, 1990.

Kelleher, Ann. "Questioning the Traditional-Modern Dichotomy: Two Thai Village Case Studies." *American Journal of Economics and Sociology* 51 (1992): 273-291.

Krasae Chanawongse. *Rural Development Management: Principles, Propositions and Challenges.* Khon Kaen, Thailand: Khon Kaen University, 1991.

Luechai Chulasai. *Migration and Rural Job Creation Programme: A Northern Thailand Study.* Chiang Mai, Thailand: Faculty of Social Sciences, Chiang Mai University, 1982.

Meer, Cornelis Lodewijk Johannes van der. *Rural Development in Northern Thailand: An Interpretation and Analysis.* Groningen, The Netherlands: Rijksuniversiteit Groningen, 1981.

Muscat, Robert J. *Thailand and the United States: Development, Security, and Foreign Aid.* New York, NY: Columbia University Press, 1990.

Parnwell, Michael J. G. and Suranart Khamanarong. "Rural Industrialisation and Development Planning in Thailand." *Southeast Asian Journal of Social Science* 18, 2 (1990): 1-28.

Ruland, Jurgen. "Municipal Government and Development in Chiang Mai." In *Urban Development in Southeast Asia.* Boulder, CO: Westview Press, 1992: 23-106.

Somsakdi Xuto et al. *Strategies and Measures for the Development of Thailand in the 1980's.* Bangkok: Thai University Research Association, 1983.

Suchart Prasith-Rathsint, ed. *Thailand's National Development: Social and Economic Background.* Bangkok: Thai University Research Association, 1989.

A Survey of Perceived Implementation Problems and Proposed Remedies in National Rural Development Planning in Thailand, 1961-1986. Bangkok: Asian Institute of Technology, 1986.

Vanpen Surarerks. *Thai Governmental Rural Development Programs: An Analysis and Evaluation of the Rural Job Creation Programs in Thailand, 1980-1985.* Chiang Mai, Thailand: Faculty of Social Sciences, Chiang Mai University, 1986.

Vuthimedhi, Yuwat. *Integrated Rural Development, Thailand.* New Delhi: Sterling Pub., 1989.

5. SOCIETY

A. Population

Amra Sunthonthada. *Ascertaining the User Perspectives on Community Participation in Family Planning Programmes in Thailand.* Bangkok: Institute for Population and Social Research, Mahidol University, 1991.

Arnold, Fred. *Revised Estimates of the 1970 Population of Thailand.* Bangkok: National Statistical Office, 1975.

Bhassorn Limanonda. *Report on a Thai Family and Household Survey.* Bangkok: Institute of Population Studies, Chulalongkorn University, 1991.

Campbell, Burnham O., Andrew Mason and Ernesto M. Pernia, eds. *The Economic Impact of Demographic Change in Thailand, 1980-2015: An Application of the HOMES Household Forecasting Models.* Manoa, HI: East-West Center, 1993.

Fertility in Thailand: Trends, Differentials, and Proximate Determinants. Washington, D.C.: National Academy Press, 1982.

Goldstein, Sidney. *Migration and Fertility-Related Attitudes and Behavior in Urban Thailand.* Bangkok: Institute of Population Studies, Chulalongkorn University, 1981.

Knodel, John E. *Thailand's Continuing Fertility Decline.* Bangkok: Institute of Population Studies, Chulalongkorn University, 1981.

____. *Thailand's Reproductive Revolution: Rapid Fertility Decline in a Third-World Setting.* Madison, WI: University of Wisconsin Press, 1987.

Kulthida Lertphongwathana. "Integration of Population, Education and Manpower Policies in Thailand: The Case of the 15-19 Years Age Group." *Asian Profile* 18, 1 (1990): 29-49.

Mason, Andrew. *Demographic and Economic Forecasting: A Pilot Study for Thailand.* Honolulu, HI: East-West Population Institute, East-West Center, 1988.

____. *Households and Their Characteristics in the Kingdom of Thailand: Projections from 1980 to 2015 Using HOMES.* Honolulu, HI: East-West Population Institute, East-West Center, 1987.

Nibhon Debavalya. *Fertility Transition in Thailand: A Comparative Analysis of Survey Data.* Bangkok: National Statistical Office, 1978.

Nipon Poapongsakorn. *Household Projections and Housing Needs in Thailand.* Honolulu, HI: East-West Population Institute, East-West Center, 1988.

Ogawa, Naohiro. *Population Change and the Costs of Health Care in Thailand.* Honolulu, HI: East-West Population Institute, East-West Center, 1988.

Overview of Population Research, Thailand, 1979-1984. Bangkok: National Family Planning Programme, 1984.

Population and Development Interactions in Thailand. Bangkok: Microlevel Studies Program on Population and Development Interactions in Thailand, 1983.

Population and Economic Development in Thailand: Some Critical Household Behavioral Relations. Bangkok: Thailand Development Research Institute Foundation, 1991.

Preeya Mithranon. *Special Report on Fertility and Mortality Changes in Thailand: An Analysis of the 1985-1986 and the 1989 Survey of Population Change.* Bangkok: National Statistical Office, 1991.

Report of the Second Evaluation of the National Family Planning Program in Thailand. Washington, D.C.: International Health Programs, 1983.

A Study of the Interrelationships of Population, Environment and Development in Thailand. Bangkok: s.n., 1981.

Suchart Prasith-Rathsint. Experiences with Development Projects and Their Demographic Impacts in Thailand. Bangkok: Published by the Author, 1986.

The Thai Elderly Population: A Review of Literature and Existing Data. Bangkok: Institute of Population Studies, Chulalongkorn University, 1985.

Thailand Population Research Inventory, Volume 2. Bangkok: National Family Planning Programme, 1984.

Thailand: Report of Second Mission on Needs Assessment for Population Assistance. New York, NY: United Nations Fund for Population Activities, 1983.

Thailand's Population Planning Project II, 1982-1987: Mid-Term Project Evaluation. Bangkok: Agency for International Development, 1984.

Thongtip Ratanarat, Khunying. Population Policy Background Paper for the Sixth National Economic and Social Development Plan. Bangkok: Thailand Development Research Institute and Human Resources Institute, Thammasat University, 1987.

Trends and Strategies of Action in Population Education for 1992-1995: Report of a Regional Consultative Seminar on Population Education, Bangkok, 21-28 May, 1990. Bangkok: UNESCO Principal Regional Office for Asia and the Pacific, 1991.

Wilawan Kanjanapan. A Study on the Relationship between Fertility Behavior and Size, Structure, and Functions of the Family in Thailand. Bangkok: Institute for Population and Social Research, Mahidol University, 1985.

Yawarat Porapakkham. *Review of Population/Family Planning Related Needs of Adolescents in Thailand.* Bangkok: Institute for Population and Social Research, Mahidol University, 1985.

B. Anthropology and Archaeology

Archaeological Excavations in Thailand: Surface Finds and Minor Excavations. London: Curzon, 1988.

The Archaeology of Peninsular Siam: Collected Articles from the Journal of the Siam Society, 1905-1983. Bangkok: The Siam Society, 1986.

Bougas, Wayne A. *Islamic Cemeteries in Patani.* Kuala Lumpur, Malaysia: Malayan Historical Society, 1988.

____. "Some Early Islamic Tombstones in Patani." *Journal of the Malaysian Branch of Royal Asiatic Society* 59, 1 (1986): 85-112.

Green, Jeremy, Rosemary Harper and S. Prishanchittara. *The Excavation of the Ko Kradat Wrecksite Thailand 1979-1980.* Fremantle, Australia: Dept. of Maritime Archaeology, Western Australian Museum, 1981.

Hanks, Lucien M. and Jane R. "The Gabled Roofs of Thai Temples." *Journal of the Siam Society* 76 (1988): 202-216.

Harper, Rosemary. *A Study of Painted under Glaze Decorated Sherds, Sisatchanalai, Thailand.* Adelaide, Australia: Research Centre for Southeast Asian Ceramics, 1986.

Hein, Don. *Report on the Excavation of the Ban Tao Hai Kilns, Phitsanulok, Thailand.* Adelaide, Australia: Research Centre for Southeast Asian Ceramics, 1986.

Hideo, Noguchi. "Historical Cities and Architecture in Thailand." *East Asian Cultural Studies* 29 (Mar. 1990): 163-182.

Higham, C. F. W. and R. Bannanurag, eds. *The Excavation of Khok Phanom Di: A Prehistoric Site in Central Thailand.* London: Society of Antiquaries of London, 1991.

Higham, Charles and Amphan Kijingam. *Prehistoric Investigations in Northeastern Thailand.* 3 v. Oxford, U.K.: B. A. R., 1984.

Higham, Charles, Rachanie Bannanurag and Graeme Mason. "Human Biology, Environment and Ritual at Khok Phanom Di." *World Archaeology* 24 (1992): 35-54.

Historical and Archaeological Sites and Monuments of Southeast Asia: A Compilation. Bangkok: Southeast Asian Ministers of Education, 1986.

Kijngam, Amphan. *Prehistoric Settlement Patterns in Northeast Thailand: The Result of Site Surveys Undertaken in January and February 1980.* Dunedin, New Zealand: Dept. of Anthropology, University of Otago, 1980.

Krom Sinlapakon. *Art and Archaeology in Thailand.* Bangkok: Fine Arts Dept., 1974.

Moore, Elizabeth H. *Moated Sites in Early North East Thailand.* Oxford, U.K.: B. A. R., 1988.

Oliver, Tony. *Twenty Centuries of Coins: Thailand's Currency through the Ages.* Bangkok: White Lotus, 1978.

Pornchai Suchitta. *Past and Present Use of Khok Di Mound, Thailand: An Anthropological-Archaeological Assessment.* Bangkok: Thai Khadi Research Institute, Thammasat University, 1980.

Prasert Na Nagara and A. B. Griswold. *Epigraphic and Historical Studies.* Bangkok: Historical Society, 1992.

Seminar in Pre-History of Southeast Asia (T-W11): Bangkok, Surat Thani, Phangnga, Phuket and Krabi, Thailand, January 12-25, 1987: Final Report. Bangkok: SPAFA Co-ordinate Unit, 1987.

Surin Pookajorn. *The Hoabinhian of Mainland Southeast Asia: New Data from the Recent Thai Excavation in the Ban Kao Area*. Bangkok: Thai Khadi Research Institute, Thammasat University, 1984.

Vincent, B. *Prehistoric Ceramics of Northeastern Thailand, with Special Reference to Ban Na Di*. Oxford, U.K.: B. A. R., 1988.

Wanat Bhruksasri. *Highlanders of Thailand*. New York, NY: OUP, 1983.

Welch, David J. and Judith R. McNeill. "Archaeological Investigations of Pattani History." *Journal of Southeast Asian Studies* 20 (Mar. 1989): 27-41.

____. "Excavations at Ban Tamyae and Non Ban Kham, Phimai Region, Northeast Thailand." *Asian Perspectives* 28, 2 (1988-1989): 99-123.

White, Joyce C. *Ban Chiang: Discovery of a Lost Bronze Age*. Philadelphia, PA: University Museum, University of Pennsylvania and Smithsonian Institution, 1982.

Wilen, Richard N. *Excavations at Non Pa Kluay, Northeast Thailand*. Oxford, U.K.: B. A. R., 1989.

Woodward, Hiram W., Jr. "Monastery, Palace, and City Plans: Ayutthaya and Bangkok." *Crossroads* 2, 2 (1985): 23-60.

C. Chinese

Amyot, Jacques. *The Chinese and the National Integration in Southeast Asia*. Bangkok: Institute of Asian Studies, Chulalongkorn University, 1972.

Boonsanong Punyodyana. *Chinese-Thai Differential Assimilation in Bangkok: An Exploratory Study.* Ithaca, NY: Cornell University Press, 1957.

Cushman, Jennifer W. "The Chinese in Thailand." In *The Chinese in the ASEAN States: Bibliographical Essays,* ed. by Leo Suryadinata. Singapore: ISAS, 1989: 221-259.

Deyo, Frederic C. "Ethnicity and Work Culture in Thailand: A Comparison of Thai and Thai-Chinese White-Collar Workers." *Journal of Asian Studies* 34, 4 (Aug. 1975): 995-1015.

Gosling, L. A. Peter and Linda Y. C. Lim, eds. *The Chinese in Southeast Asia.* 2 v. Singapore: Maruzen Asia, 1983.

Kasian Tejapira. "Pigtail: A Pre-History of Chineseness in Siam." *Sojourn* 7, 1 (Feb. 1992): 95-123.

Landon, Kenneth Perry. *The Chinese in Thailand.* London: OUP, 1941.

Purcell, Victor. "The Chinese in Siam." In *The Chinese in Southeast Asia.* 2nd ed. London: OUP, 1965: 81-165.

Skinner, G. William. *Chinese in Thailand with Supplements on the Chinese Haws and the Kuomintang Chinese.* Bangkok: Social Research Institute, Chulalongkorn University, 1983.

____. *Chinese Society in Thailand: An Analytical History.* Ithaca, NY: Cornell University Press, 1957.

____. *Leadership and Power in the Chinese Community of Thailand.* Ithaca, NY: Cornell University Press, 1958.

____. "Thailand." In *Report on the Chinese in Southeast Asia.* Ithaca, NY: SEAP, Cornell University, 1951.

Tong Chee Kiong. *Perceptions and Boundaries: Problematics in the Assimilation of the Chinese in Thailand.* Singapore: National University of Singapore, 1988.

D. Muslims

Anderson, Wanni Wibulswasdi. "The Social World and Play Life of Thai Muslim Adolescents." *Asian Folklore Studies* 47, 1 (1988): 1-17.

Ariff, Mohamed, ed. *The Islamic Voluntary Sector in Southeast Asia.* Singapore: ISAS, 1991.

____. *The Muslim Private Sector in Southeast Asia.* Singapore: ISAS, 1991.

Arong Suthasasna. "Occupational Distribution of Muslims in Thailand: Problems and Prospects." *Journal-Institute of Muslim Minority Affairs* 5, 1 (1983/84): 234-242.

Brown, David. "From Peripheral Communities to Ethnic Nations: Separatism in Southeast Asia." *Pacific Affairs* 61, 1 (1988): 51-77.

Burr, Angela. "The Relationship between Muslim Peasant Religion and Urban Religion in Songkhla." *Asian Folklore Studies* 43, 1 (1984): 71-83.

Chaiwat Satha-Anand. *Islam and Violence: A Case Study of Violent Events in the Four Southern Provinces, Thailand, 1976-1981.* Tampa, FL: USF Monographs in Religion and Public Policy, 1987.

____. "Pattani in the 1980s: Academic Literature and Political Stories." *Sojourn* 7, 1 (Feb. 1992): 1-38.

Chaveewan Vannaprasert, Perayot Rahimmula and Manop Jittpoosa. *The Traditions Influencing the Social Integration between the Thai Buddhists and the Thai Muslims,* tr. by Prachitr Mahahing and Khate Ratanajarana. Pattani, Thailand: Faculty of Humanities and Social Sciences and Center for Southern Thailand Studies, Prince of Songkhla University, 1986.

Che Man, W. K. "The Malay Muslims of Thailand." *Journal-Institute of Muslim Minority Affairs* 6, 1 (1985): 98-112.

____. *Muslim Separatism: The Moros of Southern Philippines and the Malays of Southern Thailand.* Singapore: OUP, 1990.

____. "The Thai Government and Islamic Institutions in the Four Southern Muslim Provinces of Thailand." *Sojourn* 5, 2 (Aug. 1990): 255-282.

Diller, A. V. N. "Islam and Southern Thai Ethnic Reference." *South East Asian Review* 13, 1-2 (1988): 155-167.

Farouk, Omar. "The Historical and Transnational Dimensions of Malay-Muslim Separatism in Southern Thailand." In *Armed Separatism in Southeast Asia*, ed. by Lim Joo-Jock and Vani S. Aldershot. Singapore: ISAS, 1984: 234-260.

Forbes, Andrew D. W. "Thailand's Muslim Minorities." *Asian Survey* 22, 11 (1982): 1056-1069.

____, ed. *The Muslims of Thailand: v. 1. Historical and Cultural Studies; v. 2. The Politics of the Malay Speaking South.* Gaya, India: Centre for South East Asian Studies, 1989.

Gunn, Geoffrey B. "Radical Islam in Southeast Asia: Rhetoric and Reality in the Middle Eastern Connection." *Journal of Contemporary Asia* 16, 1 (1986): 30-54.

Kraus, Werner. "Islam in Thailand: Notes on the History of Muslim Provinces, Thai Islamic Modernism and the Separatist Movement in the South." *Journal-Institute of Muslim Minority Affairs* 5, 2 (1984): 410-425.

Matheson, Virginia and M. B. Hooker. "Jawi Literature in Patani: The Maintenance of an Islamic Tradition." *Journal of the Malaysian Branch of Royal Asiatic Society* 61, 1 (1988): 1-86.

Nantawan Haemindra. "The Problem of the Thai Muslims in the Four Southern Provinces of Thailand (Parts I & II)." *Journal of Southeast Asian Studies* 7, 2 (1976): 197-225 and 8, 1 (1977): 85-105.

Pawee Thim Kham, Dolmanach Baka and Phayom Petkla. "Muslim Society, Higher Education and Development: The Case of Thailand." In *Muslim Society, Higher Education and Development in Southeast Asia*, ed. by Sharom Ahmat and Sharon Siddique. Singapore: ISAS, 1987: 177-219.

Scupin, Raymond. "Interpreting Islamic Movements in Thailand." *Crossroads* 3, 2-3 (1987): 78-93.

____. "Islam in Thailand before the Bangkok Period." *Journal of the Siam Society* 68, 1 (Jan. 1980): 55-71.

____. "Islamic Reformation in Thailand." *Journal of the Siam Society* 68, 2 (July 1980): 1-10.

____. "The Politics of Islamic Reformism in Thailand." *Asian Survey* 20, 12 (1980): 1223-1235.

Suhrke, Astri and Lela Garner Nobel. "Muslims in the Philippines and Thailand." In *Ethnic Conflict in International Relations*, ed. by Astri Suhrke and Lela Garner Nobel. New York, NY: Praeger, 1977: 178-212.

Surin Pitsuwan. *Islam and Malay Nationalism: A Case Study of the Malay Muslims of Southern Thailand.* Bangkok: Thai Khadi Research Institute, Thammasat University, 1985.

____. "The Lotus and the Crescent: Clashes of Religious Symbolisms in Southern Thailand." In *Ethnic Conflict in Buddhist Societies: Sri Lanka, Thailand and Burma*, ed. by K. M. de Silva et al. Boulder, CO: Westview Press, 1988: 187-201.

Thai Muslims. Bangkok: Ministry of Foreign Affairs, 1979.

Thomas, M. Ladd. "Cultural Factors Affecting the Rural Development Interface of Thai Bureaucrats and Thai Muslim Villagers." *Contemporary Southeast Asia* 7, 1 (1985): 1-12.

____. *Political Violence in the Muslim Provinces of Southern Thailand.* Singapore: ISAS, 1975.

Uthai Dulyakasem. "Muslim-Malay Separatism in Southern Thailand: Factors Underlying the Political Revolt." In *Armed Separatism in Southeast Asia*, ed. by Lim Joo-Jock and Vani S. Aldershot. Singapore: ISAS, 1984: 217-233.

Wilson, H. E. "British Perceptions of Malay-Muslim Separatism in Thailand: A Conflict of Sub-Loyalties." In *Contemporary and Historical Perspectives in Southeast Asia*, ed. by Anita Beltran Chen. Ottawa, Canada: Carleton University Printshop, 1985: 127-143.

____. "Partisan Imperialists and Islamic Separatism in South Thailand, 1945-49." *Canadian Journal of History* 20 (Dec. 1985): 369-391.

E. Ethnic Groups

Andersson, Edward F. *Plants and People of the Golden Triangle: Ethnobotany of the Hill Tribes of Northern Thailand.* Portland, OR: Dioscorides Press, 1993.

Aran Suwanbubpa. *Hill Tribe Development and Welfare Programmes in Northern Thailand.* Singapore: Regional Institute of Higher Education and Development, 1976.

Chiang Mai and the Hill Tribes. Bangkok: Sangdad Pub., 1989.

Gehan Wijeyewardene, ed. *Ethnic Groups across National Boundaries in Mainland Southeast Asia.* Singapore: ISAS, 1990.

The Hill Tribes of Thailand. Chiang Mai, Thailand: Tribal Research Institute, 1986.

The Hmong. Bangkok: Artasia Press, 1991.

Hmong Voices: Hilltribes of Northern Thailand: A Collection of Interviews with the People of a White Hmong Village in Northern Thailand. Chiangrai, Thailand: Paisal Printing, 1988.

Hussain, Zakir. *The Silent Minority: Indians in Thailand.* Bangkok: Chulalongkorn University, 1982.

Lewis, Paul and Elaine. *Peoples of the Golden Triangle: Six Tribes in Thailand.* New York, NY: Thames and Hudson, 1984.

McKinnon, John. *Hill Tribes Today: Problems in Change.* Bangkok: White Lotus, 1989.

McKinnon, John and Wanat Bhruksasri, eds. *Highlanders of Thailand.* Kuala Lumpur, Malaysia: OUP, 1983.

The Mons: Collected Articles from the Journal of the Siam Society. Bangkok: The Society, 1986.

Nai Pan Hla. "The Major Role of the Mons in Southeast Asia." *Journal of the Siam Society* 79, 1 (1991): 13-21.

Rajah, Ananda. "Commensalism as Practical Symbol and Symbolic Practice among the Sgaw Karen of Northern Thailand." *Southeast Asian Journal of Social Science* 17, 1 (1988): 70-87.

Renard, Ronald D. "Tai Lü Self, House, Village, and Moeng." *Crossroads* 5, 1 (1990): 43-58.

Sams, Bert F. "Black Tai and Lao Song Dam." *Journal of the Siam Society* 76 (1988): 100-120.

Scupin, Raymond. "Thailand as a Plural Society: Ethnic Interaction in a Buddhist Kingdom." *Crossroads* 2, 3 (1986): 115-140.

Suchart Prasith-Rathsint. *Ethnicity and Fertility in Thailand.* Singapore: ISAS, 1985.

Sumet Chumsai Na Aytthaya. *Naga: Cultural Origins in Siam and the West Pacific.* Singapore: OUP, 1988.

Tannenbaum, Nicola. "The Heart of the Village: Constituent Structures of Shan Communities." *Crossroads* 5, 1 (1990): 23-41.

Tapp, Nicholas. *The Hmong of Thailand: Opium People of the Golden Triangle.* London: Anti-Slavery Society, 1986.

____. *Sovereignty and Rebellion: The White Hmong of Northern Thailand.* Singapore: OUP, 1989.

Walker, Anthony R. *Farmers in the Hill: Upland Peoples of North Thailand.* Taipei, Taiwan: Chinese Association for Folklore, 1981.

Walker, Anthony R., ed. *The Highland Heritage: Collected Essays on Upland North Thailand.* Singapore: Suvarnabhumi Books, 1992.

F. Education

Aspects of Development: Islamic Education in Thailand and Malaysia. Bangi, Selangor, Malaysia: Institut Bahasa, Universiti Kebangsaan Malaysia, 1989.

Duggan, Stephen J. "Education and Economic Development in Thailand." *Journal of Contemporary Asia* 21, 2 (1991): 141-151.

Innovation in Construction of Small Secondary Schools in Thailand. Bangkok: UNESCO Principal Regional Office for Asia and the Pacific, 1990.

Samart Nitsmer. *Economics Curricula and Their Relevance to Policy-Making in Thailand.* Singapore: Regional Institute of Higher Education and Development, 1984.

Towards Universalization of Primary Education in Asia and the Pacific, Country Studies--Thailand. Bangkok: UNESCO Regional Office for Education in Asia and the Pacific, 1984.

Varaphon Bovornsiri. *An Analysis of Access to Higher Education in Thailand.* Singapore: Regional Institute of Higher Education and Development, 1985.

Wichit Srisa-an. *Innovations in Higher Education for Development in Thailand.* Singapore: Maruzen Asia, 1982.

G. Philosophy and Religion

Anuman Rajadhon, Phraya. *Popular Buddhism in Siam and Other Essays on Thai Studies.* Bangkok: Thai Inter-Religious Commission for Development, 1986.

Aye Kyaw. "The Sangha Organization in Nineteenth Century Burma and Thailand." *Journal of the Siam Society* 72 (1984):166-196.

Buddhism and Society in Thailand. Gaya, India: Centre for South-East Asian Studies, 1984.

Buddhism in Northern Thailand. Chiang Mai, Thailand: Thippanatr Pub., 1980.

Buddhism in Thai Life. Bangkok: National Identity Board, 1981.

Chawiwan Wannaprasoet. *The Traditions Influencing the Social Integration between the Thai Buddhists and the Thai Muslims.* Pattani, Thailand: Faculty of Humanities and Social Sciences and Center for Southern Thailand Studies, Prince of Songkla University, 1986.

The Chronicle of the Emerald Buddha, tr. by Camille Notton. Bangkok: Bangkok Times Press, 1932.

Cumming, Joe. *The Meditation Temples of Thailand: A Guide.* Bangkok: Wayfarer Books, 1990.

Damrong Rajanubhab, Prince. *A History of Buddhist Monuments in Siam,* tr. by S. Sivaraksa. Bangkok: The Siam Society, 1962.

Dej Tulavardhana. *Buddhism, an Intellectual Approach.* Bangkok: Thai I. E., 1987.

Desai, Santosh N. *Hinduism in Thai Life.* Bombay, India: Poplar, 1980.

Gehan Wijeyewardene. "The Theravada Compact and the Karen." *Sojourn* 2, 1 (Feb. 1987): 31-54.

Gosling, David L. "Redefining the Sangha's Role in Northern Thailand: An Investigation of Monastic Careers at Five Chiang Mai Wats." *Journal of the Siam Society* 71 (1983): 89-120.

Hughes, Philip J. *Proclamation and Response: A Study of the History of the Christian Faith in Northern Thailand.* 2nd ed. Chiang Mai, Thailand: Payap University Archives, 1989.

Ishii, Yoneo. *Sangha, State, and Society: Thai Buddhism in History.* Honolulu, HI: University of Hawaii Press, 1986.

Jackson, Peter A. *Buddhism, Legitimation, and Conflict: The Political Functions of Urban Thai Buddhism.* Singapore: ISAS, 1989.

Keyes, Charles F. *Thailand: Buddhist Kingdom as Modern Nation-State.* Boulder, CO: Westview Press, 1987.

Lando, Richard P. "'The Spirits Aren't So Powerful Any More': Spirit Belief and Irrigation Organization in North Thailand." *Journal of the Siam Society* 71 (1983): 121-148.

Luangpor Teean. *To One That Feels: The Developing of Sati: The Teaching of Luangpor Teean.* Bangkok: Mukkason, 1984.

Olson, Grant A. "Cries Over Spilled Holy Water: 'Complex' Responses to a Traditional Thai Religious Practice." *Journal of Southeast Asian Studies* 22 (March 1991): 75-85.

Phra Lithai: Trai Phum Phra Ruang: Three Worlds According to King Ruang. A Thai Buddhist Cosmology, tr. from the Thai with an introduction and notes by Frank E. and Mani B. Reynolds. Berkeley, CA: University of California, 1982.

Phra Ratchawaramuni. *Social Dimension of Buddhism in Contemporary Thailand.* Bangkok: Thai Khadi Research Institute, Thammasat University, 1983.

Phra Ratworamuni. *Thai Buddhism in the Buddhist World: A Survey of the Buddhist Situation against a Historical Background.* Bangkok: Mahachulalongkorn Buddhist University, 1984.

Rutnin, Mattani Mojdara. *Transformation of the Thai Concepts of Aesthetics.* Bangkok: Thammasat University, 1983.

Seri Phongphit. *Religion in a Changing Society: Buddhism, Reform and the Role of Monks in Community Development in Thailand.* Hong Kong: Arena Press, 1988.

Suchira Payulpitack. "Changing Provinces of Concern: A Case-Study of the Social Impact of the Buddhadasa Movement." *Sojourn* 7, 1 (Feb. 1992): 39-68.

Sulak Sivaraksa. *Siamese Resurgence: a Thai Buddhist Voice on Asia and a World of Change.* Bangkok: Asian Cultural Forum on Development, 1985.

____. *A Socially Engaged Buddhism.* Bangkok: Thai Inter-Religious Commission for Development, 1988.

____. *Understanding a State and Its Minorities from a Religious and Cultural Perspective: The Case of Siam and Burma.* Bangkok: Sathaban Santi Prachatham, 1988.

Suwanna Satha-Anand. "Religious Movements in Contemporary Thailand: Buddhist Struggles for Modern Relevance." *Asian Survey* 30, 4 (1990): 395-408.

Tambiah, Stanley J. *Buddhism and the Spirit Cults in North-East Thailand*. Cambridge, U.K.: Cambridge University Press, 1970.

____. *The Buddhist Saints of the Forest and the Cult of Amulets*. Cambridge, U.K.: Cambridge University Press, 1984.

____. *World Conqueror and World Renouncer: A Study in Buddhism and Polity in Thailand against a Historical Background*. Cambridge, U.K.: Cambridge University Press, 1976.

Tapp, Nicholas. "Hmong Religion." *Asian Folklore Studies* 48, 1 (1989): 59-94.

Taylor, J. L. "New Buddhist Movements in Thailand: An 'Individualistic Revolution,' Reform and Political Dissonance." *Journal of Southeast Asian Studies* 21, 1 (1990): 134-154.

Textor, Robert B. *Patterns of Worship: A Formal Analysis of the Supernatural in a Thai Village*. New Haven, CT: Human Relations Area Files, 1973.

____. *Roster of the Gods: An Ethnography of the Supernatural in a Thai Village*. New Haven, CT: Human Relations Area Files, 1973.

Thailand, Buddhist Land. Bangkok: National Identity Board, 1983.

Warren, William. *Images of Thailand*. Hong Kong: Asia Book, 1981.

Young, Ernest. *The Kingdom of the Yellow Robe: Being Sketches of the Domestic and Religious Rites and Ceremonies of the Siamese*. New York, NY: OUP, 1982.

Zehner, Edwin. "Reform Symbolism of a Thai Middle-Class Sect: The Growth and Appeal of the Thammakai Movement." *Journal of Southeast Asian Studies* 21, 2 (1990): 402-426.

H. Sociology and Social Conditions

Chavalit Siripirom. *Fertility Studies and Influence of Wife's Employment on Family Decision-Making Patterns: A Family Planning Perspective.* Singapore: ISAS, 1982.

Cheah Yanchong. "The Ancient Culture of the Tai People." *Journal of the Siam Society* 76 (1988): 227-244.

Cherlin, Andrew W. *Variations in Marriage Patterns in Central Thailand.* Bangkok: Institute for Population and Social Research, Mahidol University, 1987.

Chou Meng Tarr. "The Nature of Structural Contradictions in Peasant Communities of Northeastern Thailand." *Southeast Asian Journal of Social Science* 16, 1 (1988): 26-62.

Cohen, Erik. "International Politics and the Transformation of Folk Crafts - The Hmong (Meo) of Thailand and Laos." *Journal of the Siam Society* 77, 1 (1989): 69-82.

____. *Thai Society in Comparative Perspective: Collected Essays.* Bangkok: White Lotus, 1991.

Cooper, Robert and Nanthapa. *Culture Shock: Thailand.* 3rd ed. Singapore: Times Books International, 1990.

Cost of Public Family Planning Services and Scope of Private Sector Provisions. Bangkok: Institute for Population and Social Research, Mahidol University, 1991.

DaGrossa, Pamela S. "Kamphaeng Din: A Study of Prostitution in the All-Thai Brothels of Chiang Mai City." *Crossroads* 4, 2 (1989): 1-7.

The Development of Tambon Huay Haeng, Saraburi Province. Bangkok: Asian Institute of Technology, 1987.

Family Size and Family Well-Being: The Views of Thai Villagers. Bangkok: Institute of Population Studies, Chulalongkorn University, 1991.

Fraser, Thomas M. *Fishermen of South Thailand: The Malay Villagers.* Prospect Heights, IL: Waveland Press, 1984.

Hitchcock, Michael, Victor T. King and Michael J.G. Parnwell, eds. *Tourism in South-East Asia.* London: Routledge, 1993.

Hutheesing, Otome Klien. *Emerging Sexual Inequality among the Lisu in Northern Thailand: The Waning of Dog and Elephant Repute.* New York, NY: E.J. Brill, 1990.

Kemp, Jeremy H. *Community and State in Modern Thailand.* Bielefeld, Germany: University of Bielefeld, Faculty of Sociology, 1988.

____. "Peasants and Cities: The Cultural and Social Image of the Thai Peasant Village Community." *Sojourn* 4, 1 (Apr. 1989): 6-19.

Khin Thitsa. *Providence and Prostitution: Image and Reality in Buddhist Thailand.* London: Change, 1980.

Kingshill, Konrad. *Ku Daeng - Thirty Years Later: A Village Study in Northern Thailand 1954-1984.* DeKalb, IL: Center for Southeast Asian Studies, Northern Illinois University, 1991.

Korff, Rudiger. *Bangkok: Urban System and Everyday Life.* Fort Lauderdale, FL: Breitenbach, 1986.

____. "Urban or Agrarian? The Modern Thai State." *Sojourn* 4, 1 (Apr. 1989): 44-54.

Lehman, F. K. "Symposium on Societal Organization in Mainland Southeast Asia Prior to the Eighteenth Century; Freedom and Bondage in Traditional Burma and Thailand." *Journal of Southeast Asian Studies* 15 (Sept. 1984): 233-244, 266-270.

Maniemai Tongsawate. *Coordination between Governmental and Non-Governmental Organizations in Thailand's Rural Development: A Study of Planning and Implementation of Integrated Rural Development at the Local Level.* Bangkok: Asian Institute of Technology, 1985.

Muecke, Marjorie A. "Thai Conjugal Family Relationships and the Hsu Hypothesis." *Journal of the Siam Society* 71 (1983): 25-41.

Mulder, Niels. *Inside Thai Society: An Interpretation of Everyday Life.* 3rd rev. ed. Bangkok: Editions Duang Kamol, 1990.

Peerasit Kamnuansilpa. *Contraceptive Use and Fertility in Thailand: Results from the 1984 Contraceptive Prevalence Survey.* Bangkok: National Family Planning Program, 1985.

Phra Ratworamuni. *Looking to America to Solve Thailand's Problems.* Santa Monica, CA: Thai-American Project, 1987.

Seri Phongphit. *Thai Village Life: Culture and Transition in the Northeast.* Bangkok: Mooban Press, 1990.

Sinith Sitthiraksa. "Prostitution and Development in Thailand." In *Gender and Development in Southeast Asia,* ed. by Penny and John Van Esterik. Ottawa, Canada: Canadian Council for Southeast Asian Studies, 1991: 93-108.

Siriporn Chirawatkul. "The Meaning of Menopause and the Quality of Life of Older Rural Women in Northeast Thailand." In *Gender and Development in Southeast Asia,* ed. by Penny and John Van Esterik. Ottawa, Canada: Canadian Council for Southeast Asian Studies, 1991: 109-132.

Strategies and Structures in Thai Society. Amsterdam, The Netherlands: Antropologisch-SociologischCentrum, Universiteit van Amsterdam, 1984.

Suntaree Komin. *Social Problems in Thailand.* Bangkok: National Institute for Development Administration, 1989.

Tourism Prostitution Development: Documentation. Rev. ed. Bangkok: Ecumenical Coalition on Third World Tourism, 1985.

Truong, Thanh-Dam. *Sex, Money, and Morality: Prostitution and Tourism in Southeast Asia.* London: Zed Books, 1990.

Van Esterik, Penny. "Thai Prostitution and the Medical Gaze." In *Gender and Development in Southeast Asia,* ed. by Penny and John Van Esterik. Ottawa, Canada: Canadian Council for Southeast Asian Studies, 1991: 133-152.

Van Esterik, Penny and John. "Gender and Development in Thailand: Implications for Gender Studies in Southeast Asia." In *Gender and Development in Southeast Asia,* ed. by Penny and John Van Esterik. Ottawa, Canada: Canadian Council for Southeast Asian Studies, 1991: 205-212.

Walker, Anthony R. "Lahu Nyi (Red Lahu) Rites for Establishing a New Village." *Journal of the Siam Society* 71 (1983): 149-207.

Wilawan Kanjanapan. *Youth Profile, Thailand.* Bangkok: UNESCO Regional Office for Asia and the Pacific, 1986.

Wisoot Wiseschinda. *Social Development in Rural Economies in the Upper Central Region.* Bangkok: Chulalongkorn University Social Research Institute, 1990.

I. Women

Aphichat Chamratrithirong. *Thai Marriage Pattern: An Analysis of the 1970 Census Data.* Bangkok: Mahidol University, 1984.

____. *When to Marry and Where to Live?: A Sociological Study of Post-Nuptial Residence and Age of Marriage among Central Thai Women.* Bangkok: Institute for Population and Social Research, Mahidol University, 1986.

Bencha Yoddumnern-Attig et al. *Changing Roles and Statuses of Women in Thailand: A Documentary Assessment.* Nakhonpathom, Thailand: Institute for Population and Social Research, Mahidol University, 1992.

Bhassorn Limanonda. *Analysis of Thai Marriage: Attitudes and Behavior: A Case Study of Women in Bangkok Metropolis.* Bangkok: Institute of Population Studies, Chulalongkorn University, 1987.

Bunloet Lieopraphai. *Contraceptive Practise of Thai Women 1987: Results of the Study on Determinants and Consequences of Contraceptive Use Patterns in Thailand.* Nakhonpathom, Thailand: Institute for Population and Social Research, Mahidol University, 1989.

Chai Podhisita et al. *Women's Work and Family Size in Rural Thailand.* Bangkok: Institute of Population Studies, Chulalongkorn University, 1990.

Darunee Tantiwiramanond and Shashi Ranjan Pandey. *By Women, for Women: A Study of Women's Organizations in Thailand.* Singapore: ISAS, 1991.

____. "The Status and Role of Thai Women in the Pre-Modern Period: A Historical and Cultural Perspective." *Sojourn* 2, 1 (Feb. 1987): 125-149.

Eberhardt, Nancy, ed. *Gender, Power, and the Construction of the Moral Order: Studies from the Thai Periphery.* Madison, WI: Center for South and Southeast Asian Studies, University of Wisconsin-Madison, 1988.

Education Media for Young Women in Slum Communities. Bangkok: Women's Information Centre, Foundation for Women, 1989.

First National Assembly on Women in Development in the Year of Thai Women 1992: Report. Bangkok: The National Commission on Women's Affairs, Office of the Prime Minister, 1992.

Forward Together: Women's Education Media. Bangkok: Women's Information Centre, Foundation for Women, 1990.

Jordt, Ingrid. "Bhikkhuni, Thilashin, Mae-chii: Women Who Renounce the World in Burma, Thailand, and the Classical Pali Buddhist Texts." *Crossroads* 4, 1 (Fall 1988): 31-39.

Junsay, Alma T. and Tim B. Heaton. *Women Working: Comparative Perspectives in Developing Areas.* New York, NY: Greenwood Press, 1989.

Kanitta M. Meesook. *The Economic Role of Thai Women.* Bangkok: Dept. of Economic Research, Bank of Thailand, 1980.

Mills, Mary Beth. "Modernity and Gender Vulnerability: Rural Women Working in Bangkok." In *Gender and Development in Southeast Asia*, ed. by Penny and John Van Esterik. Ottawa, Canada: Canadian Council for Southeast Asian Studies, 1991: 83-92.

Omvedt, Gail. *Women in Popular Movements: India and Thailand during the Decade of Women.* Geneva, Switzerland: United Nations Research Institute for Social Development, 1986.

Rangson Prasertsri. *Political Elites in Thailand: A Comparative Study of Male and Female Parliamentarians.* Songkla, Thailand: Dept. of Public Administration, Prince of Songkla University Haad-Yai, 1983.

Shahand, Assadullah et al. *The Role of Women in Slum Improvement: A Comparative Study of the Squatter Settlements at Klong Toey and Wat Yai Sri Suphan in Bangkok, Thailand.* Bangkok: Asian Institute of Technology, 1986.

Supatra Masdit, Khunying. *Politics in Thailand with Special Reference to the Role of Women*. Singapore: Times Academic Press, 1991.

Swanson, Herbert R. "A New Generation: Missionary Education and Changes in Women's Roles in Traditional Northern Thai Society." *Sojourn* 3, 2 (Aug. 1988): 187-206.

Thai Women. Bangkok: National Commission on Women's Affairs, 1993.

Thai Women. Bangkok: National Identity Board, 1983.

Thorbek, Susanne. *Voices from the City: Women of Bangkok*. London: Zed Books, 1987.

Usaneya Perngparn. *Beliefs and Attitudes Concerning Fertility Behaviors among the Hilltribes in Thailand*. Bangkok: Institute of Health Research, Chulalongkorn University, 1989.

Van Esterik, Penny. *Ideologies and Women in Development Strategies in Thailand*. North York, Canada: Dept. of Anthropology, York University, 1987.

Vitit Muntarbhorn et al. *Status of Women, Thailand*. Bangkok: UNESCO Principal Regional Office for Asia and the Pacific, 1990.

Women in Asia: Beyond the Domestic Domain; Survey of Women's Outside Roles in India-Indonesia-Thailand. Bangkok: UNESCO Principal Regional Office for Asia and the Pacific, 1989.

Women's Legal Position in Thailand. Chiang Mai, Thailand: Faculty of Social Sciences, Chiang Mai University, 1991.

Women's Work and Family Size in Rural Thailand. Bangkok: Institute of Population Studies, Chulalongkorn University, 1990.

J. Drugs and Public Health

Abstracts on Medicinal Plants in Thailand. Bangkok: Institute of Scientific and Technological Research, 1980.

Bamber, Scott. "Metaphor and Illness Classification in Traditional Thai Medicine." *Asian Folklore Studies* 46, 2 (1987): 179-195.

Bongkotrat Techatraisak and Wilbert M. Gesler. "Traditional Medicine in Bangkok." *Geographical Review* 79 (Apr. 1989): 172-182.

Boyes, Jon and S. Piraban. *Opium Fields.* Bangkok: Silkworm Books, 1991.

Chawalit Tantinimitkul. *The Provincial Rural Health Services Planning Process and Its Implementation in Thailand.* Bangkok: Asian Institute of Technology, 1986.

Crooker, Richard A. "Forces of Change in the Thailand Opium Zone." *Geographical Review* 78 (July 1988): 241-256.

Drug Control: U.S. Supported Efforts in Burma, Pakistan, and Thailand. Washington, D.C.: Report to Congress, 1988.

Farnsworth, Norman R. and Nuntavan Bunyapraphatsara, eds. *Thai Medicinal Plants: Recommended for Primary Health Care System.* Bangkok: Medicinal Plant Information Center, 1992.

Ford, Nicholas and Suporn Koetsawang. "The Socio-Cultural Context of the Transmission of HIV in Thailand." *Social Science and Medicine* 33, 4 (1991): 405-414.

Krasuang Satharanasuk. *Thailand Health Profile.* Bangkok: Ministry of Public Health, 1980.

Mollica, Richard F. "Communities of Confinement: An International Plan for Relieving the Mental Health Crisis in the

Thai-Khmer Border Camps." *Southeast Asian Journal of Social Science* 18, 1 (1990): 132-152.

Mulholland, Jean. "Ayurveda, Congenital Disease and Birthdays in Thai Traditional Medicine." *Journal of the Siam Society* 76 (1988): 174-182.

____. *Medicine, Magic and Evil Spirits: Study of a Text on Thai Traditional Paediatrics.* Canberra, Australia: Australian National University, 1987.

Sombat Topanya. *Traditional Thai Massage.* Bangkok: Editions Duang Kamol, 1990.

Terwiel, B. J. "Acceptance and Rejection: The First Inoculation and Vaccination Campaigns in Thailand." *Journal of the Siam Society* 76 (1988): 183-201.

Thai Index Medicus, 1975-1979. Tokyo: Southeast Asian Medical Information Center, 1988.

Wichai Posayachinda. *Heroin in Thailand.* Bangkok: Drug Dependence Research Center, Chulalongkorn University, 1982.

____. *Illegal Opiate Consumption in Thailand: Population and Use Pattern.* Bangkok: Drug Dependence Research Center, Chulalongkorn University, 1981.

6. CULTURE

A. Art and Architecture

Apinan Poshyananda. *Modern Art in Thailand.* New York, NY: OUP, 1992.

Art and Archeology in Thailand. 2 v. Bangkok: Fine Arts Dept., 1974-75.

Boribanburiphan Luang. *Thai Images of the Buddha.* 3rd ed. Bangkok: National Culture Institute, 1956.

Bowie, Theodore Robert, ed. *The Arts of Thailand: A Handbook of the Architecture, Sculpture, and Painting of Thailand (Siam).* Bloomington, IN: Indiana University Press, 1960.

Chand, Emcee. *Thai Imageries of Suwanbhumi.* Bangkok: Yodtow Studio, 1987.

Damrong Rajanubhab, Prince. *Monuments of the Buddha in Siam.* Bangkok: The Siam Society, 1973.

Dhanit Yupho. *Quartzite Buddha Images of the Dvaravati Period.* Bangkok: Dept. of Fine Arts, n.d.

Di Crocco, Virginia M. "Ceramic Wares of the Haripunjaya Area." *Journal of the Siam Society* 79, 1 (1991): 84-98.

Dumarcay, Jacques. "The Palaces of Thailand." In *The Palaces of South-East Asia: Architecture and Customs*, tr. by Michael Smithies. Singapore: OUP, 1991: 21-39.

Felten, Wolfgang. *Thai and Cambodian Sculpture from the 6th to the 14th Centuries.* London: P. Wilson Pub., 1989.

Fickle, Dorothy H. *Images of the Buddha in Thailand.* Singapore: OUP, 1989.

Ginsburg, Henry. *Thai Manuscript Painting.* Honolulu, HI: University of Hawaii Press, 1989.

Itoi, Kenji. *Thai Ceramics from the Sosai Collection.* Singapore: OUP, 1989.

Muay Thai: The King of All Martial Arts. Bangkok: Rajadamnern Stadium, 1984.

No Na Paknam. *The Relationship between the Art and History of the Thai People*. Bangkok: Office of the National Culture Commission, 1985.

Phillips, Herbert P. *The Integrative Art of Modern Thailand*. Berkeley, CA: Lowie Museum of Anthropology, University of California at Berkeley, 1992.

Piriya Krairiksh. *Art in Peninsular Thailand Prior to the Fourteenth Century A.D.* Bangkok: Dept. of Fine Arts, 1980.

Robinson, Natalie V. *Sino-Thai Ceramics in the National Museum, Bangkok, and in Private Collections*. Bangkok: Dept. of Fine Arts, 1982.

Shaw, J. C. *Northern Thai Ceramics*. 2nd rev. ed.. Chiang Mai, Thailand: Duangphorn Kemasingki, 1989.

____. *The Ramayana through Western Eyes*. Bangkok: Distributed by D.K. Today, 1988.

Smitthi Siribhadra and Elizabeth Moore. *Palaces of the Gods: Khmer Art & Architecture in Thailand*. Bangkok: River Books, 1992.

Sombat Phlainoi. *Mural Paintings*. Bangkok: Office of the National Culture Commission, 1985.

Sonthiwan Inthralip. *An Outline of the History of Religious Architecture in Thailand*. 2nd ed. Bangkok: Sonthiwan Intralib, 1987.

Stratton, Carol. *The Art of Sukhothai: Thailand's Golden Age, from the Mid-Thirteenth to the Mid-Fifteenth Centuries: A Cooperative Study*. New York, NY: OUP, 1981.

Subhadradis Diskul, M. C. *Art in Thailand: A Brief History*. 4th ed. Bangkok: Amarin Press, 1978.

____. *The Art of the Srivijaya*. Singapore: OUP, 1980.

Subhadradis Diskul, M. C. et al. *The Suan Pakkad Palace Collection,* photographs by Chusak Warapitak. Bangkok: Princess Chumbhot of Nagara Svarga, 1982.

Thai Style. Bangkok: Asia Books, 1988.

Treasures of Thailand. 4th ed. Bangkok: National Identity Board, 1985.

Van Beek, Steve and Luca Invernizzi Tettoni. *The Arts of Thailand.* Rev. and updated ed. New York, NY: Thames and Hudson, 1991.

Viboon Leesuwan. *Thai Folk Crafts.* Bangkok: Office of the National Culture Commission, 1986.

____. *Thai Traditional Crafts.* Bangkok: Office of the National Culture Commission, 1981.

B. Customs and Festivals

Anuman Rajadhon, Phraya. *Essays on Cultural Thailand.* Bangkok: Office of the National Culture Commission, 1990.

Benedict, Ruth. *Thai Culture and Behavior: An Unpublished War-Time Study Dated Sept. 1943.* Ithaca, NY: SEAP, Cornell University, 1952.

Boyes, Jon and S. Piraban. *A Life Apart: Viewed from the Hills.* Chiang Mai, Thailand: Jareuk Publications, 1989.

Breazeale, Kennon and Snit Smuckarn. *A Culture in Search of Survival: The Phuan of Thailand and Laos.* New Haven, CT: Yale University Southeast Asia Studies, 1988.

Bumrongsook Siha-Umphai. "A Survey of the Impact of Radio and Television on Grass-Root Culture in Thailand." *East Asian Cultural Studies* 26 (Mar. 1987): 133-142.

Cadet, John. *Monks, Mountains and Magic: Explorations of Thailand.* Chiang Mai, Thailand: Browne International, 1990.

Eckardt, James. *Waylaid by the Bimbos, and Other Catastrophes in Thailand.* Bangkok: Post Pub., 1991.

Essays on Cultural Thailand. Bangkok: Office of the National Culture Commission, 1990.

Gerini, G. E. *The Tonsure Ceremony as Performed in Siam.* Bangkok: Bangkok Times, 1895.

Heinze, Ruth-Inge. *Tham Khwan: How to Contain the Essence of Life: A Socio-Psychological Comparison of a Thai Custom.* Singapore: Singapore University Press, 1982.

Klausner, William J. *Reflections on Thai Culture: Collected Writings of William J. Klausner.* 4th ed. Bangkok: The Siam Society, 1993.

Lee, Gary Y. "Household and Marriage in a Thai Highland Society." *Journal of the Siam Society* 76 (1988): 162-173.

Lefferts, H. Leedom, Jr. "The Cultures of Boxes: Information Flow and Social Organization among the Northeast Thai and Lao." *Crossroads* 5, 1 (1990): 59-68.

Mulder, Niels. *Inside Southeast Asia: Thai, Javanese and Filipino Interpretations of Everyday Life.* Bangkok: Editions Duang Kamol, 1992.

Pilon-Bernier, Raymond. *Festivals and Ceremonies of Thailand,* tr. from the French by Joanne Elizabeth Soulier. Bangkok: Sangwan Surasawang, 1973.

The Royal Barge Procession. Bangkok: Tourism Authority of Thailand, 1987.

Segaller, Denis. *New Thoughts on Thai Ways: And Some Old Ones Too.* Bangkok: MKE, Magazine Distribution Service, 1989.

Sombat Phlainoi. *Sorties into Thai Cultural History*. Bangkok: Office of the National Culture Commission, 1982.

Sommai Premchit and Pierre Dore. *The Lan Na Twelve-Month Traditions: An Ethno-Historic and Comparative Approach: A Research Report*. Chiang Mai, Thailand: Faculty of Social Sciences, Chiang Mai University, 1991.

Srisurang Poolthupya. *Thai Customs and Social Values in the Ramakien*. Bangkok: Thai Khadi Research Institute, Thammasat University, 1981.

Successful Living in Bangkok. Bangkok: Community Services of Bangkok, 1989.

Suntaree Komin. *Psychology of the Thai People: Values and Behavioral Patterns*. Bangkok: Research Center, National Institute of Development Administration, 1990.

Symposium on Environment and Culture with Emphasis on Urban Issues. Bangkok: The Siam Society, 1993.

Tannenbaum, Nicola. "Tattoos: Invulnerability and Power in Shan Cosmology." *American Ethnologist* 14 (Nov. 1987): 693-711.

Terwiel, B. J.   *Monks and Magic: An Analysis of Religious Ceremonies in Central Thailand*. 2nd rev. ed.   London: Curzon Press, 1979.

____. "Tattooing in Thailand's History." *Journal of the Royal Asiatic Society of Great Britain and Ireland* 2 (1979): 156-166.

Thai Culture, Songkran Festival. Bangkok: Office of the National Culture Commission, 1989.

Thai Customs and Beliefs. Bangkok: Office of the National Culture Commission, 1988.

Thai Games and Festivals. Bangkok: Public Relations Dept., 1968.

Wales, H. G. Quaritch. *Divination in Thailand; The Hopes and Fears of a Southeast Asian People.* London: Curzon Press, 1982.

____. *Siamese State Ceremonies.* London: B. Quaritch, 1931.

C. Music and Dance

Chen Duriyanga, Phra. *Siamese Music in Theory and Practice as Compared with That of the West, and a Description of the Piphat Band.* Bangkok: Dept. of Fine Arts, 1948.

____. *Thai Music.* Bangkok: National Culture Institute, 1956.

Dhaninivat Kromamun Bidyalabh Bridhyakorn, H. H. Prince and Dhanit Yupho. *The Khon.* 3rd ed. Bangkok: Dept. of Fine Arts, 1962.

Dhanit Yupho. *Classical Siamese Theatre,* tr. by P. S. Sasti. Bangkok: Hatha Dhip, 1952.

____. *The Khon and Lakon: Dance Dramas Presented by the Department of Fine Arts.* Bangkok: Dept. of Fine Arts, 1963.

____. *Pictorial Figures Depicting Basic Postures of Thai Dancing from Treatise on Dancing by H. R. H. Prince Damrong Rajanubhab,* collected and arranged by Dhanit Yupho. Bangkok: Dept. of Fine Arts, 1959.

____. *Thai Musical Instruments,* tr. from Thai by David Morton. 2nd ed. Bangkok: Karnsasana Press, 1971.

Mattani Rutnin, ed. *The Siamese Theatre: A Collection of Reprints from the Journal of the Siam Society.* Bangkok: The Siam Society, 1975.

Morton, David. *The Traditional Music of Thailand.* Berkeley, CA: University of California Press, 1976.

Renard, Ronald D., Ruthjaporn Prachadetsuwat and Soe Moe. *Some Notes on the Karen and Their Music.* Chiang Mai, Thailand: Center for Arts and Culture, Payap University, 1991.

Rutnin, Mattani Mojdara. *Dance, Drama, and Theatre in Thailand: The Process of Development and Modernization.* Tokyo: Center for East Asian Cultural Studies for UNESCO, 1993.

Sweeney, Amin. *Malay Shadow Puppets: The Wayang Siam of Kelantan.* London: British Musuem, 1972.

Wong, Deborah. "The Evening Overture in Hindu-Buddhist Thai Ritual." *Ethnomusicology* 35 (1991): 326-339.

D. Language and Literature

Abha Bhamorabutr. *Foreign Words Are Pronounced the Same as Thai Words: The Etymological Relationships of Thai and Foreign Words.* Bangkok: Distributed by D. K. Today, 1988.

Allison, Gordon H. *Compact Thai-English Dictionary: A Useful Concise Dictionary of the Thai Language.* Bangkok: Professional Services Publishers and Translators, 1972.

____. *Simplified Thai.* Bangkok: Nibondh, 1961.

Anderson, Benedict R. O'G. and Ruchira Mendiones, eds. *In the Mirror: Literature and Politics in Siam in the American Era.* Bangkok: Editions Duang Kamol, 1985.

Anuman Rajadhon, Phraya. *Thai Language.* Bangkok: National Culture Institute, 1954.

____. *Thai Literature and Swasdi Raksa.* 4th ed. Bangkok: National Culture Institute, 1956.

Bauer, Christian. "Notes on Mon Epigraphy." *Journal of the Siam Society* 79, 1 (1991): 31-83.

Benedict, Paul K. *Austro-Thai Language and Culture: With a Glossary of Roots.* New Haven, CT: HRAF Press, 1975.

Bickner, Robert. "Changing Perspectives on Language and the Poetic Arts in Thailand." *Crossroads* 3, 1 (1986): 104-117.

Bofman, Theodora Helene. *The Poetics of the Ramakian.* DeKalb, IL: Northern Illinois University, Center for Southeast Asian Studies, 1984.

Bradley, Dan Beach. *Dictionary of the Siamese Language.* Bangkok: s.n., 1971.

Brown, Adam. *Homophones and Homographs in Thai, and Their Implications.* Hamburg, Germany: H. Buske, 1988.

Brown, James Marvin. *AUA Language Center Thai Course.* 3 v. Bangkok: American University Alumni Association Language Center, 1967-69.

Brown, Marie-Helene. *Reading and Writing Thai.* Bangkok: Editions Duang Kamol, 1988.

Cummings, Joe. *Thai Phrasebook.* South Yarra, Victoria, Australia: Lonely Planet Publications, 1984.

Davies, John R. *Thailand: A Hilltribe Phrase Book.* Salisbury, Wiltshire, U.K.: Footloose Books, 1990.

Dias, Erika. *On Liberty: Poems.* Bangkok: Mahamakut Rajavidyalaya Press, 1991.

Gedney, William J. "Patrons and Practitioners: Chakri Monarchs and Literature." *Crossroads* 2, 2 (1985): 1-22.

____. *Selected Papers on Comparative Thai Studies.* Ann Arbor, MI: Center for South and Southeast Asian Studies, University of Michigan, 1989.

____. *The Yay Language: Glossary, Texts, and Translations.* Ann Arbor, MI: Center for South and Southeast Asian Studies, University of Michigan, 1991.

Haas, Mary R. *The Thai System of Writing.* Ithaca, NY: Spoken Language Services, 1980.

Hartmann, John F. "The Spread of South Indic Scripts in Southeast Asia." *Crossroads* 3, 1 (1986): 6-20.

Hartmann, John F., George M. Henry and Wibha Senanan Kongananda. "Lexical Puzzles and Proto-Tai Remnants in an Old Thai Text." *Crossroads* 4, 2 (1989): 71-85.

Henry, George. "A Proposal for a General Computer-Based Romanization for Southeast Asian Indic-Derived Scripts." *Crossroads* 3, 1 (1986): 62-79.

Hudak, Thomas John. "Internal Rhyme Patterns in Classical Thai." *Crossroads* 3, 2-3 (1987): 94-105.

____. "Spelling Reforms of Field Marshall Pibulsonkram." *Crossroads* 3, 1 (1986): 123-133.

Jumsai, M. L. Manich. *History of Thai Literature: Including Laos, Shans, Khamti, Ahom, and Yunnan-Nanchao.* Bangkok: Chalermnit Press, 1992.

____. *Seven Hundred Years of Thai Writing, or, the Story of "Lai Su Thai."* Bangkok: Chalermnit Press, 1983.

Karnchana Nacaskul. "Works in Thailand Commemorating the 700 Years of Thai Writing." *Crossroads* 3, 1 (1986): 21-39.

Kornvipa Boonsue. *Buddhism and Gender Bias: An Analysis of a Jataka Tale.* Toronto, Canada: York University, 1989.

Levy-Ward, Annick et al. "Some Observations on the Map of the Ethnic Groups Speaking Thai Languages." *Journal of the Siam Society* 76 (1988): 29-45.

Manot Tiengladdawong and Mary Lou Robertson. "The Thai Braille Writing System." *Crossroads* 3, 1 (1986): 134-153.

Matisoff, James A. *The Dictionary of Lahu*. Berkeley, CA: University of California Press, 1988.

Modern Standard English-Thai Dictionary. Bangkok: Prae Pittaya Pub., 1966.

Montri Umavijani. *The Domain of Thai Literature*. Bangkok: Prachandra Printing Press, 1978.

____. *Poems from Thailand, 1988-1991*. Bangkok: Pradipat Poetry Press, 1991.

____. *A Poetic Journey through Thai History: Based on Prince Bidyalankarana's Sam Krung*. Bangkok: National Identity Board, 1981.

Nanthana Danwiwat. *The Thai Writing System*. Hamburg, Germany: Buske, 1987.

New Model Thai-English Dictionary, compiled by So Sethaputra. Krung Thep Maha Nakhon, Thailand: Thai Watthana Phanit, 1987.

Ngampit Jagacinski. "Tai Lue Scripts: The Old and New." *Crossroads* 3, 1 (1986): 80-96.

O'Connor, Richard A. "Siamese Tai in Tai Context: The Impact of a Ruling Center." *Crossroads* 5, 1 (1990): 1-21.

Olson, Grant A. "Thai Cremation Volumes: A Brief History of a Unique Genre of Literature." *Asian Folklore Studies* 51 (1992): 279-294.

Phillips, Herbert P. *Modern Thai Literature: With an Ethnographic Interpretation.* Honolulu, HI: University of Hawaii Press, 1987.

Pira Sudham. *Siamese Drama and Other Stories from Thailand.* 5th ed. Bangkok: Shire Books, 1989.

Primary Word Book, English-Hmong. 2nd ed. Iowa City, IA: University of Iowa, 1989.

Purnell, Herbert C. *A Short Northern Thai-English Dictionary (Tai Yuan).* Chiang Mai, Thailand: Overseas Missionary Fellowship, 1963.

A Study of Thai Heroes from Thai Classical Literature. Bangkok: Office of National Culture Commission, 1986.

Treasury of Thai Literature: The Modern Period. Bangkok: National Identity Board, 1988.

7. JOURNALS AND NEWSPAPERS

A. Thai Journals and Newspapers

Bangkok Post. Post Publishing Co., Bangkok Post Building, 136 Na Ranong Road, Off Sunthorn Kosa Road, Klong Toey, Bangkok 10110, Thailand.

Business in Thailand. Business (Thailand) Co., 927 Soi Saeng Cham, Rama IX Road, Bangkok 10310, Thailand.

Business Review. Nation Publishing Group, 44 Moo 10 Bangna-Trat Road, K.M. 4.5, Bnagna, Phra Kanong, Bangkok 10260, Thailand.

Journal of the Siam Society. Amarin Printing Group, 65/16 Soi Wat Chaiyapruk, Pinklao-Nakhon Chaisi Road, Taling Chan, Bangkok 10170, Thailand.

The Nation. Nation Publishing Group. 44 Moo 10, Bangna-Trat Road, K.M. 4.5, Bangna, Phra Khanong, Bangkok 10260, Thailand.

Sawaddi. 33 Rajadamri Rd., Bangkok 10330, Thailand.

Thailand Illustrated. Foreign News Division, Government Public Relations Dept., 236 Vibhavadi Rangsit Highway, Bangkok 10400, Thailand.

B. Foreign Journals

Asian Studies Review. Asian Studies Association of Australia, Inc. Griffith University, Queensland 4111, Australia.

Asian Survey. University of California Press. Berkeley, CA 94720, USA.

Asian Wall Street Journal Weekly. P.O. Box 15, Chicopee, MA 01020, USA.

Contemporary Southeast Asia. Institute of Southeast Asian Studies, Heng Mui Keng Terrace, Pasir Panjang, Singapore 0511.

Crossroads: An Interdisciplinary Journal of Southeast Asian Studies. Center for Southeast Asian Studies, Northern Illinois University, DeKalb, IL 60115, USA.

Journal of Asian Studies. Association for Asian Studies, 1, Lane Hall, University of Michigan, Ann Arbor, MI 48109, USA.

Journal of Southeast Asian Studies. (Follows Journal of Southeast Asia History.) Singapore University Press, Yusof Ishak House, Kent Ridge, Singapore 0511.

Pacific Affairs. University of British Columbia, Vancouver, B.C. V6T 1W5, Canada.

Sojourn: Social Issues in Southeast Asia. Institute of Southeast Asian Studies, Heng Mui Keng Terrace, Pasir Panjang, Singapore 0511.

Southeast Asian Journal of Social Science. Chopmen Publishers, 865 Mountbatten Road #05-28, Katong Shopping Centre, Singapore 1543.

APPENDICES

Appendix 1

Kings of Ayutthya, Thonburi and Bangkok

KINGS	REIGN DATES
Ramathibodi I (U Thong)	1351-1369
Ramesuan	1369-1370
Borommaracha I	1370-1388
Thong Chan	1388
Ramesuan (2d reign)	1388-1395
Ramaracha	1395-1409
Intharacha	1409-1424
Borommaracha II	1424-1448
Borommatrailokanat	1448-1488
Borommaracha III/Intharacha II	1488-1491
Ramathibodi II	1491-1529
Borommaracha IV	1529-1533
Ratsada	1533-1534
Chairacha	1534-1547
Yot Fa	1547-1548
Khun Worawongsa	1548
Chakkraphat	1548-1569
Mahin	1569
Mahathammaracha	1569-1590
Naresuan the Great	1590-1605
Ekathtosarot	1605-1610/11
Si Saowaphak (?)	1610-1611?
Song Tham	1610/11-1628
Chettha	1628-1629
Athittayawong	1629
Prasat Thong	1629-1656
Chai	1656
Suthammaracha	1656
Narai the Great	1656-1688
Phra Phetracha	1688-1703
Sua	1703-1709

283

Phumintharacha (Thai Sa)	1709-1733
Borommakot	1733-1758
Uthumphon	1758
Suriyamarin	1758-1767

King of Thonburi

KING	REIGN DATES
Taksin	1767-1782

Kings of Bangkok, Chakri Dynasty

KINGS	REIGN DATES
Phra Phutthayotfa (Rama I)	1782-1809
Phra Phutthaloetla (Rama II)	1809-1824
Phra Nangklao (Rama III)	1824-1851
Mongkut (Rama IV)	1851-1868
Chulalongkorn (Rama V)	1868-1910
Vajiravudh (Rama VI)	1910-1925
Phrajadhipok (Rama VII)	1925-1935
Ananda Mahidol (Rama VIII)	1935-1946
Bhumibol Adulyadej (Rama IX)	1946

Appendix 2

Kings of Sukhothai

KINGS	REIGN DATES
Sri Indraditya	c. 1240-1270
Ban Muang	c. 1270-1279
Ramkhamhaeng	1279?-1298
Lo Thai	1298-1346/47
Ngua Nam Thom	1346/47
Mahathammaracha I (Luthai)	1346/47-1368/74
Mahathammaracha II	1368/74?-1398
Mahathammaracha III (Sai Luthai)	1398-1419
Mahathammaracha IV	1419-1438

Appendix 3

Kings of Lan Na

KINGS	REIGN DATES
Mangrai	1259-1317
Chai Songkram	1317-1318
Saen Phu	1318-1319
Khrua	1319-1322
Nam Thuam	1322-1324
Saen Phu (second reign)	1324-1328
Kham Fu	1328-1337
Pha Yu	1337-1355
Ku Na	1355-1385
Saen Muang Ma	1385-1401
Sam Fang Kaen	1401-1441
Tilokaracha	1441-1487
Yot Chiang Rai	1487-1495

Muang Kaeo	1495-1526
Ket Chettharat	1526-1538
Chai (Sai Kham)	1538-1543
Ket Chettharat (second reign)	1543-1545
Queen Chiraprapha	1545-1546
Setthahirat (of Lan Sang)	1546-1551
Queen Ku	1551
Mekuti	1551-1564
Queen Wisutthithewi (under Burma)	1564-1578
Tharawaddy Prince (of Burma)	1578-1607
Two sons of Tharawaddy Prince	1607-1613
Thadogyaw (of Burma)	1613-1615
Si Song Muang	1615-1631
Phraya Thipphanet	1631-1659
Ruler of Phrae	1659-1672
Burmese Crown Prince	1672-1675
Burmese ruler	1675-1707
Nara (Burmese officer)	1707-1727
Thep Sing	1727
Ong Kham (from Lang Sang)	1727-1759
Chan	1759-1761
Khi Hut	1761-1762
Abhayagamani (Burmese)	1762-1768
Mayagamani (Burmese)	1768-1771
Revolt in Lan Na	1771-1774

Kings of Chiang Mai

Kavila (1775-1781 in Lampang)	1781-1813
Thammalangka	1813-1821
Kham Fan	1821-1825
Phutthawong	1825-1846
Mahawong	1846-1854
Kavilorot	1856-1870
Intanon	1871-1897
Suriyawong	1901-1911
In Kaeo	1911-1939

Appendix 4

Population of Thailand by Province and Enumeration Region
(in thousands)

	1990	1991	1992	1993
Whole Kingdom	56,304	56,962	57,789	58,336
Bangkok Metropo-				
litan and Vicinity	8,539	8,702	8,661	8,769
Nakhon Pathom	658	665	672	710
Nontha Buri	669	704	699	718
Pathum Thani	453	466	485	500
Samut Prakan	855	883	872	896
Samut Sakhon	359	366	373	374
Central Region:	2,834	2,855	2,823	2,836
Chai Nat	357	358	340	349
Phra Nakhon -				
Si Ayutthaya	686	692	694	692
Lop Buri	748	754	739	734
Sara Buri	536	540	546	558
Sing Buri	231	232	222	221
Ang Thong	280	281	285	283
Eastern Region:	3,691	3,741	3,739	3813
Chanthaburi	440	447	456	460
Chachoengsao	583	590	594	598
Chon Buri	911	925	928	948
Trat	198	202	202	203
Nakhon Nayok	229	231	231	233
Prachin Buri	878	888	894	413
Rayong	454	460	438	464
Western Region:	3,306	3,337	3,424	3450
Kanchana Buri	698	709	725	725
Prachuap Khiri Khan	425	431	452	453

Phetchaburi	428	431	439	441
Ratcha Buri	721	728	778	784
Samut Songkhram	207	207	207	206
Suphan Buri	828	834	826	842
Northern Region:	10,994	11,076	11,682	11,815
Kamphaeng Phet	669	677	732	756
Chiang Rai	1,040	1,049	1,230	1,242
Chiang Mai	1,377	1,387	1,531	1,534
Tak	354	359	426	428
Nakhon Sawan	1,089	1,092	1,094	1,110
Nan	450	456	458	460
Phayao	504	507	513	511
Phichit	559	561	588	590
Phitsanulok	787	796	842	839
Phetchabun	956	964	997	1,038
Phrae	494	495	494	491
Mae Hong Son	173	176	207	209
Lampang	773	778	777	798
Lamphun	418	418	398	403
Sakhothai	593	596	607	613
Uttaradit	461	464	476	475
Uthai Thani	305	308	319	319
Northeastern Region:	19,829	20,045	20,059	20,171
Kalasin	895	906	926	921
Khon Kaen	1,682	1,695	1,663	1,637
Chaiyaphum	1,060	1,074	1,087	1,087
Nakhon Phanom	635	645	650	676
Nakhon Ratchasima	2,385	2,405	2,467	2,432
Buri Ram	1,442	1,459	1,418	1,429
Maha Sarakham	901	910	870	873
Mukdahan	289	294	300	309
Yasothon	528	533	529	526
Roi Et	1,229	1,242	1,239	1,255
Loei	552	560	596	615
Si Sa Ket	1,337	1,359	1,336	1,366
Sakhon Nakhon	975	989	1,015	1,021
Surin	1,289	1,294	1,342	1,317

Nong Khai	880	892	837	854
Udon Thani	1,826	1,836	1,846	1,399
Ubon Ratchathani	1,933	1,962	1,945	1,660
Southern Region:	7,113	7,208	7,402	7,484
Krabi	299	304	312	315
Chumphon	398	403	416	421
Trang	520	527	540	545
Nakhon Si Thammarat	1,428	1,437	1,478	1,476
Narathiwat	566	578	577	595
Pattani	538	546	542	554
Phangnga	213	215	218	219
Phatthalung	461	466	475	486
Phuket	169	175	189	194
Yala	357	363	376	381
Ranong	118	121	131	135
Songkhla	1,091	1,098	1,130	1,126
Satun	223	227	231	237
Surat Thani	739	752	792	802

Source:
Statistical Yearbook: Thailand. Bangkok: National Statistical Office, 1994.

Appendix 5

Population of Thailand, 1910-1993
(in thousands)

Year	Total	Annual growth rate	Sex ratio	Population density per sq. km.
1910	8,087		101.7	16
1920	9,409		100.0	18
1930	11,747		101.5	23
1942	16,066		101.0	31
1950	19,635		100.4	38
1960	26,392	3.1%	100.4	51
1970	35,550	3.0%	101.4	69
1975	42,392	2.6%	101.6	83
1980	46,861	1.8%	101.3	92
1985	51,796	2.4%	101.3	101
1990	56,303	1.4%	100.2	108
1991	56,961	1.2%	99.9	111
1992	57,789	1.5%	100.9	113
1993	58,336	0.9%	100.3	114

Source:
Statistical Yearbook: Thailand. Bangkok: National Statistical Office, 1994.

Appendix 6

Expenditure on Gross Domestic Product (in million baht)

	1990	1991	1992
Government final consumption expenditure	206,841	233,322	283,215
Private final consumption expenditure	1,223,922	1,390,199	1,544,910
Fixed capital formation	881,764	1,033,160	1,113,691
Change in stocks	18,150	19,775	11,705
Expenditures on consumption and gross capital formation	**2,330,677**	**2,676,456**	**2,953,521**
Exports of goods and services	745,286	887,170	1,019,603
Less Imports of goods and services	909,582	1,064,253	1,146,501
Total domestic expenditure	**2,166,381**	**2,499,373**	**2,826,623**
Statistical discrepancy	24,713	6,256	-21,688
Gross Domestic Product(GDP)	**2,191,094**	**2,505,629**	**2,804,935**

Sources:
Statistical Yearbook: Thailand. Bangkok: National Statistical Office, 1994.
Quarterly Bulletin of Bank of Thailand 34, 3 (Mar. 1994)

Appendix 7

Gross Domestic Product by Industrial Origin (in million baht)

	1990	1991	1992
Agriculture, forestry and fishing	279,268	316,781	332,917
Mining and quarrying	34,638	39,004	41,755
Manufacturing	595,181	708,868	793,449
Construction	136,235	165,338	186,447
Electricity and water	47,757	53,486	63,925
Transport and communications	156,565	176,671	201,901
Wholesale and retail trade	386,078	427,878	465,940
Banking, insurance and real estate	120,551	133,343	174,556
Ownership of dwellings	66,238	71,589	76,374
Public administration and defence	76,560	86,498	106,291
Other services	292,023	326,173	361,380
Gross Domestic Product	2,191,094	2,505,629	2,804,935

Sources:
Statistical Yearbook: Thailand. Bangkok: National Statistical Office, 1994.
Quarterly Bulletin of Bank of Thailand 34, 3 (Mar. 1994)

Appendix 8

Parties and Number of Seats for the Elections of 1983-1992

Parties	Seats				
	1983	1986	1988	1990	1992
Chart Pattana	-	-	-	60	
Chart Thai	108	63	87	74	77
Community Action Party	-	15	9	-	-
Democrat Party	57	100	48	44	79
Ekkaparb	-	-	-	6	8
Liberal Party	-	1		3	-
Muan Chon (Mass Party)	-	3	5	1	4
National Democracy Party	15	3	-	-	-
New Aspiration Party	-	-	-	72	51
Palang Dharma Party	-	-	14	41	47
Prachachon Party	-	-	19	-	-
Prachakorn Thai	36	24	31	7	3
Progressive Party	-	-	8	-	-
Puangchon Chao Thai	-	1	17	1	-
Rassadorn Party	-	18	21	4	1
Ruam Thai	-	19	35	-	-
Samakkhi Tham	-	-	-	79	-
Seritham Party	-	-	-	-	8
Social Action Party	101	51	54	31	22
United Democratic Party	-	38	5	-	-
Other Parties/ Independents	7	11	1	-	-
Total....................	324	347	357	360	360

Source:
Europa World Yearbook 1982-1994

Appendix 9

Elections Since 1932

1.	November	1933
2.	November	1937
3.	November	1938
4.	January	1946
5.	August	1946
6.	January	1948
7.	June	1949
8.	February	1952
9.	December	1957
10.	February	1969
11.	January	1975
12.	April	1976
13.	April	1979
14.	April	1983
15.	July	1986
16.	July	1988
17.	September	1992
18.	July	1995

Appendix 10

A Chronology of Coups d'Etat in Modern Thailand

1.	April 6,	1782
2.	February 29,	1912
3.	June 24,	1932
4.	June 20,	1933
5.	October 11,	1933
6.	November 8,	1947
7.	October 1,	1948
8.	February 26,	1949
9.	June 29,	1951
10.	November 29,	1951
11.	September 16,	1957
12.	October 20,	1958
13.	November 17,	1971
14.	October 14,	1973
15.	October 6,	1976
16.	March 26,	1977
17.	October 20,	1977
18.	April 1,	1981
19.	September 29,	1985
20.	July 3,	1989
21.	June 11,	1990
22.	February 23,	1991

Appendix 11

Prime Ministers, 1932-94

Prime Ministers	Term of Office
Phraya Manopakonnitithada	1932-33
Phraya Phahonyothin	1933-38
Luang Phibunsongkhram	1938-44
Khuang Aphaiwong	1944-45
Thawi Bunyaket	1945
Seni Pramoj	1945-46
Khuang Aphaiwong	1946
Pridi Phanomyong	1946-46
Luang Thamrongnawasawat	1946-47
Khuang Aphaiwong	1947-48
Luang Phibunsongkhram	1948-57
Pote Sarasin	1957
Thanom Kittikachorn	1958
Sarit Thanarat	1959-63
Thanom Kittikachorn	1963-73
Sanya Dharmasakti (Sanya Thammasak)	1973-75
Seni Pramoj	1975
Kukrit Pramoj	1975-76
Seni Pramoj	1976
Thanin Kraivichien	1976-77
Kriangsak Chomanan	1977-80
Prem Tinsulanonda	1980-88
Chatchai Choonhavan	1988-91
Anand Panyarachun	1991-92
Suchinda Kraprayoon	1992
Chuan Leekpai	1992-1995
Barnharn Silpa-Archa	1995

ABOUT THE AUTHORS

MAY KYI WIN (B.Sc., Dip. Lib. University of Rangoon) was appointed in 1990 as curator of the Donn V. Hart Southeast Asia Collection at Northern Illinois University at DeKalb, Illinois. She formerly worked as librarian at the British Council Library, Rangoon, and as Chief of the English Cataloging Department at the Universities' Central Library, University of Rangoon for sixteen years. Her publications include an article on the "Publishing Industry in Burma" and bibliographies on Burma in *CORMOSEA Bulletin* (Committee on Research Materials on Southeast Asia), the *Bulletin of the Burma Studies Group*, and numerous checklists for referencing bibliographical materials in the Donn V. Hart Southeast Asia Collection. She is also the editor of the *Bulletin of the Burma Studies Group*.

HAROLD E. SMITH (Ph. D. Cornell University) is Emeritus Professor of Sociology at Northern Illinois University. His published articles include six that deal with Thailand. He authored the *Historical and Cultural Dictionary of Thailand* (Scarecrow Press, 1976) and was a visiting Fulbright professor in Thailand 1964-66 and 1975-76.